The Complete Idiot's Reference Card

Catching and Releasing a

There are a few simple rules to follow once the trout is on you

- ➤ Do not play a trout to total exhaustion; it will probably d
  more quickly, use the strongest tippet possible for the situ

- ➤ Make sure your hands are wet before grabbing a fish. Oth
  protective coating.

- ➤ The best way to hold a fish is with one hand under its belly and the other under its tail,
  taking care not to squeeze. Keep the fish close to the water, never over any hard objects,
  in case you lose your grip.

- ➤ If you use a net, try to keep the fish in the water while releasing the hook. Fine mesh
  nets work best to prevent injury to gills or fins.

- ➤ Remove the hook very carefully. Barbless hooks are the least detrimental to a fish, your
  body, and your clothing.

- ➤ If it is impossible to get the hook out, cut your line as close to the hook as possible
  before releasing the fish.

- ➤ When releasing a fish, hold it facing upstream in the water until it can swim on its
  own. If you play a fish until total exhaustion, you are responsible for reviving it, no
  matter how long it takes.

- ➤ When releasing a fish in deep water (while boating), make sure the fish is completely
  revived. When exhausted, most fish sink to the bottom and never recover.

The Nail Knot

Since this knot works so well for tying together different diameters of line, use it to tie the
leader to the fly line. Here are the steps used:

1. Firmly pinch the tube, fly line, and backing parallel to each other with one hand. The
   tag ends should face opposite directions.

2. With your other hand, tightly wrap the tag end of the backing (use at least 6" for the
   tag end) around itself, the fly line, and the tube for five full rotations.

3. While holding all of the wraps in place with one hand, pass the tag end of the backing
   through the tube, back under the wraps you just made.

4. Pull the tag end of both the fly line and the backing in opposite directions and carefully
   slide the tube out.

5. Pull the knot tight and clip off both tag ends.

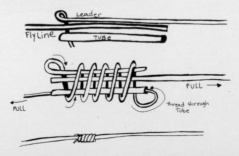

alpha
books

The Surgeon's Knot

The Surgeon's Knot is the strongest and easiest knot to tie for connecting two pieces of material with different diameters. It is commonly used to add pieces of tippet to the leader.

1. Place the tag end of the leader and two to three feet of new tippet parallel to each other so the tag ends point in opposite directions. Have them overlap by at least five inches.
2. Using the two strands as a single line (and a little saliva so they stick together), make one Overhand Knot pulling both the tag end of the leader and the standing end of the tippet through the loop.
3. Make another Overhand Knot the same way.
4. Tighten the knot by pulling on both strands on each side of the knot. Clip both ends closely.

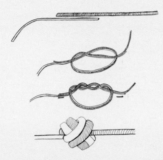

The Improved Clinch Knot

The Improved Clinch Knot is one of the best knots for tying your fly to the leader. It is easy to tie and doesn't waste much tippet in the process.

The figure above shows the basic steps for tying the Improved Clinch Knot. Here's how it's done:

1. Hold the fly in your left hand and run the end of the tippet through the eyelet of the fly.
2. Make at least five wraps around the standing part of the tippet, using your left hand to hold the loop formed by the first wrap.
3. Pass the tag end of the tippet through the first loop above the eye and through the large loop just formed.
4. To tighten, slowly pull the standing line while pinching the tag end with two fingers on your left hand so it doesn't pull through the loop. The coils should form a neat spiral and not overlap. Clip off the excess tippet.

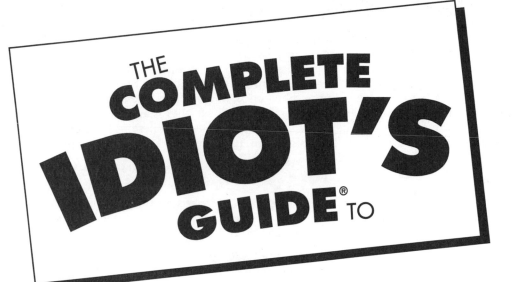

Fly Fishing

by Michael Shook

alpha books

A Division of Macmillan General Reference
A Pearson Education Macmillan Company
1633 Broadway, New York, NY 10019-6785

Macmillan General Reference books may be purchased for business or sales promotional use. For information please write: Special Markets Department, Macmillan Publishing USA, 1633 Broadway, New York, NY 10019.

International Standard Book Number: 0-02-862953-1
Library of Congress Catalog Card Number: 99-64166

01 00 99   8 7 6 5 4 3 2 1

Interpretation of the printing code: The rightmost number of the first series of numbers is the year of the book's printing; the rightmost number of the second series of numbers is the number of the book's printing. For example, a printing code of 99-1 shows that the first printing occurred in 1999.

Printed in the United States of America

Alpha Development Team

Publisher
Kathy Nebenhaus

Editorial Director
Gary M. Krebs

Associate Publisher
Cindy Kitchel

Associate Managing Editor
Cari Shaw Fischer

Acquisitions Editors
Randy Landenheim-Gil
Amy Gordon

Development Editors
Phil Kitchel
Amy Zavatto

Assistant Editor
Georgette Blau

Production Team

Development Editor
Al McDermid

Technical Editor
Brant Oswald

Production Editor
Mark Enochs

Copy Editor
Anne Owen

Cover Designer
Mike Freeland

Photo Editor
Richard H. Fox

Book Designers
Scott Cook and Amy Adams of DesignLab

Indexer
Maro Riofrancos

Layout/Proofreading
Angela Calvert
Su Wright

Contents at a Glance

Contents

Foreword

"Have you ever thought, not only about the airplane, but about whatever man builds, that all his computation and calculation, all the nights spent working over thoughts and blueprints, invariably culminate in the production of a thing whose sole and guiding principle is the ultimate principle of simplicity?

"In anything at all, perfection is finally attained not when there is no longer any thing to add, but when there is no longer anything to take away, when a body has been stripped down to its nakedness."

—Antoine de Saint-Exupery

Despite my feeling that the style and flair of brownstones and Victorians have more appeal than the efficient geometric shapes of modern buildings, there is the strong ring of truth in Saint-Exupery's principles of simplicity. Fly fishing—essentially only a flexible rod, line, and weightless lure—is the epitome of that principle.

We must consider the unusual and unique focus that presently exists in fly fishing. "Catch and Release" fishing, first introduced as a conservation measure, has now become our rallying cry—our *raison d'etre*. We have taken the reward and eliminated it from our sport. No longer is the hooked dead fish our badge of accomplishment. No longer is fly fishing listed as a "blood sport." Our focus is no longer a matter of "keeping score." The top of our mountain now is very simple—the experience. Factor in "the dance of flycasting" and it is little wonder that our sport is now described as "the poetry of fishing."

The poetic, simplistic dichotomy of fly fishing is not without its scientific context. One can fly fish for the beauty of the motions involved or probe more deeply into educational activities surrounding the sport—from aquatic entomology and tying flies to fish behavior and fly line design.

The danger to beginners is that this wide range of information can easily be overwhelming and intimidating. Tread lightly new fly fishers; start simply and grow at your own pace—or not. The beauty of our sport is both its extreme simplicity and the many wondrous avenues of limitless growth.

This very comprehensive reference book offers a simple introduction to many aspects of these delights.

—Mel Krieger, head of the Mel Krieger International School of Flyfishing

Mel Krieger has taught fly fishing for over 25 years and presently heads the Mel Krieger International School of Flyfishing. He has taught in Europe, Asia, South America, Australia, New Zealand, and North America. His widely acclaimed book and videotapes *The Essence of Fly Casting* and the video *Beginnings—An Introduction to Flyfishing* have been used as curriculum for casting schools all over the world. In 1994, he and his wife Fanny were inducted individually in the Northern California Council/ Federation of Fly Fishers Hall of Fame. Mr. Krieger lives in San Francisco, California.

Introduction

Every time someone asks me what I do for a living, I chuckle to myself and tell them, "I'm a fly fisherman."

The reaction is pretty much always the same. There's a long pause. Then I explain, "I'm a fly-fishing guide, and I also write books on fly fishing."

"What was that movie that came out a few years ago?"

"*A River Runs Through It,*" I tell them in mid-sentence.

"Yeah, that's it. It was one of my favorites," they usually say, but I just know they're trying to be polite and make small talk.

Whether you've seen the movie or not, chances are, you're interested in fly fishing. Why else would you be reading this book? And if you're interested in getting into the sport and want to take a no-nonsense approach, keep reading. The purpose of this book is to cut through all of the technical mumbo-jumbo that is often associated with the sport and walk you through it step-by-step in an easy-to-read manner. Whether you've been fly fishing your entire life or are a beginner who just doesn't understand how to get a fly to stay on the hook, this book's for you. I promise that *The Complete Idiot's Guide to Fly Fishing* will teach you just about everything you ever wanted to know about the incredible sport of fly fishing.

Beware, however. The information you are about to learn will change your life forever. You are about to enter a lifelong journey into a different world. A world full of discovery, guided by addiction. If you thought smoking cigarettes or gambling was tough to quit, you haven't seen anything; once hooked, you will soon be eating, breathing, and sleeping fly fishing.

How to Use This Book

The Complete Idiot's Guide to Fly Fishing is a quick and easy-to-read book for all fly fishermen, beginner to expert. The book starts off with the absolute basics, geared for someone new to the sport, then slowly builds on these fundamentals until a veteran fly fisherman will become glued to its contents.

Although the first four parts of the book build upon themselves, experienced fly fishermen may want to skip around as they read, looking in the table of contents for the information desired. I suggest that people new to the sport, however, read these chapters in order so they don't become confused with terminology, tips, or techniques explained earlier in the book.

Here is how the book breaks down:

Part 1 gives the basic information and history behind the sport, tells you what's needed to begin, and goes over the basic knots that all fly fishermen need to know.

This part is a must-read for all beginners as it gently acquaints you to the sport and the equipment used.

Part 2 is essential reading for anyone who has never tried the sport, or for anyone who has, but has also developed bad habits along the way. Step by step, these few chapters go over the basic casts needed before hitting the water and graduate to some more advanced casting techniques.

Part 3 is a must-read for all fly fishermen, no matter their skill level. We finally get our feet wet and learn how to read the water, figure out where the fish are holding, and learn how to sneak up on them. There are also chapters on fishing in the backcountry, what to do when the fishing's slow, and how to hook, play, and land the fish you are after.

Part 4 goes over the "fly" part of fly fishing. It starts with the basics, the hooks they are tied on, then takes you through the patterns used, when to use them, and how to tie them. You will also learn about the insects you will be imitating.

Part 5 is dedicated to the most popular freshwater gamefish you can catch on a fly rod. You will learn all about the different types of fish you will be pursuing, where they live, what they eat, and how to catch them, ranging from trout to carp.

Part 6 covers saltwater fly fishing. Here you'll learn why saltwater fly fishing is on the boom and what you'll need to get started. We will then hit the water and cover the various types of water, the tides that affect them, and the flies used to fool the fish. Finally, you'll learn how to hook, play, and land these powerful creatures, and we'll briefly go over the most popular saltwater gamefish.

Extras

On many pages throughout this book, you'll find "bonus boxes." These contain information that deserves your special attention, as follows:

Fish Tails

These large boxes provide extra bits of information related to the text: interesting facts and trivia, short stories, and other related information.

Reel Good Advice

These boxes give tips, techniques, and shortcuts related to the topic at hand.

Catch Words

These small boxes contain essential vocabulary and definitions of terms related to fly fishing.

Cut Bait

Look in these boxes for cautions, warnings, and dangers.

Acknowledgments

Several people have contributed in some way to the making of this book, including my agent Jeff Herman; my editors, Gary Krebs, Al McDermid, Mark Enochs, and Brant Oswald; Mel Krieger for the foreword; Jim Watson of Umpqua Feather Merchants for all of his assistance; my dad and Elinor for their unconditional support; Ann Geupel for her generous hospitality, computer, and "office"; George Brown, Bill Hamilton, and my brother, R.J. for their technical assistance; Mark Aiken for his hard work and perseverance; Anne Christiansen for her outstanding artwork and patience; and all of my Colorado fishing buddies and clients with whom I've shared tight lines. This book is for my beautiful wife Sarah for supporting my fly-fishing madness.

Trademarks

All terms mentioned in this book that are known to be or are suspected of being trademarks or service marks have been appropriately capitalized. Alpha Books and Macmillan General Reference cannot attest to the accuracy of this information. Use of a term in this book should not be regarded as affecting the validity of any trademark or service mark.

Part 1
Before Heading Out to the Water

If you are a total newcomer to fly fishing or have only been briefly introduced to it, it can be downright intimidating. Where do you even begin to dive into a sport that you have heard was so demanding?

Well, you've come to the right place. But before going any further, you need to know the very basics. This crucial part of the book is dedicated to answering any question you may have about the sport, the equipment, and putting the two together before heading out to the water. You will find out how to get started, how it's done, where to go, what equipment to buy and why. Then you will learn how to tie what every beginner fly fisherman naturally resents: the naughty knots. Only then will you be ready to hit the water.

Chapter 1

What Is Fly Fishing and Why Do It?

In This Chapter

➤ What is fly fishing?

➤ How and when it originated

➤ How to get started

For those of you who have never picked up a fishing pole, don't worry; you can still learn how to fly fish. And you don't have to be an old bass fisherman or accomplished saltwater fisherman. In fact, your lack of experience may come as an advantage—you don't have any bad habits to break. What's more, since you don't have any expectations, your patience level may work in your favor.

Whatever the case, the information in this chapter is essential—so don't skip over it because you're over-anxious to get going. If you're only going to retain one thing from this book, let it be this chapter.

How Do You Catch the Flies?

A good question, but you don't. This type of *angling* (fishing done with a rod and reel) is called *fly fishing* because artificial flies are used to deceive the fish. Unlike bait fishing, you don't use live creatures to entice the fish. The flies are hand-tied on a sharp *hook* (a small piece of metal with a sharp, pointed end). Fur, feathers, and various synthetic materials are used to fool the fish into thinking that the "fly" is a live insect and *striking* at it.

From Homo Erectus to the Fly Fisherman

Even though fly fishing may be new to you, people have been using artificial flies to fool trout going back to the third century. That's right, over 1,700 years ago people were fly fishing with wooden rods and fly lines made from horsehair! Little is known about the technique or equipment of the time, but one thing is certain: our ancestors noticed trout feeding on insects in the water and eventually devised a way to use insects as bait. Of course, it wasn't possible to actually tie a live insect around a hook, so fake ones were designed and tied around the hook to make artificial flies.

While fly fishing was invented in ancient times, the English take credit for evolving the art of fly fishing to what it has become today. In 1653, Izaak Walton wrote *The Compleat Angler,* a collection of fly-fishing stories enhanced by Walton's personal philosophy on life. This well-known book became somewhat of a bible for England's tightly knit fly-fishing community; it was followed by dozens of other books on the subject of fly fishing. It wasn't until the late 1800s, however, that the fine art of fly fishing really took hold in America—New York in particular. The poor trout in both the Beaverkill and the Catskill streams of New York were among the first fish in this country to get deceived by imitation flies.

Before long, anglers all over the country learned the beauty of fly fishing, and trout all over the country were being pursued with a fly rod. Both the equipment and the technique have progressed substantially since then, and fly fishermen are now seeking game fish ranging from trout to tarpon, salmon to sailfish.

Catch Words

A **strike** occurs at the moment a fish bites your fly. To the dismay of the fisherman, strikes don't always end up in hook-ups. If the fisherman always won, it wouldn't be a sport.

Fish Tails

Although the sport started with the use of artificial flies made to look like natural insects, today the term "fly" encompasses other living creatures. It didn't take long for fly fishermen to realize the fish were also feeding on other types of food such as shrimp, frogs, and even other fish. Hence, man started tying "flies" to fool the fish. Presently, fly fishing is enjoyed all over the world with flies ranging from crabs and mullet (used for saltwater fishing) to mice and frogs (used for freshwater fishing); but no matter what baits are used, they are referred to as flies.

What's the Difference Between Fly Fishing and Other Types of Fishing?

The main difference that sets fly fishing apart from other forms of angling is how you present the lure. Unlike bait fishing or spin casting where you use the rod to cast the weight of the lure or bait, in fly fishing, you use the weight of the line to *cast* the fly.

You see, the flies you will be using are virtually weightless. As a matter of fact, you couldn't even throw the typical fly more than a few feet; it would be like trying to throw a ball of cotton. But a fly rod outfit makes it all possible. By casting the fly line back and forth, gaining momentum on every cast, fly rodders can cast a fly on target from 30 feet or more.

Furthermore, since the fly line has weight, fly fishermen can manipulate the line to make the fly do what they want, much like a bullwhip. For instance, say you are fly fishing with a grasshopper pattern; that is, a fly tied to imitate a grasshopper. Since grasshoppers land on the water and immediately try to get away, fly fishermen can imitate their actions simply by manipulating the fly line. In doing so, their grasshopper *pattern,* or imitation, looks like it is struggling to get out of the water.

Catch Words

Fly fishermen refer to the different flies they use as **patterns**. They are named from the materials used to tie it or are named for the inventor of the specific fly. For example, a popular pattern used to imitate the caddis fly is called the Elk Hair Caddis because elk hair is used as a material to tie the fly. The Royal Wulff, however, was named after the inventor of the pattern, Lee Wulff.

Spinning rod

The spinning rod vs. the fly rod.

Fly rod

How to Get Started

Congratulations on your desire to become a fly fisherman and welcome to the club. There are many ways to get started in this sport, and you have chosen the first step correctly. But besides reading this book, I also recommend talking to other fly fishermen. Be careful who you ask, however.

Fly fishermen, whatever their actual ability, have the tendency to all be experts in the field. I have overheard many novice fly fishermen explain improper technique, false knots, and erroneous *hatches* to other beginners in an attempt to impress them. This does nothing more than prolong the learning curve for these eager students and teach them poor habits, many of which are nearly impossible to kick.

Catch Words

A **hatch** is the time when a large number of insects emerge out of the water.

If you don't have any friends or family who know how to fly fish, your local fly shop, or sporting goods store that specializes in fly fishing, is your next alternative—and in most cases, the best. Fly shop employees are a great source of knowledge and are used to beginners picking their brains for tips and technique.

Many fly shops also offer guided fly-fishing trips for all levels of ability. Along with this book, I highly recommend hiring a professional fly-fishing guide. They will teach you on-the-water tips and techniques that would otherwise take you years to learn on your own. But be ready to pay; guided fly-fishing trips range anywhere from $150 to $300 per guide per day. Many shops, however, offer free fly-casting clinics in an effort to lure people into the sport (yes, you can get hooked, too). Top-quality fly-fishing guides are true professionals who eat, breathe, and sleep fly fishing. Follow these guidelines before seeking dependable fly-fishing information or hiring a local guide:

Find a Reputable Fly Shop

Pick a reputable shop that specializes in fly fishing. Many bait stores carry a small supply of fly-fishing tackle but know very little about the sport; they are simply reacting to the current trends in fishing. This is especially true in coastal areas where saltwater fly fishing is quickly growing.

Reel Good Advice

Watch your tongue! Calling your lure "bait" is not acceptable in the world of fly fishing; it is now called a *fly*.

I was recently in Florida on a saltwater fly-fishing trip seeking Redfish, Snook, and Jack Crevalle. Upon arriving, I drove to the nearest bait store to get a tide chart and to poke around for fly-tying materials. Although the gentleman sold a few different pre-packaged fly patterns, he didn't know the first thing about fly fishing. As a matter of fact, he sent me to the nearest fly shop, almost a half-hour away, for reliable information.

Tell Them Your Needs

Make sure you tell the shop your exact level of experience and what skills you want to work on. This will enable them to match you up with an appropriate guide and put you on water that best suits your needs. Some guides specialize in beginners, while others don't have the patience and only take out experienced fly fishermen. If possible, talk to the guide yourself and try to get a feel for their personality. Remember, you'll be spending several hours in an intimate setting with whatever guide you end up choosing.

Give It Up

Most guides don't bring a rod for themselves on guided fishing trips; they expect to use yours to demonstrate certain techniques and casts. Although it can be tough, be a sport and give up your fly rod for a few moments to let them teach you. There are certain techniques that are much easier to pick up by watching than by hearing. It is also a treat for your guide to have a rod in his or her hands, but be wary; some have a difficult time giving it back.

Fish Tails

The Compleat Angler was so popular that at one time in history, it was outsold only by "the Bible and *The Pilgrim's Progress*. This gave Izaak Walton the distinction of being "the father of fly fishing" when, in fact, it was his good buddy, Charles Cotton, who gave Walton all the information needed on fly fishing. Sorry, Charlie!

Be a Curious George

Be sure to drill them with questions before you book the outing. Ask exactly what's included with the price of the trip. Do you have to rent the equipment, buy the flies, or bring your own lunch? Also, ask them how long you'll actually be on the water, how far of a drive it is to get there, and who's driving. I know some outfitters that spend half the day getting to the river and only a few precious hours on the water.

Find out if you are going to be fishing on public or private water. Many outfitters lease water rights from private property owners or pay a certain fee per trip that may be passed on to you. Private property usually offers better fishing because the fishing pressure is lower and it may be privately stocked. If this is the case, I recommend shelling out the extra money to gain access to this water.

If you are going out on a guided trip and want to cut down on the cost, ask the shop to pair you up with another fly fisherman with similar experience. Although you won't get quite the attention, it is usually only a small fee for an additional angler, making the trip cheaper for both of you.

Go When the Fish Are Hitting

Find out how the fishing has been and what time of day has been most productive. If it has been really happening in the morning and slow in the afternoon, maybe it's only worth booking a morning half-day trip. Or if the river is still swollen from spring run-off or excess rain has made the water murky, it may be worth saving your guided trip for another day. Also, find out the shop's cancellation policy due to bad weather. Some will give you a rain check while others abhor such a policy.

Listen Up for Heaven's Sake

Listen to your guide and let them do the talking. I know it may be tough to be a student again, but swallow your ego and come to terms with your ability level. Professional guides have heard every fishing story in the book and have ten better ones for every one that you tell (and their stories are probably true!).

Don't Be a Cheapskate

On behalf of all of my fellow fly-fishing guides, give a tip! I know the trip is expensive enough as it is, but the guide only gets a fraction of the money. If the guide is good (and that doesn't necessarily mean you catch a lot of fish), give at least a 10 to 20 percent tip—in cash. Taking your guide out for beers or dinner afterward doesn't help him pay his bills and may get him in trouble with his spouse (ask my wife).

Cut Bait

Before hiring a guide, ask the fly shop if they have an outfitters license and permits for any public water you will be fishing. These are state-regulated and required for all outfitters. For whatever reason, some shops offer guided services on water they are not permitted to fish. By supporting these shops, you take the risk of your trip being cancelled by the Department of Fish and Game.

Fly-Fishing Schools?

You got it. Just like you can go to school to become a doctor or a lawyer, you can also go to school to become a fly fisherman. Well, sort of. I guess they're more like camps than schools, but if you have the time and resources, I highly recommend it. They vary in length from introductory half-day courses to four-day weekend courses. And best of all is their classrooms. Most fly-fishing schools have their own stocked ponds or access to other productive water.

If you're serious about learning the sport, there is no better way to learn it quickly than by attending one of these schools. The instructors are true professionals, and the courses cover everything from fly casting to actually playing and landing fish on *your* fly rod.

There are certain preliminary questions to ask yourself before signing up for such classes. First of all, you must decide what type of fly fishing you want to learn about. Are you going to do most of your fly fishing in the salt water or in freshwater rivers and lakes? Are you after warm water species like bass and bluegill or cold water species like trout and salmon?

After deciding your specific needs and wants, you must then contact a fly-fishing school and get answers to the following questions:

1. Is the instruction on a one-to-one basis? If not, find out how many people are in each class and if they are grouped by ability levels.

2. Do they take place on the water or mostly in a classroom? The first part of the class may take place in a classroom, and that's okay. But be sure the majority of the lessons are in the field.

3. Do you have to bring your own equipment, or is it provided? Most fly-fishing schools have a large arsenal of fly-fishing equipment to choose from that may be included with the class.

Be sure to ask for a course curriculum and see if it meets your needs before signing up for a fly-fishing school. And like taking classes for anything these days, fly-fishing school is *not* cheap. After all, the professors (fly-fishing junkies) have to make a living, too.

Reel Good Advice

Stock up on flies and equipment the day before your trip. Why spend precious fishing time on the morning of your trip trying on waders and filling your tackle box? And if you don't have a fishing license, get one beforehand (they take a long time to fill out).

Where There Are Fish, There Is Fly Fishing

You don't have to live on the banks of a trout stream in Colorado to be a fly fisherman, although it's not bad. Any body of water that contains fish deserves to be fly fished, and this country abounds with rivers, creeks, streams, ponds, lakes, reservoirs, and coastal areas full of great fishing. The only problem you may encounter is finding access. Unfortunately for most fly fishermen, a large portion of this country is privately owned and marked with either "No Trespassing" or "Private Property" signs.

Public Water

Although fly fishing has become sort of an elite sport, you don't have to join a club or have a friend with a river running through his property to find a place to fish. While some states offer more public water than others, you can just about always find a decent place to go fishing. And contrary to popular belief, public water can be as productive or more productive than private water.

I hate to burst your bubble, but except for saltwater fly fishing, most of the fish you are going to catch aren't native fish. More than likely, they were introduced to the area and have successfully taken hold, considered "wild" now by some; or they are hatchery-raised fish and have been stocked regularly ever since. And since our tax dollars (or fishing license revenue) pays for the stockings, states are only supposed to stock public water; hence, there is often more fish in public water than in private water. Most private property, on the other hand, is only stocked if the landowner personally stocks the water and buys the fish from a private hatchery, which is quite expensive.

Public water can, however, get an enormous amount of fishing pressure. This, of course, has an adverse affect on the fishing. Stay away from areas that resemble more of a circus than a gift from Mother Nature. A *tail-water* (the river immediately below a lake or dam where water is released from a reservoir) usually offers outstanding trout habitat because the water is so cold and nutrient rich. It is called a tail-water because the river looks like a tail coming out of a large body of water.

Fish Tails

A tail-water I used to fish years ago now gets so much pressure, the fish no longer get spooked and swim away when you wade in the water. They have simply gotten used to it. As a matter of fact, it gets fished so heavily that the fish have developed highly selective eating habits and reject all but the most convincing fly imitations.

Cut Bait

Never go fishing without an up-to-date fishing license. Not only is the fine hefty, you also stand the chance of your fly-fishing equipment getting confiscated. This money is also much needed by state agencies to manage fisheries.

If you are having a difficult time finding public water, keep reading. You can find a place to fish by checking the following:

➤ **Fishing stores or sporting goods shops.** Pay a visit to your local fly shop or sporting goods store. They should be able to give you a whole list of public water to fish, along with directions on how to get there and what to use once you're there. They may even have a local fishing guidebook to steer you in the right direction.

➤ **Friends or family.** You must have some friends or family members who fish. Even if they don't fly fish, they should know of a few spots to go fishing. Who knows? They may even invite you on their next outing. (Warning: If you don't have any friends who fish, make some new ones—you're hanging out with the wrong crowd!)

➤ **Your local State Department of Fish and Game.** They will be able to tell you all of the public waters in your area, along with various access points, stocking schedules, season dates, and any other questions you may have. Although they may not be able to give you any fishing tips, they closely monitor these waters and are the best source of information on what species are where. They can also provide you with a free fishing directory for your state. It includes vital information such as public and private water, license information, and specific fishing regulations. It is available free from any licensed fishing agent (just about all tackle stores and sporting goods shops) or department office.

Fishing Private Water

As noted earlier, a large portion of this country is privately owned. This doesn't necessarily mean that it is off limits to fishing. Although many landowners mark their property with "No Trespassing" or "Private Property" signs, they may be willing to let you fish their water. All you have to do is ask. There are, however, certain guidelines to adhere to when gaining permission to fish private property.

➤ Only have one person in your fishing party approach the landowner. No matter how harmless you are, a group of camouflaged men holding rod tubes can be pretty intimidating.

➤ When you ask landowners to gain access to their property, tell them that you will respect their land and leave it in as good as or better shape than you found it. Most farms or ranches have livestock that need to stay in particular areas, so be sure to leave all gates the way you found them.

➤ Tell the owner how long you plan on fishing and how many people are in your party. The fewer of you there are, the more prone you are to get a positive response.

Fish Tails

Access laws vary from state to state. Some states, like Texas, for example, which is just about all privately owned, have very little public water. Other states, like my home state of Colorado, have laws that say you can't own the water, just the land beneath. This means that I can float through sections of private property in my boat as long as I stay in the water. Once I anchor the boat or step foot on the bank, I have trespassed.

➤ Assure the landowner that you will release all fish caught. There is a good chance that a landowner with quality water is a fellow fisherman. Why would he want other people fishing his water if they are going to kill his jewels?

➤ If the landowner denies permission to use his land, thank him for his time and ask if another time would be more appropriate. He may have plans to fish that day or doesn't want his cattle or livestock disturbed at that particular time. If you still get denied, thank him again and politely leave. Remember, private property owners have the right to refuse access to their land.

Pay to Fish?

That's right. You have to pay to fish at some places. Although as sick as it sounds, entrepreneurs across the country have opened up pay-to-fish places for people who need to catch fish the easy way. This water, usually nothing more than a half-acre pond, is so overly stocked with fish (usually trout) that it is hard not to catch one on every cast.

These are actually excellent places for a beginner fly fisherman to practice the basics of catching fish—that is, setting the hook, playing and handling the fish, and getting the hook out. Unfortunately, these places have severe disadvantages for people getting into the sport. First of all, since there are fish everywhere, there is no need to read the water. Just make a cast, and you will catch one. That is not the real world (heck, it's barely considered fishing; shouldn't it be called "catching" instead?). Furthermore, it doesn't matter how you present the fly. And what about deciphering what the fish are actively feeding on? There are so many hungry trout in these ponds, they will hit just about anything (throw a pebble in the water, and you will see). In the real world, you must present the fly as naturally as possible and keep casting until you get a strike.

Cut Bait

Private property boundaries and certain fishing regulations are usually well marked, but not always! It is your responsibility to know the fishing restrictions and regulations before you head out to the water. Always adhere to posted signs along the water!

The worst part, of course, is that you have to pay to fish. This should inherently be one of the few things in life that is free. Most places charge an entrance fee and another fee for every fish you catch, depending on its length. And the catch and release ethic doesn't exist; every fish is a keeper! How else would they make their money?

I will never forget the one and only time I went to a pay-to-fish place. About ten years ago, a good friend and I were on our way to Rocky Mountain National Park for a week-long fishing trip. On the way, we passed through the tourist town of Estes Park, which had one of those places. Since it was near dinnertime, my buddy joked about catching a few trout for dinner.

"Why not?" I asked philosophically. "When was the last time you actually kept a fish? And how much could it cost, anyway?"

"The sign said 60 cents a pound." He said matter-of-factly.

"That's cheaper than the grocery store," I said, "Let's hit it."

Five fish later (that took about three minutes), we went up to the counter expecting to pay about five bucks at the most.

"That will be $34." The woman said without expression.

My buddy read the sign wrong. It was 60 cents an inch, not a pound!

There are other kinds of fisheries that also cost money, but these types are a little different. The small fee that is collected is merely used to appropriately manage the resource.

From Trout to Tarpon

Although the sport is most commonly associated with trout and salmon, just about any species of fish can be sought after with a fly rod, and probably already has. As a matter of fact, you could use the same fly rod outfit for catching trout and salmon one day, bass and carp the next, and bonefish and permit (a type of saltwater fish) in the saltwater flats of the Bahamas on the following day (if you're lucky enough).

Reel Good Advice

Have a pen and paper ready whenever asking a fly shop for advice. Chances are, they will ramble off five or six hot patterns and an abundance of other information that will be difficult to remember otherwise.

The Least You Need to Know

➤ Although fly fishing has recently gained in popularity, it has been around since the third century.

➤ The main difference between fly fishing and other types of angling is that in fly fishing, you are casting the weight of the line, whereas in other types of fishing you cast the weight of the lure or bait.

➤ Hiring a guide or enrolling in a fly-fishing school is the best way to get hands-on instruction.

➤ Fly fishing can be done anywhere there are fish, and finding a place to do it can be as easy as asking a friend, visiting a local fishing store, or getting in touch with your state's Department of Fish and Game.

➤ Assemble everything you need, including a valid fishing license, before the day of your trip. You won't want to waste precious fishing time.

➤ Never fish on private property without permission.

Chapter 2

Gearing Up

In This Chapter

➤ Choosing a new rod

➤ Different types of line

➤ How a reel works

➤ The significance of leaders and tippet

Ask any fly fisherman new to the sport what the most difficult part of beginning was, and they will inevitably tell you it was deciding what gear to buy. To save you the hassle, they will tell you exactly what to buy and where to buy it, what to avoid and why. They will tell you how much to spend and how much your rod should bend. They will appear to be experts on the subject. After a few more minutes of gabbing, you will discover that it wasn't difficult for them at all. As a matter of fact, they make it sound like the best part. They were like kids in a candy store.

Well, welcome to becoming a kid again. Before going shopping, however, you must first decide your needs and wants. Fly rods, lines, and reels come in a variety of sizes and weights. It is important to know your needs before getting outfitted. Have answers to the following questions, or you may come home with the wrong candy:

➤ What type of fish are you pursuing?

➤ Will you be fishing small creeks and streams or large rivers and lakes?

➤ How much can you afford to spend to get outfitted?

Reel Good Advice

If you buy an entire fly-fishing outfit at a fly shop, have them put it together in front of you. There is no better way to learn how to fill a reel with backing and line than to actually watch somebody do it.

The next step is to go to your local fly shop or sporting goods store. They will be able to give you the best advice on what suits your needs. I recommend staying away from huge sporting goods stores or department stores that happen to carry fly-fishing gear. Although their prices may be better, their knowledge certainly won't be.

The Four Functions of a Fly Rod

You don't have to have the IQ of Albert Einstein to know that a fly rod is a device used to catch fish. But how exactly does the rod work? Why not just use a long stick? Good question, but a fly rod does a little more:

➤ **Casting.** A fly rod allows you to cast a weighted line with an imitation fly tied to the end. A good fly rod enables you to cast a fly line at a desired distance and let the fly land as delicately and naturally as possible.

➤ **Controlling the line.** Once the fly is on the water, a quality fly rod lets you manipulate the fly line without disturbing the natural drift of the fly.

➤ **Setting the hook.** A quality fly rod should be sensitive enough for you to feel a strike but powerful enough for you to set the hook.

➤ **Fighting and landing the fish.** A fly rod needs to be flexible enough to fight and land a fish without breaking.

Fly rod manufacturers have yet to make a rod that performs all four functions perfectly. It just isn't possible. In order to perfect one function, they have to compromise on another. The only way to choose a fly rod is to test it. You will quickly figure out what feels the best in your hand.

What the Rod Is Made Out Of

Just about every fly rod you see on the market today is made from a graphite composite or boron. And there is a reason. Graphite is the lightest, strongest, and most affordable material known today to build fly rods. Its predecessors, fiberglass and bamboo (a branch from a willow tree before that), don't compare with the overall performance (although greatly debatable—some people swear by bamboo or fiberglass) and affordability of a graphite fly rod.

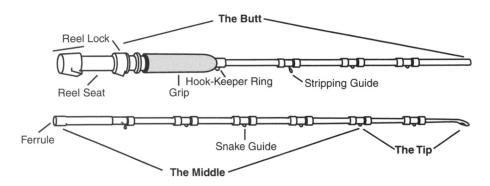

The anatomy of a fly rod.

Choosing a Rod: One Component at a Time

Before buying a fly rod, you must first understand its basic components. After learning what's available, you can then choose one that fits your needs. After all, would you buy a new car without knowing what accessories it came with?

End Plug

The very end of a fly rod has a metal cap that is called an *end plug* or *butt cap*. However, some larger fly rods used for salmon or saltwater fly fishing have a detachable butt extension used for fighting big fish for a long time. This butt extension replaces the end plug and is used to brace the rod against your abdomen when you need to relieve the pressure from your arms. Often, this butt extension is nothing more than a rubber ball. It feels better on your stomach than a metal plug. Unfortunately, these butt extensions are not necessary for most fights.

The Reel Seat

Let's start at the bottom of the rod, or the *reel seat*. The reel seat's main purpose, as its name implies, is to hold the reel securely in place. Fly rods come equipped with one of three different types of reel seats. The only difference between the reel seats is how they hold the reel to the rod.

➤ **Ring Type:** This type of reel seat is designed for light fly rods and reels. It attaches the reel with two metal rings that slide over the foot of the reel. Although the rings hold the reel much more securely than you'd imagine, they should only be used on light fly rods.

Cut Bait

Be careful when trying out a new fly rod at the store. Remember, most fly rods are between seven-and-a-half and nine feet long—sometimes longer than the ceiling of the store is high. Shop owners don't find it amusing when their fly rods get scraped on the ceiling of their store.

➤ **Down Locking:** This is the most popular type of reel seat. With this type, the reel slides into a secured metal cover at the bottom of the seat. A loose metal cover is then tightened over the top foot of the reel and screwed securely in place.

➤ **Up Locking:** This reel seat is just like the basic screw locking type, but the fixed metal hood is now on top of the reel seat. The top reel foot usually slides into the cork handle and is hand tightened with a screw band on the bottom.

Just about every fly rod you look at will have one of these three types of reel seats or one with a slight variation. It doesn't really matter which type you choose as long as the seat holds the reel firmly in place.

Get a Grip

Moving up the rod, the next part we come to is the *rod handle* or *rod grip*. Be sure to choose a fly rod with a cork grip; some of the cheaper models come with rubber grips (if they skimp out on the grip, they've skimped out on more important features as well). Cork grips are lightweight, comfortable to hold, and surprisingly durable. They come in a variety of styles and sizes, each a matter of personal comfort. Generally speaking, pick a grip with a diameter that matches the size of your hands.

Reel Good Advice

If you can't find a cork grip that is the right size for your hand, buy one that is too big rather than too small. You can always take a piece of sandpaper and sand it down to your size.

The Hook Keeper

The *hook keeper* is a small metal ring just above the grip of the rod. In case you didn't figure it out from its name, the hook keeper is used to hold your fly when not in use. Although many fly fishermen hook their fly into the cork handle, they learn quickly. The hook keeper works better and doesn't trash your grip.

Guides

The *guides* on your fly rod are the thin metal rings that hold the fly line in place while casting. They actually serve two more purposes as well: they allow you to deliver more line as you cast, and once you catch a fish, they distribute the force of the fish evenly along the rod.

The first guide you come to as you work your way up the rod is called the *stripping guide* (some rods have two or even three stripping guides). Since this guide receives the most abuse, it is usually lined with ceramic or chrome, both non-abrasive materials. The rest of the guides are called *snake guides* (except the last, which is called a *tip-top*) and aren't quite as strong or as thick. They are tied onto the rod with nylon thread, and then coated with epoxy for strength and endurance.

As a general rule of thumb, there should be as many guides on the rod as the rod is long in feet. For example, a nine-foot rod should have at least nine guides. The guides should also be spaced together more tightly as you work your way up the rod.

The Ferrules

Although I've never seen a one-piece fly rod, I've heard they're out there (although you'd have to own a hearse to fit one in your car). Most fly rods break down into two, three, or four pieces (the more pieces, the smaller they are to transport). The *ferrules* are the connections between the sections of a multi-piece fly rod. They are a male-female connection, much like an electrical outlet.

Fish Tails

Don't worry if the ferrules on your new fly rod don't seem to fit together all the way. Some fly rod companies design them like this to extend the life of the rod. The ferrules will remain snug as the joint wears.

Unless you are going to buy a rod from a top-quality manufacturer, I suggest buying a fly rod that breaks down as few times as possible. The rule of thumb is, the more ferrules in a fly rod, the less natural bend it can achieve. You can actually feel a "flat spot" or a "hinge" at the ferrules in lower quality fly rods.

Some top-end fly rod manufacturers, however, are now making graphite fly rods with such incredible ferrule systems that you can barely tell the difference between a multi-piece rod and a two-piece rod. As a matter of fact, I recently bought a three-piece fly rod that casts better than any two-piece I've ever owned. The reason: a two-piece fly rod breaks down in middle of the rod, right where the rod gets most of its power when casted. Three-piece fly rods with advanced ferrule systems can alleviate that problem because they break down in one-third sections of the rod; hence, the ferrules aren't in such a crucial spot.

Reel Good Advice

When putting your fly rod together, always hold the ferrules at a 45 degree angle, and then twist them together. This will help extend the life of your ferrules. However, if the ferrules are metal, don't twist them— just pull them snugly together.

Size Matters!

A group of numbers appears just above the reel seat of most fly rods. The numbers refer to the length of the fly rod and the line weight it was designed to cast. For example, it may say 9' #5 line or 9' 5 wt. This means it's nine feet long, built to cast a five weight fly line. It may also tell you how much the rod weighs in ounces. Don't confuse this (usually lower) number with the line weight the rod was designed to cast.

Length and weight are the most important considerations to make when choosing a new fly rod. Rods vary in length from seven-and-a-half feet to nine feet or more. As a general rule of thumb (although rules of thumb are always broken in fly fishing), the larger the water, the bigger the rod. Or, the larger the fish, the bigger the rod needed. In other words, a longer rod will let you cast line farther and more efficiently than a shorter one of the same weight. Shorter fly rods, however, also have their advantages. They are great for fishing in tight areas with brushy banks. And since they are stiffer than a longer rod of the same weight, they have a faster action (which we will get to next).

Each rod is designed to cast a specific size line, ranging from 1-weight for ultra light fishing to 13-weight for big game saltwater fishing. So before you choose a rod, you must first decide what weight line you will be using. Generally, the farther you want to cast your fly, the heavier the line weight you will need. Or the bigger the fly, the heavier the line.

Most trout fishermen use four- to seven-weight fly lines. One- to three-weight fly lines are reserved for expert fly fishermen who seek the challenge of landing fish on such light tackle. Bass, salmon, and saltwater fly fishermen usually use seven- to ten-weight fly lines, and big game (marlin, shark, and so on) fly fishermen stick to 10 to 13-weight fly lines. Unfortunately, there is not one weight fly line I can recommend for all your fly fishing needs. If you are after trout and will only be fishing small to medium sized rivers, a five-weight fly line will probably do the trick. But again, it all depends on where you will be fishing and what you will be fishing for.

All said, choosing the size of a new fly rod is a matter of personal preference. If I were to only own one rod for all of my trout fishing, I would have to choose an eight-and-a-half to nine-foot fly rod designed to cast a five-weight line.

An Action-Packed Fly Rod

When you go shopping for a new fly rod, the salesman may ask you what kind of action you like. He is not being a pervert. The *action* of a fly rod refers to its flexibility. Fly rods are rated either slow, medium, or fast action.

As the following figure illustrates, a slow-action fly rod is the most flexible. It bends throughout the entire length of the rod. This makes the rod cast line slowly and accurately, which some people prefer (especially people who grew up using bamboo or

Catch Words

The **action** of a fly rod refers to its flexibility. The action is described as either slow, for rods that are flexible throughout their entire length; fast, for rods that are flexible only in the tip; and medium, for rods that fall somewhere in between.

fiberglass rods). Slow-action fly rods take a little longer to fight a fish since they lack the backbone needed to haul one in. It would be like trying to fight a fish with a willow branch compared to a broomstick.

Medium-action fly rods bend toward the middle of the rod. These fly rods are easy to cast and will compensate for many casting errors. They are the smartest choice for beginners (although many experts prefer them as well) and are versatile enough to be used for most fishing conditions.

A fast-action fly rod, on the other hand, is somewhat stiff throughout most of its length and bends near the tip. Many advanced fly casters like fast-action fly rods because they cast quicker and farther than slower action models.

Fly rod action.

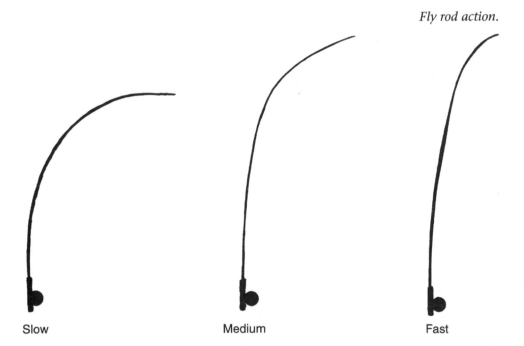

Slow   Medium   Fast

Most quality fly rods have a progressive taper. This means that the more line you cast, or the more a fish fights, the farther down the rod flexes. Unfortunately, there are no set rules for grading the performance of a fly rod. One manufacturer's fast-action fly rod may compare to another maker's medium-action of the same length. Even models made by the same manufacturer have slight variations in the action.

The Line on Lines

Now that you've decided what weight fly line to buy, your next choice is deciding what type to buy. Fly lines vary between 80 and 90 feet in length and come in a variety of tapers and densities. As you will see, each type is designed to perform a different task.

Fish Tails

Fly lines used to be made out of hair from a horse's tail. Fly fishermen would take the longest and best hair from a horse's tail and braid it together, tapering it to the tip. Luckily for the horses, silk was added to the horsehair and soon took over. All-silk lines dominated the industry until nylon lines were introduced in the late 1940's. Since then, just about all fly lines have been made out of synthetic materials.

The Truth on Tapered Lines

Just about every fly line you see on the shelves today has a *tapered* design; that is, it has a thin tip that gradually gets thicker and heavier toward the *belly* of the line. This tapered design allows the end of the fly line to delicately fall on the water at the end of a cast. Furthermore, as the line becomes thicker and heavier, it provides the weight needed to allow the rod to cast the line. There are several different types of tapered fly lines:

➤ **Weight Forward.** Weight forward fly lines have a thin tip and quickly taper for roughly 30 feet to a thick belly. The line then tapers to a thin *running line* for the duration of its length. This way, when you cast, the heavy belly easily shoots through the guides and pulls the light running line out with it. The light tip, however, allows for a delicate presentation of the fly once the line lands on the water. Weight forward fly lines have become the most popular type of tapered fly line because they are versatile and easy to cast.

➤ **Double Taper.** Double taper fly lines are similar to weight forward fly lines because they start off thin at the tip and get thicker toward the belly. The major difference is that double taper fly lines stay thick throughout the center of the fly line whereas weight forward fly lines taper down to a thin running line. This makes double taper fly lines harder to cast for long distances but good for long roll casts (which we'll get to later). The beauty of double taper fly lines is that they are the same on both ends. That is, if you folded the line in half, both sides would be identical. This makes them economical because when one side wears out, you can reverse the ends and double the life of the line. If you will only be casting short distances on small creeks and streams, a double taper may be the line for you because of its long life.

➤ **Shooting Heads or Shooting Taper.** Shooting heads are similar to weight forward fly lines, but the running line is greatly reduced in diameter, which makes them less air resistant. Because of their thin size, they are easy to cast long distances. And that is exactly what they were designed for: long distance casting. Salmon and steelhead fishermen frequently used them as well as some saltwater fly fishermen.

➤ **Triangle Taper.** These fly lines are the newest to the marketplace and are really only a specialized kind of weight forward fly line. The tip starts off thin, then gradually increases in diameter the first 40 feet or so. The line then tapers back down to a thin level line for its duration. Like shooting heads, they were designed for long-distance casting. Fortunately, they are easier to control and much more versatile.

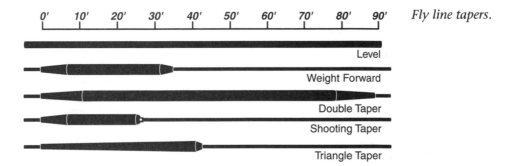

Fly line tapers.

Floating, Sinking, or In Between

Most fly fishermen use a *floating line* as their basic line for most fishing conditions. They are easy to cast, easy to control, and, of course, they float, which makes them easy to see. As a matter of fact, I know many experienced fly fishermen who only own floating lines; they just haven't found a need for a *sinking line*, or one that sinks below the surface of the water.

Floating lines are versatile because you can fish both *surface* and *subsurface* fly patterns on the same line. Since they float, they are the only lines you can use when fishing with *dry flies* on the surface of the water (sinking lines would pull the fly down). And because you attach a 6- to 12-foot *leader* to the end of your fly line, you can still fish *wet flies* several feet below the surface of the water.

Well, then, why do they make sinking lines? Good question. Sinking lines are used for water that is inaccessible to a floating line. For instance, say you wanted to fish the bottom of a 12-foot pond or a deep run on a fast moving river. A floating line just wouldn't cut it; you couldn't get the fly down deep enough or fast enough. Sinking lines sink throughout their entire length, making them accessible to very deep water. As with everything else in fly fishing, there are many different types to choose from: regular-sinking, fast-sinking, and extra-fast-sinking. Furthermore, each type is rated as to how fast it can sink, ranging from one-and-a-half inches per second for slow-moving water to over 10 inches per second for rushing water. The biggest problem with sinking lines (besides choosing one) is that they are difficult to cast once the line is in the water. You usually have to retrieve all of the line before making another cast. This is precisely why sink-tip and intermediate fly lines were invented.

Cut Bait

Be careful! Insect repellent, sun tan lotion, and the sun's ultraviolet rays are all harmful to fly line. I'm not telling you not to fish on sunny days, just be careful not to get any unnatural substances on your fly line. And store your fly line, as well as any other equipment, out of direct sunlight.

Sink-tip fly lines are like standard floating lines, but anywhere from 10 to 20 feet of the tip sinks, making them ideal for fishing deeper water. Since most of the line floats, they are much easier to cast, and controlling the line presents much fewer problems than full-sinking lines.

Intermediate fly lines are a compromise between sinking lines and floating lines. They are just denser than water and therefore sink very slowly. That makes them ideal when fishing just below the surface of the water. I also prefer them when fishing the shallows of weedy ponds and lakes. Since full-sinking or sink-tip lines sink deeper than intermediate lines, they tend to catch more weeds in the shallows.

Fish Tails

Fly lines are made to either float or sink. To get them to float, fly rod companies embed small hollow glass balls in the outer coating of the line. Sinking lines, on the contrary, have lead dust embedded in the coating.

Intermediate lines are also ultra thin, which means that they have very little air resistance when casting. Since they are so thin, they are ideal for casting on windy days (they cut right through the air). I also use them for saltwater fly fishing when the surface of the water tends to be choppy. Since an intermediate line sits below the surface, it isn't affected by the rough conditions.

Shopping for a Line

When shopping for a new fly line, you will inevitably notice some letters and numbers on the side of the box that may look like this: "**WF5F**" or "**DT6S.**" Although they may look like code, you already know what you need to decipher their meaning. The first letter indicates the taper, the number indicates the line weight, and the last letter shows the type of line, whether it's floating (F), sinking (S), sink-tip (F/S), or intermediate (I).

Don't skimp when buying a new fly line. A quality fly line suited to a high-performance fly rod will make all the difference in the world. And if you take care of it properly (washing it occasionally with a mild hand soap), a fly line should last many seasons.

Does Color Matter?

It depends on who you ask. For sinking lines, there is not much of a dispute. Since they are presented directly in the fish's line of vision, just about all sinking lines come in dark colors to blend in with the background colors of a stream or lake.

The color of floating lines, on the other hand, is a much debated topic within the fly-fishing community. Fifty percent of fly fishermen will swear that bright-colored floating lines *spook* the fish, and the other 50 percent will tell you it just doesn't matter. Whatever the case, I subscribe to the theory that it really doesn't matter one way or the other; all colors of fly lines will cast shadows on the river, and any fly line floating right over a feeding fish may spook it. To overcome this, I just try to keep as much line out of the water as possible and only present the fly to the fish (and leader if necessary).

Brightly colored fly lines do have some advantages, though. Why else would they come in fluorescent colors? They are brightly colored so you, not the fish, can see them. Fly fishing is often done in the early morning or late afternoon when the light is poor. The following reasons explain why it's crucial to be able to see your fly line:

1. If you lose sight of your fly in the water, at least you can follow the line and get a general idea of where your fly is.

Cut Bait

Be careful of cheap fly lines. Some fly line manufacturers offer low-end fly lines for beginner fly fishermen. If anything, they should be sold to expert fly fishermen who may be able to control them a little better. It would be like learning how to ride a bike with flat tires. You can get a good line for about $40.

Catch Words

To **spook** a fish is to scare a fish. Once spooked, a fish usually takes off and seeks shelter elsewhere.

2. Your fly line can tell you the behavior of your fly in the water. If the belly of your line is getting *dragged* by the current, your fly is probably getting dragged as well.

3. Rivers and streams have many obstructions. It is important to know exactly where your line is to keep clear from these obstructions.

4. By following your fly line when casting, it's possible to fix any casting ailments.

Backing

If the reel you bought didn't come assembled, you will need to add *backing* before you put the line in. Backing is a much thinner material (usually made of braided Dacron) than fly line and serves a number of purposes. Although it doesn't happen very often, a fish may run farther than the length of your fly line (80 to 90 feet). Instead of coming to an abrupt stop, your reel should have about another 100 yards of backing just in case. I know it sounds like a lot (after all, what fish is going to make a 400-foot run?) but the backing serves another purpose as well. It is also used as a filler material to take up space in the first part of the reel. This provides a cushion for the fly line and helps keep it kink-free. Since the backing goes on the spool first, it also makes it easier to reel in the fly line.

Leaders—The Crucial Link

The *leader* is a tapered piece of clear nylon monofilament that runs from the end of the fly line all the way to the fly. Usually ranging between 7 to 12 feet in length, the leader is the crucial link between the fly line and the fly. Tied to the end of the fly line at its thickest point, or its *butt* end, the leader steadily tapers down to a very thin diameter, called the *tippet* (much like the dental floss your dentist keeps whining to you about, only lighter). This is what you tie your fly to. The tapered design allows the fly to land on the water as delicately as possible while presenting the fish a fly that apparently has "no strings attached." If the fish sees that the fly is attached to something or drifts unnaturally, it will simply reject it.

Leaders come in two varieties: *knotless* or *knotted* (compound). Knotted leaders consist of different sections of progressively lighter pieces of monofilament tied together to form one long tapered piece of line. Many fly fishermen prefer these homemade leaders to the "new" knotless types because they cast more efficiently and deliver a better presentation.

Knotless leaders, as their name implies, have no knots. They are a continuous piece of monofilament that gradually decreases in diameter at a constant rate. Since they come ready to use, you don't have to tie any knots; hence, they are much easier to use for beginners and experts alike. They also don't get caught up in weeds as readily and are much easier to deal with when the inevitable knot occurs.

If you frequently change flies or accidentally lose them (most commonly in trees), you will have to tie on a new piece of tippet to return it to its original length or longer. Spools of tippet are sold for each diameter size needed. By adding new tippet, you could use the same leader for an entire fishing season. It is much easier (and more economical) to add new tippet to a leader than to add an entire new leader every time the tippet runs out. About 25 percent of a fresh leader consists of its tippet. Once the tippet gets much shorter, it's time to tie on a new piece (see Chapter 4). If you neglect to tie on more tippet, the thicker leader becomes more visible to the fish and makes the fly drift unnaturally.

Tippet thickness is described in X-numbers, ranging from 0X for the thickest, down to 8X for the finest. The higher the tippet X-number, the smaller the tippet and the smaller fly it is designed to cast. For example, tippet ranging from size 6X to 8X are designed to cast tiny flies, while tippet measuring 1X to 3X are for larger flies (usually bass bugs and saltwater flies). You also want to use a smaller size tippet when fishing super clear water or when fishing in areas that receive a lot of pressure. Here, the fish are known to be *leader-shy*; that is, wary of your leader and fly line.

Since some species of fish such as northern pike or barracuda have razor sharp teeth, a piece of abrasion-resistant shock tippet is used. Shock tippet, often made out of wire or heavy monofilament, can withstand sharp teeth that would cut through ordinary tippet.

Leader size chart.

X-Rating of Tippets

The chart below will help you understand the relationship of a tippet's X-rating to its size, or more specifically to the diameter of the monofilament used. The important thing to notice when you are looking at a leader package is the diameter and the tippet pound-test rating.

Tippet Size	Diameter	Fly Size	Pound Test*
0X	.011	#4 - #6	6.5
1X	.010	#4 - #8	5.5
2X	.009	#4 - #10	4.5
3X	.008	#6 - #12	3.8
4X	.007	#6 - #14	3.1
5X	.006	#14 - #20	2.4
6X	.005	#18 - #26	1.4
7X	.004	#20 - #28	1.1
8X	.003	#20 - #28	.75

*Approximate—a leader's *X-Rating* and *Pound Test Rating* varies from brand to brand.

Reel Good Advice

If you are unsure of what size tippet to tie on, you can generally use the rule of threes; that is, divide the size fly you want to use by three to get the size tippet you should use. For example, a size #12 fly divided by three equals a 4X tippet. A size #22 fly divided by three rounds off to a size 7X tippet, and so on.

The Reel Life

A fly reel serves many purposes. Most obviously, it stores your fly line. It also lets fly line out when needed and reels it in when necessary. And besides counterbalancing the weight of your fly rod, that's about all.

The anatomy of a fly reel is just about as simple as its use. Basically, a fly reel has two "feet" that allow it to attach firmly to your rod seat, a frame for the spool, a detachable spool that holds the line and rotates around a post attached to the frame, and a handle to turn the spool. Some reels take it a step further and add a drag system, a way of putting pressure on the spool as it releases line. If you take a close look on the outside of a reel, you will see at least one knob, and two if it has a *drag* system. The first knob simply lets you remove and change the spool (which you will use when changing lines). The second knob is used to adjust the reel's drag mechanism, which regulates the tension of the turning spool.

The drag mechanism serves two purposes. By tightening the reel's drag, you can put more pressure on a fleeing fish, making it harder to pull line out of the reel. Drag also comes in handy when casting. Without a drag system, many reels keep spinning when you pull line from them too quickly. This causes the spool to out feed too much line, which, in turn, creates unwanted tangles.

There are many different types of drag systems to choose from. The most important thing to look for, however, is a smooth one. If the drag stutters when line is pulled, or is at all jerky, your chances of snapping a leader and losing a fish are high. When shopping for a new reel, look for one that has an exposed rim on the spool. That is, make sure you can touch the rim of the spool as it spins. That way, you can set your own drag with the palm of your free hand while your other hand holds the rod. This technique is called *palming,* which can get dangerous when fighting large fish. You see, on most reels, as line is taken from the spool, the handle spins at the same rate—which can be pretty darn fast. This spinning handle often results in bloody knuckles when fighting fast-running fish.

Retrieving Your Line

You got it. You still have a few more choices to make when choosing a reel; only this one is a no-brainer. Fly reels come with one of three types of retrieval systems: single action, multiplying, and automatic. Single action is the most basic, and if you're a believer that the simpler the better, this reel's for you. Basically, a single action reel means that one turn of the handle equates to one turn of the spool. This simple design allows them to have fewer moving parts (fewer headaches) than the other types of reels. Single action reels are by far the most popular types of reels for fly fishing.

The other two types of reels, multiplying and automatic, both retrieve line faster than single action. But since retrieval speed doesn't matter too much in fly fishing, you usually don't need these kinds of reels. But just so you know, a multiplying fly reel has a multiplying gear that retrieves line faster. With these types of reels, every turn of the handle brings in more than one turn of the spool. Automatic reels do exactly as the name implies: Push a button, and the reel automatically retrieves the line. Although these types of reels sound cool, you're going to just have to trust me on this one. Buy a single action reel! After all, isn't part of the fun reeling in the fish? A single action reel with a decent drag system should cost about $100.

The Least You Need to Know

➤ Fly rods are designed to cast a particular size line, ranging from a 1-weight for ultra light tackle to a 13-weight for big-game fishing. Before buying a rod, decide what type of fishing you will be doing.

➤ The action of a fly rod is described as slow, medium, or fast, which refers to where the rod bends when you cast it.

➤ Leaders are the crucial link between the fly line and the fly. They come with a consistent taper all the way down to their smallest point, the tippet.

➤ When choosing a new reel, be sure to choose one with a nice, smooth drag to prevent losing fish.

➤ Fly-fishing gear gets abused, but with proper handling and cleaning, it can last a long time.

Chapter 3

More Essential Accessories

In This Chapter

➤ Deciding what suits your needs

➤ Don't leave home without it

➤ The non-essential essentials

Unfortunately, fly fishing is a very gear-intensive sport, and you are going to need a little more equipment than just your rod, reel, and line. This chapter goes through all the essentials you're going to need before hitting the water. As a matter of fact, it even goes over the non-essential essentials: gear that you don't absolutely need, per se, but stuff that every fly fisherman ends up with anyway.

Where Does Everything Go?

Now that you're stocking up on the rest of the accessories, we better talk about where it all goes. I know you're probably dying to get a vest and fill it with gear. After all, this is what actually makes you look like a fly fisherman. But before you do, there are a few things you ought to know.

A good vest is one that is comfortable and durable yet has the capacity to carry all of your gear. It has large zippered pockets for your fly boxes, camera, spare spools, and any other large items you may want to bring, and enough small pockets and compartments for the rest of your small items.

Vests come in a variety of styles and fabrics. Most are made out of cotton or a poly/cotton blend. Because cotton takes longer to dry, I prefer to have as little cotton as possible in my vest. As a matter of fact, I prefer vests made out of mesh for that exact reason—they dry instantly. These vests have nylon pockets for quick drying as well.

Whatever vest you choose, make sure all the large pockets have drain holes; that is, small holes in the bottom of the pockets to let water out in case they fill up—and they will at some point or another.

Vests come in two styles: regular or short. Long vests are the most popular because they have the capacity to hold more gear. Short vests were designed for fishermen who like to wade in deep water. They are cut short so your gear, especially your fly boxes, doesn't get wet when wading. There is nothing worse than a rusty fly hook. Since the eyelet and bend of the hook weaken when rusted, there is no chance to salvage them. They must be thrown away. The choice is up to you. Since I often wade in deep water, I prefer short mesh vests over longer cotton blends.

When shopping for a new vest, look for ones with the following accessories attached to them. First of all, they should have a fleece or foam drying patch to put your flies on after each use (except for your dry flies). This not only allows your flies to dry, it also keeps them conveniently located in case you want to tie them back on. A good fly-fishing vest should come equipped with a small metal ring on the outside back of the vest. This ring is used to clip a landing net onto it.

Make sure that you buy a vest that is big enough to accommodate all the clothes you'll be wearing on the coldest day of the fishing season. Otherwise, you may buy a vest that's too small once you're all geared up. It is also important to fill the pockets of a fly vest before trying it on. A full vest fits more snugly than an empty one.

Reel Good Advice

If you accidentally take a swim while wading, or if your fly boxes fill with water, immediately dry off your flies; otherwise, they may rust and must be thrown away.

Cut Bait

The fleece patch on your fly-fishing vest is for wet flies, nymphs, and streamers only. Because dry flies are so fragile, they should be put back in their appropriate fly box after each use. By keeping them on the patch, you risk the chance of crushing their wings and hackle.

Although fly-fishing vests are the most popular means to carry gear, they aren't the only way. I actually prefer to wear a chest pack; that is, a small pack (like a backpack) that fits over your chest.

Chest packs have adjustable shoulder and chest straps so you can wear them as high, when wading in deep water, or as low as you want. And since they're adjustable, they fit over any layering system. In the cold winter months, I oftentimes wear a down jacket with my chest pack over it. My old vest, however, would probably squeeze me to death if I tried to wear it over a down jacket.

Chest packs are also much more compact than vests. You have probably already learned that the more space you have, the more you will carry. The same holds true for fly fishing. I will never forget emptying out my old vest when I switched over to a chest pack. It was pretty gross. I found old disposable cameras, fly boxes, and cigar butts that I assumed were in the nearest landfill. I'm ashamed to admit it, but I even found an old peanut butter and jelly sandwich hidden in one of the pockets. The vest probably weighed close to 20 pounds. I couldn't believe everything actually fit into it. Furthermore, unlike a fly-fishing vest, you know where just about everything is in a chest pack. You don't have to fumble through a dozen pockets to find the fly you are looking for.

Waders

Unless you only plan on fishing from docks or piers, *waders* are another essential item for your fly-fishing wardrobe. They keep you warm and dry when *wading* through water and offer better traction for your feet. Waders come with either built-in boots or as stockings, where you have to purchase a separate pair of boots to wear over them. I suggest buying the stocking type of waders for two reasons. First, the boots on most built-in waders are cheap. Second, if the boots on the built-in type wear out, you have to replace the entire set of waders. With the stocking type, you can just replace the boot. My waders have outlasted three different pairs of boots. Sure, they may have patches all over them, but they are still waterproof. Wading boots can be re-felted a few times, but they usually tear apart after a few tough seasons.

Reel Good Advice

Never store your waders in the direct sunlight. The sun's ultraviolet rays can cause irreversible damage. When you store them, hang them upside down by the boots and let them dry slowly, away from any heating sources. Stuffing them with newspaper is an efficient way to absorb the inside moisture.

Catch Words

Gravel guards are worn over the top of your boots and waders to keep rocks and pebbles out of your wading shoes. They help you stay comfortable on the water and prolong the life your waders.

Waders with built-in boots are sized by the size of the boot, whereas stocking waders are sized by the height of the wader. If you're an odd size, say, short with a big foot, you don't have too many options (although a few companies are now making custom boot waders); you will have to go with the stocking type foot waders. If you do go with this type, you will also need a pair of *gravel guards*. Many stocking-type waders come with them, but if not, buy a pair. Gravel guards are used to keep small rocks and gravel out of your wading boot, which cause harm to the feet of your waders. Gravel guards are nothing more than a piece of neoprene that Velcro shut on top of your boot, making a tight seam between the top of your boots and your waders.

What Length?

Waders come in either chest, waist, or hip length. Chest waders come all the way up to your chest and are used for wading in deep water. Waist waders, on the other hand, are used for wading in water no deeper than your waist, and hip waders are used for, you guessed it, water that only comes up to your hips. If you are not sure what to get, buy a pair of chest waders since they can be used in both shallow and deep water. If your budget allows, buy a pair of chest waders and hippers. Chest waders can be an overkill in the hot summer months.

Rubber, Neoprene, or Breathable

Traditionally, all waders were made out of latex rubber or rubber-coated canvas. You would slip into the huge devices, cinch up the drawstring, and wham, instantly look like you belonged in the circus. Thankfully, you were trying to impress the fish, not other fishermen.

Although many people still use rubber waders, you now have some options. Waders are now made out of nylon, neoprene, and some new breathable materials such as Gore Tex. Lightweight nylon waders are great during the hot summer months. The only problem is they puncture very easily. The one pair of nylon waders that I owned didn't even last a season of backcountry excursions. Although they're easy to patch, you don't always have spare patches when you need them. Waders made out of an elastic material called *neoprene* are also another choice. Neoprene waders have excellent insulating properties and are quite affordable. They range in thickness from three millimeters for general uses, up to five millimeters for winter fishing. Although they may be too warm on hot days, they do keep you warm and dry on frigid days.

Breathable waders are the newest thing to hit the marketplace. They alleviate feeling like you're "standing in a sauna," which is often associated with rubber or neoprene waders. There is a catch, however. The good ones are extremely expensive, ranging in price from 200 to 300 dollars, and you have to be careful when choosing which ones to buy. I got a pair the first year they came out, and the very next day I tore them on a thorn bush while walking to the water. Fortunately, most of the good ones come with a repair kit for on-the-water emergencies and at least a one-year warranty, but I've been a bit skeptical ever since. If you opt to buy a pair of breathables, buy the pair with the longest warranty.

Cut Bait

Always wear a wading belt when wearing chest waders. If you happen to fall in, it will prevent your waders from filling up with water (which sink to the bottom of the river when full). Even if you don't fall in, a wading belt will help keep water from reaching your socks when you wade too deeply.

Reel Good Advice

Before putting on your waders, tuck your pant legs into your socks. This will alleviate the "creeping" that occurs when your pants slowly get pulled up your leg.

Wading Boots

Whatever type of waders you choose, whether the stocking type or the built-in boot type, make sure they come with felt soles. Some of the cheaper boots come with a rubber cleated sole. These were made for mud or sand bottoms so they are mostly used for duck hunting, not fishing. Every summer I get a few clients who show up with these rubber bottomed boots. I immediately outfit them with a different pair. Trust me, it is nearly impossible to get any traction on a stream or riverbed without felt soles.

If you already have a pair of boots with rubber soles, don't worry; you can buy a felt kit that glues on to your boots. As a matter of fact, I usually use old hiking boots (a size bigger) for a spare pair. All you have to do is sand the rubber bottoms down, and glue felt to the sole of the boots.

Studded cleats are also another option for traction. Personally, I have never felt a need for them, but they do make sense. They're used on fast-moving rivers that have a slick riverbed. Some boots come with both felt and studs; you could practically walk on your ceiling with these. Another option, which makes great sense, is studded sandals. They can be slipped on, laced, or buckled over your existing wading boots. These should not be worn on boats, however, as they have the tendency to tear up the floors.

The Wading Staff

Although I don't have one, there are many times I wished I did. A *wading staff* serves two purposes. First of all, it provides something to lean on when wading fast-moving rivers, acting as a third leg to help maintain your balance. Secondly, they are great tools to use to check the depth of the water. The most memorable swims that I've taken happened when I fell off a shelf in the water. A wading staff would have saved the day.

Cut Bait

If you do happen to "take a swim" while wading, don't panic. If you're in fast-moving water, keep your feet downstream and let the current take you to the slower moving water. Trying to fight the current will only prove to be fruitless.

Net That Fish!

Landing nets are a luxury item for most fly fishing situations. Depending on the quarry you are pursuing, you can usually beach a fish or grab it with your hands without too much difficulty. To land a hard-fighting fish, however, a net is often needed. It lets you land the fish without completely tiring them out.

When shopping for a net, look for one made out of a soft mesh material. Nets with abrasive meshing, or nets with too big of holes, can harm a fish. Small fish often get stuck in the holes, and abrasive materials can harm a fish's protective coating.

Nets can be attached to your vest in a variety of ways. I prefer spring-loaded cables that operate much like a tape measure. They hang off the back of your vest and stay attached when in use. The only drawback is if the net catches something when walking through thick brush. Once the cable reaches its end capacity, the net springs directly back at you. If this scares you, you can either go with a clip-on, quick-release device, a magnetic holder, or a Velcro patch. They all attach to the back of your vest. The only problem I find with these is that you have to fumble with them after each use. With spring-loaded cables, you can just drop the net, and it will retract. This comes in handy when you want to handle a fish with both hands.

Polarized Shades

Polarized sunglasses can be your most valuable piece of equipment once on the water. They help reduce surface glare, enabling you to see what's going on in the water below. They are such an important part of my fly fishing wardrobe that I keep an extra pair in my truck at all times.

Polarized sunglasses also help protect your eyes. They keep the sun's harmful ultraviolet rays out and help restrict eyestrain. They also shield your eyes from stray hooks when casting and from loose branches when walking through the brush.

Fish Tails

Some clothing manufacturers are beginning to capitalize on the latest fly-fishing trends. Shirts, pants, and even long underwear are now made specifically for fly fishing. The shirts come equipped with large pockets for fly boxes, side-venting systems to keep you cool, and a place to hang your net in the back. The pants and long underwear are lightweight and designed to breathe under your waders.

Polarized sunglasses come with either glass or plastic lenses. If your budget allows, splurge on glass lenses. They are much more scratch resistant and offer a selection of lens colors. As a rule of thumb, gray lenses work well on sunny days since they absorb so much light, and yellow or amber lenses work better on overcast days since they highlight contrast.

If you wear prescription glasses, don't worry. You can get polarized lenses that match your prescription. If you don't want to spend the money (they're quite expensive), you can always get a cheap pair of plastic clip-ons.

Fly Boxes

Fly boxes are used to store your flies. They keep them dry, protect the delicate ones from getting crushed, and hopefully keep them arranged in some kind of order.

There are many different types of fly boxes to choose from, and they all serve different purposes.

Foam Lined Boxes

These are my favorite boxes for holding *nymphs, wets,* and *streamers,* all underwater flies. The boxes are lined with foam to hold a large assortment of patterns. Large, dry flies, however, can get crushed when the box shuts.

Compartment Boxes

Compartment boxes have individual compartments to hold a wide array of flies. Since each compartment is protected, they are great for storing dry flies. They come in many sizes and styles. Some have individual lids for every compartment, and some have one lid for all of the compartments. They each have their advantages. On windy days, it's nice to have individual lids so your flies don't blow away. But these lids are fragile and bend very easily. Boxes with one giant lid are nice because you can see your entire assortment of flies and easily pick through them. Either way you go, compartment boxes were only made for certain size flies. Many large patterns simply won't fit.

Catch Words

The term **nymph** is used to describe any immature aquatic insect that lives under the surface of the water and the artificial flies that imitate them. Many fly fishermen use the terms *nymphing* or *nymph fishing* (as opposed *to dry fly fishing*) when fishing below the surface of the water.

Clip-In Boxes

These fly boxes have metal clips to hold each fly. They work well for large flies but aren't very acceptable of small ones. Most fly fishermen use these boxes to store their large streamer, nymphs, and wet flies. I don't use them. I feel they dull the point of the hook every time you insert or remove the flies.

Fleece-Lined Books

Fleece-lined books work (or don't work) just like the small piece of fleece on your vest. It is a pain to get flies in securely and even more of a pain to get them out. Furthermore, they crush dry flies and don't dry very quickly. Stay away from these!

Getting It Down

Unfortunately, there isn't always a hatch in progress that warrants the use of dry flies. You must often fish below the surface of the water to have any luck. Split shot and leader sink are both used when fishing with nymphs, immature aquatic insects that live beneath the surface of the water. When imitating this immature stage of an insect, your imitation must sink below the surface to be effective.

Split Shot

To get your fly down deep enough, it is often necessary to add weight or split shot to your leader. Split shot are little lead balls that are split in half and pinched down to your leader, or tippet, to make the fly sink.

Leader Sink

When fishing with sub-surface imitations, it is crucial for your leader to sink quickly. Leader sink removes any foreign substances from your leader that often cause it to float, like suntan lotion or *dry fly floatant*.

Catch Words

Dry fly fishing is when you use flies on the surface of the water. Dry flies, or *dries* as they're often called, usually have wings and are much more delicate than *nymphs* or *wet flies*, flies that are fished below the surface of the water.

Dry Fly Floatant

Most fly fishermen agree: there is nothing better than dry fly fishing. And there is nothing better for dry fly fishing than a fly that actually floats. Dry flies often need a little floatant to keep them buoyant. There are two types of floatant used to keep dry flies floating.

The first type is a silicon-based paste that is applied to the fly before it is used. If this gooey paste is applied too thickly, it won't work. Put a small amount on your index finger and work it with your thumb to spread it out. Then apply it to the body of the dry fly.

The second type is also silicon based but comes in a powder form. With this type, you either put the fly directly in the bottle and shake it up, or apply it with your fingers or a paint brush applicator. Silicon powders are used only after the fly starts to sink; they are not to be used when you first tie on a fly.

Although dry fly floatant works well to keep a fly floating, the best way to dry them off is with a few quick false casts. When you bring the fly in to treat it with floatant, blow on it forcefully to remove any excess water.

Strike Indicators

Strike indicators are just a classier way of saying "bobber." They are usually made of either yarn or foam and are used when fishing wet flies or nymphs. Since you can't see these sub-surface patterns, strike indicators let you know when you get a strike. For beginner fly fishermen, they are the difference between catching fish and getting skunked.

Leader Straightener

It is crucial to have a straight leader when fishing. Since leaders are anywhere from 7 to 12 feet in length and stored in a tight coil around your fly reel, they often remain that way. A leader straightener solves this problem. The leader is drawn through this small rubber patch, and the friction generates heat and takes the kinks out of your leader. Fingers also work to straighten a leader but may get cut in the process.

The Tools of a Surgeon

When people think of fly fishing, they often think you have to have the hands of a surgeon to do it. Without the following tools, they may be right.

Reel Good Advice

A **leader straightener** is nothing more than a piece of rubber with leather sides. Instead of buying one, use a small piece of rubber from an inner tube. It serves the same purpose.

Clippers

Clippers serve a number of purposes. They're used to clip off the excess material after tying a knot and are also used to trim flies. Nail clippers work well, but special fly-fishing clippers come equipped with a sharp pin that is used to unclog the cemented eyelets of fishing hooks. Clippers are an essential tool and only cost around $2.

Hemostats

The main use for a pair of hemostats is to help get the hook out of a landed fish. They are also used to grab flies out of your fly box and to hold the fly while you tie it to your leader. Hemostats come with either rough or smooth grippers. I prefer smooth grips; they cause less damage to the flies and are easier to use when crimping the barb on a hook.

Tweezers

Believe it or not, many of the flies you'll be fishing are so small, they require a pair of tweezers to handle them. Some of the biggest trout I've landed were caught on the smallest flies in my box.

Needle Nose Pliers

Needle nose pliers are used to crimp the barb on flies and to pinch split shot onto your tippet. They save your teeth, which many anglers use as a tool to pinch down the weight, and probably your health as well, since split shot are usually made out of lead, a toxic substance.

Magnifying Lens

These gadgets are for fly fishermen with poor eyesight. They are nothing more than small plastic magnifying lenses that clip on to the brim of a hat. They come in handy when tying knots or identifying insects and fly patterns.

Knot Tying Tool

Knot tying tools are handy little devices for tying knots quickly. However, I recommend first learning how to tie knots without these devices. Why end a good day on the water because you lost your knot-tying tool?

Stripping Baskets

Stripping baskets are used to hold the extra coils of fly line as you cast and retrieve line. They are nothing more than small mesh nets that attach to your wading belt and hang beside you. They work great for specific circumstances but are not needed for most. I use them when fishing from a boat or off the beach in the ocean. In both situations, the spare line becomes a nuisance. On a boat, it gets tangled on other objects very easily, and when fishing from the beach, the spare line gets dragged in the waves.

Fish Tails

Before stocking up on fly-fishing accessories, ask a few of your fly-fishing buddies what they recommend. Some of the local waters you will be fishing may not require the same accessories that are used elsewhere.

Your Lucky Hat

I'm not saying that if you don't have a lucky hat, you won't catch fish, but it sure helps. Long-brimmed hats also protect your face from the sun's harmful ultraviolet rays and reduce the surface glare on the water. Hats also provide warmth and a little protection when it rains. Speaking of protection, hats can also be used as headgear when chucking lots of weight or fishing with big streamer flies.

Since the sun is so fierce and unrelenting on the ocean, many saltwater fly fishermen wear the kind of hat with a brim in the back as well. This helps save their necks from blistering in the sun. The only problem with these hats is that you don't get to show off your farmer's tan at the end of the day.

Enough Stuff Already

I know this chapter may have been a little overwhelming; hopefully, you won't need to take out a second mortgage on your house to be able to afford it all. Just hang in there. All we need to go over now is the knots and a bit about casting, and you'll be ready to hit the water. Well, almost.

The Least You Need to Know

➤ Before buying a new vest, make sure it fits over the most amount of clothes you will be wearing during the fishing season.

➤ Waders come in either hip, waist, or chest high length. Buy a pair of chest waders if you aren't sure how deep of water you will be wading in.

➤ Soft mesh landing nets are crucial for catching and releasing fish. Stay away from cheap nylon nets; they can easily damage a fish's protective coating.

➤ Polarized glasses reduce water surface glare, allowing you to actually spot the quarry you are after. Along with a long-brimmed hat, they also reduce the harmful ultraviolet rays from the sun and protect your eyes from any stray hooks.

It's Knot a Four-Letter Word

Most beginner fly fishermen think that the hardest part of fly fishing is tying those damn knots. They're probably right; it is not a very difficult sport, but tying the knots can be tedious. However, with a little bit of practice, you only really have to learn a few basic knots that will carry you through most fly fishing situations. This chapter covers those knots, and a few more.

Filling Your Fly Reel

When most people buy their first reel, it usually comes all ready to go. But what happens if you get home and discover that you have to do it yourself? The fly line, backing, and leader all came in different packages. Don't worry, whether your fly reel came filled or not; these few basic knots are easy to learn and good to know once you have them down.

The first step in filling your new fly reel is to install the backing. But before you do anything, you must decide which side you want to crank the reel with. If you're right handed, I suggest cranking on the left side. How much backing you install depends on

Reel Good Advice

When attaching the backing to the reel, poke a pencil through the center of the spool of backing. This will enable you to spin the spool when reeling the backing in, saving both time and energy.

Catch Words

There are a few key words that are often used to describe how to tie a knot. The **tag end** of your line is the end of your line. It is the part you use to tie a knot. When you are finished tying a knot, you clip off the tag end. The **standing end** is the rest of your fishing line. It does not get clipped off.

Reel Good Advice

It is always a good idea to test your knots after they're completed. To do this, give a light tug on the standing end of the line. This is the time to catch it if it is tied incorrectly.

the size of your reel. The bigger the reel, the more backing needed. Your new fly reel should tell you how much backing it takes for the size line you use. Ideally, you want to fill your reel to about one-quarter of an inch below the rim of the spool.

If you're not sure how much backing you'll need, there is a foolproof way of figuring it out. Although it takes a little longer, you can do the process in reverse; that is, tie your fly line on the spool first with a loose knot that's easy to get undone, and then wind it up. After your entire fly line is on the reel, attach the backing and wind it up to a quarter inch below the rim of the spool. Cut off the excess backing at this point. It is the exact length you will need. Now take it all off and tie in the backing first, using the Arbor Knot. Although quite a few knots will work, this knot is easy to tie, strong, and compact in size.

Loading the Backing—The Arbor Knot

This is by far the easiest knot to learn. If you know how to tie your shoes, you already know how to tie the Arbor Knot. It is used to attach the backing around the post of your fly reel.

The figure shows the basic steps of tying an Arbor Knot. Here's how it's done:

1. Take the tip of your backing, or the *tag end* as it is now called, and wrap it around the center post on the spool of your reel.

2. Now take the tag end and make an Overhand Knot around the *standing end* of the backing.

3. Take the tag end and make another Overhand Knot around itself.

4. Pull the standing line until both knots meet each other and come tightly against the spool.

Tying the Arbor Knot.

The Nail Knot—From Thick to Thin

A number of different knots can be used to tie your fly line to the backing, but I feel the Nail Knot works best. Since this knot works so well for tying different diameters of line, I also use it to tie the leader to the fly line. It was originally tied with a nail, as its name implies, but a small tube works better. I use a one-inch piece of tube from a disposable ballpoint pen, but any small tube will work.

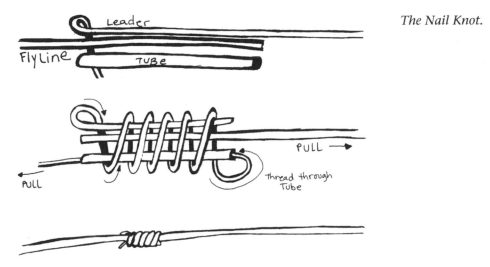

The Nail Knot.

The figure shows the basic steps of tying a Nail Knot. Here's how it's done:

1. As the figure illustrates, firmly pinch the tube, fly line, and backing parallel to each other with one hand. The tag ends should face opposite directions.

2. With your other hand, tightly wrap the tag end of the backing (use at least 6 inches for the tag end) around itself, the fly line, and the tube for five full rotations.

3. While holding all of the wraps in place with one hand, pass the tag end of the backing through the tube, back under the wraps you just made.

4. Pull the tag end of both the fly line and the backing in opposite directions and carefully slide the tube out.

5. Pull the knot tight and clip off both tag ends.

Tying Loops (Fly Line to Leader)

As I just mentioned, a Nail Knot is the best knot to use for tying your leader to the fly line. Because you may change your leader quite often, I suggest tying a 10-inch section of heavy leader material to your fly line with a Nail Knot and then tying a Loop Knot on the other end or a blood knot. There are two types of Loop Knots to use: a Perfection Loop and a Surgeon Loop. The Surgeon Loop is the easier of the two, but a Perfection Loop is a bit neater. Using loops on the end of a butt section of leader makes it quick and easy to change leaders. You also don't have to clip the end of your fly line every time you switch leaders.

Cut Bait

When tying a Nail Knot, be sure the wraps are all neatly lined up. If they are overlapping, the knot will not hold as securely.

The Surgeon Loop

The figure shows the basic steps to tie a Surgeon Loop. Here's how it's done:

Reel Good Advice

When tying loops, make them as small as possible. Leaders with large loops have a difficult time pulling through the guides on a fly rod when it's time to reel your line in.

1. Make a loop with the end of your leader. The tag end should be parallel to the standing end.

2. With the doubled portion of your leader, tie an Overhand Knot; be careful not to pull too tightly.

3. Tie one more Overhand Knot with the doubled portion of your leader. You now have a Surgeon Loop.

4. To tighten the knot, pull on the single loop with one hand and use your other hand to pull on the rest of the leader. Clip off the tag end.

5. Practice this knot until you can make it with a nice tight loop.

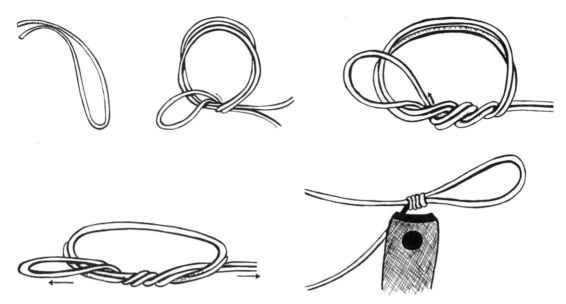

The Surgeon Loop.

The Perfection Loop

The figure shows the basic steps to tie a Perfection Loop. Here's how it's done:

1. Make a loop with the end of the leader by bringing the tag end around the back of the standing part of your leader. The tag end should end up pointing to the right.

2. Take the tag end and wrap it to the left around the front of the first loop, and then around the back. You should now have two loops.

3. Take the tag end and fold it from right to left in between the two loops.

4. Hold the tag end in place and grab the second loop (lower loop) and pull it through the first loop.

5. Tighten the knot by pulling on the standing end of the leader and the actual loop. Do not pull on the tag end. It is easier to pull on the loop if you put a pencil through it for leverage. Clip off the tag end.

6. Practice this knot until you can make it with a nice tight loop.

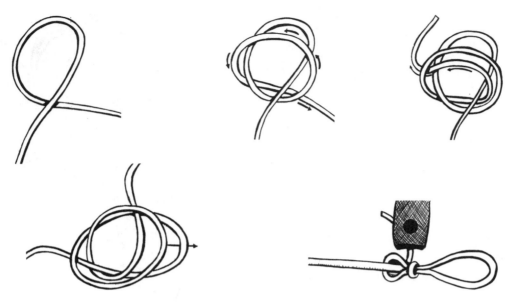

The Perfection Loop.

Fish Tails

For some reason, one of the most difficult parts of fly fishing is untangling a newly pack-aged leader. Since they're up to 12 feet in length when you buy them, they need to be tightly coiled in a small package to fit on the shelves. Most people simply pull on one end of the leader thinking it will come undone. This usually ends up making it look more like a bird's nest. I've even seen some fly fishermen get so frustrated they throw it away and start over with a new package (maybe that was the maker's intention)! To uncoil them, stick your thumb and middle finger of one hand inside the coil and stretch them out to make it tight. Then, with your other hand, carefully unwind the leader. Start with its butt section and work your way to the tippet.

Joining the Loops

Now that you have a loop in the 10-inch section of material tied to the end of your fly line and another loop in the butt section of your leader, it's time to connect them.

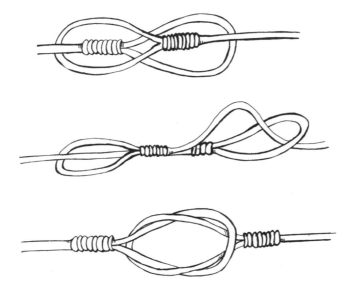

Joining the loops.

The figure shows the basic steps to connect the loops. Here's how it's done:

1. Take the loop in the butt section of your leader and pass it over the loop in the 10-inch section of monofilament attached to the end of your line.

2. Take the tippet of your leader and pass it through the loop at the end of your line.

3. Pull the leader tight until both loops are connected. Make sure the knot on your leader passes through the loop at the end of your line.

For your loop-to-loop connection to sustain its maximum durability, it must be attached correctly. The following figure shows you the right and wrong way to join the loops.

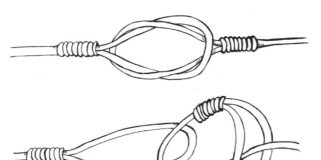

Joining loops—the right and wrong way.

Now that your loops are connected, it's easy to switch leaders. Simply take off the old leader and coil it up for future use. Now make another loop in the butt section of a new leader and attach it to the loop in the line.

Don't worry if you happen to snap your leader in its thicker section. You can still make it a tapered leader by adding new sections of tippet with a Surgeon Knot. Just make sure the tippet of each section is a little smaller in diameter than the preceding section.

Adding Tippet

Whenever you change or lose a fly, you will inevitably end up cutting off several inches of tippet to tie the knot. Once the tippet gets too short, you will have to tie on a new piece of tippet to return it to its original length or longer. As I mentioned in Chapter 2, spools of tippet are sold for each diameter size needed. If you neglect to tie on new tippet to make it the proper length, the thicker leader becomes more visible to the fish and makes the fly behave unnaturally. There are two knots to use when tying new tippet to your leader. They both work well for tying pieces of line that differ in diameter.

The Surgeon Knot

I use the Surgeon Knot for tying on new tippet. It is the strongest and easiest knot to tie for connecting two pieces of material with different diameters. It is nothing more than a double Overhand Knot.

The figure shows the basic steps to tie the Surgeon Knot. Here's how it's done:

1. Place the tag end of the leader and two to three feet of new tippet (anywhere from two to three feet) parallel to each other so the tag ends point in opposite directions. Have them overlap by at least five inches.

2. Using the two strands as a single line (and a little saliva so they stick together), make one Overhand Knot pulling both the tag end of the leader and the standing end of the tippet through the loop.

3. Make another Overhand Knot the same way.

4. Tighten the knot by pulling on both strands on each side of the knot. Clip both ends closely.

Cut Bait

Tippet serves the purpose of presenting an almost invisible connection between the fly and the fly line. If you fail to add new tippet when it gets too short, you will more than likely spook the fish.

Reel Good Advice

Believe it or not, your saliva works as a great lubricant when tying leader knots. It serves two functions: it decreases the friction when the knot is tightened—hence, makes a stronger knot—and also helps keep the different pieces of leader sticking together when working with the line.

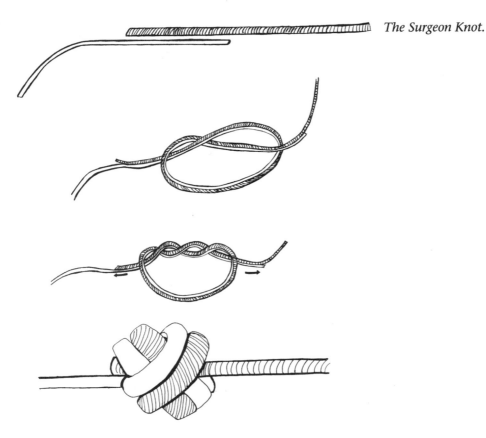

The Surgeon Knot.

The Blood Knot or Barrel Knot

The Blood Knot is another knot used for tying more tippet to the end of your leader. Although I rarely use this knot for tying on thin tippet, some people prefer it to the Surgeon Knot because it has a cleaner finish; the clipped ends on the Surgeon Knot can easily catch the line. For this reason, I use the Blood Knot when connecting thicker pieces of leader together.

The figure shows the basic steps of the Blood Knot. Here's how it's done:

1. Cross both pieces of material to make an X, leaving an extra four inches of overlap on both sides.

2. Wrap one strand around the other at least four times and pass it through the loop formed between the lines.

3. Wrap the other strand around the line another four times in the opposite direction. Pass it through the loop in the opposite direction of the first strand.

4. Using your teeth to hold the tag ends of the line, slowly tighten the standing ends in opposite directions. Clip off the excess line.

The Blood Knot.

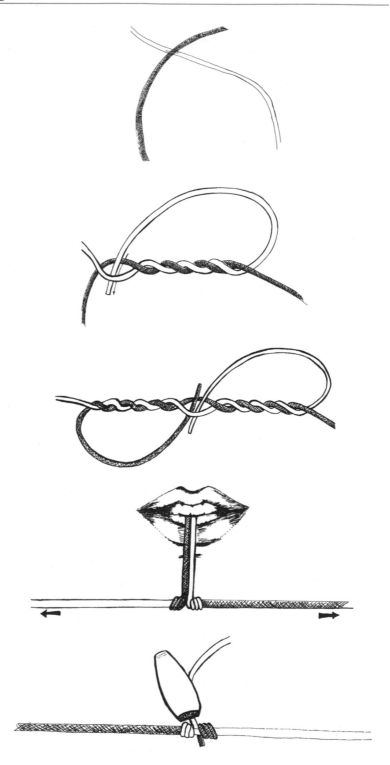

Fish Tails

I hate to admit it, but a few other fly fishing junky friends and I actually had a contest to find the strongest knot for connecting tippet to tippet (it was a cold night in late January, okay?). The Surgeon Knot beat the Blood Knot hands down. It was the only knot we tested that didn't break in the vicinity of the knot. Fortunately, it's also the easiest to tie.

Tying on Your Fly

There are two knots to use for tying the fly onto the end of the tippet: the Improved Clinch Knot and the Palomar Knot. Both are easy to tie and very durable. I use the Improved Clinch Knot almost exclusively for freshwater fly fishing and the Palomar Knot for saltwater fly fishing.

The Improved Clinch Knot

The Improved Clinch Knot is a very strong knot for its simplicity. It is easy to tie and doesn't waste much tippet in the process.

The figure shows the basic steps for tying the Improved Clinch Knot. Here's how it's done:

1. Hold the fly in your left hand and run the end of the tippet through the eyelet of the fly.

2. Make at least five wraps around the standing part of the tippet, using your left hand to hold the loop formed by the first wrap.

3. Pass the tag end of the tippet through the first loop above the eye and through the large loop just formed.

4. To tighten, slowly pull the standing line while pinching the tag end with two fingers on your left hand so it doesn't pull through the loop. The coils should form a neat spiral and not overlap. Clip off the excess tippet.

Cut Bait

Make sure you don't pull on the tag end of the tippet when tightening an Improved Clinch Knot. The knot won't hold securely, and you'll end up losing your fly.

Catch Words

Since the **Clinch Knot** is used to tie flies onto your tippet, it is the most commonly used knot in fly fishing.

The Improved Clinch Knot.

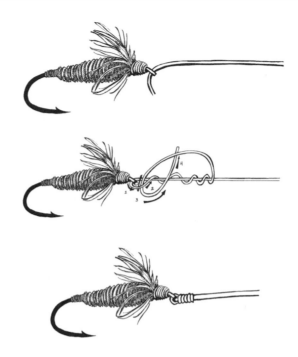

The Palomar Knot

This knot is great for large streamers and saltwater flies because it gives the fly a natural drift, letting it spin when necessary. Although the Palomar Knot uses a lot of tippet, it is strong and easy to tie.

The figure shows the basic steps for tying the Palomar Knot. Here's how it's done:

1. Double the tippet to form a loop at least four inches long. The tag end should be parallel to the standing part. Thread the loop through the eyelet of the fly.

2. Make an Overhand Knot with the loop you just threaded through the standing end of the leader.

3. Pass the fly through the loop and pull the fly gently until it clears the loop.

4. To tighten, firmly pull the tag end and standing line while holding the fly.

Cut Bait

The Palomar Knot works great for tying large flies to your tippet. Since you have to thread the tippet when it is doubled up, it is nearly impossible to pass it through the eye of a small fly.

The Palomar Knot.

Knot Easy

Congratulations, you just learned the basic knots used in fly fishing. That wasn't so bad, was it? If so, just hang in there and keep practicing them until they become second nature—like tying your shoes (hopefully you still don't have to think about the steps involved). After enough practice, these knots will seem as easy.

You're now ready to dive into the next section and learn how to cast your line. If you're getting impatient, don't worry. We'll be in the water soon.

Fish Tails

Use thick monofilament or a clothesline when practicing knots. The thicker material is much easier to work with and will help you understand how the knot works.

The Least You Need to Know

➤ Knots are the crucial link between catching and losing fish.

➤ Heavy monofilament fishing line works well for practicing knots.

➤ Loop to loop connections are the easiest way to change leaders.

➤ Although there are numerous knots to use, you will only use three easy knots on a regular basis: the Loop, Surgeon, and Improved Clinch Knot.

➤ A well-dressed knot is essential for its strength and effectiveness.

Part 2

Getting on the Water, or at Least on Your Lawn

Contrary to popular belief, casting a fly line is easy—that is, with proper instruction. Although more demanding than spin casting, you can learn the basic skills in only a few hours. Once you have the basics down, as this part of the book will show you, you can build on them and learn a variety of casting techniques.

You'll learn the very basics, from putting your fly rod together to the forward cast. Then we'll go beyond the basics and learn a variety of casting techniques for different situations. It is important that you be patient, take your time, and practice thoroughly before hitting the water. *Otherwise, you'll only learn to master your bad habits.*

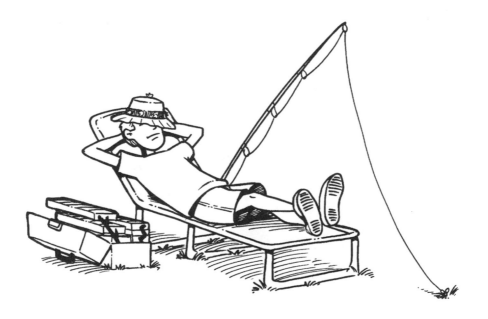

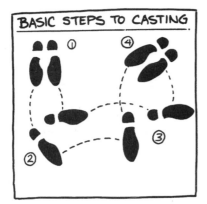

Chapter 5

Casting Basics

> **In This Chapter**
>
> ➤ Rigging your rod
>
> ➤ How the rod works
>
> ➤ Fly casting fundamentals

We all know that the point of fishing is to catch fish, right? Well, ask any fly fisherman that question, and you'll get a variety of answers. As a matter of fact, volumes of books have been written to answer that exact question. Fly fishermen will tell you that catching fish is only the icing on the cake. They'll tell you that the point of fly fishing is the actual act of doing it: being in the outdoors, closely observing the water, fish, and insects, delicately casting the fly line, watching a fish rise to your fly, and finally, if all goes smoothly, fighting and landing the fish.

Well, this chapter covers one of those points thoroughly: casting basics. Whether you think the point of fishing is to catch fish or not, keep reading. You won't even get a bite unless you know how to make a decent cast. And despite everything you've heard about how hard it is to learn, it's not. Just relax, think about what you're doing, and have fun with it.

And by the way, we're not quite on the water yet. As a matter of fact, we won't even be using our fly line in this short chapter.

Putting Your Fly Rod Together

Although putting your fly rod outfit together is easy and only takes a few moments, it is important to do it properly. The first step is to take it out of its case. If you bought a quality fly rod, it should have come in a cloth sock encased in a metal rod tube. If it didn't come with these accessories, and you want to keep your rod in good shape, buy them. The cloth bag protects the finish of your rod and keeps it from banging around in its case. The metal case prevents your rod from getting crushed in the trunk of your car or the overhead compartment of an airplane.

Now that you have the fly rod out of its case, it's time to put it together. Whether you bought a two-piece, three-piece, or four-piece fly rod, you must put it together to make one long rod. To do this, hold the pieces of the rod close to the ferrules and twist them together at an angle. Pull tightly until the guides are all lined up straight. This will prolong the life of your rod and fasten it together securely.

Cut Bait

Always be careful when your fly rod is around an automobile. Unfortunately, most fly rods break from a car door or trunk, not from a fight with a big fish. You risk breaking your rod any time you lean it against your car. Get out of this lethal habit and keep it away from all car doors and trunks.

Attaching the ferrules.

Attaching the Reel

Now it's time to put the reel on the rod's reel seat. Depending on what type of reel seat you have (see Chapter 2), you must slide the foot of the reel into the reel seat hood until it is nice and snug. Then, take the loose cover and slide it on the opposite foot. Screw the reel down with the reel seat's screw band. If you are right handed, put the reel handle to your left side. This way, you won't have to switch hands to reel in line after you cast.

Reel Good Advice

When you take your rod out of its case, put the cloth sock inside the rod tube and screw the cap back on. You may lose them otherwise.

Attaching the reel.

The Purpose of Casting

Now that you have your fly rod put together, you should probably understand why you're going to cast in the first place. There are three main reasons. The first reason is the most apparent. You need to cast so you can place the fly near the fish. Obviously, you can't just wade into the water and drop the fly line in. You would spook all of the fish. You need to cast from a distance and present the fly as naturally as possible so you can deceive the fish you are pursuing. It's the same reason you cast while spin fishing or bait fishing, but now you're casting the weight of a line instead of the weight of a bait or lure.

The second reason we cast is to keep the fly dry when fishing with dry flies. As I said in Chapter 3, dry flies float on the surface of the water. To keep them floating, you need to cast the line back and forth to shake off the excess water. This makes them more buoyant, and they look more lifelike. That's the point, right? Trying to fool the fish into believing that your fly is not an imitation with a hook stuck through it.

The third reason, which you will soon discover, is that casting is fun. The first few years I guided fly fishing, I would tell beginners they were casting too much. Frustrated, I would tell them they weren't going to catch fish unless their line was in the water, not in the air. It wasn't until a few summers ago a client told me to relax. "It's fun to cast," he said matter-of-factly.

Get a Grip!

Now that you know why you're casting and you have your fly rod rigged, you're ready to hit the water, right? Wrong. Believe it or not, you're not even ready to thread your line through the guides. First, you need to learn how to hold the fly rod.

Holding your fly rod is not much different than shaking hands with somebody. As a matter of fact, that is exactly what I want you to do. Wrap your hand around the grip of your fly rod and keep your thumb on top (opposite the reel), much like shaking hands with an old friend. Although there are several ways to hold a fly rod, the thumb-on-top method is usually the most comfortable and least tiring. It also provides the most power.

Holding the rod with thumb on top.

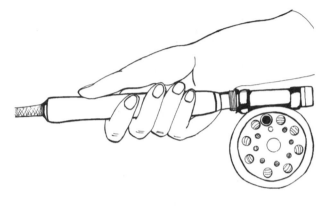

Holding the rod with index finger on top.

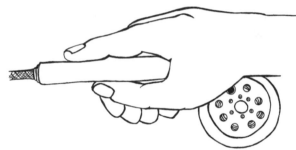

If this grip is uncomfortable for you, there are alternatives. Try gripping the rod with your index finger on top. This method helps prevent your wrist from cocking back on the back cast, one of the most common ailments for beginner fly casters. If this grip is still uncomfortable or awkward, forget the finger on top method—just wrap all of your fingers around the grip. Of course, go with whichever way feels the most natural.

The Basic Cast

I know, you still haven't peeled any line off your reel. Just hang on, you're almost there. The best way to learn the motion is without any line at all. Now that you're holding the rod correctly, it's time to learn how to actually stroke it through the air. Your hand and forearm need to move back and forth in the shape of a V. Your elbow should stay stationary at the bottom of the V, and your wrist needs to stay still. Just let your forearm do the work.

Fish Tails

Although fly fishing has been around since the third century, fly casting has changed drastically in the last few decades. Fly fishermen of yesteryear preached about the importance of the wrist snap while casting. They even taught beginners how to cast while holding a book under their arm to keep the movement of their forearm restricted. A lot of this had to do with the flexible bamboo and fiberglass rods they were using, but a lot of it was nonsense and was only used in theory; they even broke their own rules while casting.

The casting corridor.

It's About Time

Before actually practicing the motion, you first have to imagine that your forearm is the big hand of a clock. Straight up is high noon and straight out in front of you is 9:00. The V of the casting motion stays between 11:00 on your forward cast and 1:00 on your back cast. Now, with fly rod in hand, bring the rod straight up to 12:00. Your hand should be slightly higher than your shoulder and your elbow at breast level. Now practice the following steps in slow motion:

1. With your rod pointing to 12:00, slowly bring back your forearm until it is pointed to 1:00. This is as far back as your back cast will come. This is called the *back cast.*

2. Without bending your wrist, bring your forearm to the 11:00 position. This is called the *forward cast*.

3. Now pick up the speed a little, and bring your forearm back and forth from the 11:00 position to the 1:00 position, pausing in between casts. You should feel the tip of your fly rod flex when you stall on the forward and back stroke. When you are actually casting a line, this stall in between strokes allows the line to straighten out and gives you power for the next cast.

Catch Words

A **back cast** is when you propel your fly line behind you while casting. A forward cast, on the other hand, is when you cast the fly line in front of you.

The rod should be kept vertical through the entire stroke and go in a straight line rather than an arc. Practice this until you feel comfortable with it, and you can go from 11:00 to 1:00 without looking. Although this exercise may seem a little rudimentary (and boring), it will program your arm and shoulder muscles to do the basic casting motion. This will help out dramatically once in the field.

Now that you know the basic casting motion, you're ready to dig into Chapter 6 and learn how to actually cast the line.

The Least You Need to Know

➤ Be careful when assembling your fly rod outfit. Always twist the ferrules together (except metal ferrules) to increase their longevity and thread the fly line while it's doubled up.

➤ When you grip your fly rod, you will get the most casting power if you keep either your thumb or index finger on top of the grip.

➤ Hold your fly rod in a comfortable position above the reel and try not to use your wrist when casting; let your forearm do the work.

➤ The tip of the rod should follow a straight line through the air, instead of an arc, during the entire casting stroke.

Chapter 6

The Forward Cast

In This Chapter

➤ Mastering the forward cast

➤ Common casting ailments

➤ False casting

➤ Shooting line

➤ The final presentation

Now that you've learned the basic casting motion, it's time to actually learn how to cast the fly line. Besides the roll cast (which we'll get to in Chapter 7), you will be learning just about every other cast on dry land, rather than in the water where you have enough other distractions to keep you preoccupied. And don't think your back yard has to be the size of a football field to learn; we won't be casting great distances. Those casts are reserved for fly fishermen who can't drop their egos. Ninety percent of the trout you will be catching will be within a 30 to 35 foot range—most much closer.

Adding Line

Now that you know the basic casting stroke, it's time to *line your rod*; that is, feed the fly line through the guides of the fly rod. But before doing this, pull the entire leader and roughly 12 feet of fly line off the spool of your reel. This is called *stripping*. Instead of trying to thread the leader through the guides, it is much easier if you fold the fly line in half and feed the doubled up portion through first. This way, if you drop the line, it simply stops at the last guide you threaded instead of falling back through the guides. Since your rod is so long, you are going to have to set the butt end on the ground and hold the rod in its mid-section while you thread the upper guides. When you've finished threading the line, pull the rest of your leader through the tip-top guide.

If your leader looks like it just came off a tightly coiled reel, which it did, you have to straighten it out. To do this, run the entire leader through a leader straightener or piece of rubber. If you don't have one, run it through your fingers or alongside one of the tires on your car. This will get the kinks out and make your leader straight again.

Lining the rod.

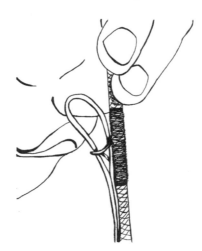

The Truth on False Casting

Now that you have practiced the basic casting stroke explained in Chapter 5, it's time to take it one step further: practice *false casting* the line. That is, cast the line back and forth without letting it touch the ground. False casting is as important to fly fishing as being able to jump is to basketball. If you can't false cast, you're at a severe disadvantage.

Cut Bait

Be careful not to miss any guides when lining your rod. It is easy to do and will greatly affect the performance of your rod.

Fly fishermen false cast for a variety of reasons. As I mentioned in Chapter 5, we cast the line to obtain distance and shake excess water off the dry fly. False casting serves a few more purposes as well; false casting allows you to progressively obtain distance without letting your fly line touch the water. It also lets you see where your fly is going to land. If your fly is going to land just shy of the fish, you can shoot line to make it hit your target, or bring line in to fish closer. Shadow casting enables you to this without splashing the water and spooking the fish.

False casting also lets you change the direction of your cast with maximum efficiency. Say you present the fly to a *rising* fish—one that is feeding on the surface of the water—and it refuses your offer. Out of the corner of your eye, you spot another fish breaking the surface of the water. You now want to cast in that direction. If you were to just pick up the line and cast it in the opposite direction, you would have a sloppy presentation. The flex of the rod wouldn't perform at such an awkward angle. You need to make a few false casts, with each forward cast working its way in that direction until you can efficiently drop the line.

Learning the False Cast

There is no need to practice false casting with a fly tied to the end of your tippet; you will only lose it in the brush. Instead, tie on a small piece of brightly colored yarn. It works well for practicing, and you won't end up piercing your ear. It will also let you concentrate on casting, instead of concentrating on not getting hooked. Once you've tied it on, you're ready to start.

We've already talked about how to hold the rod with your casting hand (shake its hand, remember?), but what do we do with the other hand? Your other hand is now called your *line hand,* and it serves a crucial purpose in fly fishing. It is in charge of controlling the fly line while you cast and of retrieving line once it's on the water. But for now, you're only going to use it to hold the fly line. Now that we know what to do with both hands, let's walk through the steps.

Catch Words

Stripping your line is a popular term used in fly fishing. It is used for either taking line off your reel or for stripping line in when retrieving it from the water.

Cut Bait

When you are first learning how to cast a fly line, don't tie a fly to the end of your leader. More than likely, it will end up stabbing you or a loved one in the face or back.

Fish Tails

Follow the fly line on both your front and backstroke to make sure it is straightening out all the way. As you get better, you will be able to feel (rather than see) when the rod is loaded.

The casting motion.

1. Find a decent size lawn to practice your casting. It should be at least 50 or 60 feet long and have no obstructions (trees, bushes, houses, and so on). Now lay out 25-30 feet of fly line on the grass in front of you.

2. Grasp the rod with your right hand (or left hand if you're a lefty), thumb on top just like before, using your left hand to hold the line. It should be held with your thumb and forefinger in between the stripping guide (first guide on your rod) and the reel. The line should be held tightly with your other hand (your line hand) at waist level.

3. Position your body so that you are angled toward your target. For example, if you cast with your right hand, your left foot and left shoulder should be angled in the direction you are casting.

4. Lift the line from the ground with a quick, smooth stroke and stop at 1:00. If you did it correctly, the line should have formed a tight loop behind you when you stopped the rod then straightened up parallel to the ground when it unrolled.

5. Before letting the fly line drop to the ground, do the same forward stroke we practiced earlier and stop at 11:00.

6. Congratulations, you have learned how to false cast. Now keep practicing the cast from the 11:00 to 1:00 position, stalling in between casts to let the line straighten out, or load the rod without letting it touch the ground.

The amount of time you pause (not stall) between casts depends on how much line you are casting. If you are only casting a short amount of line, you won't have to pause for long because it won't take long for the fly line to straighten out all the way. On the other hand, if you are casting a lot of line, you may need to pause for a little while to let the fly line straighten out. A longer line also takes a little more power to cast than a shorter line.

You are now false casting to build your coordination. Once on the water, you will be false casting for the reasons previously mentioned. But again, I can't emphasize it enough. Don't worry about distance at this stage of the game. Keep practicing your casts with about 15 feet of line.

Reel Good Advice

Have a friend watch you cast. Even if they don't know how to cast themselves, they can tell you when you bring the rod too far back on your casts (farther than the 11:00 to 1:00 casting corridor).

What Went Wrong?

Your first time casting probably looked more like you were beating something on the ground rather than casting a fly line. Don't worry, you'll get over it quickly. You are probably doing one of the following things wrong:

1. **Not keeping your rod in between the 11:00 and 1:00 corridor.** Most beginners do this (especially those with a spin casting background). They think the farther back they bring the rod, the more power they will get. They're dead wrong. To overcome this, keep a tight eye on your rod tip while casting. Make sure it stays in the 11:00 to 1:00 corridor.

2. **Using too much wrist.** Like most beginners, there is a good chance you are snapping your wrist to get the power needed rather than letting it come from your forearm. Avoid this! It will only make your fly line fall in a heap in front of

you or behind you. To correct this, think of your fly rod as an extension of your forearm and keep your wrist as rigid as possible. This will help you keep as little of an angle as possible between your rod and your elbow. If you still can't keep a rigid wrist, try placing the butt of your fly rod in your shirtsleeve while you cast. This will act as a brace to restrict wrist movement.

Fish Tails

The number one casting ailment for 90 percent of beginner fly fishermen is bringing their fly rod back too far on the back cast. This inherent trait stems from throwing a ball. The farther you cock your arm, the greater the distance you can throw, right? Well, this may be right for throwing a ball, but it doesn't work for fly fishing. Except for extra long casts, there is no reason to ever come back farther than 11:00 when casting a fly line.

3. **Not pausing between casts.** If you're hearing a snapping sound when you cast, you are more than likely rushing your casts and not pausing for a long enough period of time. Although the snapping sounds cool, it is caused by the line snapping on itself because it doesn't have time to straighten all the way. Remember our little stroking exercise we practiced before we added the fly line? Now try casting again and pause in between casts. Be sure to look behind you on the back cast to make sure the line is straightening all the way out. After a little practice, you will be able to feel the rod flex when it's time to make another cast. Otherwise, you are not getting the most power out of your fly rod.

4. **Too much or too little power into your cast.** If you put too much power into your cast, it will not make a delicate presentation on the landing. Too little power, and you won't be able to load the rod. The line won't straighten out all the way on the back or forward cast.

5. **Losing power.** If you all of a sudden lose power in your cast, you more than likely unpinched the fly line with your line hand. If you let it go, you will lose the tension in the line; hence, lose the power as well.

Reel Good Advice

Try casting with your eyes closed. You should be able to feel when the rod has been loaded and when it's time to make another cast. This will do wonders for your timing.

Shooting and Stripping Line

Now that you've mastered false casting with 15 feet of line, it's time you learn how to add more distance to your cast. After all, what if the fish are feeding 20 or 30 feet away? You obviously aren't going to lay 20 feet of line on the ground and start casting again. No, you're going to *shoot* more line through the air until you are casting the appropriate length. To do this, your line hand (the one that has been pinching the line) is going to release extra line on the forward cast. The weight and momentum of the line already out there is going to pull this line through the guides of your fly rod. Easy as that. Now let's go through the steps until you have it down.

1. To start, have 25-30 feet of fly line on the ground in front of you.

2. With your line hand, strip 8 to 10 feet off the reel and leave it in a pile next to you (be careful not to step on it). Now pinch the line in between the reel and the stripping guide.

3. Make a few false casts just as you were doing before, pinching the fly line with your line hand.

4. After you have made a few good false casts, make a forward cast and unpinch the fingers on your line hand at the same time. Point your thumb (on your rod hand) where you want your fly to land and lower your rod tip to the 1:00 position on the follow through. Your left hand should not drop the line; just unpinch your thumb and index finger and let the excess line thread through your remaining fingers.

5. If you did it correctly, the 8 to 10 feet of spare line next to your feet should have shot through the tip of your rod and landed on the ground in front of you.

6. Now that you have 25 feet of line on the ground, strip 8 to 10 feet of spare line next to your feet again. To do this, you must use the index finger on your rod hand to thread the line. This is known as your *stripping finger* or *trigger finger*. It is also used to pinch the fly line when setting the hook on a fish. Your line hand will actually feed the fly line to this trigger finger, and then pull the line through

Catch Words

To add distance to your cast, you must **shoot line** on the forward stroke; that is, feed extra line through the guides on the forward cast.

Catch Words

Your **stripping finger**, or **trigger finger** as I like to call it, is the index finger on your rod hand. It is used to slip line through on the retrieve and to pinch the line when setting the hook.

it in one to two foot increments, bringing the end of the line closer to you. As the line is being stripped, you can either let it fall to the ground (or water) next to you or coil it in your line hand.

7. Now that you have retrieved all the line that you just shot, repeat the process and shoot it out again without letting it out of your line hand, automatically passing the line to the trigger finger every time it lands on the ground. Practice this until it becomes second nature.

Stripping the line.

If you're having trouble shooting line, you're going through the steps a little too fast. Go back to false casting and practice until you can do it with your eyes shut, and then try again. Shooting line is easy to do once everything else clicks. Basically, all you're doing is false casting like before, only this time you unpinch the fingers on your line hand when the line is shooting ahead of you on the forward cast.

If you are still having a difficult time shooting line, you are more than likely unpinching your fingers at the wrong time, probably too soon. Go through the steps again, only this time shoot the line at the exact moment the line has straightened out in front of you and starts to tug on the tip of your rod. But instead of letting it tug on the end of your rod, you are going to release the tension by unpinching your fingers so the tug will pull the spare line next to your feet. Keep practicing; the timing will soon become natural and rhythmic.

Reel Good Advice

When feeding line to your stripping finger, make sure your hand actually touches the finger then strips in line below it. If not, you will waste precious time trying to flip the line to your finger and affect the natural drift of the fly in the meantime.

Casting to Your Target

Now that you know how to false cast and shoot more line for distance, it's time to learn how to cast to your target. As I mentioned earlier, casting to your target is done by pointing your thumb or index finger, whichever one you place on top of the grip, directly at your target and following through with your rod tip to the 1:00 position. It's not much different than throwing a ball. You must point directly at your target on the follow through, or you will totally miss your target.

On the water, your target will either be a feeding fish that you can see or a spot in the water that looks like a trout condominium; but for now, a small clump of grass will do. If you want to get really fancy, set up a few different casting targets on your lawn. Articles of clothing work well, but be sure to space them out at varying distances and different angles from where you are standing.

On target.

A Delicate Delivery

It is important to remember that you don't want to drive your fly, leader, and fly line into the water with a splash. This will spook every fish in the vicinity; you might as well throw a rock into the water instead. The point is to let the fly, leader, and fly line land on the water at the same time, both delicately and naturally. This way, you won't spook the fish, and your fly will stay nice and dry. In order to do this, you must aim several feet above your target (more with longer casts) and let the fly land on the water (or lawn) nice and delicately. There are, however, several circumstances where it is smart to have a sloppy cast or one with a splashy presentation, but we will get to them later.

Changing Directions

You will often need to change the direction of your cast (if you find yourself casting to the exact same spot all day, it may be time to pay a little visit to the mental hospital). To change directions, simply pivot your feet and shoulders in the direction you desire and cast to that spot. To hit a target that is more than a 40 to 50 degree change of direction, you will probably need to make a few false casts in between to hit it accurately (and not sloppily). Each forward cast should gradually work its way in that direction until you can cast to your target efficiently.

To practice changing the direction of your casts, set up several targets on your lawn and space them out at different angles to where you are standing. Then try to hit every target by moving your body and making a few false casts in between.

Modified Forward Casts

The overhand forward cast is the most basic way to cast a fly rod. But what do you do if there are bushes behind you and you can't make a decent back cast without losing your fly? Or what if the fish you are after is feeding just below a hanging branch in the water? Again, an overhand cast would snag the branch and send the fish scurrying away.

Fish Tails

There is never any reason to false cast more than four or five times. The more times you cast, the greater your chances of losing your timing and making mistakes.

Don't worry, once you have the basic overhand forward cast mastered, you can learn these slight variations very quickly.

The Sidearm Cast

Once you have the forward cast down, the *side cast* may seem easier and more natural to you. Since there is tension on the rod throughout the entire cast, this cast is easier to feel when the rod tip is loaded to its maximum. The sidearm cast is nothing more than an overhand cast that is cast to your side instead of over you; everything else is the same.

To do this, simply move the hands of the imaginary clock to your side. Instead of being directly above you, 12:00 is now straight to your side, parallel to the ground. This makes the 11:00 and 1:00 hands sit a little differently as well. They are also to your side.

Now use the same steps you used before for false casting, only this time cast to the side. Your fly rod is still performing a straight line, only now it is horizontal (parallel) to the ground instead of vertical. Be careful not to drop the tip of your rod lower than the handle, or you will cast the line directly into the ground (and possibly snap the tip).

Practice this cast at different angles: from horizontal to the ground all the way up to the vertical position you used for the basic forward cast. You may find one angle more comfortable and efficient and that you will use for the majority of your casts.

When practicing the side cast, set up a target in your yard that is four or five feet under an overhead obstruction, like the limb of a tree or bush. If your side casts still aren't low enough to reach your target without snagging the obstruction, you may need to cast from knee level. Some of the best fish I've hooked were from a side cast that only hovered two to three feet above the surface of the water.

Although this cast has a variety of uses, its main purpose is to allow you to cast to a target that would otherwise be unreachable.

Catch Words

A **sidearm cast** is a modification of the forward cast. The stroke is performed to your side (horizontally) rather than over your shoulder (vertically). The side cast is used to access otherwise inaccessible spots on the water.

The Backhand Cast

This is a great cast to use if you are standing in a tight spot. For instance, suppose you are standing on the bank of a river, and there is a large tree directly behind your right side. If you cast with your right arm, any side or overhead cast would surely snag it. This is where the backhand cast comes in to play. You can now cast over your opposite shoulder and avoid snagging the tree. It involves nothing different from the previous casts; shooting line, false casting, and the final delivery are all the same, only now you're casting over your opposite side, just like a backhand stroke in tennis, only staying in the 11:00 to 1:00 corridor.

The Law of Learning

In case you haven't come to terms with it, there is a discreet law you must abide by when learning a new skill. Although not many people have heard of it, it is called "the law of dwindling attention and coordination the longer you practice casting."

Whether you've heard of it or not, here is how it works. When you're learning how to cast a fly line, don't try to master it all at once. Four half-hour sessions spaced out through the week are much better than one two-hour session.

I can't emphasize enough how important it is to practice regular but short sessions. At some point in the learning curve, whether it is 15 minutes or a half-hour, the longer you practice casting, the more sloppy you get. Keep casting beyond that threshold, and you will only start to master those bad habits, many of which will be nearly impossible to break.

Also, there is only so much you can learn from a book. Pay a visit to your local fly shop or ask anyone who knows how to fly fish for a casting lesson.

Cut Bait

Don't get in the habit of dropping your fly line with your line hand after each cast. Just unpinch your fingers and let the line slip through your remaining fingers. If you let go of the line when the fly lands on the water, you will waste valuable time trying to recover it and feed it to your trigger finger. You also won't be able to manipulate the fly or set the hook just as it lands on the water—a time when fish often strike.

The Least You Need to Know

➤ Your back and forth casting, called false casting, should not go beyond the 11:00 to 1:00 position.

➤ It is imperative to pause between casts to let the line straighten so that you can load the rod on the next casting stroke. This is where the power comes from.

➤ If you hear a cracking sound as you cast, you are not stalling for a long enough period of time between casts.

➤ Don't be preoccupied with how far you can cast. Once on the water, presentation, precision, and timing are much more important.

Chapter 7

Beyond Casting Basics—Just Add Water

In This Chapter

➤ Distance casting

➤ The roll cast

➤ Beating wind

➤ When the fish is by your side

Now that you've learned and practiced the forward and false cast, and know how to shoot line, it's time to get on the water and practice. Obviously we're not quite fishing yet; we still need to go over the flies and patterns we'll be using, but we'll learn some advanced casting techniques in this chapter.

If you don't feel 100 percent comfortable with the casts learned in the last chapter, skip this one and keep practicing. You will use the basic forward cast and its variations just about all the time anyway. Come back to this chapter later in your fly fishing career, when you feel the need to learn more.

If you dig into this chapter too soon, one of two things will happen. You will either learn to make poor casts in a variety of advanced ways, or you will have no idea what's going on and lose interest in the sport.

Distance Casting

Even though I said earlier that long distance casting was reserved for fly fishermen with an ego, there are times when it's needed—and not just to impress your friends. Although I hesitate to teach distance casting in such a book, it wouldn't be complete without it. Although rare, there are times when the only way to catch a fish is with a distance cast, or *hero cast* as my friends call it. Remember, though, there is a direct, negative relationship between distance and accuracy. That is, the more line you have in the air, the more sloppy or inaccurate your casts will be. With this said, keep distance casting to a minimum. Remember, most fish are caught within a 20- to 30-foot radius when fishing small- to medium-sized rivers.

Reel Good Advice

When practicing distance casting, keep your false casts to a minimum. With so much line in the air, it becomes very difficult to keep your timing. Your casts will only get sloppier the more time you spend false casting.

Raise Your Arm

There are two ways to get more distance out of your cast without adding any new technique; the first is the easiest and works for most situations. It is to simply raise your arm more when casting. Rather than keep your elbow at shoulder level or below like you did before, raise it above your casting shoulder on the back cast. This serves two purposes. First, you get more ground clearance because your rod tip is now higher. This enables you to cast a longer line without smacking the ground behind you. Second, by raising your arm, you get a longer stroke, which lets you put more power into your casting. The only problem with this method is that your shoulder muscles fatigue more quickly.

The second way to obtain more distance in your cast is to bring your rod tip farther back on the back cast. Instead of stopping at 1:00, bring it all the way back to the 2:00 position. When trying this, be sure to add more power to the cast so the line doesn't drop below the tip of your rod.

The Double Haul for Distance

The *double haul*, like the side or back cast, is nothing more than a modification of the forward cast. Unlike the side or back cast, this technique is used to increase line speed when casting. Since the double haul makes your line move faster, it carries more momentum and allows you to shoot line farther. This technique is used when casting more than 60 feet of line, when casting into the wind, or when you need to shoot a lot of line quickly.

Catch Words

The **double haul** is a technique used for distance casting. It enables you to shoot line at great distances.

To execute the double haul effectively, you must use either a weight forward or shooting head fly line. As I mentioned in Chapter 2, these lines are tapered so they have roughly 30 feet of line at the end that is thicker and heavier than the thin diameter running line that comprises the rest of the line. This way, the heavier line is used to load the rod and increase the momentum of the fly line, which pulls the running line through the guides for a long distance cast.

The double haul.

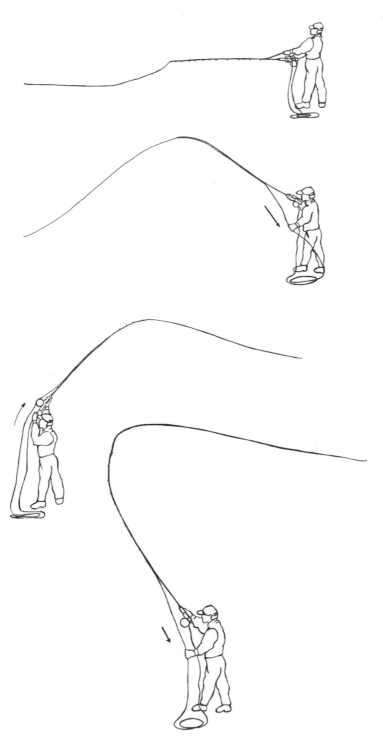

Follow these steps to perform the double haul:

1. Before trying the double haul, do some false casts to get warmed up. Once you feel comfortable and your timing is accurate, lay 30 feet of fly line on the water in front of you with another 20 feet of slack coiled up on the water next to you.

2. Making sure there is no slack in the 30 feet of line in front of you, slowly start your back cast at the 10:00 position with your elbow above your shoulder. Your line hand should be pinching the fly line very close to the stripping guide on your fly rod. Once the fly line gets taken from the water, or at about the 11:00 position, pull your line hand down to your waist with a powerful stripping motion. Be sure to keep the line pinched when pulling it.

3. As the line gets thrown behind you, bring your line hand back to the stripping guide. Nice going, you just performed your first *single haul*. I use this exact single haul quite often when there is wind at my back. It increases the line speed and makes the line cut through the wind easier on the back cast.

4. To perform the double haul, do the same thing as the single haul but haul the line on your back cast as well. Since your line hand comes back to the stripping guide on the back cast, it is already positioned for another haul. This time, wait until the line straightens out behind you at the 2:00 position and pull the line down to your waist with the same powerful motion as before, and make a forward cast. Once your rod tip hits the 10:00 position, unpinch your fingers and let the slack next to you shoot out to the water.

Cut Bait

Be careful when practicing the double haul. Since you generate so much line speed, the damage will be more severe if you hook yourself.

Congratulations, you just performed the double haul cast. With the increased line speed you gained while hauling on the fly line, you just shot 20 feet of line on a single cast. Pretty cool, huh? Now keep practicing until your rhythm and timing are in sync with the loading of your rod.

Remember, the double haul is reserved for distance casting and to help fight the wind. Unless you are fishing on large rivers or lakes, need increased line speed to cut through the wind, or are fly fishing in the salt water, there is very little use for the double haul. Again, most of the fish you catch will be in the 20- to 30-foot range.

The Roll Cast—No More False Casting

The *roll cast* is used when fishing in confined areas. Since it eliminates casting the line behind you on your back cast, a roll cast is ideal when fishing in tight, brushy areas or when there are casting obstructions behind you that would otherwise prohibit any other type of cast. It is just like the basic forward cast, only the back cast is made a little differently. And because you don't false cast when performing a roll cast, you must learn it on the water to perform it properly. Unlike the casts you learned on your lawn, the roll cast relies on your line's contact with the surface of the water. The water's surface tension helps load your rod on the forward cast. I know it sounds a little confusing, but it's not. After practicing it a few times, you'll see what I mean. First, find a body of water, preferably still, like a lake or pond.

The roll cast.

As the three pictures in the figure illustrate, here is how it is performed:

1. Before trying the roll cast, practice the basic forward cast until your casting arm is warmed up and reacquainted with your rod. Really focus on staying in between the 11:00 to 1:00 corridor.

Catch Words

Since you don't perform a back cast when performing the **roll cast**, it is a great cast to use when fishing in tight, brushy areas.

2. Once you feel comfortable with your casting, lay 25-30 feet of line on the water. Bring your rod up to the 1:00 position. Do it slowly, without lifting the line from the water. Unlike the previous casts, you are not trying to cast the line behind you. Make sure you keep the line on the outside of the rod as it comes next to you.

3. Let the line drift toward you until it forms an arc between the rod tip and the water.

4. After a brief pause at the 1:00 position, use a quick, forceful stroke to drive the rod tip down to the 10:00 position. If you did it forcefully enough, the line should have picked up off the water, and a loop should have unrolled in front of you.

5. Practice this cast until you get perfect rolls in front of you. To get more distance, extend your arm and bring the rod farther back on the back cast and make your forward cast more commanding. On long distance roll casts, your arm should be almost all the way stretched out.

Fish Tails

Long fly rods are advantageous for roll casting. Since the tip travels a greater distance, it can exert more power to the line. That is one reason I typically fish with nine-foot rods even when I'm casting a light line. They make it much easier to perform a long roll cast.

Less Commotion

The roll cast isn't only used when fishing in confined areas. It is also a great cast to use when you don't want to make a disturbance on the water. Say you are casting to a rising fish that refuses one of your offers. A conventional back cast may spook the fish since the line needs to be lifted out of the water. With a roll cast, however, you can pull the line slowly away from the fish and make as little disturbance as possible. When the fly is out of the fish's vicinity, you can make a roll cast and present it right back to the same spot.

This method is remarkably effective when fishing with poppers or large dry flies. These large, buoyant flies tend to dive under the surface of the water on a conventional back cast and make a loud splash in the process, alerting fish of their fraudulence in the process.

Take Up the Slack

The roll cast can also be used before making a sequence of false casts. To do this, make a roll cast but don't let the line touch the water on the forward cast. Instead, bring your rod tip back to the 1:00 position and start shadow casting. This method is often used when you have too much slack on the water. For instance, say you made a terrible cast and have too much slack on the water. If you were to immediately make a conventional back cast, the excess slack would make it sloppy. By doing a roll cast to start the series of false casts, you take up the slack in the process. This method is commonly called the *roll cast pickup*.

Roll Casting Sinking Lines

When you start fishing with sinking lines, you will find yourself making roll casts almost instinctively. Since it is impossible to lift 20 or more feet of line that is below the surface of the water with a single back cast, you must first bring it to the surface. You can do this with a roll cast. Remember, when you start a roll cast, you have to slowly bring your rod tip back. This pulls the line to the surface. Now perform a roll cast but don't let the fly land on the surface of the water. Once the line has completely straightened out, start making conventional back casts.

Freeing Your Fly

My favorite use for the roll cast is to free snagged flies. Say you make a beautiful cast to a pod of rising fish. The fly lands on the water just as you anticipated, but you get no strike. It begins to drift with the current until the unthinkable happens: the hook gets stuck on a branch protruding from the water. Rather than stomping through the water to save your fly, which would scare the fish away in the process, you now have an option. You can either pull on the line until you free the fly (which in most cases just snaps your tippet), or you can execute a roll cast and save your rig without spooking the fish. This doesn't always work, though; sometimes the fly is hooked just too deeply.

To execute a roll cast to release a snagged fly, lift your rod tip back to the 1:00 position (your line should be nice and tight since it is snagged on the

Cut Bait

Be careful not to bend your wrist too much when powering your forward stroke on the roll cast. This will only increase the size of your loop and cause more slack to build at the end of your line.

Reel Good Advice

When all attempts fail to release a snagged fly and you must snap your tippet, don't bend your rod to do it. Instead, point your fly rod directly at the fly and pull on the line until the tippet snaps. This will extend the life of your rod.

branch) and forcefully snap it down to the 9:00 position. Point your rod tip at the branch on the follow through. The roll cast works well in this situation by dislodging the hook from the opposite direction.

The Reach Cast

The *reach cast* is used just about as often as any other cast. In fact, many anglers use it without even realizing it. Any time you make a cast upstream from a fish and reach in that direction to prolong the drift, you are performing a reach cast. It is used to get the longest *natural drift* possible out of your fly. A natural drift is one that flows at the same rate as the current of the water, as opposed to a drift that has *drag,* or one that moves at an unnatural pace with the current of the water due to the movements of the fly line.

Here's how it's done:

1. Make sure your body is positioned properly. Your left foot (or right if you're a lefty) should be forward and pointing toward your target.

2. To get warmed up, make a few false casts aimed directly at your target. Now visualize a spot on the river roughly 10 feet upstream of your target and cast to it by making your final delivery at a 45-degree angle from your body (your right arm should reach over the front of your body on the final cast).

Catch Words

The **reach cast** is a method of casting used on moving water. It is used to place the fly line upstream of the fly to get a drag-free drift. It is called the reach cast because your rod arm actually reaches over your body to place the fly line upstream of the fly.

3. If you did it right, your rod should be pointed upstream of the fish, and your line should have made an upstream arch with your fly drifting downstream first. This way, your fly drifts naturally toward the fish before your fly line and leader.

4. With your rod tip, follow the line as it drifts downstream to the fish. This will enable you to get the longest drift possible without affecting the float of your fly.

The same steps apply if you need to make a reach cast to your right side, but you don't cross your body with your rod arm. The final cast is done away from your body.

Dealing with Wind

You will have very few days on the water when the wind doesn't act up at least once. And in case you haven't figured it out, it can be overwhelmingly frustrating. But instead of letting a windy day ruin your fly fishing outing, learn to deal with it. There are two basic principles you must know before trying to conquer the wind.

First, wind velocity gets substantially stronger the higher off the water you cast. Use this to your advantage. Instead of making a forward cast with the tip of your rod 14 feet up in the air, stay low to the water and make a series of side casts to reach your target. If you are fishing from a boat, this is probably a good time to get out and wade. It's hard to keep a low profile while standing up in a boat to cast.

Second, the tighter your loop when casting, the less effect the wind will have on your line. To make tight loops, make sure that the casting corridor stays in the 11:00 to 1:00 position and that you cast in a straight motion, not an arc. It is also important to use your wrist as little as possible throughout the casting stroke. Any slight movement of your wrist has an exponential effect on the tip of the rod. This creates large loops.

Fish Tails

Weight forward fly lines work better than their counterparts on windy days. Since the running line is a thinner diameter than the head, they are less air resistant and slice through the wind better than other fly lines.

Before discussing the different techniques to combat the direction of the wind, you must first learn the golden rule: try moving out of the wind. Too many fly fishermen call it a day when the wind picks up without even trying to find a new spot. In many cases, you can escape the wind simply by walking to the next bend in the river or fishing from the opposite bank. It doesn't take a genius to figure out which way the wind is blowing and where to stand to get optimal protection.

Casting into the Wind

If the wind is blowing in your face and you can't avoid it, make a more powerful forward cast. Obviously, your back cast won't take too much effort. A strong wind can practically make it for you. But your forward cast, on the other hand, needs to have more power and line speed to cut through the wind. When making your forward cast, try cutting through the wind with a quick downward motion with your rod tip, ending at the 9:00 position. This will help you slice through the wind without the line blowing back in your face because this drives the casting loop lower, where wind velocity is less.

Reel Good Advice

Wear a light nylon windbreaker on windy days. It will help keep the wind chill down and keep you on the water longer.

If this doesn't work and the wind is too strong to cut through with a powerful forward cast, try making a single haul on your back cast to increase line speed. Remember, to perform a single haul, your line hand must pull the line down to your waist with a forceful motion as the line loads behind you and you start your forward stroke.

If you are fighting a powerful wind on your back cast (with the wind blowing from behind), do just the opposite. That is, do a powerful back cast, using the single haul if necessary, and a lackadaisical forward cast. Often, you don't have to make a forward cast at all. You can use the wind to your benefit. Just keep the rod tip high and let your line blow into the air. Now dip the rod tip and ease your fly to the water. To pick it up, just lift the rod tip, and the wind will carry the line parallel to the water.

Fighting Crosswinds

Crosswinds should not create huge problems for fly fishermen. If the wind is coming from your left and you cast with your right, don't worry. Just cast to your side and keep the fly line near the surface of the water. When you are ready to deliver the fly to your target, you must compensate and take the wind direction into account. If the wind is coming from your left, the fly is obviously going to drift to the right on your final delivery. To overcome this, pick an imaginary target upwind of your real target and let the wind carry your fly to the right spot.

If you cast with your right hand and the wind is coming from your right side, you have another problem to worry about: hooking yourself with the fly. If the wind is so powerful that you can't side cast to your right side, you have two options. You can either perform a back-hand cast so the fly line is downwind of you, or you can switch casting arms, which, for most people, is like throwing a ball with their weak arm and is not very realistic. Whatever the case, remember to compensate. The wind is going to make your fly drift away from your target so you must move your target into the wind.

Cut Bait

Be careful when there is a strong crosswind coming from your casting side. The wind can easily tangle your entire fly line, leader, and hook around your body. To solve this, cast to your side or make a back cast.

Compensating for crosswinds.

Windy Day Success

Believe it or not, heavy winds can actually make the fishing more productive. Often, newly hatched flies either get stuck on the surface of the water or wait until the wind subsides to fly away. This, of course, gives trout a little longer to snack on these easy prey. Heavy winds also blow terrestrials such as grasshoppers and ants into the water, both of which offer easy trout meals.

Wind also ruffles the surface of the water, which makes it more difficult to spot fish. This also makes it more difficult for their predators to spot them and, believe it or not, they use this to their advantage. Some of my most productive fishing days have been when there is a light wind to ruffle the surface of the water. It seems many of the old, wise (and big) fish are a little less tentative to show themselves and will come out of cover to feed in the open areas, making them more readily available for deception by an imitation fly.

Reducing Drag

As I mentioned earlier, even though your fly is lifeless, it needs to act as naturally as possible on the surface of the water. Otherwise, it will simply be rejected by the quarry you are after. And since the surface of the moving water has various currents, your fly may get dragged at a different pace than the water. For example, say you are wading through a fast moving river and spot a rise on the far bank. The rise was in a slow moving pool behind a large rock. You try to cast your fly into the pool, but you see your line taking off downstream with the current. All of a sudden, your fly gets dragged downstream and forms a large wake behind it. Not only does the fish you are after think the fly is fake, it also probably thinks the floating object has a small motor attached to it. This is precisely why drag is bad.

Fish Tails

Believe it or not, trout have the uncanny ability to know a fly is fake if it drifts at a different pace than the natural movement of the water. If your fly is drifting any faster or slower than the current, there is a very slim chance you will catch anything.

Casting with Slack

Besides a reach cast, there are other ways to help keep your line from dragging the fly. They all do nothing more than buy you time before your line gets dragged by the moving water.

The *s-cast* is a prime example of buying more time. It is called an s-cast for two reasons. First, the *s* stands for *slack*, which is exactly what you're casting into the water. The more slack line you have in the water, the longer it takes the current to drag the fly. Think about it. If you cast a tight line into fast moving water, the faster currents will immediately form a downstream belly in your fly line, thus dragging your fly with it. It is also called an s-cast because you try to make s-curves in your fly line while it is in the air. This gives you more slack once it lands on the water.

The s-cast.

As the figure illustrates, here's how it's done:

1. Make a forward cast as you normally would, but instead of shooting line to the water, pinch your fingers on your line hand and lift the rod just as the line straightens out in front of you. If done correctly, the line should have come to an abrupt stop in mid air and sprung back toward you before falling to the water. The line should land on the water with a sufficient amount of slack to give the fly "time" for a natural drift.

2. If you need more slack next time, simply pull on your line hand while you flick the rod tip up on the forward cast or wiggle your rod back and forth before the line hits the water. Both of these techniques will give you more slack.

Cut Bait

Be careful of adding too much slack to the surface of the water. If the line is not semi-tight, a fish can actually swallow the fly and spit it out without hooking itself.

3. Once the fly line lands on the water, feed the line to your trigger finger and strip the slack at the same rate as the current without affecting the drift of your fly.

Although creating slack on the water buys you more time for a natural drift, too much slack gives the fish time to reject your fly. You have to find a happy medium where you have enough slack for a good drift but not so much that you can't set the hook in case you get a strike.

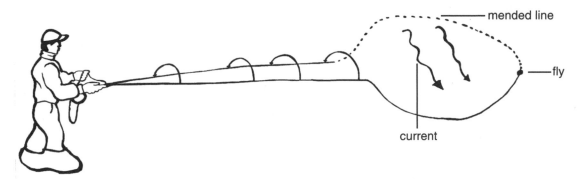

The upstream mend.

Mending the Line

Mending the line is an essential technique that can be used with any cast. Since moving water is comprised of numerous currents, you must often reposition your fly line after it lands on the water so it drifts at the same rate as the fly. This repositioning of the fly line is called *mending the line*. Mending the line is a method used to avoid drag. It is accomplished by flipping the belly of the line in the opposite direction in which the fly is getting dragged.

To see how mending the line works, it must be practiced on moving water. As the figure illustrates, here's how to mend the line:

1. Make a conventional forward cast across the river or stream. If possible, cast your fly into water that is moving slower than the main current of the water. Behind a rock usually works. Watch the belly of the line get dragged downstream. It should form a downstream arch.

2. Now flick the belly of your line upstream by making a powerful semi-circle with your rod tip (the semi-circle should go in an upstream direction). The belly of your line should now be upstream of your fly and make an upstream arch. Like the s-cast or the reach cast, mending the line buys you more time to get a natural drift.

Your first few times mending the line probably flipped the fly out of the water as well. Be careful, this will also spook the fish. If this happens, try using a little less power on your circular motion.

When fishing in really fast moving water, you often have to mend the line repeatedly to get a drag free drift. Since you get a longer drift out of your fly, mending your line enables you to cover much more water over the course of the day.

It is very important to be able to *read the water;* that is, study the flow of the water. Although not as common, sometimes you need to make a downstream mend; that is, flip the belly of the line in a downstream direction so you don't slow the fly down.

For example, say you are casting from the inside bank of a meandering river. Next to the bank is a 15-foot wide pool of slow moving water, and you cast to the faster current next to it. Although your fly quickly drifts with the current, it is soon held up by the fly line in the slow moving water. To avoid this, do a downstream mend. Follow the same steps as before, but your rod should now perform a semi-circle in a downstream direction.

Catch Words

Reading the water is an expression fly fishermen use when studying the water. You *read* the water for a variety of purposes: to figure out where fish are holding, to figure out the currents, to watch for rising fish, and so on.

High Sticking

Now that you've learned how to perform a variety of casts for different situations, it's time to know what to do if the fish you are pursuing is holding right next to you. If you cast the line, it would simply go beyond the fish.

The answer is simple: keep your rod tip as high as possible and allow as little fly line to touch the water as you can. It's as easy as that.

This technique is often used when nymph fishing in deep holes. Since you can get much closer to a fish that is holding in deep water, nymph fishermen often fish directly over their target. Instead of casting at the end of a drift, they simply pull up their line and flick it back upstream. By keeping their rod tip high, only their leader and fly are in the water.

Cut Bait

If you are getting blisters on your hand after a day on the water, you are gripping the rod too tightly. Loosen up. Your casting will improve significantly.

High sticking is also a great technique used to avoid drag and to avoid spooking fish. Since your fly line is what causes drag and often is what spooks a fish, why not keep as much of it out of the water as possible? That is exactly what high sticking does. By keeping your rod tip high, you keep all excess fly line out of the water so there is nothing to drag the fly and nothing to cast a shadow in the water. This is how fly fishing originally got started. It can also be called *dapping*, a technique that good fishermen use all the time. Dapping is covered thoroughly in Chapter 8.

Putting It All Together

The beauty of fly fishing is that no two days are the same. As a matter of fact, no two casts are even the same. Now that you have learned how to cast and have an idea of how to control the line, it is time to put it all together and rise to meet every situation the river offers.

The only way to get better now is to practice your newly learned skills. Since every fly fishing circumstance presents its own challenges, you must constantly reach into your bag of tricks to meet them. By practicing what you've learned in this chapter, your bag of tricks will get deeper and deeper.

The Least You Need to Know

➤ Roll casts are used when there is no room for an adequate back cast.

➤ Double hauls are used to further load your rod and increase line speed on both the back and forward cast. This casting technique is used for distance casting on large rivers and lakes, and for saltwater fly fishing. It is also a good technique to use when casting large flies.

➤ Reach casts are used on rivers to present the fly in a drag free manner. It also gives the angler the advantage of presenting the fly before the leader and fly line.

➤ High sticking is used to keep unnecessary line out of the water. This technique lets the fly drift as naturally as possible.

Part 3
On the Water Tactics

Everything you've learned up to now was to prepare you for getting on the water. I know it may have seemed a bit excessive—all of the gear, the casts, and so on—but this is fly fishing (if you wanted to pick up something easy, you could have tried bowling). Now that you're on the water with fly rod in hand, where do you go? Where are the fish? How do you catch them?

These are all valid questions that you should be asking yourself. After all, you want to catch fish, don't you? Well, this crucial part of the book answers these questions and more. We will start by figuring out where and when to fish and end with the techniques used to hook, fight, land, and of course, release a fish.

Chapter 8

When and Where to Fish

In This Chapter

➤ Reading water

➤ Different parts of a river or stream

➤ Fishing ponds and lakes

➤ Best times to fish

Now that you know how to cast and present your fly in a drag-free manner, it's time to talk about the water you will be fishing. Even if you know where to go, you still need to figure out where to fish once you're there.

This chapter will enable you to dissect the different parts that make up a body of water. Whether it's a high alpine lake or a fast moving river, you will learn where the fish are holding and the best times to fish for them.

Fishy Signs

When you head out to go fly fishing, whether it be at a stream or a lake, the first thing you need to do is look for signs of fish. The surface of the water can tell you a great deal about where the fish are feeding. Of course, you have to be sly and keep a low profile in order to see them. The following signs on the surface of the water indicate there are feeding fish.

➤ **Splashes.** Often you can see fish aggressively feeding on the surface of the water. When doing so, they actually make a splash. They are either feeding on aquatic insects emerging toward the surface of the water or on smaller bait fish. Bass are known to actually jump out of the water to snatch a hovering dragonfly or damselfly.

➤ **Rings.** Rings are a good indication that there are fish feeding on the surface of the water or just beneath.

➤ **Bulges.** Bulges on the surface of the water indicate that a fish is feeding just below. More than likely, the fish is feeding on aquatic insects emerging toward the surface of the water to hatch. You may even see their *dorsal fin,* or top fin, come out of the water when they are feeding.

➤ **Tailing.** When fishing in shallow water, keep your eyes peeled for a fish that is *tailing*; that is, a fish that shows its tail through the surface when feeding on the bottom. This is a great way to find fish in the saltwater flats (which we will discuss later).

➤ **Wakes or currents.** Some fish actually form a small wake behind them when they are swimming through the water. When this is the case, they are either spooked and running for shelter, lazily cruising in search of food, or aggressively chasing their next meal. When casting to a cruising fish, always cast ahead of the fish in the direction it is swimming.

Cut Bait

Just because you see rings on the surface of the water, don't immediately tie on a dry fly. Often, a ring is formed when a fish is feeding on insects just beneath the surface. When this is the case, you must present your fly beneath the surface to have any luck.

Reel Good Advice

Don't judge the size of a fish by the size of the ring, splash, or bulge it left on the surface of the water. Many large fish sip flies off of the surface, leaving only a small dimple as evidence. A small fish, on the other hand, may splash the surface of the water and create a huge racket just to grab a small meal.

Dissecting the Stream

Have you ever heard the expression that 10 percent of fishermen catch 90 percent of the fish? Well, disregard it. It's not true. It's more like 95 percent of the fish. Why, you ask?

The answer is that skilled fishermen know where the fish are holding. That is, they know how to dissect a body of water and figure out where the fish are even if they don't see them. But before we discuss where the fish hold, you must first understand two basic laws that apply to moving water:

1. For a stream or river to flow, there must be a gradient; otherwise, it would be stagnant. And the steeper the gradient, the faster the water moves (if you know the basic laws of gravity, this should be nothing new to you). Although some rivers may not appear to have a gradient, they do. Even the Mississippi and Missouri rivers have a gradient.

2. Water takes the path of least resistance. Well, of course, right? Most fly fishermen, however, don't fully understand this. It is something that can only really be learned by spending time on the water.

Catch Words

A **feeding lane** is a current that carries insects and debris to feeding fish. It is important to present your fly in a feeding lane to have a successful day on the water.

Now that you know a little bit about how rivers and streams work, it's time to understand the different parts that make them up. Whenever dissecting a part of a river, always look for its *feeding lanes* or *feeding alleys*; that is, the current that carries the most food and debris.

Pools

A *pool* is generally considered a deep, wide area of slow moving water in a stream or river. Because there is an abundance of easy-to-catch food, pools can be one big "trout condominium." There are several different parts that make up a pool, all of which hold fish.

The *head* of a pool is the very beginning, usually after a section of fast moving water. This is usually the easiest place to approach because the choppy water and the loud sound disrupt the fish's senses. The choppy water makes it more difficult for them to see you, and the rough water makes it less likely for them to feel your vibrations.

The head of the pool usually has a *lip* that the water flows over before it gets deep. Although difficult to fish, this small shelf below the lip is great holding water for trout. They simply rest in this calm water and feed on the abundance of food pouring over them in the current.

The *tongue* is the main current of water that drops into the head of a pool. Unless the main current hugs a bank before forming a pool, there will be two small areas of calm water on either side. This makes great holding water because it is calm (the fish don't have to expend much energy staying there), and there is an influx of food pouring in from the main current. It is much easier to fish these side pools off of the tongue than to fish the deep water under the shelf.

The head is followed by a broad segment of slow moving water. This is the *middle* section of the pool and usually the deepest. If the fish are rising through this section, the fishing can be phenomenal. Otherwise, the fish will stay out of the faster moving water near the surface and feed on the bottom, in which case, you must use nymphs (which we'll get to later).

It is important to locate the main current when fishing the middle of a pool. To locate it, study the surface of the water. You will see where most of the debris, bubbles, insects, and so on are most concentrated. This is the main feeding lane of the pool.

Reel Good Advice

A careful approach is absolutely necessary when approaching the tail of a pool. The best spot is just downstream at an angle or from the side on a bank. The water downstream is more than likely faster than the water in the tail of a pool. To compensate, keep your rod tip held high so the line at your feet doesn't drag your fly at an unnatural speed.

Since the water is smooth and glassy through the mid-section of a pool, the fish can easily get spooked. When you plan your approach, make sure you are out of sight and you offer your imitation with a drag-free drift.

The *tail of a pool*, or *tailout*, is its lowest section and usually the shallowest. This is where the water picks up its pace and drops into a *riffle* or *run*. Since all of the food in a pool drains into the tail, it usually houses the biggest fish.

When scouting the tail of a pool, look for its deepest channel. This is the main current, and it carries most of the food; hence, it is where most of the fish will be holding. If you can find the spot where the deep channel starts to get shallow before picking up its pace, you can almost always be assured a nice fish. If you were to take a strainer and seine the water in this spot, you would get the most amount of food. Not only is the food gathered horizontally on the surface, it is also funneled vertically in the water column.

Riffles are shallow stretches of choppy water that separate pools and runs. Their rocky bottoms create the choppy surface and make great holding water for trout. Since the riverbed has a steeper gradient, the water moves faster than in a pool. Most trout, as well as the insects they feed on, favor the highly oxygenated water in riffles.

If you look closely at a stretch of riffles, you will see spots on the surface that seem totally smooth, like someone sanded out all the choppy water. These are called *slicks,* and they are caused by a depression in the riverbed or an object on the bottom (usually a rock). If the water is deep enough, slicks can offer outstanding cover from fast moving water.

It is also important to locate *seams* in the water. Seams are formed by two currents that move at different speeds. For example, say a large rock is protruding from the water. The water just behind the rock will be moving slower than the main current. A visible line, or *seam*, will form in the water. Since trout want to expend as little energy as possible, they usually hang out in the slower moving water and dart out to grab food in the faster current. Even if there is no obstruction in the water, there is also a holding spot right at the seam of the two currents. Since both currents are pushing against each other, a trout can remain almost lifeless and be held in between the two currents.

Fish Tails

Trout have two things on their minds: food and shelter. They will hold in a spot that offers plenty of food and easy access to shelter in case of emergency (eagles, mergansers, herons, fly fishermen, and so on). But in order for the spot to be worth their while, they have to be able to take in as much food as possible, with the least amount of effort. It is all an energy game for them; they have to take in more energy than they're expending, or they will die. That is, there must be enough food for them to take in more calories than they use to get it. That's why trout rarely hold in really fast moving water. They have to waste too much energy staying there.

For most people, riffles are the easiest places to catch fish. Since the water is choppy, the fish have a more difficult time seeing you, and your vibrations don't travel as far. Furthermore, since there is such an abundance of food, the fish hold just about everywhere. And don't worry about the water being too shallow; they will hold in much shallower water than you'd imagine. I've caught large fish that were feeding in water just deeper than their dorsal fin (their top fin).

It can also be much easier to present your fly in a series of riffles. Since the current is constant and the surface flows at a uniform speed, your fly doesn't get dragged too badly.

A *run* is deeper than a riffle but narrower than a pool. The water also moves at a speed in between the two. Runs usually don't offer too much cover for fish but, at times, can offer excellent fishing.

Eddies are formed by obstructions in the flow of the water. They create a swirling flow behind them that usually moves in the opposite direction of the main current. Picture the large rock protruding from the water in our last example. The water behind the rock is called an *eddy*. Fallen trees, small islands, meandering banks, and, of course, large rocks, all create eddies in the water. Although tricky to fish because of the *drag* thing we talked about earlier, eddies can offer great holding water because of the abundance of food they tend to gather.

Reel Good Advice

When I hit a stretch of riffles, I grid them out so I end up fishing every possible spot a fish could be holding. I start by fishing the water close to me and progressively work my way out to the opposite bank, letting my fly drift through every foot of water.

When I come across a nice looking eddy, I strategically plan my approach. Usually, I will first cast to the water just upstream of the obstruction and to its sides (remember, it takes an obstruction in the current to make an eddy). It is much easier to get a drag-free drift in this water, and it can hold some nice fish. Only then will I fish to the swirling eddy behind the obstruction. Since this water is more difficult to fish without dragging your fly, it is easier to spook the fish. Why take the chance of fishing this water first since you may ruin your chances of sneaking up on fish in the calmer water.

Fish Tails

There are two types of holding water: *temporary* holding water and *permanent* holding water. Permanent holding water offers a year-round spot for fish to hold and offers plenty of food and shelter. Deep pools and runs offer permanent holding water for trout. Temporary holding water, on the other hand, is water that trout move into only when it's productive (that is, a hatch). Riffles and shallow bank water are excellent examples. At times, there is an abundance of insect activity that invites hungry trout to these areas. Other times, however, the food supply diminishes, and trout seek other holds because they offer better protection from predators. It's kind of like your mother's kitchen: visit it when there is food on the stove and retreat to the den when there's not.

On fast moving, deep meandering streams, fish stay out of the main current and retreat to the slower moving water on the inside of the bank (*bends* in the river). To save energy, the fish often hold in the margin between the fast and slow moving water and dart out into the faster moving water to feed.

Cut Bait

Be careful when fishing undercut banks. Although they hold fish, they usually have roots and other strainers that can easily snag your fly.

Fish will often move into the outside bank when the water level drops late in the season. The current isn't too powerful to hold the fish and the outside current gets a steady supply of food. The inside bank can also be too shallow to hold fish during low water conditions. Also, look for undercut banks on the outside of bends. This is great holding water for trout because it offers protection from predators and shelter from the strong current of the main channel.

Side channels are often created on large rivers from floods or high spring conditions due to a melting snow-pack. During this time, side channels offer excellent protection from the torrents or rapids that are created. Since trout can't afford to expend more energy than they're taking in, side channels offer great holding water, and they're easy to fish. Just think of them as separate smaller streams and fish them accordingly. You will be amazed at how many fish gather in side channels during this time.

Creeks and streams that contain large protruding rocks are full of *pocket water*. It is called *pocket water* because each rock will have an eddy, or *pocket*, of water behind it. These all offer great holding water for trout.

When fishing pocket water, act like there is a trout behind every rock. Believe it or not, there sometimes is. A cast or two behind every rock is usually all that's needed. But be careful. Since there are so many currents in pocket water, it is essential to keep as much line out of the water as possible. This will only create drag and possibly snag your line as well. Remember to keep your rod tip held high to keep excess line out of the water.

Rather than being *selective feeders*, fish in pocket water tend to be *opportunistic feeders*. That is, they tend to grab just about anything that resembles food that floats by. Selective feeders reject everything but the most natural, realistic looking fly patterns presented perfectly. Since the water usually moves fast through a section of pocket water, the fish don't have time for close examination. They have to either react and grab whatever comes floating by or miss the meal. If you get a strike but don't set the hook in this type of water, chances are it will strike again. The fish simply missed the fly and will often strike back with a vengeance.

More Holding Water

In moving water, trout face upstream so they can intercept food floating by them. As a matter of fact, if you look at the body of a trout, you can see that it was designed to be facing upstream. Like the fast curves on an aerodynamic racecar, the body of a trout is hydrodynamic. Although they were designed to withstand fast moving water, they will only hold in a spot where they can take in more calories than they are burning. With this in mind, always look for slower moving water that has easy access to the faster currents that carry food. Thankfully, most good trout streams are full of rocks and other obstructions that break up the current and give trout good resting places. These breaks in the current are where trout spend most of their lives.

Look for trout in the following spots:

➤ **Fallen trees and brushy banks.** Both fallen trees and brushy banks offer protection from predators and an abundance of food. Brushy banks can be full of terrestrials such as ants, hoppers, and beetles that accidentally fall into the water. Fallen trees in the water offer great forage for aquatic insects. This, of course, attracts the fish that feed on them. Fallen trees also offer a break from the main current. The slower moving water behind these obstructions is excellent trout territory.

➤ **Confluences.** Confluences are the collision of two different flows of water. They can be created by two rivers or streams that intersect or two channels of the same river that collide. Confluences give fish a choice of two food supplies and usually have an eddy that provides good holding water. When fishing confluences, keep as much line out of the water as possible. Since there are two currents of varying speed, it is easy for your fly to get dragged unnaturally. Also, spend extra time at these places. There can be so much food in the water, it will be just a matter of time before you get a strike.

➤ **Feeder streams.** The inlet of feeder streams provides great trout habitat. There is usually an abundance of food at these confluences because there are now two sources of current bringing insects in. Also, the eddy created by the merging of two bodies of water provides good holding water. There is an abundance of food, and the trout don't have to expend a lot of energy to hold their position. Furthermore, many rivers get so warm during the hot summer months that the trout seek a refuge. Besides shady areas, trout also look for small feeder streams and springs that usually offer a colder flow of water. When this is the case, the trout are usually stressed out and gathered in such places for survival. Use your best judgement. I would like to think that most fly fishermen would leave these helpless trout alone and let them survive another season.

➤ **Around rocks.** As I mentioned earlier, fish like to hold in the eddies created behind rocks. This gives them a break from the main current and offers easy access to food. They will also hold in the pillows of water that form in front of rocks and to their sides.

➤ **Near banks.** Since the banks on most trout streams and rivers aren't uniform, they offer trout an easy break from the main current. Banks also offer trout a steady food source. Many species of aquatic insects develop near the banks, and terrestrials often end up in the water adjacent to them. Banks can be the only fishable water during high water. If the main current is too powerful, fish will hug the banks until the water calms down later in the season. When this is the case, it is often necessary to keep your casts within a foot of the bank.

➤ **Tailwater.** Tailwater is the water below a lake or reservoir. It is usually fed by a dam and looks like a long tail below the larger body of water. Because

Reel Good Advice

Always make a few casts in the mouth of a feeder stream. Fish hold in these spots to escape the main current and capitalize on the influx of food.

Cut Bait

Be careful when fishing in a tail-water. A loud horn is often blown to alert anglers that an increase of water is going to be released through the dam. Read the signs by the water and get out immediately if you hear a loud horn.

of the incredible amount of food that is available, tailwaters provide excellent habitat for trout. Since the water is usually released from the bottom of a reservoir, it is well oxygenated and usually remains at a constant temperature and stable flow. Sometimes it's the only water in a river system that is cold enough to house trout.

➤ **Nervous water.** Nervous water is created by the collision of two different currents. It creates a choppy surface that actually looks "nervous" or "stressed." Nervous water makes outstanding holding grounds for fish. There is both an abundance of food and shelter from the faster moving currents.

Still Water

Rivers and streams aren't the only places to fly fish. Lakes, ponds, and reservoirs also offer excellent fly-fishing opportunities and host many more species of fish, all of which can be caught on a fly rod. Of course, there are a few major differences between the two.

First, reading the water is a whole new ballgame in still water. In moving water, it's relatively easy. For the most part, the fish are holding in spots where they have the greatest amount of food available for the least amount of effort. Unlike fish in moving water, who have a smorgasbord of food flowing past them in the current, fish in still water usually have to search for their food (except for inlets and outlets, which we'll cover in a minute). Since the water is still, the food rarely comes to them (except for the careless bait fish that offers easy prey). But fish in still water also hold in water that offers the most food with the least amount of effort.

Your tactics are also going to be much different than fishing in moving water. Remember all of those advanced casts you learned a few chapters ago (s-cast, reach cast, and so on)? Well, you won't be using those much on still water. As a matter of fact, you don't want any slack line on the water at all; you no longer have to worry about a drag free drift. Most of the time, you are going to have to keep your fly moving anyway, as most of the insects you will be imitating are much more active than insects in fast moving water. Furthermore, you will probably be fishing with patterns that imitate bait fish more often than in moving water.

Fish Tails

Unlike rivers and streams, lakes and reservoirs that are deep enough can support both warm and cold water fish. These "two-story" lakes maintain cold temperatures in the deep water and warmer temperatures toward the surface and in the shallows.

Likely Spots

Just as on rivers and streams, there are many spots on a lake or pond that hold more fish than others. If you don't immediately spot rises or see cruising fish, look for these spots before casting your line:

➤ **Shelves and drop-offs.** Shelves and drop-offs are caused by an abrupt change in the contour of a lake and are ideal spots for predator fish to sneak up on prey. Since there is an abrupt change in the depth of the water, many of the larger fish come out of their cold water zones to ambush the smaller fish above. Since streamers (which we'll get to later) are used to imitate smaller bait fish, they are excellent patterns to use in this type of water. When presenting them, give them a little time to sink before stripping them in. This way, they will be in prime view of any predator fish.

➤ **Inlets and outlets.** Inlets usually offer a fresh supply of cold, oxygenated water as well as a steady supply of snacks—both of which attract fish. Concentrate your fishing right at the mouth of an inlet. Outlets serve as the strainer of a lake and can offer an incredible amount of food for the fish you are after. Distance casting with long leaders is often necessary when fishing an inlet or outlet. Since the water below is calm and clear, the fish are easily spooked. This makes it imperative to plan your approach as stealthily as possible.

➤ **The main channel.** If a body of water has an inlet and an outlet, it has a main channel. Examine the topography of the land from the inlet to the outlet and imagine the path a river would take if it followed it. On windy days, you can sometimes see the main channel. It will often be smooth when the rest of the surface is choppy. Believe it or not, this main channel has current and can offer a steady flow of insects. If the lake isn't too deep (more than 15 to 20 feet deep), it is possible to fish this main channel with a sinking line.

➤ **Shade.** Fish seek any source of cooler water during the hot summer months. Since shade offers protection from the sun, the water is a bit cooler. The trees, bridges, docks, lily pads, and so on that offer shade also offer protection from predators. Terrestrials such as ants, hoppers, and bees also fall into the water from these sources. Some of the

Cut Bait

Be wary of shelves and drop-offs when wading in ponds or lakes. They are well hidden and dangerous if deep.

Reel Good Advice

When fishing weed beds, be sure to check your fly frequently. Make sure there are no leaves or algae caught on the hook.

best fishing on a lake can be below man-made sources. Concentrate your efforts around bridges, docks, or any other sources of shade.

➤ **Weed beds.** Weed beds offer protection from predators such as birds and bigger fish, and are a great source of food. Since insects, crustaceans, and bait fish all thrive in weed beds, game fish do, too. The lily pads and cattails that make up weed beds also offer a great source of shade.

➤ **Submerged objects.** Submerged trees, rock piles, cars, you name it, all attract bait fish and offer excellent hideouts for predator fish as well.

The Least You Need to Know

➤ Fish hold in places where they expend a minimum amount of energy yet can easily get at their prey. When fishing lakes or ponds, concentrate your fishing around steep drop-offs, obstructions in the water, and banks with lots of flora.

➤ Look for confluences in the water. Fish like to hold in these places because of the abundance of food available.

➤ Fish sense danger with either their eyes or through vibrations in the water. To sneak up on a fish, be sure to keep a low profile and wade carefully.

➤ Fishing can be slow during the hot summer months. Try to fish early or late in the day.

Chapter 9

Like a Fish in Water

In This Chapter

➤ Wading techniques

➤ How trout get spooked

➤ Sneaking up on fish

➤ Spotting a fish

I remember the first time I went fly fishing in a river. My mentor told me to go fish at the head of a pool for a pod of rising trout he claimed to have seen. I immediately tromped through the water and walked right into the calm pool. "This will be easy," I thought. After all, I had spent two hours casting on the lawn earlier in the week and could cast a fly line nearly 40 feet. Now I was standing in a small pool less than 15 feet from where I was told to fish. After a solid hour of casting and no sights of any fish, my buddy came up to me and asked if I had been standing there the whole time. "Of course not," I lied. "I got a bunch of strikes upstream but just came down here to see how you were doing." Unfortunately, I hadn't read the chapter you are about to read.

This chapter covers essential information you will need to know before actually getting in the water. Trust me and read every word of it. You don't want to feel how I felt my first time getting in the water. Without this information, you won't have a prayer of catching a fish.

Watchful Wading

There are two things you must constantly think about when wading through the water. The first is to not spook the fish. As I said earlier, spooking the fish is the number one reason fly fishermen get skunked, and there is no better way to spook the fish than careless wading. The second thing you should always be thinking about, and by far the most important, is safety. Although fishing seems like a pretty safe sport, it can be deadly. Every year, fly fishermen get in over their heads—literally!

Though you may disagree, your safety is much more important than catching fish. That's why we'll talk about it first.

Reel Good Advice

Make sure to tighten your shoelaces after you get in the water. Wading boots tend to loosen up when wet and pose a danger while wading.

Wading Safely

To the non-fisherman, wading seems like a pretty easy thing to do. After all, it's not much more than just walking with waders on. Or is it?

To tell you the truth, it is. As a matter of fact, it takes as much skill and balance to wade through a fast moving river as it does to ice skate for the first time. At some point, you're going to lose your balance and take a fall.

There are a few important things to keep in mind when wading that will decrease your chances of taking a swim.

➤ **Start in the shallow water.** I know this seems like a no-brainer, but you wouldn't believe how many fishermen hop off of a bank into semi-deep water and continue to wade until it becomes dangerous. At that point, they turn around and grimly discover the way they came in isn't much easier in reverse. Always start in shallow water. This way, if it gets too deep or rough, you can always retrace your steps to safety. Riffles and the tail ends of a pool are usually shallow and are good places to start.

➤ **Take baby steps.** Instead of taking large strides through the water, take baby steps. This way, in case you step on something that's loose or slippery, you can easily regain your balance and step elsewhere. This will also enable you to walk as quietly as possible and spook the least amount of fish.

➤ **Walk upstream.** By walking upstream, you can lean into the current as you walk and use it as a brace. By wading downstream, you stand the chance of the current carrying you into dangerous water. You also may not be able to fight the current if you decide to retrace your steps back upstream. Besides the safety factor, it is much easier to sneak up on a fish when wading upstream. When you wade downstream, the fish have a much easier time seeing and hearing you (actually feeling your vibrations). You also inadvertently kick up mud, silt, and other debris that drift downstream, all of which are red lights for wary fish.

➤ **Walk diagonally.** This minimizes the surface that the water has to push against and makes you more hydrodynamic.

➤ **Walk in between rocks, not on top.** The top of rocks and boulders are usually the slipperiest parts of a stream. Since they are closer to the surface of the water, they receive the most sun and usually house the most algae. The top of rocks and boulders also get smoothed out from the constant flow of water. This also makes them extremely slippery. Always walk in between them for the best traction.

For Safety Measures

Always wear a wading belt when wearing chest-high waders. Without one, you risk the chance of filling them up if you accidentally wade in too deep or take a swim. Also, if you plan on wading through rough or deep water, bring a wading staff or use a long, sturdy stick. Either one will significantly help your balance and can also act as a measuring device before stepping out into deep water.

Taking a Swim

In case you accidentally take a swim while wading (we all do at some point), there are a few things to keep in mind. If it is fast moving water, your first instinct will be to get out of the water. All I can say is don't panic. I know it may be tough, but the best thing to do is stay in the water and use the current to push you into slower moving water. Trying to fight a heavy current will be fruitless anyway. You will only waste precious energy and bang yourself up in the process. Instead, float downstream on your back with your feet leading the way. Use them to bounce off of rocks and other obstructions and wait until the current carries you to an eddy or slower moving water, which it always does.

Don't Spook the Fish

Since it is nearly impossible to catch a fish that has been frightened, or *spooked*, the first thing you must learn in fly fishing is stealth; that is, don't scare the fish. Unfortunately you're going to scare a few fish while you are in the water; it's almost impossible not to, but try to spook as few as possible.

Whenever you approach a new body of water, whether it be a river or a lake, fish the shallow water first. Too many fly fishermen, beginner to expert, immediately walk up to the bank to see what's going on. This only tells the fish what's going on. Remember, you are a predator to them, and they are just about always on the lookout.

Cut Bait

If you accidentally take a swim while wading in fast moving water, don't try to stand. Wait until the current brings you to shallow water or a calm eddy. If you try to stand in fast moving water, you risk the chance of your feet getting stuck in the rocks on the bottom.

Reel Good Advice

Don't spook the fish. Spooking the fish is the number one reason many fly fishermen get skunked.

Nervous Normans

Trout are inherently nervous creatures. As a matter of fact, I would even call them neurotic. The slightest stir in the water, whether it's a predator or not, can spook them for hours. They won't feed, play, or even swim away from their protected shelter until they are 100 percent sure they are safe from whatever rock, twig, leaf, or even shadow disturbed the water. If they were humans, the only safe place for them would be a psychiatric ward.

Fish Tails

Some fish don't get spooked as easily as others. The fish in areas with lots of fishing pressure seem to be much more immune to anglers than fish in backcountry streams and lakes—areas that aren't fished very often. It also depends on the type of fish you're pursuing. Trout, of course, are among the most easily spooked fish and can stay in hibernation for hours afterward. Bluegill and Sunfish, on the other hand, are much less wary. These are good "beginner fish" to pursue before tricking smarter, more finicky fish.

Trout get spooked in one of two ways. They either see something that alerts them of danger, or they feel it. Trout have an extensive system of nerves that enable them to feel vibrations in the water.

To catch a trout, you must not alert them of your presence. Trout have a built-in alarm system that goes off in the following ways:

Reel Good Advice

Take your time when approaching a nice hole or a rising fish. Many anglers can't hide their excitement and spook the fish before even making a cast.

➤ **Vibrations.** Although trout can't hear, per se, they can feel vibrations. This makes it imperative to wade cautiously. Rocks crushing against each other on the bottom of a riverbed will send a trout swimming back to its mother's womb in a heartbeat. Since vibrations get carried more easily downstream, it is much easier to sneak up on a fish while walking upstream. They are also much more sensitive to vibrations in still water than fast moving water. Sloppy casts, splashes in the water, and even loud noises all cause vibrations.

➤ **Eyesight.** Although trout can't see that well under the surface of the water, they have excellent vision above. They can see in all directions except directly behind them. But because of the refractive properties of light entering the water, they have a limited *window* of vision; that is, there is a certain angle above the water that they cannot see. This makes it essential to keep a low profile while wading and always try to approach a fish from behind.

➤ **Shadows.** Fish use shadows to alert them of oncoming predators. Be careful of the shadow you cast on the water with both your body and your fly rod.

➤ **Strange movements.** Strange movements will send a fish running for cover in a hurry. Remember, fish have excellent eyesight outside of the water. Even if they don't sense a shadow, any unnatural movements can spook them.

➤ **Mother Nature.** Thunder, heavy rains, or a quick change in the barometric pressure or water level can all scare fish.

➤ **Other fish.** In case you were wondering, fish do tell their friends. They may not say, "Hey, Joey, there is a tall human being trying to entice us with fake flies tied on a sharp hook," but they can alert other fish with their frightened behavior.

When Their Guards Are Down

Although there is just about no circumstance when you can easily approach a trout, there are certain times and places when they are the most vulnerable. Trout that receive a lot of fishing pressure tend to be less spooky than trout in backcountry streams where they have very little human contact.

Catch Words

Fish have a **window** of vision. It is important to stay out of this window so you don't frighten them.

Reel Good Advice

Make sure the sun is not directly behind you when casting. This projects your shadow to the water, an easy signal for wary fish.

Fish Tails

Since the current in slow moving pools and runs is slow, fish have an easy time nabbing their prey. This makes it a bit more difficult for the fly fisherman. Because the current is slow, the fish have more time to examine the fly and tippet. In fast moving water, they must make their decision immediately, which often results in a hookup.

I fish at many high-pressure tailwaters where the fish are simply immune to fishermen. As a matter of fact, on the Colorado River in northern Arizona, some of the trout are so used to fishermen, they actually pick food off of their waders. It has gotten to the point that some trout are even attracted to wading fishermen. They gather downstream and feast on the food that gets stirred up from the disturbance. Of course, these are major exceptions. Most trout get spooked at any sign of danger. The following times make it easier to sneak up on a trout:

Cut Bait

Be careful when fishing in the rain. Flash floods can occur without notice, and lightning is a potential threat. Get out of the water and retreat to safety when either sign becomes apparent.

Catch Words

Fish go into a **feeding frenzy** when there is a large hatch or abundant supply of another source of food (bait fish, ants, hoppers, and so on). This is when fishing is usually the most productive.

➤ **Cloudy or overcast weather.** Trout have a more difficult time distinguishing fishermen when the sky is overcast or cloudy. As a matter of fact, anytime the sun isn't high in the sky is an easier time to approach a fish. Your image is much less discernible against the bright sky, and you cast fewer shadows during these times.

➤ **Broken, choppy water.** Trout also have a much more difficult time seeing your silhouette in rough or choppy water. The water is also louder, making your vibrations much less discernible. Slow moving pools and flat water require the most caution.

➤ **Soft rain or snow.** If it isn't raining too hard, which may spook the fish, a soft rain or snow ruffles the surface of the water. This makes it more difficult for the fish to see you through the surface of the water. It is also overcast when it rains or snows, which makes you more difficult to distinguish.

➤ **Low water conditions.** Low water conditions also require more stealth than during the high water. The water is less turbulent during this time, which makes it quieter and calmer. Low water is also much clearer, thus giving the fish greater visibility than the murky water of spring runoff.

➤ **Heavy hatches.** Sometimes fish get so carried away during a *feeding frenzy*, they tend to lower their guards. Even if they are slightly spooked, they may treat it as more of a "nuisance" than an actual "danger." They simply weigh the pros and cons and decide to take advantage of the all-you-can-eat ala carte.

Fish Have Rhythm, Too

Believe it or not, fish get into a steady rhythm when feeding that must not be broken. Don't immediately start casting after you spot a rising fish or one that is sipping flies off the surface. Instead, take a moment and study its feeding patterns. You will more than likely notice the fish taking flies with a steady tempo. They do this for the same reason they do just about everything else in life. They are simply following the movements of the flies. During a big hatch, (when aquatic insects enter adulthood and fly for their first time), most of the nymphs emerge to the surface around the same time. The fish that you see rising in a steady pattern are more than likely eating the poor brothers and sisters of this particular hatch as they emerge to the surface, one at a time from the bottom of the river. This is usually the case before or after the peak of a hatch. During the thickest part of a hatch, the fish may stay at the surface and feed voraciously on flies trying to get airborne for their first time.

Figure out the timing and present your fly accordingly. For example, if you spot a fish that is rising to the surface every 10 seconds, cast your line nine seconds after the fish's last meal. This way, you increase the odds of presenting your fly to the fish's natural feeding pattern.

It's About Time

Selecting the right time to fish can be as important as selecting what to fish with. Since water is constantly in a state of change, fishing conditions change as well. Before heading out to a body of water, talk to your local fly shop and see what's going on. The time of year, time of month, and even the time of the day can all affect fishing conditions.

Time of Year

The water level in streams and rivers can change drastically throughout the season. Water that is dependent on *snow runoff* can swell hugely during the spring and early summer months, when snow in the high country melts. Many western rivers aren't fishable from the beginning of May all the way through the end of June; the water is simply too high and murky. Many of these same rivers also ice over during the winter months, again making them unfishable.

Rivers and streams that don't ice over can be fished in the winter, but when the water is too cold, fishing can be extremely slow. Fish become lethargic when the water becomes too cold, and their metabolism slows down exorbitantly. They won't make any mad dashes for a morsel of food and will only take a fly that is presented right in front of them. Sometimes you have to just about hit them on the nose for them to respond. Persistence can pay off, however, and on warm winter days the fishing can be outstanding. Both the insects and the fish take advantage of the warmer water temperatures.

Although all rivers and streams are affected by rain, some are much more dependent on rainfall than others; that is, they rely on the rainy season for the majority of their flow. These lower elevation rivers swell up during the rainy season, usually occurring during the late summer months. Again, the water is usually too high and murky for productive fishing during this time.

Time of Day

Without devoting the rest of the book to this lengthy topic, the best time of day for fly fishing is when the insects are the most active. And as you will learn in the next part of this book, they are the most active before and during a hatch.

Fortunately, insects are a lot like humans. Although there are exceptions to this crazy notion, we both tend to agree on the most comfortable temperatures for our water activities. Thankfully, the similarities stop there (although I have to admit, I am attracted to a few different types of mayflies).

In the Rocky Mountains where I live, nights are cold throughout the entire year. Except for the hottest days of the summer, the most comfortable time for fishing is mid-day. This also happens to be when most of the aquatic insects hatch. On really hot days, when I take a siesta during the heat of it, so do the insects. They tend to hatch in the mornings and evenings on these "dog days of summer." Even during the winter, when only the hardiest fly fishermen can withstand the warmest part of the day, only the hardiest insects are active.

Reel Good Advice

Fish during the morning and evening on hot summer days. The fishing is usually more productive, and the weather is more tolerable.

The same principle holds true in warmer climates as well. During the summer, fishing is usually slow during the hottest part of the day, when the weather can be unbearable for even a fly fisherman. This is when mornings and evenings are the most comfortable times to fish and the insects agree. This is their favorite time to hatch. As the weather cools down in the fall and winter, both fly fishermen and the insects get more active during the middle of the day.

*Disclaimer: This theory, as well as any other theory in fly fishing, has exceptions, and every rule of thumb has been broken a thousand times.

Never the Same River Twice

Since the flow on most rivers is constantly fluctuating, so are the fishing conditions. A large rapid in the spring may be a small riffle during the fall, while a productive eddy in the summer may be nothing more than a pile of sun baked rocks later in the season. Because the conditions are always changing, you must constantly modify your tactics.

High Water Fishing Strategies

Just about every stream or river experiences fluctuations in its water level. As I mentioned earlier, they are either rain dependent, snow dependent, or fed from natural springs. It has to be fed from something, right?

When the water is high and murky, it doesn't necessarily mean it's unfishable. It may be a bit more difficult, but as a rule of thumb, if you can see 12 inches into the water, it's fishable. You may not be able to wade in the water or be able to follow your dry fly as it gets washed downstream, but then again, you may not have to.

To escape the powerful currents during heavy spring runoff, most of the fish hug the slower water next to the banks. When I guide during this time, I make my clients hammer the banks with every cast. If their fly doesn't land within six inches of the bank, I tell them they're not hitting their target, and they won't catch fish. Unless there is a good hatch (which there seldom is during this time of year), I usually fish with streamers. Because the water is usually murky with low visibility, you can get away with short, heavy leaders.

Cut Bait

Do not wade in the river during high spring conditions. The currents can be powerful and the water much deeper than any other time of year.

Feeder streams are also a good spot for trout to escape the mighty currents during high water. Since they don't have as much water in their flows, they can offer much easier holding water for weary trout. They are usually not as rough, and some feeder creeks may run clearer than the main river.

Low Water Fishing Strategies

Fishing during the late summer and early fall months can be more difficult than spring high water. Since the water can be so low during this time, it is usually extremely clear. You have to practice extra caution when wading during this time and keep a low profile. Since the water is usually so clear, light tippet is a must. Otherwise, the fish will see your heavy tippet and reject every offering.

Usually, but not always (since there are no absolutes in fly fishing), the flies get smaller as the water level drops. For some fly fishermen, this makes late in the season the hardest time of the year. Streamer fishing can be phenomenal, though. Brown trout get very territorial when the water is low and will often hit a streamer just for invading its space.

Seeing the Fish

If you don't see any signs of fish on the surface of the water (rises, bulges, and so on), don't get discouraged. Although it takes some training, it is possible to see trout under the surface of the water. Before we talk about what to look for, I must emphasize the importance of polarized sunglasses. Even the most trained "trout eyes" will have a difficult time spotting trout without this essential piece of gear.

Search for Shadows

It is very difficult to actually spot a trout on the bottom of a river or lake. They were designed to be almost perfectly camouflaged to their surroundings and like all wild creatures, use it to their benefit. I've spooked brown trout in lightly colored riverbeds before and have actually seen them dart to the nearest dark spot or depression in the riverbed where they became nearly invisible.

Instead of searching for the trout themselves, try to spot the shadows they cast on the riverbed. Because they are much more defined, they are considerably easier to detect. I'll never forget the time an old buddy and I hiked down a narrow gorge to this remote river we hit every year. Throughout the day, we took turns being each other's "spotters." Fortunately, when we got to one of the river's biggest pools, it was his turn to spot. He hiked up to the bank above the river to see where the fish were holding while I was standing in the water downstream. He spotted a large shadow just to the left of the main tongue pouring into the pool and hand-signaled to me where to cast. After a dozen or so perfect drifts by the shadow, I started to question the sighting. I got out of the river and walked up to the bank where he was standing. "That's not a fish," I said. "It's a log in the water, you damn fool. It's too big to be a trout, and it hasn't moved in a half hour." After a small wager, I threw a rock in the water, and we both witnessed the biggest brown either of us had ever seen take off upstream. The wake it left looked like a jet ski skipping across the surface of the water. I tied a dozen flies for him that evening and apologized for my lack of confidence in his sighting. To this day, he still harasses me for throwing that rock in the water.

Look for Flashes

When trout are actively feeding under the surface of the water, you can often see a silver or white flash. They make this flash when they are doing one of two things. It is usually made when a trout opens its mouth to take in a piece of food. Once you train your eyes, this is one of the best ways to spot feeding trout. Trout can also make a flash as they roll into their feeding lane to take a piece of food drifting by. What you are seeing is the side of the fish exposed to the sun, and the fish only does this when rolling for a piece of food or moving to a new spot. Although flashes can be more difficult to detect than shadows, they are great signs of actively feeding fish.

The Least You Need to Know

➤ When wading across rivers, keep your body at an angle to the current to minimize the amount of friction.

➤ If you happen to fall in while wading in moving water, try to keep your feet downstream so they hit any obstructions first. Also, don't try to fight the water; the current will take you to slower moving water.

➤ When approaching any body of water, always make a few casts in the shallow water near the bank before stepping in. Fish often feed on insects or prey on bait fish in these shallows.

➤ Fish face into the current when in moving water. For this reason, you must always wade upstream so they don't see you first.

➤ When casting to rising fish, single out a particular fish, study its rising patterns, and cast accordingly.

➤ When searching the water for fish, it is often easier to look for shadows or silver flashes rather than the fish themselves.

The Backcountry Angler

For most fly fishermen, there is nothing better than getting away from the crowds, cars, and pollution that are associated with many of the easy-access waters in this country. After all, isn't that what fly fishing is all about? Getting a bit of solitude while getting in touch with Mother Nature and one of her natural wonders, fish?

Either a short walk or a multi-day backpack can get you into some incredible backcountry fishing. The farther you go, the less likely you will bump into other fishermen. Even a half-hour walk can weed out the hordes of fishermen that gather around easy-access fishing areas.

What Is the Backcountry

The *backcountry* is a very subjective term. My father may consider a backcountry fishing adventure nothing more than a 15-minute hike from the car down to a river. I see it a little differently. To me, a backcountry fishing trip requires at least a few hours of hiking into a wilderness setting. Other than perhaps a small trail, there are no other signs of civilization. For the sake of simplicity, let's call a backcountry fishing trip one that requires you to break a sweat to get there and is at least a half hour walk from any houses or roads.

Where to Go

Where to go depends largely on where you live. If you live in Columbus, Ohio, and want to get into the backcountry to go fishing, it may be a little difficult. On the other hand, if you live in the mountains in Colorado, you may be able to walk into the wilderness from your back door. Whatever the case, you need water that holds fish in a backcountry setting and a little knowledge of the area.

Reel Good Advice

When choosing a spot in the backcountry, make sure it is late enough in the season to be clear of snow. Many high country creeks and lakes are blocked with snow until the middle of the summer.

Cut Bait

Make sure you know how to read a topographical map before setting out for a backcountry excursion. Many streams and creeks flow through tight mountain gorges on their journey downstream, and these areas are sometimes un-navigable for the average fisherman.

Finding a place to go can be as easy as stopping at your local fly shop or outdoor gear store and asking for suggestions. They will more than likely sell you a map and an assortment of flies that may or may not work. As a general rule of thumb, the more you spend at a fly shop, the more advice they will give you. I have worked or done business with fly shops for the last decade and see this phenomenon all the time. Talking to 20 or 30 people each morning about the fishing conditions and hearing each one of their fishing stories, whether true or not, gets a little old for a salesman, especially when they don't buy anything. When a customer who has supported the shop in the past or comes in to stock up on flies wants some advice, you better believe he will get some.

If you're familiar with the area or have a good *topographical map* (and know how to read it), it isn't difficult to find a place on your own to go. A *topographical map* is an invaluable tool for backcountry travelers. It reveals the topography of the land; that is, the profile of an area's terrain. Contour lines represent the gradient of the area, giving its readers a three-dimensional layout of a given region. Just make sure there is water on the map and the gradient isn't too steep to hold fish. In the mountains, many streams and creeks are fed from high alpine lakes that may also offer good fishing. Others simply branch off like the roots of a tree as you work your way upstream. I prefer fishing creeks that are fed from a lake. This way, I can catch easy-to-fool trout in the creek and work my way to the more difficult trout in the lake.

What to Bring

This is a difficult question to answer. What to bring depends largely on what time of the year you are going and where you will be fishing. If you are only going to walk for a half hour from your car, wear your normal fly fishing garb but throw a rain jacket, a snack, and some water in the back pouch of your vest. If you need more, don't worry. Your car is close by. Always have a spare set of car keys when you venture into the backcountry. Carry one set with you and hide the other set in your car in case of emergency.

If you are going on a full day trip and plan on hiking several miles from your vehicle, bring a small daypack as well. You will need the extra space for some food, water, maps, extra layers of clothing, and a rain jacket. I also suggest packing in your waders rather than wearing them. If you wear them on a long hike, you will undoubtedly feel like you're walking in a sauna and will probably tear them up in the process. Instead, pack a pair of lightweight waders and bring a pair of sandals or lightweight tennis shoes to wear as boots. Or, if the weather is hot and you can bear the cold water, try *wet wading*; that is, don't wear waders at all. Just wade in your shorts and wear your tennis shoes, hiking boots, or a pair of river sandals.

Instead of wearing a vest on backcountry fishing excursions, I usually wear a fly-fishing shirt. Yes, that's right, they actually make shirts specifically designed for fly fishing. They are about as practical as anything I own. They are simple long-sleeved, button-down shirts with oversized pockets for fly boxes, underarm vents for hot weather, a small loop sewn in the back for a clip-on net, and some other bells and whistles for carrying various other goodies. The quality ones are made out of nylon for quick drying and increased breathability (they also don't smell so bad).

As any hiker will tell you, pack light! Remember, everything weighs something. I tend to go a little overboard on this theory but have yet to be proven wrong. Just trust me on this and pack light on backcountry fly-fishing excursions. Your shoulders will be sore enough from carrying a pack and casting all day, let alone carrying any extra weight.

Reel Good Advice

Because tennis shoes are light and small enough for a backpack; they work great as wading shoes in the backcountry. Glue felt soles on the bottom to increase their traction (available at most fishing shops) and be sure to replace the cotton shoelaces with nylon shoelaces (cotton laces won't last long).

Be sure to pack your rod in a rod tube (inside the sock) if you are going on a long hike or backpack. Most people prefer four-piece fly rods for long hikes and backpacking. They are easy to fit into a backpack and can be put together in minutes. Since most of my rods are two-piece fly rods, I bring one of them. Instead of using the expensive aluminum case that came with the rod, I use a padded piece of PVC tubing to hold the rod. It also acts as my walking stick and wading staff if needed. On short jaunts or hikes that I'll be fishing along the way, I don't bring a case at all. I just keep my rod rigged so I am ready to fish in a moment's notice.

Fish Tails

There is a certain law in backpacking that says the more space you have, the more you will carry. For this reason, don't bring a huge backpack if you are only going on a short day trip. This makes it too easy to bring the nonessentials, which will just make your pack heavier and your shoulders more tired.

Tackle

Since you will be fishing a wide variety of conditions in the backcountry, it is tough to suggest just one rod for all conditions. My last journey into the backcountry started off on a small creek for brookies and rainbows in the morning, three large beaver ponds around lunchtime, and my final destination, a medium-sized high alpine lake full of cutthroat trout in the mid-afternoon.

Which rod did I want? Well, if I had a porter, I would have brought three or four. An eight-foot, three-weight for the small tight stream, an eight-and-a-half-foot, five-weight for the ponds, and a nine-foot, five-weight for the lake. Of course, I would have preferred a nine-foot, six-weight to fight the wind when it picked up, but I can't have it all.

Which rod did I bring? My eight-and–a-half-foot, five-weight. This seems to be my rod of choice for backcountry excursions where I will be fishing a variety of conditions. It was just short enough for the brushy creek and just heavy enough to make long casts and fight a soft breeze when lake fishing.

Reel Good Advice

When deciding which rod to bring on a backcountry fishing trip, think about where you will be doing the majority of your fishing. If you will be spending most of your time fishing small creeks, there is no need to bring a long, heavy rod.

A floating line is ideal for most of the conditions you will encounter in the backcountry, but if you know you will be fishing a lake on the trip, carry a spare spool loaded with a sink tip line. I only started doing this a few years ago but have noticed a substantial increase in my fishing success. It comes in handy for reaching the big fish in the deeper water of the lake.

As far as tackle goes, there is a fine line between packing light and not packing enough. At the very minimum, be sure to pack the following items:

➤ **Flies.** You will learn what flies to bring in Part 4 of this book, but be sure to bring a variety for all fishing conditions. Bring at least two of each size; there will undoubtedly be one fly that produces the best results and if you only bring one of this pattern, you will kick yourself after losing it.

➤ **Spare leader and tippet.** Always carry at least one spare leader on backcountry trips. Although you may never use it, it takes up just about no room and is crucial if needed. Two spools of tippet in different sizes are usually sufficient for most backcountry trips. I usually bring a 4X and a 5X in the early summer months, and a 5X and a 6X when the water is low and clear later in the season (remember, the bigger the X-size, the smaller the diameter).

➤ **Strike indicators, fly floatant, and split shot.** Although most fish in the backcountry will take your fly with a vengeance, strike indicators can be useful for beginner fly fishermen who have trouble feeling a strike. Floatant, both the liquid paste and the powder form, are essential for keeping your dry fly floating. A small amount of split shot in different sizes should also be handy for getting the fly down deep.

➤ **Clippers and forceps.** Any kind of clippers are essential for trimming leader knots. I bring nail clippers on backpacking trips both for fishing and for toenails, which seem to grow exponentially faster the farther I get away from my home. Forceps work well for unhooking fish and getting small hooks out of your clothing or skin.

Cut Bait

A landing net is totally optional when on backcountry excursions. I rarely bring one on hikes simply because I don't want to carry it in my pack or wear it on my back. It only adds extra weight and ends up getting snagged on bushes and shrubs. There are a few different models of folding nets on the market, but I have yet to try them. It is easy enough to land backcountry fish in your hand and not have to deal with a net.

Essential Gear

Besides fishing tackle, you are also going to have to bring a few other necessities for survival. Assuming you are going in the summer months, make sure you don't forget the following items:

➤ **A rain jacket.** No matter how clear the sky looks when you leave, bring a rain jacket. Afternoon showers are common in the high country and even more common when you forget one.

➤ **Topographical map and compass.** An up-to-date topographical map is essential for any backcountry excursion. Unless you know the area well, bring a map. Believe it or not, if you are a good map reader, you can pick many of the good fishing spots before you even get there.

➤ **Food and water.** Bring plenty of food and water on all backcountry excursions. To lighten your load, carry water treatment tablets or a filter instead of several water bottles. On hot days, plan on at least 3/4 of a gallon per person.

➤ **First aid kit.** These are one of those items that are great when you need them and burdensome when you don't. Get a small backpacker's version that is light and doesn't take up much space. It could be a lifesaver.

➤ **Hat, polarized glasses, and sunscreen.** You should have these essentials on all of your fly fishing trips, not just in the backcountry, though the glasses are extra handy in the backcountry for protecting your eyes when walking through thick brush.

➤ **Overnight essentials.** If you are going on an overnight adventure, make sure to bring a warm sleeping bag, bedroll, and a tent or bivy sack, as well as the appropriate cooking gear.

Small Creeks and Streams

Backcountry creeks and streams offer some of the easiest trout fishing available. They are easy to read and full of hungry, non-discriminating fish—usually trout. These trout are easier to fool than easy-access areas for a variety of reasons. Since they don't receive much fishing pressure, they are more prone to be fooled by an imitation fly. Some of the fish in high-pressure areas (tailwaters) have seen just about every trick in the book and will only take the perfect presentation. Since fish in the backcountry may have never seen a fake fly, they are much more likely to strike one. Furthermore, because the streams and creeks in the backcountry usually lie in higher elevations, the insect hatches aren't quite as heavy. This makes the fish *opportunistic feeders*; that is, they have to take advantage of any food that comes their way. And since the season is shorter at higher elevations, the fish have to pack in an entire year's worth of food in a few short summer months.

Catch Words

Fish that are **opportunistic feeders** will strike a variety of fly patterns, not just natural looking imitations. **Selective feeders**, on the other hand, will only strike a fly that resembles the natural flies in the water at the time.

Most small creeks are full of pocket water and riffles, both of which hold trout. As a general rule (this one almost always holds true), the smaller the creek, the quicker you should work your way upstream. Don't be surprised if you find yourself several miles upstream of where you started on a productive day of backcountry fishing. When fishing pocket water, unless you keep getting strikes, there is no need to cast more than a few times per pocket. If a fish doesn't take your offering, it was either spooked or not interested. Whatever the case, move on after a few casts and consider changing fly patterns or switching to a smaller size tippet when the fishing gets slow.

Some creeks and streams in the backcountry are so small or shallow, you have no alternative but to fish with dry flies. Since most fly fishermen prefer dry flies to nymphs, this shouldn't be a disappointment. However, if you come to a deep run or pool, a nymph or wet fly may be the only one that will take a fish.

Backcountry streams and creeks aren't for everyone. If you measure success by the size fish you catch, stay to the more developed areas; you aren't going to catch too many trophies in backcountry creeks. The trout are usually small, ranging in size from six to 12 inches (though a 14-inch trout will seem like a trophy after catching and landing a dozen small fish).

High Mountain Lakes

High mountain lakes are one of the most beautiful places to fish, period. They usually sit in a small bowl or cirque highlighted by a beautiful peak and lush meadow in the background. They are rarely very large, usually only a few acres in size, and can offer outstanding fishing.

There are two different types of high mountain lakes: those that sit above the tree line and those that don't. Some lakes sit at such a high elevation they are above the level trees can grow. These lakes usually sit at the bottom of a talus slope and offer very little cover for fish. Since these lakes aren't as nutrient-rich as those below the tree line, food is scarce, and they tend to house fewer trout. This doesn't necessarily mean the fishing isn't as good, though. As long as you don't spook the fish (which can be quite easy), you can take advantage of the scarce food situation. Because of the fierce competition for food, some of these high alpine trout will aggressively attack almost anything that even resembles a meal.

Because lakes below the tree line offer more food, they typically house more fish. There is also usually more cover for these fish to hide. The only draw-back to these lakes is that they can be in heavily forested areas, which makes casting difficult. This can also shelter a lake from the sun.

Cut Bait

Be careful. It is very easy to lose track of time in the backcountry. Don't be stuck with a five-mile hike back to your car with an hour of light left in the day.

I remember a hike I went on a few summers ago in Colorado. I tried to time my trip just as I thought the lake was thawing out in mid-June, since this can offer some of the best fishing of the year. During this time, the fish are usually hungry and eager to attack anything that looks like food. I also think fish seem to forget some of their nervous habits over the long winter months and appear to be a bit less spooky after ice-out. Well, on this particular trip (as well as many others), I had to use snowshoes to reach the lake only to discover it was still iced over. I was probably two weeks early. Not wanting to give up, I took out my map to see if there were any other lakes in the area. Luckily, I spotted a small, unnamed lake on the map that rested just above the tree line. Although it was a little higher in elevation, it sat on a south-facing slope. What the heck, I thought, might as well give it a try since it received a bit more sun.

I reached the lake an hour later, and to my good fortune, the lake was just about ice free. I was sure I was the first fisherman to cast a line in the lake all year, but before I did, I hiked up to a small knoll overlooking the lake to scout the situation. I couldn't believe what I saw. It seemed every trout in the lake was cruising the shallows for food and probably enjoying the warmer water as well. They weren't schooled up (as brook trout rarely are); instead, it seemed as if each fish was out for their own survival. To make a long story reasonably short (I could write a book about the day), I got strikes on just about every cast. The fish were actually racing each other for my fly. I caught and released over twenty brookies that afternoon and several in the 16- to 18-inch class. What a first day of the season!

Strategy

The key to success on high alpine lakes (and on all water, for that matter) is to not spook the fish. Too many fishermen, beginner to expert, immediately walk up to the bank of a lake to see what's going on. Little do they know, they just ended what was going on and sent the fish scurrying for deeper water. This is especially true with backpackers; they get so excited they reached their final destination, they throw off their pack and immediately hit the water.

The shallows offer some of the best fishing in a lake. This is where most of the aquatic insects thrive and where most of the terrestrials (hoppers, ants, and so on) end up on windy days; hence, where most of the fish come to feed. This shallow water is known as the *littoral zone* by biologists and shouldn't be disregarded by fly fishermen.

Catch Words

The **littoral zone** of a lake is its shallow water near the banks. This water is usually rich with life and can offer incredible fishing.

Many anglers have a false notion that only small fish reside in shallow water. This is because in the past, they spooked all of the larger, wilier fish when they walked up to the bank to check out the situation. They only caught the small, gullible fish that haven't yet learned the "tricks of the trade."

When you reach a high alpine lake, plan your approach carefully. Drop your pack and put your fly rod together away from the water, so there is no chance the fish can see you. Then, keeping a low profile, delicately cast your fly into the shallow water. If possible, only let your leader and tippet fall into the water with the end of your line still on the bank. Carefully grid out the shallow water before working your way to the shelf, or drop off. If there are obstructions behind you and you can't make a decent back cast, quietly wade into the water and cast parallel to the bank to fish the shallows.

Fish are inherently more alert for predators when feeding in shallow water. They are much easier to detect and don't have much shelter for protection. This makes them extra paranoid, so a careful approach is absolutely necessary. At other times, however, it seems some fish couldn't give a hoot about your presence.

Fish Tails

I'll never forget a few non-fishing buddies of mine who went on a backpack almost a decade ago. They were in Glacier National Park and spotted a pod of hungry rainbows feeding on the surface of a high alpine lake near their camp. All they had with them for fishing equipment was a long piece of monofilament and a sharp earring, which one of them happened to be wearing. Somehow, they proceeded to eat trout on every night of their backpack, and to this day still give me grief for devoting my life to fooling these creatures.

After thoroughly fishing the shallows, it's time to search for fish in the rest of the lake. Don't get too excited if you see a few rises or bulges in the surface of the water. They are probably only small fish taking advantage of a poor, stray fly. I have even watched fish in a high mountain lake chase a blowing leaf across the surface of the water. Unless there is a major hatch, or there are lots of rises and bulges on the surface, concentrate your fishing below the surface of the water. Although you may catch a few small fish, you will more than likely spook the bigger ones down deep. We'll talk more about lake fishing and what flies to bring in the next part of this book.

Weather

Watch the weather when fishing high alpine lakes. Afternoon thunderstorms are common and if they get too heavy, can ruin the fishing in a heartbeat. They are often accompanied by lightning storms, so get out of the water at the first sign of thunder or lightning. Since lightning strikes the highest ground in the vicinity, put your fly rod away and retreat to a lower elevation. Find a dry spot if possible and wait out the storm. A common saying in the mountains is, "If you don't like the weather, wait five minutes." This is a little exaggerated, but storms usually pass within a half-hour.

The best time to be on these lakes is in the morning. For some reason, winds and thunderstorms usually occur in the afternoon in the high country. On warm summer evenings, though, the last hour of daylight until you can no longer see your fly line tends to be the best time for dry fly fishing. During this time, it seems every fish in the lake is slurping insects off the surface of the water.

At other times, however, you can use the weather to your benefit. Overcast, rainy, and uninviting weather can offer the best fishing conditions of the day. Cloudy, windy days with a slight drizzle typically make fish a little more self-assured in their feeding. These conditions are also likely to blow terrestrials into the water and keep newly hatched aquatic bugs stuck in the surface film.

Cut Bait

Watch the weather closely when fishing a high alpine lake since graphite rod material is an excellent conductor of electricity. Put your rod away and retreat to safety at the first sign of lightning. Since lightning strikes the highest point in an area, retreat to a lower elevation.

Unfortunately, you must often cast directly into the wind on windy days. Although it is a bit more difficult, this is where most of the fish tend to gather since the wind blows the insects to the *leeward* side of the lake. If you are casting with the wind to your back, you are more than likely standing on the wrong side of the lake.

I'd have to say that some of the best days of fishing I've ever had on alpine lakes were during the most border-line weather. If the fishing wasn't so incredible, I would have retreated to my warm, dry tent hours earlier. But remember, there is a fine line between being mildly uncomfortable and downright miserable. When fishing during these times, come prepared for the worst so you can stay out a little longer when weather rolls in.

Fish Tails

Fish in high alpine lakes have a tough enough time as is, let alone losing a brother or sister to a hungry angler. Because they often lie at a high elevation, the season is short, and food can be scarce. There simply aren't enough fish in these lakes to keep any, and more than likely, they are *wild fish*; that is, they reproduce naturally and are no longer stocked. Some of the fish are *natives* and have never been stocked. They were there long before man started tying flies to fool them. Respect these fish and practice great caution when releasing them. After all, only humans can ensure their survival.

Beaver Dams

Beaver dams are a bonus to any fly fishing trip in the backcountry. Since very few of them appear on a topographical map, you have to either hear about them from a friend (a good friend at that) or bump into them. Unfortunately, a beaver pond you hit one year may not be there the next. I fished the same beaver pond for four years in a row and whether you believe it or not, I am pretty sure I caught and released the same cutthroat trout every year. I went back a few summers ago to see if he was still there, but to my chagrin, the entire dam had been washed out by high water. As a matter of fact, the beautiful meadow below the dam was not fishable for several hundred yards because of all the debris that was blown downstream. I lost a half dozen flies trying my hardest to fish this meadow, which now offered excellent habitat for fish, but not for fishermen.

Strategy

Beaver dams should be approached just as if you were approaching the shallows of a small lake: from a distance. Since the water is slow, clear, and shallow, the fish seem to be extra skittish. This means you need to practice extra caution to have any luck. If you can see the fish in a beaver pond, more than likely they can see you, too. All but the very small and gullible fish will retreat to safety. Avoid the overwhelming temptation of walking up to the pond to spot the fish.

Instead, keep a low profile and delicately cast to any rising fish or bulges you see in the water. Be sure to concentrate your efforts at the pond's inlet, the main stream channel, the deeper water at the dam itself, and any other good holding water you may notice. Since beaver ponds offer such an abundance of food, the majority of trout will feed on the surface only when there is a large hatch in progress. Some of the smaller fish may feed on stray bugs, but for the most part, they will be eating nymphs under the surface of the water.

I like to stand just below the actual beaver dam and cast into the deep water behind it. It's easy to sneak up on the fish from here, and you don't need much line to present your fly. This will usually yield a fish or two, but it is a tough place to fish (although there really aren't any easy places in a beaver pond). Most of the time, you will either snag your fly on a piece of wood or hook a fish that b-lines it to its shelter under the dam. Whatever the case, plan on losing lots of flies.

I will never forget the time I hooked a large native cutthroat trout in a small beaver pond in Colorado. Again, I approached the pond just under the dam and hooked it on my first cast (which is often the case in beaver ponds). After a rather lengthy battle, I finally got the fish to within arm's reach when the unthinkable happened. The fish made one final run, but this time dove below the dam and tangled itself around a large piece of wood. I tried my hardest to untangle the leader, but to no avail. I had to snap the tippet. With a long branch, I reached the line and pulled the dying fish up to

Reel Good Advice

Remember to rest a body of water when the fishing slows down. That is, after fishing a certain area, give the fish some time to resume their normal feeding habits before fishing it again.

the surface of the water. To this day, I shudder to think about holding that poor cutthroat, thinking I might have killed it for sport. Fortunately, after a solid 10 minutes of holding the fish upright in the water, I finally revived it.

Fishing below a beaver dam.

Besides a sly approach, the key to successful fishing on beaver ponds is to give them a break. Unless it is a huge pond, don't plan on fishing for more than 10 to 20 minutes before all the fish are spooked. Instead, catch a few trout, give it a break, and then come back. I usually fish a beaver pond pretty thoroughly when I first get there, and then give it a break for a half-hour or so. During this time, I either have lunch, nap, or more than likely fish my way up the creek until I hit some more beaver ponds. If there are several beaver ponds in a given area, some of the best fishing can be in the channels that connect them. Concentrate on these channels while you give the ponds a break. I can't remember a time that I only fished a beaver pond once in day.

Leave No Trace!

As Wallace Stegner once wrote, the wilderness doesn't need any defense, just more defenders (at least he wrote something to that effect). I will spare you a list of reasons as to why to leave the backcountry just the way you found it; just do, period. If you need a list of reasons, put down this book. You shouldn't take up fly fishing in the first place.

Pack out everything that you packed in. If you want to go above and beyond your call of duty (although we're all in the same boat), pack out anything else you see that doesn't belong in the backcountry.

The Least You Need to Know

➤ Because they are not as accessible, fish in the backcountry are typically much easier to catch than fish in crowded, easy-access areas.

➤ Pack as light as possible when heading into the backcountry on a fishing trip. You will very likely end up wearing the backpack as you work your way up the stream or creek.

➤ When fishing beaver ponds, be careful you don't get your fly stuck in the beaver dam. Smart fish will make a run for the dam to free themselves from the hook.

➤ Keep an eye out on the weather. The higher up you get in the backcountry, the greater your chances are of running into bad weather. Retreat to safety at the first sign of lightning.

➤ Leave no trace when you enter the wilderness. Pack out everything that you packed in and clean up after others.

Chapter 11

When the Fishing's Slow

In This Chapter

➤ Natural reasons for a slow day on the water

➤ Is it your fault the fishing is slow?

➤ Changing your outfit

➤ Animating your flies

➤ Calling it quits

Sometimes, even for a veteran fly fisherman, the fishing is slow. Don't take it personally; there are just times when the fish aren't biting. It's as simple as that. It happens to anyone who has ever spent any time fishing, no matter what they are fishing for or what flies they are fishing with. It's just a part of the sport. If it were easy and we caught fish consistently every trip, we wouldn't turn into fly fishing junkies. It would simply get old after a while. This chapter talks about why the fishing may be slow and what to do when it is.

Why Did It Slow Down?

Although sometimes the fish really aren't biting, most of the time there is a good reason why the fishing slows down (or never picks up for that matter). The following reasons can be to blame.

Human Factors

Although it's easy to blame a number of external factors for a slow day on the water, most of the time it's you, not the fish, that makes them want nothing to do with your fly. When the fish reject all of your offerings, try to correct one of the following things before blaming it on the River gods:

➤ **You're spooking them.** Often, fish don't bite because they simply know you're there. As I mentioned earlier, fish can be alerted by your presence either by seeing you or by feeling your vibrations. If this is the case, move to another spot and plan your approach more carefully, or take a break and wait until the fish calm down.

➤ **Already fished.** Before getting on the water, make sure the stretch is virgin water; that is, make sure no one has already fished the water that day. Sometimes it is necessary to walk upstream and see if you see any fishermen. If you do, walk a good distance downstream or leap frog the other fishermen, giving them lots of space to fish.

Reel Good Advice

Before changing patterns, change the size of your fly. Fish are usually more picky to fly size than fly pattern.

Cut Bait

Make sure the tippet you are using is not too large for the given situation. If so, it is unlikely to fool the fish. You want your fly to look like it has "no strings attached."

➤ **Wrong fly.** Believe it or not, fish, especially trout, can be very finicky eaters. Sometimes the fish aren't biting your fly because you have the wrong one tied on. If your imitation looks nothing like the natural flies in the water during that time of the year, it will very likely be refused. Try to match the size, color, shape, and behavior of the natural insects in the water before calling it a day.

➤ **Your fly looks unnatural.** If your fly doesn't drift like a natural insect, it will probably be rejected. For your fly to look natural, it doesn't only have to be the right color and shape, it also has to act like a natural fly. For example, if you're using a streamer (a pattern that imitates another fish) and you're stripping it too fast or too slow, the fish you're after may know it's fake. Or if you're fishing with a dry fly, it may look unnatural to a feeding fish if it's getting dragged or drifting at a different pace than the main current.

➤ **Tippet is too big.** When fishing over selective fish, you often must use a very light tippet. When the water gets clear, still, or low, your tippet becomes much more visible. Your fly will also drift unnaturally if your tippet is too big. Switch to a smaller tippet size during these times.

➤ **Fishing to the wrong spot.** This seems like a no-brainer, but many beginner fly fishermen have slow spells because there are no fish where they are casting. I remember going fishing with my friend's father a few summers ago. It must have been one of the biggest hatches of the summer when I came across him fishing the biggest rapid in the river. He turned to me and said, "There's no fish in here!" Not wanting to show him up, I abstained from telling him about all of the beautiful rainbows I'd caught downstream. "You're right," I said.

When the Fishing Really Is Slow

You will be happy to know that at times, the fishing really is slow. No matter who is casting, fish can be stubborn and reject all offerings, real or not. What makes the fish stubborn, you may ask? Well, that's a difficult one to answer, but the following things all have a major impact:

➤ **The water is too warm or too cold.** Many fish become inactive when the water becomes too warm or too cold. Trout won't survive in water that is colder than 35 degrees or warmer than roughly 75 degrees Fahrenheit. Most trout favor water that is around 58 to 59 degrees Fahrenheit and feed most voraciously during this time. Brown trout can withstand warmer temperatures than rainbows, while cutthroats and brookies prefer the coldest water. All trout, no matter what species, slow down their feeding patterns if the water is colder than 50 degrees or warmer than 70 degrees Fahrenheit. It isn't warm water that kills trout; it's the lack of oxygen that warm water fails to hold. Trout can survive in warmer water only if it is well oxygenated.

➤ **Wrong time of year.** This goes hand in hand with the last reason. The water may be too warm or too cold during that time of the year. For example, if you are fishing during the dead of winter, the fish may be totally inactive.

➤ **Drastic change in the weather.** A change in the weather will often slow down the fishing. A sudden rain or hailstorm can spook the fish and make them stop feeding in a hurry, as can

Reel Good Advice

If the fishing is slow due to the temperature of the water, look for any spot that may be colder or warmer. For instance, cold feeder creeks and springs may offer a break from warm water conditions during the hot summer months.

Catch Words

Stockers is a term used to describe fish that are hatchery raised and have been stocked in the water. They are usually less gullible than wild fish and not as easily spooked.

a sudden drop in the temperature. When the temperature quickly drops, aquatic insects usually become very inactive. Of course, this makes trout inactive as well. After all, why would they waste precious energy swimming if there is little or no food available?

➤ **Other fish or birds spooked them.** Humans aren't the only predators to trout. Other fish and birds also prey on them and can send a trout into hiding for hours.

➤ **An indigestion session.** That's right, fish get full, too. After snacking down several dozen flies during a big hatch, they often retreat to deeper water and go into a food coma—much like we do after pigging out at an Italian restaurant. The fishing may get slow for a little while, but it doesn't last for very long.

Fish Tails

I will never forget a great day of trout fishing I had early in the season when just about everything else was too high and murky. Several thousand rainbow trout were just stocked at the inlet of a large reservoir. My buddy Dom and I must have caught 20 of these *stockers* the first half hour we were there when a huge pike came out of the shallows for a little feeding frenzy. Although this put a small damper on the trout fishing, we fished for pike the rest of the day with extraordinary success.

A New Rig?

Ever thought of trying a new rig when the fishing gets slow? Sometimes that's all it takes to get things moving again. Although it can be a pain in the rear to keep changing your rig, don't be lazy. I've seen fly fishermen stay with the same setup all day and only have luck when it coincidentally happened to be the right one. As fishing conditions change, so must your fly-fishing setup.

Adding or Losing Weight

It is usually necessary to add weight to your leader when fish are feeding on the bottom of the water. Unless you are fishing with a *weighted nymph*—that is, one that has weight tied on to the body of the fly—your fly may not sink down to the fish's level.

Catch Words

A **weighted nymph** is a fly that has weight tied to it in the fly tying process. Weighted nymphs are often preferred because they drift more naturally than adding split shot to the leader.

If your fly is not bouncing along the bottom when nymphing or occasionally snagging weeds and debris, chances are, you need to add weight. How much, you may ask? Well, that's a difficult question to answer, but at least enough to get the fly bouncing on the bottom of the river but not so much it gets snagged at every drift. As you will learn in the next part of this book, aquatic insects spend just about their entire lives on the bottom of the water before emerging to the surface to hatch. Since this is where most of the food is, you better believe this is where most of the fish will be found feeding.

Sometimes your fishing will improve just by moving your weights up or down the leader. If you're fishing the bottom of a shelf or quick drop-off or in really fast moving water, your weights need to be near the fly so it sinks quicker. If you're fishing a slow moving run or pool, you may need to move your weights up the tippet to get a good natural drift.

New Leader Already?

Some fishermen get so into the fly fishing "zone" that they forget to check the condition of their leader. Remember, leaders are tapered down to a very fine tippet. Every time you tie on a new fly, you lose several inches of tippet material. Once you run out of tippet or it gets too short, fish have a greater chance of seeing it. Make sure your leader is always in good condition and you have enough tippet to fool the fish.

It is also important to fish with tippet that is light enough for the given situation. If you're fishing when the water is clear and low during the fall months, it may be necessary to use lighter tippet than you're used to. You may not get a strike all day if you're fishing with 3X tippet in water that calls for 6X; the fish will simply be on to you. And if you are fishing with small flies, a lighter tippet will allow your fly to drift more naturally.

Reel Good Advice

Use unleaded weight. That's right, most of the split shot on the market are made out of lead, which adds toxins to the water (and your mouth when you bite on them to clamp them down). Most quality fly shops and sporting goods stores have non-toxic shot (made mostly out of tin) and they are growing in popularity.

Cut Bait

Get all knots out of your leader; they are the weak link in your setup. Since tippet knots are almost impossible to untie, you must cut the section off and add a new piece.

I Just Tied It On!

Before switching fly patterns, switch fly sizes. Most fly fishermen fish with a pattern that is at least one size too big. Sure, it's easier to see, but they don't get as many strikes. I know this sounds nit-picky, but fish are nit-picky creatures. They are usually more discriminating to the size of the fly and its presentation than they are to its pattern and coloring. If you're still having no luck after switching to a smaller size, it may be time to switch to a new pattern.

The most important choice when deciding what fly to tie on is to figure out where the fish are feeding. If the fish are feeding on nymphs on the bottom, you will have better luck with a nymph imitation. If you see fish feeding on the surface or just below, use either a dry fly or one that can be fished below the surface of the water.

Reel Good Advice

When fishing with two flies at once, your dropper fly should be at least one size smaller than the first. This will enable you to get the best drift possible.

Grid the Water

Sometimes it's necessary to *grid* the water when the fishing is slow. Try to present your fly to every likely feeding lane, both on the surface of the water and in the water column. It's easy to grid the surface. After all, you can see all of the feeding lanes. Gridding the water column can be a different story. To do this, you must present your fly at varying levels beneath the surface of the water.

There are a few ways to do this. You can either change the amount of weight or move the weights up or down your leader. Either way will present your nymph at a different depth. Another way to fish different depths of water is to fish with two flies at once. When you do this, the second nymph, or *dropper fly*, will be suspended higher in the water than the first fly. To do this, tie roughly 15 inches of tippet on to the hook of the first fly with a Clinch Knot, then tie on the dropper fly, again with a Clinch Knot. When tying on your second fly, use either the same size tippet or one size smaller. It is a little more difficult to cast and much easier to get tangled up, but you increase your odds of hooking a fish.

Cut Bait

Minimize your casting when using a two-fly rig. Because there are two flies, it is very easy to get them tangled and create a rat's nest.

Moving to New Water

Moving to new water may be your best alternative to a slow day of fishing. A short walk to the next bend in the river may be all it takes to find more productive water, but most of the time it takes a little more effort than that. If a body of water really is fishing slow and it's not just you, your best bet may be getting into your car and driving to another part of the river or lake or a whole new body of water altogether. For a reason only Mother Nature truly knows, some rivers or lakes simply turn off; that is, they quit producing quality fishing for some reason unknown to man.

Changing Tactics

When the fishing is slow, it is very likely due to your tactics, not the fish. Thankfully, it is easier to change your tactics than it is to change the fish's feeding habits. Analyze what you have been doing since the fishing slowed down. Are you still using a dry fly even though the hatch ended an hour ago? Are you using a streamer even though you are now fishing a shallow riffle? Asking a few questions like this may help you figure out why the fishing has been slow.

It is also necessary to analyze the fish's feeding patterns. For example, say you are lake fishing and have spotted several rainbows cruising the shallows for food. Study their behavior and answer questions like how fast are they swimming, what depth of water are they holding in, and what are they feeding on? Even if you have no idea what they are feeding on or what species of insects are in the lake, at least you know a little about their behavior. You can now present your fly at the correct depth and give it the same action as the fish. That is, if the fish are quickly darting around, mimic their actions with your fly. Chances are, they are swimming as fast or as slowly as the creatures they are feeding on.

Take a Break or Call It a Day

As any angler will tell you, there are certain times of the day when the fishing is slow. Heck, there are certain days that are slow altogether. No matter what you try, there is absolutely nothing you can do to get the fish to take your fly. What should you do during these times? I guess that depends on how patient you are.

Fish Tails

No matter what anyone tells you, fly fishing and dogs don't go hand in hand. Although I occasionally bring my two well-trained Labrador Retrievers, I never catch as many fish as when I leave them at home. They either spook the fish or don't let me concentrate on the task at hand.

If the fishing is slow and you have nothing better to do (although a bad day on the water is still better than a good day at work), use this time to hone your skills. Work on the different casts you learned earlier in the book. Pick up some rocks and sticks in the water and try to identify the different species of insects. Or simply take a break from fishing altogether and just relax, enjoy the solitude and sounds of Mother Nature. Sometimes this is all it takes for you to figure out why the fishing has been slow. It's like frantically searching your house for your car keys or wallet and having no luck. Once you relax and assess the situation, you often find them right out in the open.

If you don't have the patience to take a break or did and the fishing is still slow, call it a day. There is no point staying on the water if you are just going to get frustrated and angry.

The Proverbial "Last Cast"

Before calling it a day, every fly fisherman, no matter what sex, race, creed, or experience level, must make the proverbial last cast. Or, in most cases, the proverbial last dozen casts. It's like that potato chip commercial a few years ago, "Bet you can't eat just one," only in this case it's, "Bet you can't cast just one more time." Every fly fisherman thinks he deserves one last fish, and for some reason, that last cast should be the lucky cast of the day. This is almost never the case and will often only get you in trouble. Just ask my wife.

The Least You Need to Know

➤ There are many reasons the fishing may be slow. It may be something you're doing or something you have no control of, such as the weather.

➤ If the fishing is slow, step back and analyze the situation. Maybe you need to add more weight to fish deeper water, or maybe your fly is too big or too small.

➤ Check your fly frequently. It may be too haggard to use or damaged from getting snagged. Don't wait until you've had a half-hour slow spell before checking your fly.

➤ Grid out the water to increase your odds of finding fish. Do this both on the surface of the water, letting your fly drift in a different feeding lane every cast, and in the water column, varying the depth of water in which you're presenting the fly.

➤ Take a break when the fishing gets slow. Use this time to analyze the situation and figure out why it's slow, or to hone some of your other fly fishing skills.

Chapter 12

Icing on the Cake—Hooking, Playing, and Releasing Fish

In This Chapter

➤ Setting the hook

➤ Playing your fish

➤ Landing your fish

➤ Releasing it alive

Now that you know where the fish are holding and how to present your fly to them, it's time to learn what to do next. What do you do when you do hook the fish? How are you going to bring it in? How do you get the hook out? Then what do you do with the fish?

This chapter covers all of the information needed to answer these questions and more. From setting the hook, to releasing the fish unharmed, this chapter covers it step by step.

Setting the Hook

I am pretty sure the phrase "beginner's luck" has its origins in fly fishing. All fly fishermen can remember one of their first outings when they just happened to catch more fish than the rest of their party. The fact that this was the day they turned into a fly-fishing junky is no coincidence. The sheer thrill of fooling a fish, watching it take the fly, and playing it changed their lives forever. They now measure success by how many days they spend on the water rather than how much money is in their bank accounts.

Fish Tails

Setting the hook too quickly is the number one reason fly fishermen lose fish. What's the second reason? You got it, not setting the hook fast enough. Most beginner fly fishermen either see the take and strike too quickly out of excitement, or miss the strike all together because they weren't paying attention.

Maybe it wasn't luck at all when they first started out. Maybe they just did what they were instructed and simply fooled the fish. I subscribe to another theory. I think beginner fly fishermen, with their sometimes slow reflexes, simply let the fish take the fly. Because they may have seen the take after the fact or felt the strike a second late, they were able to set the hook, or actually, let the fish set the hook. As the beginner hits the water a little more often, his reflexes quicken, and he now feels and sees more strikes. This is precisely why beginners go through a slump after their first few days of beginner's luck. Now that they know what's going on, they simply set the hook too fast for their own good.

You're Not Bait Fishing!

Setting the hook with a fly rod takes a delicate touch. If you have a spin casting background or have done a lot of bait fishing, you may be at a severe disadvantage.

Reel Good Advice

Make sure your hooks are nice and sharp. If they are dull or rusted, they may be sharpened with a file. This will increase your strike-to-hook-up ratio dramatically.

You must forget everything you learned in the past about setting the hook, and start from scratch. Otherwise, you'll set the hook way too forcefully and probably miss a majority of the strikes. If you do happen to set the hook on a fish the way you did on your spin casting setup, you will either rip its lips off or send it flying through the air behind you.

Unless you'll be doing most of your fly fishing in the salt water (which we'll get to later), most of the hooks you'll be using will be very small with extremely sharp points. Because the hooks are so sharp, it only takes a small amount of pressure to set them firmly in a fish's mouth. In some cases, the fish will simply hook themselves.

Tight Lines

No matter how perfectly you think you set the hook, you will catch very few fish with slack in your line. Too much slack in your line will allow the fish to actually taste the fly (or feel its texture) and spit it out before you have time to react. And if you have too much slack when you lift the rod tip to set the hook, you'll only move the fly line, not the hook.

Remember the stripping finger on your rod hand we talked about earlier? Well, don't forget to use it. You must continuously strip line in with your line hand using this stripping finger as a guide. If you are fishing upstream in a fast moving current, you must strip line in as fast as the current is carrying it toward you.

You Don't Have to Be Arnold Schwarzenegger

No matter how much force is needed, you don't have to be a muscle-head to set the hook. Even if the situation calls for a forceful set (which it rarely does), it is still nothing more than lifting your rod tip from the 9:00 position up to the 12:00 position while pinching the line with your trigger finger. Or if you are using a high-sticking technique we talked about earlier, pull the rod back to the 1:00 position. If you forget to use your trigger finger or are using it but forget to pinch it, you won't apply any force to set the hook. The line will simply slip back through the guides on your fly rod.

How much force is needed to set the hook depends on a number of factors. The size hook you are using is a major influence; large hooks require more power to set than small hooks. If you are fishing for bony-mouthed fish like pike, bass, and most saltwater fish, you must also set the hook more forcefully. Not only will you be using larger hooks, it is also harder to penetrate their bony mouths. It also depends on how much line you have in the water. Obviously, you are going to have to pull on the line more forcefully if you have 50 rather than 15 feet of line on the water.

Cut Bait

Be careful of how hard you set the hook. If you set it too hard, you will simply pull the fly right out of the fish's mouth or break the tippet.

In most cases, though, especially if you are using small hooks and a light tippet (which is usually the case for trout fishing), you must set the hook fairly gently. Otherwise, you will either pull the hook right out of the fish's mouth or snap the tippet and lose both the fish and your fly.

It's All in the Timing

As I said earlier, most missed fish are a result of setting the hook too quickly, though some fly fishermen, usually those thinking about their cold feet instead of catching fish, miss the majority of their fish by not reacting quickly enough. There is a fine line between the two, and it varies according to what you are fishing with. Dry flies, nymphs, streamers, and wet flies all require a slightly different approach to setting the hook. And to make matters worse, different fish take flies in different ways. Some slurp them while others sip them. And some charge them while others inhale them. At least they all take flies with their mouths!

Dry Flies

It is much easier to detect a strike when using dry flies than any other type of flies. Since you actually witness the fish take your fly, or see a disturbance on the water in the vicinity of your fly, you should be able to catch the fish every time, right? Well, unfortunately that's not the case. It takes a little more skill than that. As I said earlier, most beginner fishermen lose the majority of their fish by setting the hook too quickly. The act of witnessing a fish charge the fly is too much to handle, and they simply set the hook too fast. They lose the fish out of sheer excitement rather than waiting for the right moment to set the hook.

The right moment varies from species to species, but with all fish, you must wait until they actually take your fly. Although it may be difficult to hide your excitement and immediately yank on your fly rod, it's essential to relax and wait until you see the fly disappear or actually feel the weight of the fish on the end of your line. This is the time to set the hook. Simply pinch the trigger finger of your rod hand and lift the rod tip.

Reel Good Advice

If you lose your fly to a fish, tie on the same pattern that you lost. It is obviously a winner. If you are out of that pattern, choose a fly of similar size that resembles its silhouette and coloring.

Nymphing

Since you very rarely see a fish take your nymph, detecting a strike can be much more difficult when *nymphing* than when dry fly fishing. As a matter of fact, most fly fishermen only know when they get a fraction of their strikes. When nymph fishing, you must either feel the weight of the fish on the end of your line or use a strike indicator to detect any strikes.

If you actually feel a fish on the end of your line, there is no need to wait. Obviously, they have already taken the fly. Just pinch your trigger finger and lift the rod tip. Once the fish makes a run, use your stripping hand to control how much line is fed and use your trigger finger to feed it through the guides.

If you are using strike indicators (which I recommend for all beginner fly fishermen), closely follow the indicator. If it even stalls, bounces, bobs, jerks, hesitates, or gets pulled in any direction, set the hook. Be careful, however, that you don't pull too hard. You will know

Catch Words

As you know, a **nymph** is the immature stage of an aquatic insect. Nymphs live below the surface of the water. **Nymphing** is when you fish with flies, nymphs or not, below the surface of the water.

you have a fish the instant you lift the rod tip. If it was a false alarm, no big deal. Just lower the rod tip and let the nymph continue on its drift.

Fish Tails

Most fly fishermen only detect a fraction of the strikes they get while nymphing. I guided a client a few summers ago who kept missing strikes while nymphing. She wouldn't even believe me when I told her the strikes were fish. To prove my point, we walked downstream to a small wooden bridge crossing a nice pool. I let her wear my polarized glasses and told her to cast to the head of the pool. We both witnessed a large, brown trout take the fly within the first two feet of the first drift. Although she missed the strike, she let the fly continue its drift. As she picked up the line to cast again, she got one more strike, only this time set the hook properly. In both instances, the strike indicator did nothing more than briefly hesitate. Obviously, she got the point; we headed back upstream, and she proceeded to land six more beautiful wild browns.

You will often get strikes when you lift the rod tip on a false alarm or when you pull the line up to make another cast. This is not a sheer coincidence. The action makes the fly look like it's swimming to the surface of the water to emerge into adulthood. Insects are highly visible to a fish during this time and virtually defenseless, making them an easy target.

Wet Flies

Although we'll talk about *wet flies* more in the next section, you must first understand what they are before knowing how to fish them. Remember, nymphs are immature aquatic insects that live below the surface of the water. Wet flies, on the other hand, are winged adult insects that have already lived outside of the water. They have already gone through their mating rituals and have come back to the water for one of two reasons. Some dive through the surface of the water to lay their eggs, while others come back to the water to mate and die soon thereafter. Wet flies imitate both of these insects (as well as emerging nymphs), which are highly vulnerable to hungry trout as they get swept through the current of the water.

Catch Words

Flies that imitate adult winged insects that sink beneath the surface of the water are called *wet flies*. These flies can also be used to imitate a nymph as it emerges toward the surface of the water. They are some of the oldest fly patterns in fly fishing history and are having a resurgence in popularity.

To imitate the naturals, wet flies are most successful when swung in the current just below the surface of the water. Because your line is tight when fishing with wet flies, it's easy to detect a strike. To take the fly in the swift current of the water, fish also have to race to it and end up striking it with force. You will immediately feel the fish on the end of your line. All you have to do is lift the rod tip and pull the line. Be careful, though; many of the fish you take on wet flies will be downstream. If you set the hook too hard, you will pull the fly right out of the fish's mouth. It is also impor- tant to give them some slack after you set the hook and don't try to muscle them in. Because you are fighting the current when fishing downstream, it is easy to snap the tippet if you don't let them run.

If you get a strike directly downstream of you, it's often necessary to pull the rod at an angle; otherwise, you will pull the fly right out of the fish's mouth. To do this, hold your rod just as you would when performing a sidearm cast. When you get a strike, pull the rod tip back to the 12:00 position, or facing the opposite bank.

Streamer Fishing

As when fishing with wet flies, it's easy to detect a strike when fishing with streamers. Since streamers imitate bait fish, they are usually taken with a vengeance so the meal doesn't escape, or in retaliation for invading the fish's territory. Whatever the reason, it is easy to set the hook when fishing with streamers. Since you are already stripping the line in, the fish will usually hook them- selves. And since the line is already tight, you will immediately know when you've gotten a strike.

Unlike dries, nymphs, and wet flies, you will usually only get one or two tries when fishing with streamers. The fish you are after will either take it or they won't. If they reject it the first few times, it is usually futile to keep trying. Because you only get a try or two at each spot, you must cover a lot of water when fishing with streamers. That is why streamers are best fished from a boat; you cover much more territory, and it's easier to cast to the banks.

Reel Good Advice

If you see a fish following your streamer but not taking it, change the speed of your stripping or change the direction of the fly. This will often entice a strike.

Cut Bait

Be careful when fishing with streamers from a boat. Because of their large size, you will inevitably have a few sloppy casts. You, your boat, and any of your fishing companions will be at the mercy of a wild hook.

Strike One, You're Out!

Unless the fish you're pursuing is extremely gullible, a fish will only strike your fly one time before realizing it's fake. If the fish happens to miss your fly, you may get a second chance. If you do, the fish will most likely race to your fly and strike with aggression so it doesn't miss it a second time.

The Big Fight

Next to seeing a fish rise to your dry fly, playing a fish is one of the biggest thrills in fly fishing. The fight is so exciting with a fly rod that this is one of the many reasons people take up the sport. Unlike fishing with a spinning rod, where you just crank on the reel until the fish is by your side, you must fight the fish with extreme delicacy, letting it run when necessary so it doesn't snap your tippet.

The first thing to remember when fighting a fish is to keep the rod pointed toward the sky. Depending on the action of your rod, the tip may bend clear down to the water, but as long as the handle is still between the 10:00 and 11:00 position and you don't give the fish any slack, you shouldn't lose the fight. If you are fishing in a weedy or rocky area, you may need to hold your rod high and pointed at 12:00. When a fish makes a run, lower the rod tip and point it directly at the fleeing fish. Give him as much slack as he needs but keep constant tension on the line so he can't shake the fly loose. Also consider the following:

➤ **Small fish.** Small freshwater fish can be played with your hands. Using your line hand, simply strip the line in through your trigger finger. If the fish takes a run, let him. Just let out line by unpinching your fingers and threading it through your trigger finger. Small fish won't run very far before tiring out. Once the fish is within close range, use your net or hand to land it.

➤ **Large fish.** Large fish can also be played with your stripping hand, but your reel works more efficiently. Like when fighting a small fish, you must also use your trigger finger to let out line on a run. Once the fish takes up all of your spare line, it's time to fight him with your reel. If a large fish fails to make a quick run and you want to reel him in, simply pinch the line with your trigger finger and reel in your spare line. Be careful, though; if you give the fish any slack, he will either spit out your fly or snap the tippet on a head shake. Make sure you give a steady amount of tension throughout the entire fight and let him run when needed.

Cut Bait

Be careful when you are fighting a fish with a leader longer than the length of your rod. If you bring in the line past the tip top guide, the leader to fly line knot may get snagged. If the fish decides to take one more run and the knot gets caught on your last guide, the increased stress may break the tip of your fly rod.

Setting Drag

The beauty of using a quality reel to fight fish is its drag mechanism. Remember when we talked about drag in Chapter 2? Well, then, you should have been paying attention. Anyway, as I mentioned earlier, a good reel will have a smooth mechanical drag that doesn't take much power to get started. In other words, it shouldn't require much energy to initially pull line from the reel, and once the reel is spinning, the tension should be smooth and constant, without any jerks or delays.

If the drag is not smooth and abruptly stalls or stops, the game is over. More than likely, the fish will snap the tippet. A nice, smooth drag will keep steady pressure on a fish no matter how fast or slow it runs.

Setting the drag depends largely on what size tippet you are fishing with. Light tippet requires a light drag setting. If you are fishing with 6X or 7X tippet, use little or no drag. A heavy drag may snap the tippet on a quick run. Heavy tippet, on the other hand, can go either way. You don't necessarily have to have the drag set on a heavy setting, although you more than likely will be pursuing large fish or fighting heavy currents. It's also possible to set the drag as you are fighting the fish. If you know your reel well enough without stumbling around too much, you can simply adjust the setting during the fight.

Although not all reels come equipped with a drag mechanism, it's possible to apply drag manually if the spool has an exposed rim. Even if your reel does have a drag mechanism, this is a good technique to know to give additional drag. To give drag manually, also called *palming*, simply place the palm of your line hand underneath the reel and slow down the spinning spool as much as needed. Be careful, though; as I mentioned earlier, a spinning reel handle can be a deadly weapon to exposed fingers.

Catch Words

Using the palm of your hand to manually create drag on the reel is called **palming**. Many fly fishermen prefer this method because they feel more active in the fight and because it gives them a very fine control on the amount of drag pressure.

Watch Those Legs

Fly line has the magical ability to creep its way around any possible object it could get snagged on. It's important to always know exactly where your excess fly line is so it doesn't get tangled up. What's the big deal, you may ask? More than likely, you'll figure it out the first time you hook a powerful fish that makes a run. Just as you yell to your buddy to check out the monster on the end of your line, the fish will undoubtedly snap your tippet and set itself free. It's a component of Murphy's Law that sooner or later happens to every fly fisherman. It seems that whenever your line gets snagged on something, a large fish will take your fly, make a run, and snap the tippet once the spare line runs out. It will happen so fast, you won't know what hit you until your friend finally catches your attention and glances over to see your fly line dangling in the air. Line has the tendency to wrap around the following things:

➤ **Legs.** Fly line can easily get wrapped around your legs when wading in the water.

➤ **Rod handle or rod butt.** It's easy to get your line wrapped around the rod handle or butt. Be especially careful after you tie a fly on or when you are performing the double haul cast.

➤ **Boat.** Your fly line will find any object, rope, chair, or d-ring on a boat to wrap itself around.

➤ **Weeds, brush, and rocks.** Whether you're wading in the water or casting from the bank, watch out for these line catchers.

➤ **Chest pack or vest.** At the least opportune time, your fly line will wrap around anything that dangles off of your chest pack or vest.

Always keep an eye out for these obstructions. It seems that every time you have a fish on your line, the excess line will get into trouble.

Reel Good Advice

Some larger species of fish require you to haul on the line as you set the hook. To do this, pull on the line with your line hand as you lift the rod to set the hook.

Don't Over-Play Your Fish!

A fish that gets hooked is going to do all it possibly can to survive. It doesn't know if you plan on releasing him (although I'm not sure about some fish that have been caught over and over in some regulated waters). It's going to run, jump, dive, shake, and squirm until it wears itself out or is landed. As ethical anglers, our job is to land the fish as quickly as possible before it totally wears itself out.

This is probably the number one reason many fish don't survive after being released. They're simply too exhausted to swim away on their own. To keep from overplaying your fish, use the heaviest setup possible for the given situation. This includes your rod, line, leader, and tippet. If you're fishing for monster rainbows in a good size river, don't bring your three-weight fly rod. You won't be able to bring the fish in quickly enough without totally exhausting it.

Unfortunately, these light fly rods are growing in popularity, and many of the buyers are using them to enhance their fight. Sure they may land the fish, but by the time it gets netted, the fish looks like it has been through nine rounds with Mike Tyson. It is both unethical and cruel, even if you plan on keeping the fish.

Bow to Your Fish

Although you should treat any large fish that gets airborne like a king, I'm not talking about *bowing* as a sign of respect. When a large fish treats you with an acrobatics show, temporarily bow to him and point the rod at him while he is in the air. This will give him extra slack for his jump. If you fail to give him the much needed slack, chances are he will snap the tippet. Only after the fish lands back in the water should you raise your rod tip and tighten the line.

Fish Tails

Although I have never heard of it happening, or at least never believed the person telling the story, it's possible for a strong fish to take you to the end of your backing. What do you do? Well, if this really is the case, you will most likely lose the fish. Rather than worrying about losing the fish, you should be worried about losing your line. If a fish does take you to the end of your backing, wrap your line hand around the end of backing to get a firm grip. Then point the rod directly at the fish and give a hard pull. If your knots are all tied correctly, the fly should break off at the tippet connection.

Power Steering

When fighting a powerful fish, you often have to steer it in the right direction in order to land it. If you are fishing in an area that has lots of snag-likely obstructions on the bottom, you must have a plan of attack for when you hook up. Coral, weeds, sharp rocks, or fallen timber can all snag your line or snap your leader in a heartbeat and they all make great cover for a scared fish.

Many ponds and lakes also have weedy banks that can create a mess when landing a fish. To keep your fish out of these lethal areas, raise your rod high in the air and keep it pointed at 11:00 or keep your rod horizontal to the surface of the water. This will keep the fish close to the surface of the water and away from any possible snags.

In rivers and creeks, fish will also use the heavy currents to their advantage. But if you are tactful, you won't let them. Keep your rod horizontal to the water and steer their head away from the heavy current. If the fish gets into the current, try to keep it upstream of you. This way, the fish will have to fight the current, not you. If he gets downstream of you, you will probably have to follow him. Be sure to keep a tight line and let him run if needed as you work your way to the shore. Then, once you're on the bank, walk downstream and steer the fish into slower moving water before netting him.

If the fish gets himself wrapped around a rock or other obstruction, try to untangle the line or leader. If you can wade out to the obstruction, use a stick, wading staff, or any other device to get it undone. Sometimes you can net the snagged fish right there. If you can't reach the fish, try giving it some slack. It may try to make another run and free your line from the snag in the process. If it doesn't, use any means possible to get it to do so. I have even gone as far as throwing rocks in the water to make the fish run.

Landing Your Fish

Chances are, a fish will make one final run when you get him close to you or your boat. It's his last struggle to survive before succumbing to death. After all, he doesn't know he may be released.

Once the fish surrenders, it's time to land him. This can be done in a variety of ways, but the most popular means are to land him by hand, beach him, or use a landing net. Whatever the case, always follow these guidelines when landing a fish:

1. Take in any extra slack and keep the line tight.

2. Lift your rod high in the air over your head. Make sure the butt section of the rod doesn't drift past the 12:00 position, or the increased stress may snap the tip.

3. Wait until the fish is in close range before trying to land him.

If you plan to release the fish, reach down and try to pull the fly from the fish's mouth. To do this, you must grab the fly near its bend and back the fly out the same way it went in. If you have trouble holding the fly with your fingers, use a pair of hemostats or forceps to grip the hook. If you plan on releasing the fish but can't get the hook out without damaging the fish, cut the line as close to the fly as possible and release the fish. The hook will either fall out or corrode within a week, and the fish should survive.

Cut Bait

When fishing with light tackle, don't try to lift the fish out of the water to land it. The weight alone will likely snap your tippet, losing the fish and your fly.

Fish Tails

It is much easier to remove barbless hooks than barbed hooks, and the fish will sustain much less injury. With most flies, you must crimp down the barbs with either a small pair of pliers or a pair of forceps. Barbless hooks are also much easier to get out of skin, clothing, and trees.

151

Barbed vs. barbless hooks.

If you are landing the fish by hand, hold it in its mid-section with a firm grip, but be careful not to squeeze it. If you plan on releasing the fish, keep it in the water as long as possible and handle it with care. Hold the fish in the water until it can swim away on its own. If the fish is exhausted, this may take several minutes.

A landing net is the most guaranteed way to land most fish. It is also the easiest way to keep a fish in the water while you remove the hook. There are several things you must keep in mind, however:

1. Don't try to net a fish prematurely. If he is still fighting aggressively, wait until he wears himself out.

2. Don't try to swipe the fish in the water. This almost never works and will only lead to tangles. Plunging a net into the water will also spook a fish and send him running one last time, possibly breaking your tippet in the process. Instead, gently put the net in the water and lead the fish in head first. If possible, try to get the fish upstream of you so you don't have to fight the current.

3. Don't try to lift the fish in the air and drop him into your net. You'll probably break your tippet.

If you use a landing net, make sure it is made out of a soft material with small holes. Many of the nets on the market do more harm than good. Their sharp nylon material can damage the fish and make it virtually impossible to release it in good shape.

Plan your attack carefully if you're beaching a fish. Make sure you end the fight in shallow water and the bank has a gentle slope. If you plan on releasing the fish, make sure the bank won't damage the fish and get him back in the water as soon as possible.

Catch and Release!

Fortunately, most fly fishermen catch and release most of their quarry. Although their reasons vary, they all agree on one thing: a dead fish can't be caught a second time. If properly done, catch and release fishing can help ensure the future of the sport. The days of long stringers filled with fish are over; there are simply too many fishermen fishing over a limited supply of fish.

Handling the Fish

In order to ensure a fish's survival, you must handle it very carefully and release it unharmed. Fish have a protective coating on their skin. This delicate coating protects them from disease but can get damaged very easily. Always make sure your hands are wet before handling a fish. Dry hands and nets can do irreparable damage to this layer of protective coating.

Take the Picture Already!

If you need to take a photograph of the fish, wait until the camera is all set up and ready to shoot before removing the fish from the water. And always take the picture while holding the fish over water rather than the hard ground. This way, if the fish falls, he will land on water instead of rocks.

Resuscitating the Fish

A fish will be exhausted after losing a hard-fought battle. Its blood will be deoxygenated, and it will have little energy left to swim. This is the number one reason many fish die after being released: they simply weren't revived. To ensure his survival, you must carefully revive him and only let him go when he's ready. Follow these guidelines if you need to resuscitate a fish:

1. Hold the fish upright in the water with both hands under his belly. Move his body back and forth just under the surface of the water. This will allow the oxygenated water to flow through his gills and bring him back to life.

2. The longer the fish fought, the longer it will take to revive him. This usually takes no longer than a minute or two but may take much longer if the fish is totally starved of oxygen.

3. Don't worry when holding him; he will not struggle too hard to free himself until he is ready. Let go of your grip when he tries to swim away on his own.

4. If possible, don't release a fish in deep water or in fast currents. He will have a slimmer chance of surviving.

The Least You Need to Know

➤ Fly fishermen miss fish because they set the hook too fast out of excitement or because they don't know they got a strike.

➤ When nymph fishing, watch your strike indicator very carefully. If it stalls, dives, bounces, or even twitches, set the hook.

➤ When fighting a fish, bring it in as fast as possible; overly exhausted fish are more prone to die.

➤ Always wet your hands before handling fish. Fish have a protective coating that gets damaged from a dry hand or net.

➤ If you plan on releasing a fish, make sure it has been revived and can swim away on its own.

Part 4

The Fly Part of Fly Fishing

This part of the book unravels what most fly fishermen agree is the most complicated part of the sport: the flies. That is, both the natural flies you see on the water and the patterns you are using to imitate them. Unlike much of what has been written about this aspect of fly fishing, this part of the book is written in an easy-to-understand manner, without anything too scientific.

I know how intimidating this subject can be for beginners, so we'll take it very slowly. We'll first start by going over the different types of fly patterns and learn how to pick one that works (by far the biggest enigma for most fly fishermen). Then you will get a crash course on entomology (in layman's terms) and learn how to tie a few favorite patterns, and get the recipes for several more.

Chapter 13

Hooked on Flies or Flies on Hooks

In This Chapter

➤ All about hooks

➤ Types of fly patterns

➤ Choosing the right fly

➤ Switching patterns

➤ What the fish look for

This important chapter really dives into the heart of fly fishing. It covers everything from the actual hooks that are used to catch the fish to the different types of flies that are tied on them. You will finally learn what kind of foods the fish eat and what they examine before striking your fly. And yes, they do think before they strike. Despite the fact that a trout's brain is smaller than a pea (they just fit more into that small space), they still discriminate more than most humans I know.

Most importantly, this chapter will help you answer the question that makes every fly fisherman scratch his head in wonderment. The question that leads to more frustration than any other known to man. The question that has probably caused more fly rods to be broken over knees than any other. This not so simple question is: what fly do I tie on?

The Hook on Hooks

Now that we finally get to talk about the "fly" part of fly fishing, we should start things off with the hooks they are tied on. After all, this is one of the most crucial pieces of equipment in the entire link; without a hook, we wouldn't catch any fish.

Like every other piece of equipment used for fly fishing, hooks come in an assortment of sizes and varieties. Some are designed so small you need a hemostat to handle them, while others are large enough to land a 200-pound tarpon in the ocean. Before we discuss the imitation flies we tie around these hooks, we must first go over the different parts of a hook. Believe it or not, even a basic hook has an entire set of terms used to describe its various parts.

Parts of a hook.

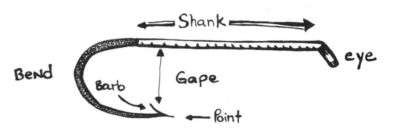

➤ **Eye.** The eye of a hook is the loop in the very front. As you have probably guessed, this is the hole that you tie your leader to. Of course, in fly fishing there are different eye styles to choose from. Some are turned up from the shank (common for salmon) while others are turned down (for trout). Most saltwater hooks usually have straight eyes that are even with the shank. Although these different styles are made to perform differently, I've never noticed a difference.

Reel Good Advice

If you can't thread your tippet through the eye of your hook, try threading the point of another hook through it first. After the fly is tied, a strong glue (called head cement) is applied that sometimes clogs the eye of the hook.

➤ **Shank.** The shank of a hook is the top straight part that most of the fly tying materials are tied around. Shanks vary in length for different types of flies.

➤ **Bend.** Hopefully you know what the bend of the hook is. If not, put this book down and take up something that involves a little less brainpower, like clapping. There are several styles of hooks that have different shaped bends for specific purposes.

➤ **Barb.** Unfortunately, most hooks come with a *barb*. To me, barbs do little more than damage the mouth of a fish. They were designed to help keep the fish on the hook, but they will stay on anyway. Some manufacturers make *barbless hooks*.

If your fly has a barb, crimp it down with a small pair of pliers or forceps. It will also penetrate the mouth of a fish easier since there is less resistance.

➤ **Point.** The point of a hook is what actually penetrates the mouth of a fish. It should always be sharp and in good shape. A good way to test its sharpness is to run it on the top of one of your fingernails. If it doesn't scratch your nail, sharpen it with a hook hone or a sharpening stone.

Catch Words

Barbless hooks are, as the name suggests, hooks without a barb. The barb of a hook lies just behind the point and is designed to help keep a hooked fish from slipping off. Since barbs can harm a fish, many ethical anglers crimp the barb of the hook down with pliers before heading out to the water.

Hook and Fly Sizes—One in the Same

The size of a fly is based on the size hook it is tied on. There is no such thing as a size 6 fly tied on a size 10 hook. It is simply called a size 10 fly. Therefore, when your buddy says he caught a fish on a size 16 fly, he is really talking about the size of the hook he caught it on. Or when you ask what size caddis is hatching from the water, the response will be, "A size 14," rather than how many millimeters long the fly is.

Some flies look much larger than the hook they are tied on. For example, a streamer pattern may be tied on a size 6 hook, but it looks much larger. Although its feathers are several inches longer than the length of the hook, it is still a size 6 fly.

Standard hook sizes for trout vary from size 2 for the largest down to a size 28 for the smallest, using even numbers the entire way (there is such thing as a size 3 fly). The only odd size is a size 1, but the measuring system changes here to the *aught system*. Unlike the other system, the aught system increases the larger the number hook size; you just say aught after the hook size (the old way of saying zero). So a size 1 aught hook (written 1/0 for ease) is larger than a size 2 hook, but a 2/0 is larger than both of them. Although the system may sound a little confusing, it isn't once you study the figure.

Shank Size

Although this probably isn't too important to you right now, it may be later on in your fly fishing career. As if the sizing system isn't difficult enough, some hooks are made with extra long hook shanks for specific flies. These hooks are measured with a special X-system for ease, and the numbers range from 1X to 6X. The larger the X size, the longer the shank of the hook. For example, a size 8 2X long hook has an extra long hook shank, but it is still considered a size 8 fly because the gap between the point of the hook and the hook shank is the same as every other size 8 fly. The X system starts at 1X and ends at 8X, the longest hook shanks made. The first few X sizes are generally used for long bodied nymph imitations. The larger X sizes are used almost exclusively for streamer patterns.

Fish Tails

As with the length of the shank of a hook, the diameter of the wire used to build hooks is measured on an X system. Standard diameter wire hooks are generally used for flies that sink. Special hooks are designed for dry flies that are measured 1X, 2X, or 3X fine-wire. That is, a 2X fine-wire hook is two sizes finer than a standard wire hook of the same size. Of course, even though the fly becomes more buoyant, the hook loses some of its strength with each size smaller in diameter. Hooks for strong-fighting fish like salmon, steelhead, and most saltwater fish are made 1X and 2X stout. That is, they are either one or two sizes heavier than standard hooks for extra durability.

Fly Patterns

Flies are tied to look like just about anything a fish will eat or strike at. The different variations in flies are called *fly patterns*. There are thousands of different fly patterns, each hand tied for a specific purpose. Some have been around for centuries and are still popular today, while others are being invented as I finish this sentence. Some patterns are successfully fished all around the world, while others are made specially for certain areas.

Although they are called flies, not all of them are tied to imitate insects. It is called "fly fishing" because that is what our ancestors started off with, flies. Some are tied to look like bait fish, while others are tied to look like a frog or mouse. Nonetheless, they are all called *flies*.

Aquatic Insects

Most fly patterns are tied to look like *aquatic* insects. These insects are born on the bottom of the water and go through different stages of development before developing wings and flying through the air. Fly fishermen imitate these flies in the following stages of development:

➤ **Nymphs.** These patterns imitate immature flies that live on the bottom of the water. Since this stage of development is by far the longest for aquatic insects, this is when they are most prone to be eaten. Nymph patterns need to sink to be successful. To get them down, fly fishermen often tie them with weight or add weight to the leader. The term *nymph* has become generic, and fly fishermen use it to describe any pattern that is fished below the surface of the water, even if it's not the nymph stage of an aquatic insect they are fishing with.

➤ **Emergers.** These fly patterns are tied to imitate a nymph on its journey, or *emergence,* to the surface to hatch. Most *emerger patterns* are fished just below the surface of the water.

➤ **Adults or dry flies.** Dry fly patterns are used to imitate winged flies that have emerged through the surface of the water or adult insects that come back to the water to lay their eggs. Most fly fishermen agree, because you can see the take, there is nothing better than dry fly fishing.

➤ **Wet flies.** Wet fly patterns are the oldest fly patterns in existence. They are tied to imitate drowned winged insects or other winged insects that swim below the surface of the water (usually to lay eggs). Wet flies can also imitate small minnows, emergers, or any other food that lives below the surface of the water.

➤ **Terrestrial insects.** Land insects live their entire lives on land. Some unlucky ones are either blown into the water or accidentally fall in and quickly become fish food. These are the insects fly fishermen are representing when fishing with *terrestrial patterns*. Ants, beetles, grasshoppers, and crickets are the most common land insects that fly fishermen imitate.

Catch Words

Anglers fish with flies that imitate a wide variety of **aquatic** insects. Unlike land insects, which are born on land, aquatic insects are born in the water.

Catch Words

A **weighted nymph** is tied with lead (or unleaded) wire to help it sink. Many anglers prefer weighted nymphs because they are easy to fish and behave more naturally than nymphs that are dragged by split shot when drifted on the bottom of a river.

Fish Tails

During the late summer months, terrestrials can make up a large portion of a trout's diet. Look for an increase of ants, beetles, grasshoppers, and crickets in the water on windy days. These patterns should be fished in middle of the river as well as on the banks.

➤ **Attractor patterns.** These patterns don't resemble any particular fly at all. Rather than looking like a particular natural insect, *attractor patterns* are tied with bright colors to attract *opportunistic* fish rather than *selective* fish; that is, fish that are not highly selective but instead seize the opportunity for an easy meal.

➤ **Streamers.** Most fish eat other smaller fish, even their own kind. These smaller fish are called *bait fish*. Fly fishermen use long streamers to imitate a wide variety of bait fish, including minnows, sculpin, and darters. Streamers can also be used to irritate a fish into striking it. Territorial fish will attack a streamer just to "teach it a lesson" or get it out of its private stash of water. Fish that are spawning may strike a streamer because it is a potential threat to their precious eggs. Whatever the case, streamers can be successful.

➤ **Crustaceans.** Many fly patterns imitate crustaceans, both freshwater and saltwater. Saltwater fly fishermen use these patterns to resemble crabs, shrimp, and other shellfish. Freshwater crustaceans include scuds, or freshwater shrimp, crayfish, and aquatic sow bugs. They are most often found in streams and lakes with weedy bottoms and since they live their entire lives in the water, they are available food throughout the year.

➤ **Worms and leeches.** Believe it or not, many fly fishermen tie patterns to imitate worms and leeches. Of course, these patterns are not very difficult to tie. Worm and leech patterns work great when fished at the tail of a pool. They are mostly found in slow moving water and can offer outstanding, if not easy, fly fishing. Since these invertebrates prefer slow moving water, use them accordingly.

Cut Bait

Be careful when fishing with a streamer pattern. Since these flies can make such a disturbance when they land in the water, they often spook the fish.

Fish Tails

Many fly fishermen feel that worm patterns are unsportsmanlike for fly fishing. They think worm patterns are just too easy to fool fish with or that worm and egg patterns are too much like bait and shouldn't be included in the sport.

➤ **Animals.** That's right, trout, bass, and many other freshwater fish will strike mice, salamanders, snakes, and small rodents that end up in the water. Be prepared for a ravenous strike by these large fish.

Which Type to Use?

Should you tie on a nymph or a dry, a streamer or a terrestrial, a crustacean or a worm? These are common questions fly fishermen face once out on the water. And unless you know exactly what the fish are feeding on, these questions can be very intimidating.

Many patterns can be ruled out quite easily. If you are fishing a river during the early spring months and you haven't seen a grasshopper since last fall, a hopper pattern is probably not your best bet. And if you are fishing a small creek or river that doesn't contain any crustaceans, a shrimp pattern wouldn't be the best fly to use. I could go on and on with these examples, but you get the point.

A number of factors should go into your decision of what fly to use:

➤ **Available food.** A basic understanding of what types of food the body of water you are fishing holds will help out dramatically when deciding what fly to use. Talk to a local fly shop or fishing buddy for this information.

➤ **Time of year.** Many sources of food also change with the seasons. If you are fishing during the winter months, you will probably not have as many options to choose from as during the summer months.

➤ **Type of water.** Your choice of patterns may vary depending on what type of water you are fishing. For instance, a high alpine lake may call for different patterns than fast moving creeks.

Fish Tails

Although fly patterns are designed to be fished either wet or dry, it depends on how they are used. I remember a float trip I was on a few summers ago in Colorado. Since the water was high and murky, we used streamers for most of the day with great success. Just before dusk, we noticed a large hatch of size 10 brown caddis flies. Not being prepared to match the hatch, I took the brown streamer (Wooly Bugger) I had been using and blew on it until it was dry then I treated it with floatant and skated it across the water below me. It was some of the best fishing of the day. As a matter of fact, I got more strikes fishing the streamer as a dry fly than I did underneath the surface of the water.

➤ **Type of species.** Although there is crossover, many fly patterns were designed for specific types of fish. For instance, the flies you will use when fishing for pike will be much different than the flies used for small brook trout.

➤ **Depth of water.** Some patterns should be fished deep in the water column, while others were designed for surface feeding.

➤ **Type of tackle used.** If you are fishing with an eight-foot, three-weight fly rod outfit, casting a size 1/0 streamer is probably out of the question.

Your First Fly of the Day

Before tying on a fly, the first thing you want to do is see if you see any rises, bulges, or boils in the water. If so, try to identify what the fish are feeding on and act accordingly. Even if you can't identify exactly what type of fly the fish are eating (most fly fishermen can't), try to match its size, shape, color, and behavior as closely as possible (more on this in a minute).

Signs of surface feeding may tell you if you should fish below the surface or on top, but not always. If I'm fishing in shallow water, I just about always start off with a dry fly. Even if the fish in shallow water are not concentrating their feeding on the surface, they won't have far to go for an easy meal. And since the water is shallow, the fly is also highly visible. Even when the water isn't necessarily shallow, many attractor dry fly patterns will entice fish to the surface.

If I don't see any surface activity when I first approach a piece of water with any depth, I usually tie on a pattern that is fished below the surface of the water, like a nymph, wet fly, or streamer, depending on the layout of the water. If it is deep pocket water, I will usually reach for a box of streamers, especially if it is brown trout water. Browns tend to get highly territorial in this type of water and strike streamers accordingly. If I approach a nice stretch of riffles and don't see any rises or hatches, I will assume the fish are feeding on nymphs on the bottom.

Cut Bait

Just because you see a little surface activity doesn't necessarily mean you should tie on a dry fly. It is usually the small, dumb fish that come up to feed first while the larger ones stay on the bottom to feed on nymphs until the majority of insects rise to the surface to hatch.

Other times, I will start off fishing with a terrestrial. If I see hoppers jumping on my walk down to the river, you bet I'll start off with a hopper pattern, especially if there is a slight breeze in the air that may send them to their deathbeds. Since they are only available at certain times of the year, fish take these large flies with greed, and this point must not be overlooked.

As you can see, choosing the right fly depends on a number of factors, none of which can be set in stone. Follow your instincts, think like a fish, and observe your surroundings before choosing what fly to tie on.

When to Change Patterns

It is usually best not to change patterns at all if you are having some luck. But what should you do if you are only getting an occasional strike or no strikes at all? The answer isn't always to change patterns. What if you aren't getting any strikes because the fish have been spooked? What if it's because you're not fishing in the right spot, or not presenting it convincingly enough? You may end up swapping a winning pattern for one that will only decrease your chances.

Knowing when to change a pattern and what to change it to can be difficult questions for many fly fishermen, if not all fly fishermen. Unfortunately, there aren't any general rules to follow that will tell you when to switch patterns. There are, however, several things to keep in mind that may give you some clues:

Reel Good Advice

Before switching to a new pattern, take a moment and think about why you are changing patterns in the first place. This may help you in the pattern choosing process.

1. You have carefully fished a piece of water and have gotten no strikes. If this is the case, it's probably time to switch patterns or the type of fly you are using. For instance, if nothing rose to your dry fly, it may be time to try a nymph or streamer.

2. Fish are rising to your fly but not taking it at the last moment. If this is the case, your fly is most likely the wrong size, usually too big. Switch to a smaller size of the same pattern before switching patterns.

3. Fish are rising to other insects but not your fly. Switch patterns and, if possible, try to imitate the natural insects on the water. Even if you can't identify what type of flies they are, try to catch one and imitate its size, color, shape, and behavior as closely as possible.

4. You are fishing with a dry fly and see several flashes on the bottom of the water. This should immediately tell you the fish are feeding on nymphs below the surface. Switch to a nymph pattern when this is the case.

5. If you change to a new type of water. For example, if you have been fishing with a nymph in a deep pool or run and work your way upstream to a shallow set of riffles, you may want to switch to a dry fly.

6. Change habitats. Make sure the pattern you are using lives in the type of water you are fishing. If you are fishing with stoneflies in a fast moving river in the morning and hit a pond in the afternoon, you will have to switch patterns to a type of fly that lives in that habitat.

165

7. See a new type of insect that dominates the water. For example, if you have been fishing with a mayfly pattern and see a huge swarm of caddis hatching from the water, switch to a caddis pattern (more on these insects in the next chapter).

8. Fishing over a new type of fish. If you are fishing with dry flies for gullible brook trout in one spot and move downstream to fish for wily browns, you will probably want to change your pattern for the new occasion.

As you can see, the list could go on and on. It is up to you to decide when the pattern you are fishing is not working and needs to be changed.

Cut Bait

When switching fly patterns, make sure your tippet hasn't gotten too short. Remember, every time you tie on a new pattern, you lose some tippet material in the process.

What Fish Look for in a Fly

Fish, especially trout, can be downright finicky eaters. But what makes them picky? What makes them reject one fly and devour another? Who knows? There has been much written on the subject, but what it comes down to is that we don't have the ability to think like a fish. We can only speculate.

Since aquatic insects usually offer the most abundant supply of food for fish, they are the most easily recognized as counterfeits. After all, they share the same habitat and see these food sources all of the time. When fishing with flies that imitate aquatic insects, your pattern must look and act like the natural insects, or they may be rejected. The fish may not know it's fake, but they will sure realize it's different from the others and may not want to take their chances. The same holds true for humans. Say you are like many friends I have and eat pasta five nights a week. It wouldn't be very difficult for you to realize if all of a sudden, the noodles that were served to you were either too big or too small, a different color or a different shape. Well, as off the wall as this analogy is, this is exactly what fish take into account when deciding whether to strike at your imitation fly.

Catch Words

Searching patterns work well when there is no hatch in progress and you want to lure a fish. A searching pattern is used to imitate any stray fly that may be in the water.

Size Matters

The size of the natural insects you see on the water (or on rocks on the bottom) should tell you what size fly to tie on. Most fly fishermen, myself included, have the tendency to fish with a fly that is at least one size bigger than the situation calls for. It is extremely important to match the size of your pattern to the size of the naturals in the water, especially when there is a large hatch in progress. During a hatch, fish will easily recognize if your fly is too large or too small.

Size isn't as important if you are fishing with a *searching pattern*; that is, a pattern that is used to entice fish to the surface when there is no hatch in progress. Since this pattern is imitating a random fly in the water rather than a particular hatch, it can imitate a variety of insect sizes.

Color

Although probably not as important as size, try to imitate the general color of the natural insects in the water. Remember, when fishing with dry flies, the trout's vantage point is the bottom of the fly. No matter how colorful and exact the top of your fly is, this isn't what the trout sees. Look at the underside of the natural insect you caught and match your pattern accordingly.

If you are fishing with nymphs, pick up a few rocks or sticks in the water and try to match the color of your nymph with the naturals. If you can't find any or will spook the fish if you do, match the color of your nymph with the color on the bottom of the river or lake. They are often the same color. Mother Nature has a way of camouflaging prey for maximum protection.

Shape

Just about all insects in the same order have the same body shape. As you will learn in the next chapter, all adult caddis flies have tent shaped wings, all adult mayflies have upright wings, and so on. This makes it important to be able to match the shape of the naturals when there is a hatch in progress. Even if you don't know what type of insect you are trying to imitate, picking an artificial out of your box that resembles the shape of the naturals will greatly increase your chances for success.

Behavior

The way you fish a certain pattern should reflect the behavior of the naturals in the water. If the insect you are imitating twitches in an upstream direction on the surface of the water, yours should do the same (or at least as closely as possible). If the insect looks lifeless and simply drifts at the whim of the current, again, yours should do the same. If in doubt, fish with a drag-free drift. Rather than trying to fight the current, most insects drift rather smoothly in the surface of the water.

The behavior of a fly isn't just limited to the way it moves (or doesn't move) in the water. It also reflects its course of action in the water. For example, many flies that emerge to the surface to hatch get caught in the surface film and spend a great deal of time trying to get free. Imitating this behavior and fishing these patterns in or just below the surface film will change your fishing forever.

There are many factors that increase the selectivity of a feeding fish:

➤ **A large hatch in progress.** As I just mentioned, it is crucial to match the exact size of the naturals when there is a hatch in progress. Since the fish have so many flies to choose from, why would they take their chances on a fly that doesn't look like the rest?

167

➤ **High pressure waters.** Fish become highly selective in easy-access waters that receive a high amount of fishing pressure. They are less likely to take their chances on a snack that is different than the rest. And if there are catch and release regulations, it probably made the mistake in the past and has learned from experience.

➤ **Clear water.** The clearer the water, the greater the visibility for fish. Since fish have an easy time seeing your imitation in clear water, you must be extra careful to fish with the correct size.

➤ **Smooth water.** It is also much easier for a fish to see your fly if the surface of the water is smooth.

➤ **Slow moving water.** Fish in slow moving water have time to closely examine the size of the fly. Fish in fast moving water, on the other hand, have to react much quicker for a meal and so there is a greater chance of it taking a "fake" fly.

The Least You Need to Know

➤ The size of a fly is dictated by the size of the hook it is tied on.

➤ A hook has many different parts including its eye, shank, bend, barb, and point.

➤ Fish eat a variety of foods including aquatic insects, land insects, crustaceans, other fish, and more. Flies are tied to imitate all of these different types of food.

➤ Terrestrial insects, such as ants, grasshoppers, and beetles, are all land dwelling creatures. They end up in the water on windy days, during water levels changes, or by accidentally jumping or falling in.

➤ It is important to know what the fish are feeding on before you decide what type of fly to use.

➤ The size, shape, color, and behavior of your fly are all important ingredients to catching fish.

Entomology 101

During the first few years of my fly fishing life, just hearing the word *entomology* scared me. I was sure that I was never going to be able to learn about all of these flies. So I just kept fishing and slowly, very slowly, started learning about the flies I was imitating. Although I read everything I could get my hands on, I learned more while observing the insects on the river than through the books I was reading. I found that while I was spending a lot of time flipping through the pages of fly mags and other entomology books, I spent more time and effort trying to decipher words such as *Ephemerella* and *Trichoptera* than actually learning about the insects themselves. Unfortunately, I had to learn the hard way; there was nothing written for the absolute layman.

Well, the next two chapters are dedicated to all of you laymen out there who want to learn the absolute minimum about entomology and still have a grasp on the insects you will be fishing. It's not the intention of this book to teach you how to identify a fly down to its genus and species. After all, there are more species of insects than taxonomists can keep up with. Let's face it, you just want to know what pattern to choose to imitate a particular insect and how to use it. Besides, big words like *Ephemerella* and *Trichoptera* won't help you catch fish.

This chapter starts with the very basics to help get you going and the next will help you identify which major orders of aquatic insects are important to fly fishermen and the fish that eat these insects.

Catching Those Little Critters

In order to properly identify an insect, or even see what type of pattern will imitate it, you must first know what it looks like. And in order to know what it looks like, you must often have to catch it. What?!! I'm having a hard enough time catching fish, let alone the insects, you may say. Well, I know it sounds difficult, but it isn't. We don't bother with the ones that are. After all, some flies are harder to catch than the fish themselves. We're just after the easy ones.

If there is no hatch in progress, shake the branches of a bush or tree next to the water. More than likely, adult mayflies, caddis flies, or stoneflies will be present, as will an assortment of terrestrials. Since aquatic insects have such short lives as adults, the flies you find in the bushes probably hatched within the last few days, if not earlier that day. If there is no hatch in progress and you want to fish with dries, try to match your pattern with the adult flies you see in the bushes. Chances are, the fish will recognize these flies and strike accordingly.

Reel Good Advice

If you're not sure what fly to use, shake the branches of a bush or tree next to the water. The flies you shake loose have more than likely hatched in the last few days and are still familiar food sources for trout.

Catch Words

Fly fishermen call the net they use to collect insects a **seine**, not a net.

During a large hatch, swiping at a fly in the air can be the easiest way to catch them. If you can't swipe one with your hands, try your hat. If this doesn't work, forget about it and just keep reading. We will go over the major insects in a minute and describe them so thoroughly that you won't have to have one in your hands to identify it. You will simply be able to tell what it is by its size, shape, and behavior.

Since it's nearly impossible to see what aquatic insects fish eat under the surface of the water, you must go down and see for yourself. Fortunately, nymphs are easy to catch. You can simply pick them up with your fingers. Look for them in the following places:

➤ **Branches and trees.** Nymphs feed on downed trees and branches. Pick one up out of the water and look closely. Most likely, you will see a variety of nymphs squirming around or a bunch of small cases (that look like cocoons) that house them.

➤ **Plants.** If the water you are fishing has a decent supply of aquatic plants, you will surely find nymphs feeding on them.

➤ **Underneath rocks.** Many aquatic insects feed on the bottom of a river or lake and hide beneath rocks to escape the current and predatory fish. Pick up a few rocks in the water, and you'll see what I'm talking about.

➤ **Silty bottoms.** Many aquatic insects live in the silt on the bottom of the water. Simply scoop a handful up and sift it through your hands. More than likely, you will see several aquatic insects move around in the palm of your hand.

Using a Net

Although it's easy to grab nymphs off of rocks or branches with your hands, it is just about impossible to grab them when they are drifting in the current. The only way to collect insects drifting in the current is with a small net, or *seine*. This will prove to be an invaluable tool for figuring out what the fish are actually feeding on. Even though you may see an abundance of one type of nymph living on a rock you pick up, the ones drifting in the current may be something else. And these are the nymphs that are most vulnerable to a hungry trout, hence, the ones you should be imitating.

Now That I've Caught It, What Do I Do with It?

Now that you know where to find aquatic insects, we should probably discuss what to do with them once you've caught them. The next step is to observe the fly's attributes before choosing a pattern to match it.

1. **Its size.** Flies vary greatly in size. Once you have caught a predominant insect, match its size to a fly you have in your box.

2. **Its shape.** The shape of an insect is one of its most important attributes for identification. Look at the fly's shape and compare it to the flies in your box. How many tails does it have? Does it have a wide body or a thin body? Match the shape of its body to a pattern in your box.

3. **The color of its body.** Different species of flies vary greatly in color. As a matter of fact, two flies of the same species can vary in color as well. Choose a pattern that matches the color of the natural insect you are trying to imitate.

Cut Bait

Make sure the size of your fly isn't larger than the naturals you are trying to imitate. Fish can be extremely finicky when it comes to size.

Reel Good Advice

If you are fishing in water that is too deep or too fast moving to catch a nymph to check out its colorings, just match the color of your imitation with the bottom of the river. To avoid predators, most insects blend in with their habitat.

171

There have been many excellent books written on the subject of insect identification but, unfortunately, most of them are too scientific in nature. After all, most fly fishermen don't give a hoot what the Latin name is for a particular insect. They only really want to know what pattern will work to imitate it. If you want to take entomology a step further, which I highly recommend, pay a visit to your local fly shop or bookstore and look for books written for fly fishermen, by fly fishermen, not by biologists.

Aquatic Insects

Don't let the hundreds of fly patterns you see at a fly shop intimidate you. Sure, they will all work at some point or another, but a handful of those patterns in different sizes are all that's needed to match just about any hatch you see on the water sufficiently enough to catch fish. The rest are reserved for obsessed fly-junkies who need to match every insect they see on the water to a tee. I have to admit, I'm one of them. But I'll just as readily admit that I probably wouldn't catch any fewer fish if I deleted half the patterns in my fly boxes.

There are really only four orders of aquatic insects that are of utmost importance to the trout fisherman. A few more will be mentioned, but they aren't nearly as valuable food sources in most waters as the big four: mayflies, caddis flies, stoneflies, and midges. Once you can identify the shape of these different types of insects and match a pattern to imitate the size and color of the naturals, you will be on your way to fooling more fish than you ever thought possible. I must emphasize, it's not important to be able to identify every species of insect within these orders. No fly fisherman in the world can do it. Heck, professional taxonomists who devote their entire lives to the subject can't even do it. There will be a few species of insects within each order that you will hear of repeatedly, but that's as far as most fly fishermen go.

The Two Lives of an Aquatic Insect

Aquatic insects live a dual life. In their immature stage of development, they live and feed on the bottom of the water. When they mature, or *hatch* as most fly fishermen call it, they live in the same world as us (only for a much shorter amount of time). Since they spend the majority of their time developing under the surface of the water, they are much more available to fish in this stage of development.

Nymphs, Larvae, Pupae—What's the Difference?

You will often hear fly fishermen refer to flies as *nymphs*, *larva*, or *pupa* (*larvae* and *pupae* are plural, pronounced like "Harvey" and "soupy"). These are just the different stages of development an aquatic insect goes through before becoming an adult. It is important, however, to

Catch Words

A **hatch** is when a large group of similar insects emerge out of the water at the same time. This is usually the most opportune time for fly fishermen.

understand these life cycles, as each stage of development presents the fish a different looking piece of food.

Aquatic insects develop in one of these two ways:

➤ **Complete metamorphosis.** Remember learning about the life cycle of a caterpillar in grade school? Well, the word *metamorphosis* was used to describe the process. Let me remind you how it goes. Aquatic insects such as the caddis fly and midge go through complete metamorphosis; that is, they go through three stages of development: larva, pupa, and adult. After they hatch out of their egg, they go through a larval stage. The larva then wraps a cocoon around itself and begins to pupate. When it is ready to enter adulthood, it emerges from its cocoon to the surface of the water and emerges as an adult. Pretty fascinating, huh?

➤ **Incomplete metamorphosis.** Unlike caddis flies and midges, mayflies and stoneflies go through *incomplete metamorphosis* before entering adulthood. These insects emerge from their eggs as nymphs and forage underneath the surface of the water until they are ready to enter adulthood where they mate and repeat the process. Mayflies, however, go through one more stage of development before they are considered adults. They are called *duns* when they emerge from the water and aren't considered adults, or *spinners* until they go though one more *molting*, or stage of development. They are the only aquatic insects that go through two winged stages of development.

Catch Words

Newly emerged mayflies are called **duns** when they hatch from the water. They aren't considered adults until they go through one final stage of development and are able to reproduce. Then they are called *spinners.*

Fish Tails

As you will learn, fly fishermen call any fly (except streamers) that is fished below the surface of the water a nymph. We now know that this isn't exactly true. Insects that go through complete metamorphosis are never nymphs; they are called larvae and pupae before entering adulthood. The term has become generic, just as the term *flies* is used for patterns that imitate shrimp, crabs, and other fish.

Hang in There

Hopefully some of the words in this introductory chapter didn't scare you. After all, they're just words. Although this information may seem a little overwhelming right now, if you continue your fly fishing journey, you will someday want to know all of this and more. But for now, a basic understanding of the flies you will be imitating will go a long way.

The next chapter covers in semi-great depth the major insects you will be fishing. If this chapter doesn't make complete sense, reread it before diving into the next chapter.

The Least You Need to Know

➤ Catching adult insects can be as easy as swiping your hand or hat through the air. Nymphs can be found on the bottom of the water under rocks, branches, roots, or other vegetation. Once caught, try to match the insect's shape, color, size, and behavior with a similar fly pattern.

➤ A small aquarium net can be used to catch insects on the surface of the water or just beneath.

➤ A nymph is the immature stage of development for aquatic insects that go through incomplete metamorphosis. Insects that go through complete metamorphosis go through a larval and pupal stage before becoming adults.

➤ The term *nymph* is used to describe many fly patterns that are fished underneath the surface of the water, whether they are true nymphs or not.

Chapter 15

The Basic Food Groups

In This Chapter

➤ Mayflies

➤ Caddis flies

➤ Stoneflies

➤ Midges

➤ Lake dwelling insects

➤ Land insects

One look at the assortment of fly patterns at your local fly shop is enough to intimidate even the most avid fly fisherman. Row after row of flies in various shapes, colors, and sizes lie lifelike in the bins, forming one giant collage. Most beginner fly fishermen take one look at the flies and shake their heads in bewilderment. How am I ever going to learn about all of these insects, they ask themselves?

Let me give you a little good news. First of all, each fly pattern doesn't represent a different type of fly. As a matter of fact, most of the flies you see in the bins imitate only four groups of insects: mayflies, caddis flies, stoneflies, and midges, all in various stages of development. With few exceptions, the rest of the flies are either streamers or terrestrials. This crucial chapter highlights these four basic food groups and more. We will discuss their various life cycles, descriptions, habitats, sizes, and behavior, and most importantly, how to fish each one of them. So keep reading, and don't let those bins of fly patterns fool you.

The Graceful Mayfly

There has been more literature written about these graceful insects than any other part of fly fishing. As a matter of fact, the word "mayflies" has become just about synonymous with trout throughout the history of the sport. And there is a reason. Not only are both of them beautiful, they also share the same habitats. They both thrive in cold, unpolluted water.

Mayflies are also one of the easiest aquatic insects to observe. Since most species sit peacefully on the surface of the water after their emergence, they are easily seen by both fly fishermen and trout.

Fish Tails

Most species of mayflies have a one-year life span. They spend just shy of a year as nymphs on the bottom of the water and anywhere from one day to a week as adults on land. The hatches on many famous rivers are so predictable, occurring at exactly the same time every year, that many fly fishermen plan their trips accordingly.

The Complete Incomplete Life of a Mayfly

The mayfly goes through incomplete metamorphosis before entering adulthood. I briefly mentioned this earlier, but the better the understanding you have of this insect's life cycle, the better you will be able to imitate it.

Reel Good Advice

Most newly emerged insects have to wait until their wings dry off before taking flight. Dry fly fishing can be phenomenal on windy, cloudy, or rainy days because these insects get stuck on the surface of the water longer.

Once the egg of a mayfly hatches, the tiny nymph scavenges for algae and plant matter on the bottom of a river or lake. As it grows, it sheds its old skin and forms a new layer. The time in between these sheddings is called *a stadium* and the individual during this interval is referred to as an instar.

In the nymph's final stage of growth, it develops its wing pads and keeps them folded beneath its tight skin. When it is finally ready to emerge as a dun, it gets restless and increases its activity level. This restlessness is what often leads to its death. Because it moves around more during this time (often in the view of trout), it is more vulnerable to being munched on. As I said earlier, this usually happens at the time of the day that's most comfortable for us; mornings and evenings during the hot summer months and midday during the spring and fall. Nymph fishing can be incredible during these few hours of increased activity before a hatch.

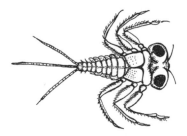

The mayfly nymph.

After nearly a year of growth, the nymph eagerly swims to the surface of the water to emerge. Once there, it faces the chore of breaking through the surface film while it frees itself from its nymphal shuck. Once free, the dun floats on the surface of the water and spreads its wings out before taking flight; exhibiting the same silhouette as a miniature sailboat. Of course, it has to wait for its wings to dry before lifting off and if it's cloudy or rainy out, this may take a while. A slight wind can also keep these poor duns on the surface of the water, praying not to be inhaled by the mouth of a trout.

An adult mayfly.

Mayflies are highly vulnerable during all three stages of development. If they don't get munched down on their swim to the surface of the water, they face the risk as they are stuck in the surface film, trying to break away from their nymphal shuck. And if they don't get munched then, they are lucky to survive the first few seconds of adolescence.

The fortuitous mayfly duns that do survive these feeding frenzies immediately fly for safety in the nearby streamside foliage. Their journey doesn't stop there though. After a short break, ranging from a few precious minutes to a few days, the lucky duns that have escaped the ravenous birds shed their skin one last time before qualifying as mature reproductive adults, called *spinners*. Spinners look much like the duns but they now have longer tails, transparent wings, and a thinner body. Their flight patterns also change. Rather than the slow, gawky flight that duns exhibit, spinners hover much faster over the water and systematically dip their bodies up and down while hovering over the water.

Spinners have one thing on their tiny minds: reproduction. The male spinners immediately fly back to the water and bounce up and down until a female comes to the rescue. The male then seizes a female and they mate while flying through the air. The female then deposits her eggs in the water, either by dropping them from a distance, lowering to the surface of the water and releasing them, or in a few cases, crawling through the water and depositing them on the bottom. Whatever the case, most of the female spinners lay *spent* on the surface of the water or drift with the current underneath the surface before ending up as trout food. The males, on the other hand, immediately look for another mate before flying back to the bushes for their last few hours of life.

When fishing with dry mayfly patterns, you want to mimic either a freshly emerged dun or an adult spinner that has already reproduced, usually a female. Whatever the case may be, it usually calls for a drag-free, dead-drift.

Fish Tails

The restlessness of birds can be a great indication that a hatch is about to occur. Somehow (although I've learned not to question Mother Nature), birds know when aquatic insects are about to emerge and if you know what to look for, you will be able to predict it as well. Birds tend to gather in the vicinity of a hatch and get fidgety in anticipation. If you see them jumping back and forth on rocks, making quick flights over the water, or gathering in the trees, chances are, some bugs are about to hatch.

The Four Types of Mayfly Nymphs

There are four groups of mayfly nymphs. Each group has miraculously adjusted to its environment (who said they don't believe in Darwinism?). If you can mimic both the looks and behavior of the species you are fishing, you will increase your success with that nymph pattern.

1. **Swimmers.** Like their name implies, these active mayfly nymphs dart around as they swim through the slow moving water they prefer. They are the most common types of mayflies in lakes and ponds and thrive in weed beds and mossy areas. Their bodies are long and skinny; thick in the thorax area and tapered down to their tails, of which they have two or three. When picked up out of the water, they squirm more than other mayfly nymphs. Since swimmer nymphs dart around from place to place, your fly should do the same. Short retrieves or a small twitch in the rod tip will achieve this; otherwise they will look lifeless.

2. **Crawlers.** This type of mayfly nymph lives in moderate to fast moving water. Its body is short and bulky with thick, strong legs to grip rocks in the current. Like the fish you are pursuing, their eyes are to the side of their heads. These nymphs are lousy swimmers when they get swept away in the current. Their fat bodies simply fall back to the bottom and bounce until they get a grip. Your imitation should do the same. A dead drift on the bottom is the most effective way to fish these imitations. A strike indicator is often necessary for the subtle takes on a crawler nymph.

3. **Clingers.** This type of mayfly is a perfect result of evolution. Since they live in fast moving rapids and riffles, and cling to the top of rocks, their bodies are as flat as pancakes. Unlike crawler nymphs, their eyes are on top of their heads and their heads are the thickest part of the body. Since clinger nymphs rarely drift in the current, they aren't readily available trout food until they make their emergence toward the surface. At this time, they leave the powerful currents of the fast moving water. Unlike the other three types of mayfly nymphs, most clinger nymphs leave their nymphal shuck on bottom of the river, and the duns, with their wings to their sides, feebly swim to the surface of the water to enter the outside world. It is during this journey to the surface of the water when they are most vulnerable to trout. Since these clingers expose their wings on the bottom of the river and swim to the surface for emergence, traditional wet flies are the most successful patterns for imitation.

4. **Burrowers.** These large nymphs bury themselves in the bottom of lakes or rivers with slow moving water. They dig small tunnels in the muddy or silty bottoms that they live in and only come out to feed. Since they live such obscure lives, they aren't readily available trout food until their emergence. At this time though, these large flies rise in mass numbers and can attract every large trout in the water for a late evening happy hour meal. When imitating these nymphs, you will have more success if your fly mimics the behavior of the naturals. Burrowers are only available to trout on their journey to the surface and are best fished in this manner. Since they are found in slow moving water, let your imitation sink to the bottom of the river or lake and bring it to the surface with a pulsing motion in the rod tip.

Reel Good Advice

If you are not sure of how to imitate the nymph you are fishing, fish it with a dead-drift. Nearly all aquatic insects get taken downstream with a dead drift at some time or another.

The Fluttering Caddis

Along with the mayfly, the caddis fly is one of the most abundant sources of food for trout. Unfortunately this fly has never gotten the respect it deserves; it has always been placed a distant second to the mayfly.

Why the lack of respect? Well, first of all, the caddis fly isn't as pretty as the mayfly. It looks more like a household moth you want to swat at than a source of food for hungry trout. I know it sounds a little off the wall to be judging the beauty of an insect, but it's not at all. You'll someday understand.

The caddis fly is also much more evasive than the mayfly. It doesn't usually hatch in great numbers (although I have seen hatches as thick as a cloud hovering over a river) and rarely hatches during the brightest part of the day, favoring the darker after hours for its emergence. Caddis hatches are more sporadic than their mayfly counterparts and can also tolerate much dirtier water.

Cut Bait

Be careful when fishing with poorly tied caddis fly patterns. Most of them are tied with elk hair, a very rigid fur. If the hair hangs over the hook too much, the fly will only get bumped when a fish strikes, making it almost impossible to set the hook.

Unlike the slow flight of a mayfly dun or the graceful dance of a spinner, the caddis fly moves through the air with no flight pattern at all. Its erratic flight makes it much more difficult to see when it's flying through the air and just about impossible to catch. Fortunately, you don't have to catch it at all. It's flight pattern alone should tell you it's a caddis fly.

Since there are so many species of caddis flies and the hatches are so inconsistent and random, fly fishermen don't even attempt to classify them. You very rarely have to match the exact species with an imitation, just the size and predominant body color. This makes it much easier for the beginner fly fishermen to fool a trout with a caddis pattern than a mayfly pattern; you don't have to be as exact. And because caddis flies hatch with such irregularity, it also makes them a great dry fly pattern to use when there is no hatch in progress. In a trout's eyes, it is simply less peculiar for a stray caddis fly to be on the surface than a lone mayfly.

The Complete Life Cycle of a Caddis Fly

Unlike mayflies, caddis flies go through complete metamorphosis before emerging as adults. They are deposited as eggs in the water then hatch into larva anywhere from a few days to several weeks later. This stage is by far the longest stage of development for the caddis fly. This is when they do all of their growing and preparation for their next phase of life, the pupal stage. There are two different types of caddis fly larva:

1. **Case builders.** Most species of caddis larva build cocoon-like shucks around their bodies. Depending on the species, the cases are made out of sticks, pebbles, sand,

leaves, or other debris, and are used for protection against predators and to counterweight the pull of the current. During the summer months, pick up any stick or rock and you will more than likely see some caddis cases.

2. **Free-living caddis.** These caddis larva don't form a casing at all. They simply wander the bottom of a river in search of food; most commonly, smaller aquatic insects. Some species of free living caddis larva hide out in small crevices and burrows, then build small nets to catch food, much like the web a spider makes.

The caddis larva.

After almost a year in the larval stage, the caddis fly goes through its pupation. This is when all of its adult structures are formed (wings, antennae, reproductive organs, and so on) and it is ready to emerge into the outside world. Once ready, with the help of buoyant gases trapped in the pupal shuck, the pupa emerges to the surface and flies away. It is during this emergence that the caddis pupa is most prone to being eaten. Once the caddis fly reaches the surface of the water, it immediately takes flight and heads for the streamside vegetation for its mating rituals.

The adult caddis fly looks more like a moth than any other insect. Unlike mayflies, caddis flies have tent shaped wings that fold parallel to their bodies and they don't have tails. Instead, they have two long antennae. If you want to see a caddis fly when they are not hatching, simply shake any bush next to the water and you should see an entire swarm of different species.

Catch Words

The **caddis fly** is an important source of food for trout, hence, an important pattern for fly fishermen. It has tent shaped wings and looks like a moth in flight.

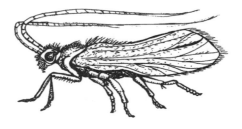

The adult caddis.

Because they immediately take flight after hatching, adult caddis flies are most vulnerable to trout when they come back to the water to lay their eggs, not when they've just hatched. Depending on the species, the eggs are deposited in a variety of ways. Some adults drop them through the air from a distance while others dip to the surface of the water to release them. Other species dive through the water and crawl along the bottom before releasing their eggs.

Imitating the Caddis Fly

When imitating the different stages of life a caddis fly goes through, it is important to duplicate their natural behavior as closely as possible. Follow these guidelines for imitating these insects in their different stages of development:

➤ **Caddis larvae.** Since most caddis fly larvae live in a casing, they aren't big swimmers. Free-living caddis, on the other hand, squirm about like worms, but still lack any real swimming capabilities. In moving water, both varieties move more or less at the whim of the current and should both be fished in a dead-drift manner. These patterns can be fished with a slight twitch in slow moving rivers and lakes, where their movements may be more pronounced.

➤ **Caddis pupae.** Caddis pupae should be imitated just like they behave. In fast moving water, they propel themselves to the surface while drifting downstream in the current. To imitate this behavior, let your pupa imitation sink to the bottom of the river with a dead-drift. Once the fly reaches the end of the line downstream of you, lift your rod tip and let the imitation rise to the surface. You should get strikes in both stages of the drift, but they will be more frequent and aggressive when it swings below you.

In slow moving rivers or lakes, the caddis pupa rises with more conviction. When imitating these insects, let your pattern sink to the bottom then lift your rod tip so it follows the line back to the surface. When doing this, its possible to bounce your fly like this several times per drift.

Catch Words

Soft-hackled flies are used to imitate winged insects underneath the surface of the water. They look very life–like when fished and are presented just like wet flies.

There are many excellent fly patterns used to imitate the caddis fly larva and pupa. As a matter of fact, the same patterns are often used to imitate the fly in both stages of development. It is just fished differently. When imitating the caddis pupa in rivers, I seem to have the best luck with *soft-hackled flies*. These flies have a thin body and a few wraps of a feather, or *hackle*, around the head of the fly. The fly is easy to tie and closely resembles a caddis pupa; the hackle looks just like the fly's wings, legs, and antennae as it drifts toward the surface of the water.

Just about all adult caddis flies can be imitated with the infamous Elk Hair Caddis. This fly is so life-like that a few variations of it are all that's needed to consistently take fish. Carry the appropriate sizes for the naturals you see hovering over the water or in the bushes; sizes ranging from 10 through 16 cover most circumstances. The wings are just about always tan or brown, with a few species leaning toward gray. If possible, match the color of the natural's body. Tan, brown, green, and gray bodies work well for covering just about all caddis flies.

Since caddis flies move very erratically, just about any presentation you give your fly on the surface of the water can imitate them. Some drift motionless in the current, some flutter in an upstream direction, while others simply skitter in circles until they get airborne or eaten. There are three excellent ways to present an adult caddis fly:

➤ The first is with a drag-free, dead-drift. This, of course, imitates caddis that float at the whim of the current.

➤ The second is to fish it like a wet fly. This style imitates caddis that dive through the water to deliver their eggs.

➤ The third, and often most deadly, is to fish the pattern below you in an upstream direction, letting it skitter across the top of the water. This will often induce strikes when nothing else is happening.

The Rolling Stonefly

Ask any fly fisherman familiar with the Gunnison River in Colorado, the Deschutes River in Oregon, or the Madison River in Montana what the best hatch of the year is, and they will more than likely tell you the giant stonefly. If they don't, they have simply never fished these rivers in the early summer months or they don't know what they're talking about.

Stoneflies can be, without a doubt, some of the best hatches of the year. They range in size from more than two inches long down to a size 18 and favor clean, fast-moving, well-oxygenated, rivers and creeks. Because of their sheer size, it seems every large trout in the river is on the prowl for these easy meals during their emergence.

Cut Bait

Be careful when fishing with stoneflies. They are most often associated with fast moving, rocky water that can be very difficult to wade.

As their name implies, stoneflies live on rocks on the bottom of the river. The larger species have a two- to three-year life cycle while some of the smaller species live only for one year. They offer trout a good source of food throughout the entire year.

The Stonefly's Life Cycle

Like mayflies, stoneflies go through incomplete metamorphosis. That is, they go from nymph to adult and bypass the pupal stage. They do not however, emerge as duns. They simply emerge as adult flies that have one thing on their minds: reproduction.

183

A stonefly nymph.

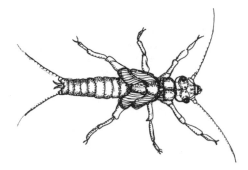

Stonefly nymphs live in fast moving, rocky (or stony) water, preferably with lots of oxygen. For this reason, few species are found in lakes and ponds. The nymphs forage the bottom of rivers for any vegetation they can get their hands on, or mandibles in this case. Some have carnivorous diets and feast on other aquatic insects while others are strict vegetarians.

After anywhere from one to three years in the water (depending on the size of the species), the nymphs are finally ready to hatch, or in this case, migrate. Instead of hatching through the surface of the water like most aquatic insects, stoneflies crawl out onto the banks. It is during this migration, that stonefly nymphs are most vulnerable to trout.

The stonefly adult.

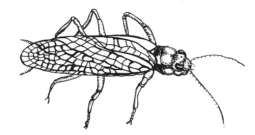

Once on land, the stoneflies emerge from their nymphal shuck and leave a quite life-like exoskeleton behind. To escape being devoured by birds during the daylight, this usually happens at dusk or after dark. The adults then retreat to streamside vegetation, usually willows or tall grass, and begin their mating procedures. Once the female is ready to lay her eggs, she flies back to the water and either drops her eggs from the air or dips her body through the surface of the water and expels them.

Imitating the Stonefly

Remember, stoneflies live anywhere from one to three years so their nymph forms are available to trout throughout the entire year. And since stoneflies inhabit fast moving water, they often get carried in the current, tumbling on the bottom as they try to regain their hold. Stonefly nymph imitations fished with a dead-drift in fast moving water mimic this action to a tee. Make sure that your nymph is heavily weighted so it bounces along the bottom of the river.

When stonefly nymphs are ready to migrate towards the banks, they leave the fast moving water and gather in the shallows before their final emergence. The fish, of course, follow suit and gather in the shallow water as well—feasting on the abundant supply of food. This is when stonefly fishing is at its best; just before the main hatch and consequently before the hordes of anglers that come to match it. If possible, hit the water during this time and hammer the shallow water with your nymph imitations. You will be amazed at how good the fishing can be.

Like I said earlier, when the nymphs break out of their exoskeletons they head for the tall grass or willows to mate. Their hormones get them into trouble during this time. As they clumsily fly from willow to willow in search of a partner, they often end up in the water as trout food, especially on windy days. I have seen giant stoneflies (also known as salmonflies or willowflies) congregate so thickly on a hanging willow that they actually dragged the branch into the water and subsequently, into the mouths of awaiting, hungry trout.

Fishing with adult stonefly patterns can be some of the most exciting fly fishing ever. During the larger hatches, such as the Golden Stone or Salmonfly hatch, it seems every monster trout in the river will come up for these huge meals. These patterns should be fished along the banks, mimicking the behavior of the naturals during mating activity. At dusk, or when the females come back to lay their eggs, these imitations should be fished in the riffles and choppy water.

Adult stonefly imitations should be fished with a dead-drift, or with a slight twitch to give them some life. Believe it or not, I have also had good luck fishing these huge insects just below the surface of the water, mimicking drowned adults that drift in the current.

Reel Good Advice

When fishing with stonefly nymphs, it's important to make sure they are weighted enough to bounce on the bottom. Otherwise, they will be out of the view of feeding trout.

Midges

If trout see stoneflies as steak dinners, they see midges as an afternoon snack, like a bowl of popcorn. Although these insects can be aggravatingly small—down to a size 28—their great numbers make up for their small sizes. If you have the patience (and eyes) for midge fishing, you may be rewarded with some of the best fly fishing you've ever had.

Midges thrive in just about all types of water, from nasty sewage tanks to crystal clear spring creeks, and the cold water of most trout streams and lakes is no exception. These hardy insects are available

Catch Words

Midges are miniscule insects that offer trout and various other fish an abundance of food. They are the smallest insect a fly fisherman imitates.

year-round and under all weather conditions. When there is no other readily available food source, they can be the mainstay of a trout's diet, especially during the winter.

The Life of a Midge

To properly understand how to fish with midge imitations you must first understand their life cycle. Like the caddis flies we discussed earlier, midges go through complete metamorphosis before adulthood. The swarms of adults you may see flying through the air are mating adults that only live a day or two. They deposit their eggs (how and where depends on the species) then the larvae hatch and grow before pupation takes place.

The midge pupa.

The larva looks like a tiny worm or tube and comes in just about every color imaginable. They live in, on, or near the bottom of the water or aquatic vegetation.

Cut Bait

The biggest mistake fly fishermen make when fishing with midges is fishing with patterns that are too large. When fish key in on a midge hatch, they will reject any offering that is too large.

After the larvae grow, they go through a few days of pupation and then are readily available trout food on their slow journey to the surface of the water. If the pupae don't get devoured along the way, they still face the difficult task of breaking their way through the surface of the water before emerging into their reproductive adulthood. And this is no easy feat for these tiny insects, especially on calm days when the tension on the surface is greatest. Once the midge pupa gets its head and thorax through the surface film, it tries to liberate itself from the pupal shuck it no longer needs. It is during this precious time that the tiny insect is most vulnerable to trout, hence one of our (us trout junkies) favorite times as well. During the summer, mornings and evenings can often provide the hottest midge fishing. During the winter months, they emerge most frequently at mid-day.

The adult midge.

Imitating the Midge

Since midge larvae have no legs to help them swim, they get around with a seemingly directionless flick of the body motion. Because of the area they inhabit, the larvae can be tough to imitate but should be fished deep with a long leader (10 to 12 feet in deep water), with a dead-drift or a slow hand twisting retrieve. Trout aren't going to strike this small meal with a vengeance. The take will be dull, one that you may or may not even notice. Watch your strike indicator closely and set the hook frequently simply by lifting your rod tip. Also, your odds of detecting a strike will increase dramatically if you take the time to straighten out your leader before casting. Any kinks in the leader will delay movement of the indicator, allowing the fish more time to reject the artificial.

Trout won't exert too much energy for such a small meal or they will be expending more energy than they're taking in. This makes it imperative to fish at various depths until you find where they are feeding. And don't expect a huge tug on the end of your line. Remember, these fish aren't going to make a mad dash for such a small snack. They aren't giant stoneflies! The take will be very subtle; half the time you won't even know you have a fish on.

Reel Good Advice

When fishing with small flies such as midges, it's extra important to make sure your leader is kink–free. Your odds of detecting a strike will increase dramatically.

Presenting the midge pupa depends on which stage of development you want to imitate. If you wish to fish it deep, when the pupae are on the rise, you must use a long leader (10 to 12 feet). A dead-drift works well for most situations and a strike indicator is a must. And remember, make sure your leader is kink-free for greater success.

Imitating the midge pupae just below the surface or in the surface film requires a different approach. It can be a difficult task to keep this small fly from sinking too deep or riding too high in the surface film. Luckily, there are a few good techniques to keep it from sinking too deep. The first is to treat your leader to within 6 to 10 inches (depending on where you want your fly) of your fly with fly floatant. This will let your pattern hang just below the surface film while the rest of the leader stays afloat. Another good way to keep the pupa from sinking is to tie it from the bend of a dry fly with 8 to 12 inches of light tippet. The dry fly helps keep the dropper fly suspended in the water and also acts as a great strike indicator. Don't be surprised if the fish strike the dry fly as well (probably mistaking it for a cluster of adult midges or a mayfly dun).

Only after the midge pupa emerges through the surface and frees itself from its pupal skin is it considered an adult. The adult then flies to nearby foliage and comes back a day or two later to repeat the mating process. Fishing adult midges can be a difficult task. They are not only difficult to see, but it is hard to tell if the fish are feeding on midge pupae below the surface or adults on the surface. When in doubt, fish with a pupa pattern just below the surface or in the surface film. You will be amazed at the difference.

Catch Words

Sight fishing is when you are pursuing visible fish. **Blind fishing**, on the other hand, is fishing to an area that looks promising, but no fish are in sight.

If you are *sight fishing* (pursuing a visible fish) with midges (or any other small flies for that matter), you must literally put the fly right in front of the feeding fish. If casting to a bunch of rising fish, you must often single out one particular fish to cast to and set the hook if you see the fish make any subtle body movements or open its mouth. Because of their minute sizes, sight fishing with midges can be some of the most technical fly fishing known to man.

A Few Honorable Mention Stillwater Flies

As any fly fisherman will tell you, most trout feed on the big four insect groups: mayflies, caddis flies, stoneflies, and midges. There are times, however, when it seems every fish in the water is feeding on something else, especially in ponds or lakes. If you plan to do a lot of lake or pond fishing, keep reading; learning about the following stillwater insects will increase your fishing profoundly.

Dragonflies

Just about everyone knows what a dragonfly is. A large insect that flies around ponds and lakes, right? Well, yes. But not everyone knows (or cares to know) that they can be a great source of food for the fish that feed on them. Even fewer people know their life cycles (just nerdy entomologists and taxonomists, right?).

Like mayflies and stoneflies, dragonflies go through incomplete metamorphosis. They have two- to three-year life cycles which makes their nymphs available fish food throughout the year. Usually in the spring or early summer, when the water warms up to roughly 60 degrees, the emerging nymphs migrate toward the bank of the water. Once the sun sets, these hour-glass shaped nymphs crawl out to land and exit their nymphal shucks (sound familiar? hint: stoneflies). Unlike the other aquatic insects we discussed, the adults actively feed on other insects before reproducing.

Fish Tails

In both their nymph stage and adult stage of life, dragonflies actively hunt and gobble any smaller insects they may catch. Fortunately, mosquitoes are a delicacy for them. Believe it or not, some parts of this country (New England in particular) have used dragonflies to combat their mosquito infestations. They simply introduced thousands of dragonfly nymphs into infested waters. These carnivorous nymphs feast on the mosquito larvae under the water, and once they emerge as adults, feed on the annoying adult mosquitoes.

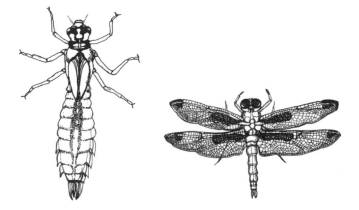

The dragonfly nymph and the adult dragonfly.

Since dragonflies hatch on land, they are rarely available fish food as adults. Their nymph forms are of primary interest to the fly fisherman. The best dragonfly nymph fishing is when they migrate to the shallows. Fish feed voraciously on these defenseless nymphs as they make their way through the weed beds for shore. Large nymph patterns, ranging in size from 6 to 10, should be fished near the shore during their emergence. At all other times, they should be fished in the deep water. Whatever the case, fish these nymphs with a stripping motion, varying the speed and length of strips until you start hooking up.

Damselflies

Damselflies are very similar to their cousins, the dragonflies. They both share the same habitat (ponds and lakes) and both go through incomplete metamorphosis, migrating to the bank to hatch. This is usually after dark to avoid the birds. They are also both carnivorous eaters, both as nymphs and adults, eating whatever they can catch with their legs.

The damselfly nymph and adult.

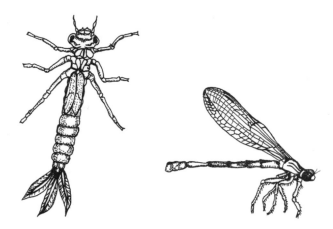

The main difference between the two is their looks. Dragonflies are usually much larger than damselflies, both in their adult and nymph stages. And dragonfly nymphs have an hour-glass shape, while damselfly nymphs have long slender bodies and three large gills instead of tails, where they take in their oxygen. This makes them easy to distinguish from any other type of nymph.

The adults also look much different. Damselflies just about always have a light blue slender body and keep their wings folded parallel to their bodies at rest. Dragonflies, on the other hand, have a much thicker body and keep their wings spread horizontally at rest.

Unlike dragonflies, damselfly adults are readily available fish food, even during their hatch. Once they leave the water and crawl out of their exoskeletons as winged adult flies, they rest to dry their wings. If there is a slight breeze in the air, they can get blown right back in the water and gobbled up by awaiting fish. Even if they survive this vulnerable period, they often get blown back in the water later in life.

Catch Words

Damselflies are aquatic insects that live in ponds and lakes. They are a close relative of the *dragonfly* and share the same habitat.

Fish Tails

Dragonflies and damselflies have two pairs of wings and flap their front pair of wings separately from their hind pair. They can change direction almost instantly, hover and fly backwards. Some species of dragonflies cruise through the air at 35 miles per hour while hunting other insects.

Adult damselfly patterns should be fished near the shore or in the shallows on windy days. Fish them with a dead-drift, giving them a little twitch once in a while to entice a strike. Their nymph imitations should be fished in the shallows during a hatch, and out in deeper water during other times of the year. Fish these patterns with a slow retrieve or a slight twitch with your rod tip.

Water Boatmen and Backswimmers

Ever look into a pond or lake and notice those little beetle-like insects moving around like little drift boats in the water? Well, if you didn't already guess, the two types of insects that match this description are called water boatmen and backswimmers. As you can see by watching them swim, the oars that power these little boats are their legs.

The nymphs and adults of these insects are just about identical, except for their size. They both share the same habitat, and although the adults have fully formed wings, they only use them for emergencies. The adults trap a small air bubble under their bodies for oxygen and dive through the surface of the water in search of aquatic vegetation. When their air runs out, they simply swim (or row) to the surface for more. Because of their high need for oxygen, both the nymphs and adults of backswimmers and water boatmen live in shallow water.

When fishing with these patterns, it's crucial to imitate the behavior of the naturals. The most successful way to do this is in shallow water while stripping the line two inches at a time or with a slight twitch of your rod.

Reel Good Advice

When fishing with water boatmen or backswimmer patterns, make sure you twitch them through the water just as they swim. Otherwise, the fly won't look real.

The water boatman.

Terrestrials—The Land Rovers

Unlike aquatic insects, terrestrials live their entire lives on land—and often end their lives in water. These land insects are, at times, a major food source for hungry trout, especially during the late summer months. These insects, including grasshoppers, crickets, ants, and beetles, most often end up in the water by accident. The wind, rising water levels, a misjudged flight, or simply falling from the overhanging branches all send these juicy morsels to their death.

A grasshopper.

Because terrestrials live on land, I will spare you a discussion of their various stages of development. Only the adults are of importance to fly fishermen. Concentrate your efforts near the bank or shore of rivers and lakes when fishing with terrestrial patterns. On really windy days, don't ignore the middle of the river or small lake. A strong gust of wind can send these poor insects flying (no pun intended).

Like all fly imitations, your patterns should mimic the same action as the naturals you see on the water. And since terrestrials land in the water by accident, they try their hardest to get out. Unfortunately for them, their efforts are usually futile. Sure, they give it their all, but they don't have much to give it with. Remember, these creatures have evolved on land, hence, they don't swim very well. After a few minutes of struggling, they run out of energy and simply drift at the whim of the current. The lucky ones may catch an eddy and escape the deadly water, but most of them end up as fish food. Fish these patterns with either a slight twitch, imitating their struggle for freedom, or with a dead-drift, the same behavior as the exhausted naturals.

Now that you've finished your crash course in entomology, it's time to learn how to fill your fly box with patterns to match these major food groups. Turn the page. Chapter 16 covers this and more.

The Least You Need to Know

➤ Most aquatic insects have a one-year life cycle and develop at the same time each year.

➤ Mayfly nymphs hatch from the water with wings as mayfly duns. They go through one more molting before becoming mature adults, or spinners.

➤ Mayflies have upright wings and look like little sailboats on the water while caddis flies have tent shaped wings.

➤ Stoneflies live in fast moving oxygenated water. They live anywhere from one to three years, depending on the species.

➤ There are many factors that dictate when a fly will hatch. Weather conditions, sunlight, water temperature, time of year, and time of day are all major influences.

Chapter 16

Fly Selection

In This Chapter

➤ Filling your fly box

➤ Arranging your flies

➤ Caring for your flies

➤ Animating your flies

➤ Recommended Flies

Being caught without the right fly pattern is one of the biggest crises in a fly fisherman's life. Not being able to find a pattern quick enough is a close second. These are some of the biggest causes of stress that many of my fly-fishing friends face in life. Not a bad life, huh?

The goal of this chapter is to help alleviate some of these inconveniences. I am not going to tell you exactly what flies to buy simply because I don't know where you will be fishing. I will give you a few basics that you shouldn't leave home without, but after that, it's your duty to pay a visit to a local fly shop and get some local advice.

Once you've bought all of the flies needed (and have gotten a second mortgage on your house), it's time to learn how to take care of them and organize them so you can easily find them.

Getting Organized

It took me several seasons of avid fly fishing (counting the number of days in the summer I wasn't on the water rather than the days I was) before I realized I was carrying too many fly boxes to the stream. It hit me on a gorgeous mid-summer day. The fishing had been slow (over an hour since my last fish), when all of a sudden a pale morning dun (a type of mayfly) flew right in front of my nose. I then looked out in the riffles and saw more rising slowly through the air. I dug through every pocket of

Reel Good Advice

Keeping your flies properly organized will save you much aggrava-
tion once on the water. There is nothing
worse than to not be able to find
the right pattern because your fly
box is so messy!

my vest, frantically searching for a size 16 pale morning
dun (PMD for short). After unsuccessfully flipping
through four or five fly boxes, I glanced back at the
river. The sporadic rises had turned into a feeding
frenzy; every trout in the river seemed to be rising for
these little flies. I continued to search, sweating bullets
the entire time.

"What's the problem," my buddy Dom called out "It
looks like you're searching for your drivers' license with
a cop over your shoulder."

"Got a size 16 PMD?" I yelled out. He pulled out two fly
boxes from his chest pack, a green one and a blue one.
Within three seconds he grabbed a size 16 PMD from
the green one. That day taught me a valuable lesson.

Two Boxes Only

There are probably several different ways to organize your flies. Unfortunately, I don't
know them. It wasn't until that humbling day on the river that I assumed any responsibility for my flies at all. As soon as I got home, I went through my vest and found
four large fly boxes and three little compartment-sizes boxes. I then dumped every box
out on my fly-tying table. Over four hundred flies sat in a small pile; enough to catch
every trout in the entire county. I then weeded through them and picked out the
damaged ones. I was down to about half. Pretty pathetic, I thought. I just threw away
about twenty five hours worth of fly tying (I'm a pretty slow tyer) or about three
hundred dollars in flies.

With the salvageable flies laid out neatly in front of me, I began to categorize them. To
make it easy, I put them into two piles: flies for down under and flies for on top. Every
nymph, larva, pupa, streamer, emerger, soft-hackle, and wet fly went into the
"nymph" pile and every dry fly went into the other, larger one. I then went through

Cut Bait

Don't keep your dry flies in sheep-
skin wallets. They were designed for
nymphs and only crush the wings
and hackle on dry flies.

the flies and categorized them further before arranging
them back in their boxes. Only this time, I put them all
in two boxes.

I put all of the dry flies in a large green box labeled
"dries" and arranged them according to type and size. I
came up with six categories, the four major food groups
we talked about earlier: mayflies, caddis flies, stoneflies,
and midges plus two more, terrestrials and "various
others." The "various others" pile included patterns that
didn't fit anywhere else, like attractor flies, damselflies,
dragonflies, and so on. I then arranged them by size,
making sure I had an array of sizes for each pattern and
at least two or three of each size. Wham, I was done
with my dry box.

For a quicker withdrawal, I purposely arranged all of my "down under" flies in a gray box, a different color than my box of dry flies. I arranged the nymphs the same way as my dries, by the type insect they matched, then according to size. I then arranged the streamers and other odd flies according to size and color. Since I vowed to keep it down to two boxes, I bought the ones with foam liners; they hold more flies and let you view them all at once. I even found a safe one for dry flies, it is thick enough not to crush their hackle and wings when closed.

I have to admit, I have a few extra boxes of flies for special circumstances, and of course a few more for saltwater, but those two boxes carry me through most freshwater fishing excursions.

I'm not saying this is the only way to organize your fly boxes, it just happens to be the one that works for me. I also followed Dom's suggestion and now wear a chest pack; it doesn't let me be such a pack rat!

Reel Good Advice

Make sure your fly boxes are different colors for easy identification. Better yet, label them with a permanent magic marker so you don't waste time digging through the wrong boxes once on the water.

Caring for Your Flies

Flies should be treated just as you treat your pet, with tender love and care. Otherwise, just like your dog, they will become undependable. It breaks my heart just thinking about how many fish have broken off from a rusty hook or how many strikes I've missed because my fly was beaten up or the point wasn't sharp enough. I could go on, but I'll spare you the lecture. Just take care of your flies as you should take care of any equipment.

Getting to the Point

Fly hooks need to be sharpened periodically. As a matter of fact, they usually need to be sharpened when they're brand new from the factory. For some reason (I have yet to figure out), they just don't come with a very sharp point (except many of the newer chemically sharpened hooks). Invest in a good hook sharpener or hook hone and carry it in your vest or chest pack all times.

It's ironic how most fly fishermen don't start sharpening their hooks until later in their fly fishing lives when it's as beginners that they need it the most. Hooks become dull from snags on rocks and trees, a common trait with beginner fly casters. They will become dull regardless; hooks lose their sharpness when bounced and snagged on rocks on the bottom of a river, things no fly fisherman can avoid.

Most fly shops sell high quality flies. I advise you not to buy cheap flies from a large department store or sporting goods store because that's exactly what you'll get, cheap flies. These flies are tied with inferior materials on lousy hooks. Sure, you may save money, but don't expect to get it back when that Parachute Adams (a type of fly) falls apart after three drifts. Trust me, this is not the place to cut costs. If you need to save money for fly fishing, drive a less expensive car or don't go out to eat as much, just don't skimp on the flies.

Flies cost anywhere from $1.50 to $2.25 at a fly shop (more for salt water flies and poppers). Although you may find them cheaper at a large sporting goods store or discount store, more than likely they will be tied with poor quality hooks and materials. These flies aren't durable and are usually poor imitations of the naturals. If you really want to save money, learn to tie your own. The flies will end up costing a fraction of the price and your satisfaction level will be much greater when catching a fish on your own creation.

Keeping Them Dry!

When storing your flies, keep in mind that a dry fly is a good fly. Flies that are put away wet have a higher chance of rusting than flies that are dried off first. I'm not saying you have to carefully hand dry your flies after every use; just give them a good blow before putting them away. If you happen to drop your box of flies in the water, get as much water out as possible then bring them to the bank to dry off. Keep the box open and let the combination of sunlight and fresh air do the work. Just be sure to sharpen them before using them again.

Fish Tails

Although I don't usually bring my labs on fishing trips, they have saved the day. I'll never forget one particular outing during a Salmonfly hatch in mid-June. After bending over to release the first fish of the day, my entire box of dry flies fell into the fast moving current. Since the water was still high from spring runoff, I couldn't wade in after it. I helplessly watched a box full of 150 flies slowly drift away. Suddenly, my older black lab Otis jumped into the frigid water and retrieved the box. I couldn't believe my eyes; he brought it back to me without letting one fly get wet.

Revitalizing Your Flies

Your flies don't necessarily have to be thrown away after getting smashed or chewed up by a fighting fish. Some of them can be revitalized.

Dry flies with smashed wings or tails can be made into nymphs or wet flies simply by cutting off the wings and adding weight. Nymphs that have been crushed can still be used with success as well. As a matter of fact, in many cases, a haggard nymph looks more lifelike than one that has been neatly tied and cared for.

Types of Flies

If you have a difficult time making choices, picking out flies at a fly shop may be the hardest shopping experience of your life. Not only are there several patterns and sizes to match each insect you want to imitate, there are also several different styles in which they are tied.

If you feel a little overwhelmed when you walk into a fly shop, ask for some assistance. Most fly shop employees are eager to share their knowledge of flies and patterns. You will be amazed at how much they seem to know.

Reel Good Advice

Don't throw away flies that have been smashed or crushed. They can be brought back to "life" with a little manipulation from your fingers. If a dry fly is too haggard to use, clip off its wings, add weight, and fish it as a wet fly or nymph.

Surface Flies

Since fish are more discriminating when they have to rise for their food, there are many more different types of dry flies than nymphs. Here are some of the different families of dry fly patterns:

➤ **Traditional dry.** These, of course, are the most traditional dry flies used today. Since the mayfly has always been of primary significance to the fly fishermen, these flies have traditionally been tied to imitate this beautiful insect. The flies are tied with upright wings and a tail, just like the silhouette of an adult mayfly.

The traditional dry.

➤ **Parachutes.** These flies are tied for their increased visibility and flotation. They are actually tied with an upright fur post that is easy to see in even the roughest of water.

A parachute pattern.

➤ **Variants.** These flies are very similar to traditional dry flies but their tails and hackle fibers are longer and they are tied without wings. The long hackle gives the impression of wings and makes them float higher in the water. Because they are so buoyant, they are great patterns to use in rough water. Beginner fly fishermen also have an easy time with them because they are easy to see.

➤ **Spent wings.** These dry flies imitate dead insects that float on the surface of the water after mating. Rather than being tied with their wings upright, like a live insect, spent wings are tied with their wings spread out on the water to imitate a dead insect.

➤ **Compara-duns.** These no-hackle flies are tied to float in the surface film, rather than on top. They are great patterns for highly selective fish in calm water. They have upright deer hair wings that resemble a newly emerged mayfly dun.

➤ **Compara-spinners.** Like Compara-duns, these no hackle flies are tied to float directly in the surface film. This gives the fish an unobstructed view of the fly's silhouette. Their wings lie flat to the side to imitate spent mayflies that have fallen to the water after reproducing. Because they lack the buoyancy of hackled flies, they should only be used in slow-moving water. Both compara-duns and compara-spinners are probably considered specific patterns rather than types of patterns, but they are now tied to imitate a wide array of mayflies.

Catch Words

Compara-duns are a type of pattern tied to float flush in the surface film. They are tied with upright deer-hair wings and no hackle. **Compara-spinners** float in the same fashion, only their wings lie to the side to imitate a spent mayfly spinner.

Reel Good Advice

Compara-duns and compara-spinners should only be fished in slow-moving water. They aren't buoyant enough to float in rough water.

A compara-spinner.

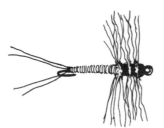

➤ **Spiders.** These flies are tied with extra long, stiff hackle on small hooks. They are usually tied without tails or a body and are extremely buoyant. Because they float so well, they are great patterns to use for skating flies across the surface of the water to induce strikes.

A spider pattern.

➤ **Midges.** As we discussed in the last chapter, this is a type of small aquatic insect. Because of their miniscule size, the term "midge" has become generic. It is used to describe any miniscule fly pattern.

➤ **Down-winged flies.** These flies are tied with their wings to their side, parallel to their bodies, rather than upright like a mayfly. Caddis fly and stonefly patterns are tied in this manner to more exactly imitate their body styles.

A down-winged fly.

➤ **Terrestrials.** These flies are tied to imitate the wide variety of terrestrial insects that fall or get blown into the water. Their imitations include ants, beetles, crickets, and grasshoppers.

A terrestrial pattern (ant).

➤ **Attractor patterns.** These patterns don't imitate any specific insect at all. They are tied with either flash or bright colors to entice a strike by any opportunistic fish that is not feeding selectively.

An attractor pattern (the Royal Wulff).

Catch Words

Flies that are tied to induce strikes are called **attractor patterns.** Although they don't resemble any specific natural food, they look life like and are highly visible.

Sub-Surface Flies

Since nymphs are available fish food throughout the entire year, at all times of the day, they comprise most of a trout's diet; hence, are the most effective flies for fly fishermen. Fortunately, the color and shape of nymphs don't vary as much as their dry fly counterparts. This makes fish much less fussy when it comes to striking flies that are fished below the surface of the water. As a matter of fact, a few patterns, such as the Hare's Ear in various sizes, can be used to match several different types of insects in various stages of development. Although fly fishermen call just about all flies fished below the surface of the water "nymphs," there are still several different families of sub-surface flies that must be mentioned.

➤ **Larva and pupa patterns.** As you learned in the previous chapters, larva and pupa patterns imitate insects such as the caddis fly and midge in immature stages of development. Although they are still considered nymph fishing, these patterns are tied to imitate insects that go through complete metamorphosis.

A pupa pattern.

➤ **Wet flies.** Wet flies can be used to imitate just about anything in the water, such as drowned adult insects, emerging insects, or even minnows. Although these patterns have wings, they are fished below the surface of the water. They are the original patterns used for fly fishing.

A wet fly.

➤ **Soft-hackles.** Fished like wet flies, these imitations are sparsely tied with a few wraps of hackle (feathers) around the head. They resemble most emerging insects as well as drowned adults.

A soft hackle.

➤ **Emergers.** As their name implies, these patterns imitate insects emerging toward the surface of the water. To get them to ride just below the surface of the water, emerger patterns are usually tied on fine wire dry fly hooks. Unlike nymphs, most emerger patterns have short wings or a ball of fur or synthetic material to imitate the emerging wings.

➤ **Streamers.** Streamer patterns are tied to imitate bait fish. Whether they look like other fish or not, there is no question that they seduce a fish into striking. They are tied with long feathers that pulsate when retrieved. There are several variations of the basic feathered streamer, all tied to look and behave differently in the water.

Cut Bait

Be careful when fishing with small emerger patterns. Because of their size, fish won't make aggressive strikes. They are often just sipped in the surface film.

A streamer pattern.

201

Making Your Flies Look Alive

Remember what I said earlier about the size, color, shape, and behavior of a pattern? Well, I'll still hold to it; the behavior of your fly is more important in fooling a fish than anything else. After all, a fly that drifts unnaturally in the current has no chance of getting munched no matter how close its size, color, or shape is to the natural.

Although a dead-drift works well for imitating the behavior of many aquatic insects, other patterns need to be fished with some animation. The following techniques should be used to make your fly appear to be alive.

➤ **Swimming.** If the species you are imitating swims or darts through the water, your fly should do the same, especially if you are streamer fishing. If possible, observe the movements of the minnows, sculpin, or dace you are trying to imitate. If the fish make short dashes, your fly should mimic this behavior. To do this, cast upstream of your target (usually directly across or slightly downstream of you in a river), let the fly sink for a few seconds, then use your line hand to strip it in with short retrieves. If you want your fly to look like it is fleeing from a predatory fish, increase the speed and distance of your strips or mend the line downstream so the current drags your fly.

➤ **Fishing with emergers.** If you are trying to imitate caddis, mayfly, or midges that are emerging toward the surface of the water, your imitation needs to rise toward the surface as well. To do this, cast upstream of the fish you are pursuing and let the fly sink to the bottom. Once it reaches your target, lift the rod tip and let the fly appear to be swimming toward the surface of the water. This often induces a strike whether the fish are actively feeding or not.

➤ **Dapping.** This aged technique was invented when fly fishermen used long rods and very short lines to present a fly. When dapping, the idea is to bounce your fly on the surface of the water without letting any line or leader touch the water. This way, there is no chance for your fly to get dragged. It is a great technique to use to imitate the caddis fly bouncing up and down on the surface of the water. The only trick is to not spook the fish; you must stalk them very carefully, usually by crawling up to the bank or hiding behind a bush or tree.

➤ **Skating your fly.** This technique works well to induce strikes when nothing else seems to be working. To skate your fly on the surface of the water, cast it downstream and across. Then, keeping your rod as high as possible to keep all excess line off the water, lift your rod tip and let

Catch Words

Dapping is the original method used for fly fishing. When you *dap* a fly, you simply dangle the fly in the air and let it bounce on the surface. Because you don't cast the line, *dapping* is only done next to the banks and is great for achieving a drag-free drift.

the fly skitter across the river. This presentation works great for imitating adult caddis flies who seem to fly upstream. Make sure your fly is well treated with floatant and don't set the hook too prematurely.

➤ **Jigging.** This technique can be deadly when fishing with heavily weighted streamers. The idea is to have the fly bounce up and down on the bottom of the water. This mimics the action of many bait fish and crawfish. To do this, cast across the current and let the fly sink to the bottom. Then, lift up and down with your rod tip and let the fly pulsate as it bounces on the bottom.

➤ **Creating a splash.** This technique is used to get the attention of a predatory fish. It works well for attracting largemouth bass and hungry brown trout feeding at night. I have also used it during large Salmonfly hatches to mimic adults crashing to the water. To make your fly splash when it lands, you need to drive it with a downward stroke on your final cast. Just make sure the fly lands first so you don't spook the fish with your line.

Don't Leave Home Without Them

The following is a very basic list of fly patterns that have stood the test of time; they have proven to be successful over and over. It is only a recommended list and will vary according to where you fish. Some of the patterns suggested won't be suitable for where you fish, while others that are may not be listed. I recommend carrying at least two patterns of each size and try bringing the whole array of sizes for each pattern. Remember, there are thousands of patterns to choose from; this is only a minimum list of the basic flies you should bring to the water.

Table 16.1   Recommended Dry Flies

Standard Adams #12-18	Parachute Adams #12-16
Green Drake #10-14	March Brown #12-14
Gray Drake #12-14	Blue Dun #10-20
Light Cahill #14-16	Blue Wing Olive #14-20
Pale Morning Dun #16-20	H&L Variant #12-16
Elk Hair Caddis #12-16	Goddard Caddis #14-16
Bucktail Caddis #12-16	Royal Humpy #10-14
Royal Wulff #10-14	Royal Coachman #12-16
Soft Pillow #6-10	Stimulator #6-14
Griffiths Gnat #16-20	Midge Adams #16-24
Black or Cinnamon Ant #14-20	Black Beetle #12-18
Joe's Hopper #6-12	Letort Hopper #6-1

Table 16.2   Recommended Nymphs

Pheasant Tail #14-20	Gold Ribber Hare's Ear #8-16
Zug Bug #12-16	Prince Nymph #6-16
Green Caddis Larva #12-16	Soft Hackles #12-16
Brassie #14-20	Bitch Creek #4-8
Box Canyon Stone #6-10	Kaufmann's Black Stone #4-10
Royal Coachman Wet Fly #12-16	Scud #10-14
Black Woolly Bugger #4-10	Black Woolly Worm #4-12
Green Damsel Nymph #10-12	

Table 16.3   Recommended Streamers

Muddler Minnow #2-8	Matuka Sculpin #2-4
Zonker #2-8	Black Nose Dace #6-12
Mickey Finn # 4-10	

Fish Tails

The Jackson Hole One Fly contest is held every year on the Snake and South Fork Rivers in Jackson Hole, Wyoming. Like its name implies, participants are only allowed to use one fly per day for this multi-day extravaganza. If he or she loses the fly or the fly is damaged, the participant is disqualified for that day of the contest. The scoring system is based on a point system; the longer the fish, the more points awarded. All fish are released back to the water after they are landed. Points are deducted for any mortally wounded fish.

The Least You Need to Know

➤ Keeping your fly boxes properly organized will save you time and frustration once on the water.

➤ Keep your hooks sharp and rust-free to increase your strike to hook up ratio. A small file or hook sharpener works well.

➤ Think twice before throwing damaged dry flies away. Often, they can either be revitalized or made into nymphs simply by cutting off the wings.

➤ There are many different families of dry flies. The traditional dry fly is tied with upright wings to imitate an adult mayfly.

➤ Wet flies can be used to impersonate just about anything in the water. They are used to imitate drowned adult insects, emerging insects, and even minnows.

➤ Jigging is a way of presenting your fly. The idea is to have the fly bounce up and down on the bottom of the stream to mimic the actions of many bait fish and crawfish.

How to Tie a Fly

You are about to enter another world. It consists of people who talk floss, feathers, and tinsel more than they talk about sports or worldwide events. It consists of fanatics who screech their cars to a halt when they see a roadkill, look around to make sure no one is watching, and then collect its fur. Welcome to the world of fly tying.

This chapter eases you into this new, often intimidating world with ease and comfort. It goes through all of the steps in the fly tying process, starting with the merits of tying your own versus buying them at a store and ends with your first hand-tied fly, the Woolly Bugger. Whether you thought flies were made with machines before picking up this book or are a seasoned fly tyer, I guarantee that you will learn something. And if you have no interest whatsoever, skip the next few chapters. Or maybe you should at least read the next section.

Why Tie When You Can Buy?

Good question and good timing. Many fly fishermen find they have no time or energy to tie flies after they've invested in all of the equipment and materials. Don't be one of these victims. Before you dive into the hobby, make sure it is something you think you will actually do. Sure, it sounds neat and rewarding, but will you actually find time to do it? And like all hobbies, fly tying takes time and patience. I couldn't even begin to count all of the hours I've spent in front of a vise, not to mention the time spent searching for quality materials.

Fish Tails

Every fly pattern in existence was invented by an innovative fly tyer while sitting at a vise. The tyer usually gets the honor of naming the fly, which in most cases, is named after the tyer or the materials that are used. For instance, the Royal Wulff is named after its creator, the fly-tying legend Lee Wulff. The Elk Hair Caddis, on the other hand, was named after the material used to imitate the wings of a caddis: elk hair.

The following are all good reasons to tie your own flies:

➤ **It's relaxing.** Like reading a good novel, fly tying is a peaceful and relaxing way to pass time; but once you get started it will turn into a lifestyle, not a pastime.

➤ **It's rewarding.** Only one thing beats catching a nice fish; that is, catching a nice fish on a fly that you tied. It is both gratifying and rewarding.

➤ **You can be creative.** Fly tyers have the ability to create their own patterns. They can be as creative and artistic as they choose to be.

➤ **It keeps you in the sport.** Fly tying is an excellent way to keep you connected with the sport, especially during the long winter months. Fly tying classes and seminars are also a great way to meet fellow fly fishermen.

➤ **It's economical.** The materials used to tie your own flies only cost a small fraction of what a fly costs at a fly shop (roughly ten percent). It is expensive to get started, however, so it takes a while before you start saving money.

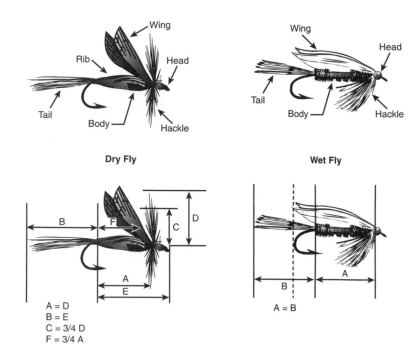

The anatomy of a fly.

Dry Fly

Wet Fly

A = D
B = E
C = 3/4 D
F = 3/4 A

A = B

Anatomy of a Fly

In Chapter 13, you learned just about everything there is to know about hooks; now let's go over the anatomy of a fly (a fake one). Here are the different components that make up a fly:

➤ **Head.** Most flies are tied with the head of the fly right behind the eye of the hook. The head is usually made with the thread that is used to tie the rest of the fly. This is where most flies start and end in the fly tying process.

➤ **Body.** The body of a fly is its main meat and is tied around the length of the hook shank. For nymphs, it is divided into two sections, the abdomen and the thorax.

➤ **Wings.** Wings are tied on most dry flies, wet flies, and streamers. Nymphs are usually tied with wing cases to imitate the undeveloped wing of the insect.

➤ **Tail.** Many dry flies, nymphs, and streamers are tied with tails to imitate the naturals.

➤ **Legs.** Many nymphs are tied with feathers on the bottom of the fly to imitate the natural legs of a nymph.

➤ **Hackle or collar.** Hackle is wrapped around a fly to imitate its legs, wings, and so on. It also makes a dry fly more buoyant for rough water and more visible.

209

Tools of the Trade

If you've decided to get into fly tying, there are two ways you can go about it. You can either buy a beginner fly tying kit or buy everything separately. If you're not one hundred percent sure that you will continue with the hobby or have limited resources, I suggest buying a fly tying kit. They have all of the tools and materials necessary to get started; most of them even include a small book or pamphlet on how to tie flies. There is one drawback however, the tools are usually low quality and the materials are sparse. Most avid fly tyers that start off with a kit soon replace just about all of the tools with higher quality versions.

Reel Good Advice

Fly tying kits are a great way to get into fly tying. They are much more economical than buying all of the tools and materials separately.

A Vise

There are many things to look for when buying a decent fly tying vise. Perhaps the most important quality, however, is a firm clamp on the hook. The jaws should either tighten by pushing a lever, releasing a lever, or rotating a knob. Whatever the case, the jaws should securely clamp any size fly with ease and release it the same way. Before buying a vise, test its holding power by placing a hook in it jaws and pushing down on the eye of the hook. If clamped properly, the hook should bend before it slips out of the jaws.

Vises come in two styles. They either come with a clamp-on mount or a pedestal style heavy base-mount. This second type is probably the sturdiest but when traveling, you don't always have a solid object to mount them to. I use both: a clamp-on type for traveling (the clamp also works well on my steering wheel for riverside tying sessions) and a heavy base-mount for my fly tying table.

Your last decision is whether or not you want to splurge on a rotary vise. Unlike stationary vises, rotary vises swivel to let you look at the fly from different angles. Rotary vises are nice, but expensive and not necessary for beginner fly tyers.

Scissors

Out of all of the equipment needed for fly tying, this is the one not to skimp on. Being the cheapskate I am, I originally laughed at the outlandish prices of fly tying scissors at the fly shop and bought my first pair at a fabric supply store. They worked fine, I thought. Then I tried a buddy's scissors. I couldn't believe the difference. I ran back to the fly shop the next day and bought the pair I originally laughed at.

Cut Bait

Only use your good fly tying scissors for tying flies, not to cut stiff or hard materials. Otherwise, you will dull the blades and make them useless.

A good pair of fly tying scissors should have large finger loops and a super fine point so you can clip with great accuracy. The blades should also be stiff enough not to bend when cutting stiff material. To extend their life, don't cut stiff materials near the point of the scissors. Instead, cut them near the hinge and only use the points to cut fine material like feathers and dubbing. Better yet, use an old pair (or nail clippers) to cut the hard stuff and save the good ones for delicate materials.

If you do splurge on a good pair of scissors, by all means keep them away from any non-fly tyers (because only fly tyers treat them like fly tying scissors).

Hackle Pliers

This essential tool has jaws to clamp on to the end of a feather, or *hackle*. They are used to help wrap the hackle around the shank of a hook and are invaluable for wrapping small hackle. Standard hackle pliers have metal serrated jaws to grab the feather. They work for most purposes, but tend to snip the end of the hackle when wrapped, making you start the wraps from scratch. If you can afford the few extra bucks, buy hackle pliers that have a rubber jaw. Since their jaws aren't sharp, they work much more efficiently.

Catch Words

Fly fishermen call feathers **hackle** when they are tied around a hook.

Bobbin

A *bobbin* is as important as a vise for tying flies. It is what holds the spool of thread as you tie the fly. It is nothing more than a metal clamp to hold the spool with a long tube that holds the tag end of the thread in place. A bobbin can be tailored to the exact tension you want on the spool of thread simply by bending its metal legs for a tighter or looser fit. That is, you can set it loose enough to easily unroll the thread but stiff enough to let it hang from your hook without unraveling. This will make much more sense when you actually start tying flies.

Since it is easy to change spools of thread on a bobbin, you won't need to buy more than one. Another bobbin for flosses and other spooled materials may come in handy, but is not necessary. And besides thread, most other materials can be hand wrapped.

Reel Good Advice

A round toothpick or hatpin works just as well as a bodkin and is much less expensive.

Bodkin

A *bodkin* serves many purposes. It is used to apply head cement to the finished fly, tease fur or dubbing on nymphs, free trapped hackle fibers under thread, and more.

The Non-Essential Essentials

You don't really need the following tools to tie a fly, but they make life much easier. Sure you can do without them, but why? You will eventually own most of them anyway, so why not just buy them now?

➤ **Hair stacker.** This should probably be in the essential category, but I guess you can tie a fly without it. A hair stacker is used to even the tips of hair so that they're even when tied. They are easy to use. Simply insert the clump of hair in the tube, tap it a few times, and remove the cap.

➤ **Pliers.** Long needle-nose pliers are used to make barbless hooks by crimping the barb of the hook. Make sure to do this before the fly is tied. If the hook breaks (which they sometimes do) all you have lost is a hook, rather than the time spent to tie a fly. Smooth flat pliers work better than those with serrated edges.

➤ **Hackle gauge.** Anyone who has been tying flies for a long time will tell you that a hackle gauge isn't needed; they can simply judge the size of the hackle by eye, but a gauge will certainly help a novice avoid wasted hackle. Hackle gauges are used to measure the lengths of hackle, an important step before tying a fly.

➤ **Magnifier.** Magnifying lenses are great for tying small patterns. You can get just a lens or a lens on an adjustable arm. Some of the adjustable models have built in overhead lights.

➤ **An overhead light.** This is one of those pieces of equipment that should probably be on the essential list. A powerful, adjustable light is crucial for tying flies.

➤ **Whip finisher.** This tool makes it easy to complete the *whip finish*, one of the final steps in tying a fly. The whip finish can also be done by hand, which I recommend learning before using the tool.

Fish Tails

A close fishing companion and I went on a fishing trip to the San Juan River, a trophy trout stream in northern New Mexico. We both ran out of much needed Blue-Winged Olives (size 22–24) on the second day of our week-long trip. We decided to do some tying when we got back to camp late that night. My buddy, a much faster tyer than I, had a small anxiety attack just after he finished tying his first fly; he couldn't find his whip finisher tool to execute the last step of the fly. I couldn't believe my eyes; one of the most proficient tyers I knew didn't know how to tie a whip finish by hand! This is why it's crucial to learn it manually, the old-fashioned way, in case a crisis arises.

Believe it or not, this is only a brief list of the fly tying tools used, and every year I see more and more tools at the trade shows. These tools will get you through all of the flies in this book and more.

Materials

Just about everything that is used to make the body of a fly is considered a fly tying material. This includes everything from the thread that starts the fly to the head cement that finishes it. Fly-tying materials are nearly infinite; I've heard of people using the fur from their dogs to the feathers from their pet parakeet. An entire series of books could be written on the different materials used to create a fly so I promise to only cover the basics.

Thread

There is a variety of fly tying thread on the market. Fortunately, you only need a few to get you through most fly tying situations. As far as size goes, you only need two to get started. Buy a 3/0 monocord (pronounced three aught—remember, aught is the traditional way of saying zero) to start off with. This is a heavy thread primarily used for large flies. I think beginners should start off with this size because it is much more difficult to snap; a common, very frustrating occurrence when tying a fly. As soon as you get a little better handling the thread or want to tie smaller flies, move up to 6/0 nylon thread. It's a little finer and easier to break but your flies will turn out much better looking. Both of these threads come either waxed or unwaxed. Stick with waxed thread; it is easier to work with.

Thread also comes in several colors. A spool of black and a spool of tan will carry you through most of your fly tying needs. Although many fly tyers make a big fuss over the thread color, I personally don't think the fish do.

Birds of a Feather Tie Together

Most feathers, or *hackle* as it is now called, come from different parts of a rooster or chicken that has been genetically bred for fly tying. Two kinds of feathers are harvested; those that are used for dry flies and those that are used for flies below the surface of the water. The feathers are also graded for their quality, ranging from No. 1 grade to No. 3 grade. Since each manufacturer grades their own hackle, the grading scale varies dramatically.

The best dry fly feathers usually come from the neck or *saddle* (just in front of the rump) of a rooster. These feathers are usually tied around the hook to create a collar with the fibers of the feather but are also used for creating tails and wings. For dry flies, long, stiff, shiny hackle is most desirable.

Cut Bait

Use caution when examining a neck of feathers at a fly shop and handle them with care. If you want to take a closer look at the feathers, pick the neck of feathers up with one hand and sort through the feathers with your other; just don't bend it. Necks can be very brittle and break easily, especially when dyed.

Hackle used for flies that sink usually come from the neck and saddle of a hen or the saddle of a rooster. The feathers are used to make wings, legs, and collars. A variety of land birds, such as Hungarian partridge and grouse, are also used for these flies. Their feathers are often short and referred to as soft hackle. Hackle for subsurface patterns is usually soft, dull, and absorbent.

The following list covers the most common varieties of colors and markings you will have to choose from:

➤ **Brown**—Usually a medium brown or reddish coloring.

➤ **Coachman Brown**—A very dark shade of brown.

➤ **Blue Dun**—A bluish gray coloring that ranges from light to dark.

➤ **Badger**—White, tan, or cream with a black stripe running up the center.

➤ **Furnace**—Brown with a black center stripe.

➤ **Grizzly**—Alternating stripes or bars of white and black across the feather.

➤ **Ginger**—Ranging from a light cream coloring to a medium tan.

➤ **Variant**—Any color with other random color patterns.

➤ **White**—White.

Reel Good Advice

If you don't want to spend a small fortune, only buy a few different colors of hackle. Just make sure they are different shades of colors when you buy them.

I don't know many people who own saddles in all of these colors or marking patterns. A few usually does the job. If possible, start with three; a light color like ginger or a blue dun, a dark brown and a grizzly. These *necks* (feathers usually come attached to the skin and the sum is called a *neck*) will cover most fly patterns.

The Perfect Body

The body of a fly is important in the fish's eyes. It will quickly get rejected if it doesn't look or feel like something tasty to eat. Several materials are wrapped around the shank of a hook to make the body of a fly, but most are made with real or synthetic fur. Animal fur comes from a variety of animals including rabbit, goat, opossum, beaver, muskrat, otter, badger, mole, seal, and others. Wool is also commonly used for the bodies of wet flies and nymphs because it is absorbent and therefore helps the flies sink.

Herls from the fanlike tails of peacock and ostrich are used to create a fuzzy body that reflects light. The fibers from the tail of a pheasant are also used to create a natural looking, durable body.

There is a wide array of synthetic materials used to tie flies. Polyester fiber dubbing is one of the most popular for imitating fur. It is strong, buoyant, and lifelike; great qualities for tying dry flies. Other synthetic materials such as Larva Lace, "V" Rib,

Antron, Latex, Krystal Flash, Flashabou, and Fly Bright are also used for tying the bodies of flies and dozens of new ones come to the marketplace every year.

Chenille is one of the most popular materials used for tying subsurface patterns like the infamous Woolly Worm and Woolly Bugger. The fiber is woven into a thick furry rope and comes in an arsenal of colors. Wool, synthetic yarn, and rayon floss are also very popular materials for creating the body of a fly.

Many subsurface patterns are also *ribbed* (wrapped in a spiral down the fly) with tinsel or wire to give the fly an added flash. They are available in different diameters and widths and include colors such as gold, copper, and silver. You can also get them in oval, round, flat, or braided. New colors, types, and patterns are showing up in the market-place every year.

Catch Words

Fly fishermen use the word **dubbing** in two ways: Dubbing is a fur or synthetic material used on the body of a fly and also a verb used to describe the method by which fur is applied to a hook in the fly tying process.

Wings and Tails

A variety of materials are used to tie the wings and tail of a fly. Feathers are the most traditional and are usually taken from the wings of a mallard or the *flank* (feathers from the side of the body) of a wood duck.

Marabou feathers are popular with fly tyers for subsurface patterns. The material is soft and downy, and very life-like for the long wings and tails of many streamer patterns. It comes dyed in a variety of colors.

Fish Tails

Over the last few decades, many of the exotic fly tying materials have become unavailable. In most cases the animal or bird has become extinct or endangered. The United States government and other worldwide agencies are working to protect these species, but year by year, the list continues to grow.

Animal hair from moose, elk, deer, antelope, and caribou also make excellent materials for wings and tails. They are both stiff and hollow (contain small air pockets within the hair) and come in an array of natural colors. Hollow hair has the advantage of both increased buoyancy and a consistency that makes it easy to work with. It is important to follow a fly recipe closely when using these hairs as their properties vary. Some are more hollow, long, stiff, and brittle than others. One of the most popular patterns of our time, the Elk Hair Caddis, popularized the use of such hair.

The hair from several other animals is also used to tie hair-wing flies and tails. The possibilities are almost endless, but some of these animals include:

➤ **Bucktail.** Usually taken from white-tail deer, these long hairs are used for the wings and tails of many dry flies and the wings on bucktail flies; flies that are fished beneath the surface of the water to imitate bait fish and other food sources.

➤ **Calf Tail.** Often substituted for bucktail, calf tail is finer and more translucent. Like bucktails, calf tails come in a wide selection of already dyed colors.

➤ **Fox Tail.** Arctic, red, and gray fox tails are used for the wings on many streamer, steelhead, and salmon patterns.

➤ **Mink Tail.** Mink hairs are great hairs for dry fly wings such as the caddis fly.

➤ **Moose.** Hair from both the mane and body work great for dry fly tails and wings.

➤ **Squirrel and woodchuck.** The hair from these small animals is used for the tails and wings on many dry fly patterns.

Other Key Ingredients

Before we actually learn the steps to tie our first fly, a few other key ingredients are needed that didn't really fall in any other categories of this chapter. These few materials are essential items for the beginner fly tyer:

➤ **Weight.** In order to get a fly to sink properly, weight is often added to the fly before it is tied. Lead wire (or preferably the non-toxic, unleaded version) is wrapped around the hook shank to add weight. Some tyers also use beads for the head of a fly. This helps them sink and gives the fly some flash under the surface of the water.

➤ **Cements.** This is the last step in the fly tying process. It is applied to the head of the fly to give it a better appearance and to keep the thread from unraveling. Other glues and cements are used to add gloss to a fly, increase its durability, and strengthen fragile materials.

➤ **Dubbing wax or bees wax.** When tying the body of a fly, waxes are applied to thread to help keep the fur dubbing in place.

➤ **Waterproof markers.** These can be purchased at both fly shops and art supply stores. They are used to instantly change the color of a fly or to add realistic markings to the fly.

Catch Words

Dubbing wax is used on thread to help keep the dubbing, or fur, in place while it is wrapped on the hook.

Basic Fly Tying Steps

There are many steps involved in tying even the simplest of flies. Before we dive into the Woolly Bugger, I want to go over a few very basic steps that are used to tie all flies.

The first step in the fly tying process is to thread your bobbin. Your bobbin should hold the spool of thread with the proper amount of tension. If it is too loose, thread will unravel when hung; too tight and it will break. To thread your bobbin, follow these steps carefully:

1. Free the tag end of the thread out of the notch cut in the rim of the plastic spool.

2. Mount the spool on the legs of the bobbin. Adjust the tension of the bobbin so the spool will release thread with a light tug.

3. Pull out five or six inches of thread and put the tag end through the barrel of the bobbin. Suck the air out of the end of the barrel, the thread should get sucked out as well.

Once you have threaded your bobbin with the appropriate thread, you must decide if you want to fish with barbless hooks. Many fly fishermen started fishing with barbless hooks because they wanted to minimize the damage done to the fish they caught. Although they thought they may lose more strikes, they soon discovered that they were hooking more fish; without the barbs, the hook seems to have an easier time penetrating the fish. If you decide to fish with a barbless hook, smash the barb with a pair of pliers. It is important to do it now, in case the hook accidentally breaks in the process, rather than later, when you jeopardize losing the finished product.

Now take the hook and clamp its bend in the jaws of your vise. The hook should be clamped so the point sticks out just behind the base of the barb and firm enough so that it doesn't shift or fall when manipulated. These steps should be done for every fly you tie.

You are almost ready to tie your first fly, but first, let's go over some basic guidelines.

➤ Always wrap thread away from your body over the hook, and toward your body underneath the hook. This is a clockwise direction if you are looking at the eye of a fly toward the bend. And be careful not to catch the thread on the point of the hook.

➤ Although your vise should firmly hold the hook, hooks are flexible and may need additional support with your free hand. This is especially true with long-shank hooks and fine wire dry fly hooks.

Reel Good Advice

If you have a difficult time pulling the thread through the barrel, it is usually because the thread is either frayed or the barrel is clogged with wax. If this is the case, re-clip the thread with sharp scissors or unclog the barrel by pushing a thick fishing line through it.

➤ Don't worry if you accidentally break the thread in the middle of a fly, it happens to everyone. Just make several wraps around the broken piece with new thread and continue with the fly. Hackle pliers work well for putting tension on the broken piece while you add the new thread.

➤ When tying material to the hook, make sure your wraps are nice and tight.

➤ If you make a mistake while tying a fly, go back and fix it even if you have to reverse several steps. Fly tying mistakes result in a loss of durabililty or a fly with incorrect proportions when ignored.

➤ It is much easier and time effective to tie several of the same pattern in one tying session rather than switching patterns every fly.

➤ Wrapping hackle around the whole length of a fly is called *palmering*. It is either done in a forward direction, which is toward the head of the fly or in a backward direction, which is toward the bend of the hook.

➤ Instructions in most fly tying books are for right handers. If you are a lefty, simply reverse the directions.

Catch Words

Palmering is a fly tying technique used to wrap hackle around a fly.

➤ Don't leave a hook clamped in your vise for a long period of time. When not in use, the jaws of your vise should be free.

➤ Make sure all hair tips are even before tying them in. The fly will look and behave much more naturally.

➤ And last but not least, a good fly is quick and easy to tie, durable, and effective in catching fish.

Tying Your First Fly—The Woolly Bugger

If you were to ask 10 fly tyers what the first fly they tied was, nine will tell you it was the Woolly Bugger. Why, you may ask? Well, first of all, it's a simple pattern to learn, and the steps that are used work for many other flies as well. Second, it's a proven success. Depending on how it is fished, it can be used to imitate leaches, worms, nymphs, and other fish. It is easy to use and looks alive in the water.

Any book on fly tying or fly patterns will give a basic recipe for the flies. Here is the recipe for the Woolly Bugger:

Thread: Black 3/0 monocord

Hook: Standard streamer hook, 2-3x long

Size: 4-12

Tail: Black marabou

Hackle: Black

Body: Black chenille

Tying the Woolly Bugger.

After reading the recipe for a given fly, it's important to have all of the appropriate materials at hand. Here are the steps to tying the Woolly Bugger:

1. With the bobbin in your right hand and your thumb and forefinger of your left hand clenching the end of the thread parallel to the hook, wrap the thread around the hook. Make sure to overlap the thread a few times so it doesn't unwind. Cover the entire shank of the hook with thread, leaving your bobbin hanging just in front of the bend.

2. Wrap lead (or unleaded) wire around the middle two thirds of the hook (between the eye and the bend). One layer should do the trick.

3. Pinch a small clump of black marabou and wrap it with thread just above the bend of the hook.

4. Tie on a three-inch piece of chenille just behind the lead wire and wrap the thread backwards, toward the bend of the hook.

5. Select the appropriate size hackle with your hackle gauge (if you don't have one yet, just wrap the feather around the hook; the barbs should be one and half to two times as long as the gape on the hook). Strip the fuzzy fibers from both sides of the feather's base and attach it to the hook just in front of the bend. The stem of the feather should point toward the eye of the hook.

6. Now wrap the thread forward to just behind the eye of hook. Then wrap the chenille forward along the hook shank and tie it off with several wraps. Clip off the excess chenille.

219

7. Holding the tip of the feather with your hackle pliers, wrap the hackle (called *palmering*) around the chenille and tie it off with several wraps at the front of the hook. Clip off the excess feather.

8. Now make several half hitches by forming a loop of thread at the end of your finger and placing it over the head of the fly. Do this four or five times then clip the excess thread. Use these half hitches to finish your flies until someone teaches you how to do a whip finish (it is nearly impossible to learn from a book).

9. Now apply a small amount of head cement to the head of the fly. Make sure the head cement doesn't clog the eye of the fly. To remove head cement from the eye, thread a feather through it or clear it with the tip of another hook.

Congratulations, you've just tied your first fly. It may not be pretty, but you sure did learn a lot. Now tie several more Woolly Buggers until the steps become smooth and easy. You will be amazed at how quick they will start to look good. The basic steps you have learned will be used to tie a variety of flies. We will tie a nymph, a wet fly, and a dry fly in the next chapter.

The Least You Need to Know

➤ A quality pair of sharp, durable scissors is essential for fly tying.

➤ Once outfitted, tying flies is much cheaper than buying them from a store.

➤ Flies are made out of fur, feathers, and yarn and other synthetic materials. Thread is used to tie the materials to the hook.

➤ Materials used for tying nymphs should absorb water so they sink more easily. Dry flies, on the other hand, should be tied with materials that are buoyant.

➤ When tying flies, it is much more efficient to tie several of the same pattern rather than switching every time.

A Few More Patterns to Tie

I remember when I first learned how to tie flies; the only pattern I knew how to tie was the Woolly Bugger. Several hundred Woolly Buggers later, a friend of mine showed me how to tie a standard nymph. I couldn't believe how easy it was. How could I have wasted so many hours tying Woolly Buggers when it didn't take much more to tie a nymph? I then got a book with several different fly recipes and quickly went to work.

Now that you know the basic steps for tying a Woolly Bugger, it's time to broaden your horizons. After all, you don't want to fish the Woolly Bugger forever. This chapter will teach you how to tie nymphs, wet flies, dry flies, and streamers. Once you've learned them, you will be able to tie most other flies.

Tying Your First Nymphs

Just about every aquatic insect spends most of its life under the surface of the water. And since trout eat 80 to 90 percent of their diet below the surface of the water, it is important that you learn how to tie nymphs. They are among the easiest flies to tie and often work when nothing else does.

The Gold Ribbed Hare's Ear

This scruffy nymph has probably caught more trout in this country than any other nymph, period. Not only does this pattern look lifelike, it is also easy to tie and very

Catch Words

A fly's **recipe** is a list of the exact materials used to tie the fly. The materials are usually given in the order in which they are used.

Reel Good Advice

Always leave room just behind the eye of the hook to tie the fly off.

Tying the Gold Ribbed Hare's Ear.

durable; the essential ingredients of a good pattern. If fished properly, the Gold Ribbed Hare's Ear can be used to imitate just about any type of aquatic insect.

This pattern will teach you how to add dubbing, rib a fly, and add a wing-case; all important techniques for future flies. Here is the *recipe* for the Gold Ribbed Hare's Ear:

Thread: Black 6/0

Hook: Any heavy wire hook, 1X, 2X or standard length

Size: 8-18

Tail: Hare's mask or woodduck flank

Rib: Gold oval tinsel

Abdomen: Hare's mask

Wingcase: Brown mottles of turkey quill

Thorax: Hare's mask

Here are the steps for tying the Gold Ribbed Hare's Ear:

1. Thread the hook, starting from the eye and working your way back toward the bend. Add weight if desired.

2. Cut a small clump of hare's mask guard hairs (the long, stiffer hairs that stick out beyond the underfur) and pinch it by the tips with your left hand. With your right hand, pull the excess fuzzy underfur out of the clump. Now tie the tail on the hook (it should be roughly one-half the hook's total length).

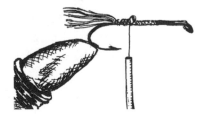

3. Cut off a three-inch piece of gold tinsel and tie it to the back of the hook.

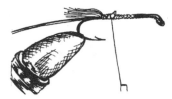

4. Cut a clump of fur off the hare's mask and blend it together to make dubbing (you can also buy it as pre-mixed dubbing). Now wax the thread and spin a small amount of fur on to it with your thumb and index finger. Try to taper the dubbing, thin near the tail and thicker toward the abdomen. Wrap it half way up the hook shank.

5. Spiral the tinsel over the dubbing and tie it off half way up the hook.

6. Cut a section of turkey quill that is roughly a quarter inch wide (or narrower) and tie it on the hook (halfway up the hook shank) so the butt section is facing the front of the hook.

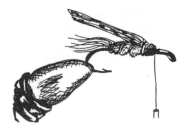

7. Now dub the rest of the hook with hare's mask leaving enough room behind the eye to tie off the fly. The thread should end up at the very front of the hook.

8. Now fold the turkey quill over the thorax, tie it off just behind the hook and trim excess quill.

9. Tie several half hitches to finish it off and add head cement. If necessary, clear excess head cement out of the eye of hook.

10. Take your bodkin and pick out some dubbing at the sides of the thorax to create legs.

Congratulations, you just tied one of the most successful nymph patterns ever used. Now tie several more until they start looking good. A well-tied one should be tapered toward the tail and dubbed thickly in the thorax area. You will use these new techniques to tie a wide array of flies.

Fish Tails

Fish can be much less fussy about the aesthetics of a fly than a fly tyer can. Some fly tyers are so meticulous with their work that it seems they are trying to impress themselves rather than the fish. Other tyers, however, are the extreme opposite. They measure their flies by how many they can tie in an hour and don't worry too much about the finished product. I suggest to try to be somewhere in between; tie flies that are proportionate and good looking, but don't spend too much time on each pattern.

The Pheasant Tail

The pheasant tail nymph is a mayfly imitation that is easy to tie and extremely effective. It closely resembles the shape and color of most mayfly nymphs and is a must fly in every box of nymphs.

Here is the recipe for the pheasant tail nymph:

> **Thread:** Black 6/0
>
> **Hook:** Nymph hook, standard 1X or 2X long
>
> **Size:** 12-18
>
> **Tail:** Pheasant tail fibers
>
> **Rib:** Small copper wire
>
> **Abdomen:** Pheasant tail fibers
>
> **Wingcase:** Pheasant tail fibers
>
> **Thorax:** Peacock herl

Here are the appropriate steps in tying a pheasant tail:

1. Wrap thread to the back of the hook. Tie several strands of pheasant tail fibers for the tail and clip off excess.
2. Tie a 4-inch piece of copper wire to the back of the hook then a clump of pheasant tail strands for the body.

Catch Words

A **pheasant tail** is a nymph pattern that is used to represent a variety of mayfly nymphs. Of course, it is called a *pheasant tail* because the major ingredient in the fly is from the tail of a pheasant.

Cut Bait

Most mayflies only have three tails. When tying mayfly nymphs, make sure your imitation's tail isn't too large or bushy.

225

3. Wrap the pheasant tail strands 2/3 of the way up the shank of the hook. Now counter-wrap (wrap in opposite direction as pheasant tail strands for increased durability) the copper wire over the pheasant tail fibers, evenly spiraling it as you wrap. You've just completed the tail and body of the fly.

4. Tie on another long clump of pheasant tail in front of the body; this will be used for the wing case. Now tie two strands of peacock herl in front of the last clump of pheasant tail.

5. Wrap peacock herl forward to front of hook, tie off, and trim (always leave enough room to tie off the fly).

6. Pull pheasant tail fibers forward to make a wing case and make several wraps to keep it there. With the excess fibers, separate them into two equal bunches, then pull a bunch back on each side of the body. These will imitate the legs of the nymph. Make several wraps to keep them in place.

7. Finish the fly with several half hitches and add head cement. Clean eye of hook.

The Old Timer's Flies

Wet flies are the original flies for fly fishing. As I mentioned earlier, they are tied to imitate drowned winged insects or other winged insects that swim below the surface of the water (usually to lay eggs). Wet flies are also used to imitate emerging insects, and small bait fish. Actually, just about anything that lives below the surface of the water.

What Makes Them Sink?

Wet flies are usually tied without weight. They sink because of the materials that are used to tie them. Unlike dry flies, the materials are highly absorbent and the hook is a little heavier. Wet flies, of course, are also not treated with fly floatant for buoyancy. As a matter of fact, in order to keep them wet, it helps if you keep casting to a minimum.

Fish Tails

Believe it or not, the wet fly patterns tied today are much like the ones tied during the 15th century.

A Classic Wet Fly: The Leadwing Coachman

This all around wet fly will teach you the basic steps for tying just about all other wet flies. Here is its recipe:

Thread: Black 6/0

Hook: Standard wet fly

Size: 10-16

Tail: None

Body: Peacock herl

Hackle: Coachman Brown

Wing: Mallard duck wing quill sections

Follow these steps to tie the Leadwing Coachman:

1. Thread the hook, starting from the eye and working your way back toward the bend.

> **Cut Bait**
>
> Peacock herl is very fragile. When tying with it, be careful not to wrap the herls too tightly as they break very easily.

Tying the Leadwing Coachman.

2. Where you would tie in the tail, tie in a three- to four-inch piece of silver tinsel. With the tinsel, make three wraps toward the bend then reverse the direction and wrap it back to the original starting point. Tie it down and cut off any extra.

3. Just in front of the silver tinsel, tie in three to four strands of peacock herl then wrap the thread to the front of the hook. Now wrap the peacock herl to the front of the hook, tie it off, and clip off the tag ends.

227

4. Tie in a loose, soft, webby strand of brown hackle (with fibers the length of the hook shank) and wrap it three or four times before tying it off. Wrap the hackle two or three turns, tie it down, and clip off excess. Pull the hackle down and back, and secure it with three or four wraps of thread.

5. Pick out two matched wing quill feathers from a right and left wing. Hold them together so they match up and tie them to the hook with their tips up and extending just beyond the bend of the hook. Six or seven wraps should hold them in place sufficiently. Clip off any excess quill.

6. Keep wrapping thread until you have a decent sized head behind the eye. Make several half hitches to tie thread off and clip. Apply head cement and if necessary, clean out the eye of the hook.

All of Our Favorites: The Dry Fly

As you hopefully know by now, dry fly patterns are used to imitate adult aquatic insects or terrestrials. They are a little more difficult to tie, so if your nymphs or wet flies look like they've been through the washing machine, keep practicing before moving on. Luckily, many of the steps you've learned for the previous flies are used in dry flies. The biggest difference, however, is that it is crucial for these flies to be proportionate, or they won't drift, look, or act naturally.

I will give instructions on how to tie two different types of dry flies; the Adams and the Elk Hair Caddis. After learning how to tie these two patterns, you will be able to tie a variety of others.

The Adams: The Classic Dry Fly

The Adams family of dry flies are some of the most popular patterns used for fly fishing (and they are much prettier than the Adams family you are probably thinking of). They are used imitate many different species of mayflies. Fortunately, once you learn the Adams, you've learned how to tie most dries. That is why I've chosen to include it. Here is the recipe for the standard Adams:

Thread: Black 6/0

Hook: Standard length dry fly hook

Size: 12-18

Wings: Grizzly hen saddle tips

Tail: Brown or grizzly hackle fibers or a mix of both

Body: Muskrat fur

Hackle: Grizzly and brown

Here are the basic steps used for tying a standard Adams:

1. Thread the hook, but instead of working your way back to the bend like the previous flies we tied, stop the wraps halfway down the hook. Now wrap the thread forward until it is one quarter the hook shank from the eye.

Cut Bait

Be careful not to select too long of hackles for the wings of a dry fly. Measuring wings and hackle is perhaps the most difficult part for beginner fly tyers. If they are disproportional, the fly will look and behave much differently than the naturals.

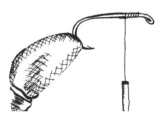

Tying the Adams.

2. Select two dry fly grizzly hackles for the wings. Line up the hackles back to back so the tips turn away from one another. Pinch them with your left fingers and measure them to the hook; they should be as long as the distance from the eye to the bend in the hook (most beginners tie them in way too long). Tie in the wings so the point faces the eye of the hook. When the feathers are tied in, the barbules (the strands of a feather) should be nearly vertical. Clip off excess feather.

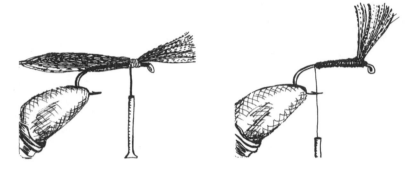

Reel Good Advice

Keep this in mind when tying in the tail of a dry fly: the tighter you make your wraps, the more flared the tail will be; the looser you make your wraps the more bunched up they will be. Try to tie your tails somewhere in between.

3. Wrap the thread to the bend of the hook and tie in the tail. The tail is made from individual barbules of the feather. Tie in a small clump of grizzly and a clump of brown (maybe 10-15 altogether) so they are as long as the wings. When tying in the tail of a dry fly, make a few wraps of thread underneath the tail toward the bend. This helps keep them aligned with the hook shank.

4. Dub the body with muskrat fur to just behind the wings. Now pinch the wings and put them in a vertical position with several wraps of thread in front of and behind the stem.

5. Select two hackles for the wings, one brown and one grizzly. Measure them with your hackle gauge so that the barbules are as long as the hook shank (shorter than the wings). Tie them in behind the wing with their shiny sides facing the bend of the hook. Make one light wrap then continue with a few secure wraps. This loose wrap method helps keep them in place and should be practiced regularly.

6. Pinch the tip of one of the hackles with your hackle pliers and make two to three wraps behind the wing and three to four wraps in front of the wing. Leave a small amount of space in between the wraps for the second hackle. Now tie it off and repeat the process with the second hackle.

7. Make several half hitches or a whip finish to tie the thread off and clip it. Apply head cement.

Congratulations! You just tied your first dry fly. Don't worry about how it looks; your next one will look prettier. More than likely, you made the wings or hackle too long. You will get more proficient before you know it. Now let's tie a different type of dry fly, one with hair wings.

Fish Tails

One of the most difficult parts about tying flies is not breaking the thread or feathers. Don't worry, though; even professional fly tyers still do it on occasion. It won't take long before you develop the right touch; that is, being able to wrap thread and hackle without breaking it (most of the time).

The Elk Hair Caddis

This may be the hottest pattern in the west. Developed by Al Troth, the Elk Hair Caddis effectively portrays the silhouette of the caddis fly. Furthermore, it has excellent flotation properties and is highly visible. This pattern can be fished with a dead-drift, a drift with an occasional twitch, dapped, or skittered and danced across the surface of the water.

Here is the recipe for the Elk Hair Caddis:

> **Thread:** Gray or tan 6/0
>
> **Hook:** Standard length dry fly
>
> **Size:** 12-18
>
> **Tail:** None
>
> **Rib:** Fine gold wire
>
> **Body:** Hare's ear fur; olive, gray, brown or tan
>
> **Hackle:** Brown
>
> **Wing:** Tan elk hair

Follow these steps to tie the Elk Hair Caddis:

1. Thread the hook, starting from the eye and working your way back toward the bend. Tie in a 4-inch piece of gold wire at the rear of the hook.

Tying the Elk Hair Caddis.

2. Dub the hare's ear fur for the body of the fly. Stop 1/16 of an inch from the eye.

3. With the shiny side forward, attach the brown hackle just in front of the body. Palmer the hackle toward the rear of the hook with four to six wraps. Then take

233

the wire and make two tight wraps to hold the hackle in place. Spiral the wire forward to the front of the fly. Tie off the wire and clip off excess wire and hackle.

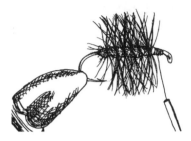

4. Cut a bunch of elk hair and even it out in your stacker. Pinching the bunch, tie in the hair so the points extend just beyond the bend in the hook. Clip off excess hair leaving a small flared head.

5. Make several half hitches or a whip finish to tie thread off and clip it. Apply head cement.

Congratulations—you have just learned to tie some of the most successful patterns ever developed. Now get to work and fill up those empty fly boxes! And remember, practice makes perfect.

The Least You Need to Know

➤ A good fly is easy to tie, durable, and catches fish.

➤ A list of the exact materials used to tie the fly is called the fly's recipe. It is usually given in the order in which the materials are used.

➤ Don't be too forceful when palmering hackle around a fly; otherwise, it may break.

➤ When tying flies, it is important to make all of the materials proportional to each other and proportional to the size of the hook.

Chapter 19

Some More Delicious Recipes

<table>
<tr><td colspan="2" align="center">**In This Chapter**</td></tr>
<tr><td>➤</td><td>A few essential dry flies</td></tr>
<tr><td>➤</td><td>Recipes for nymphs</td></tr>
<tr><td>➤</td><td>Recipes for wet flies</td></tr>
<tr><td>➤</td><td>Streamer and bucktail recipes</td></tr>
</table>

Now that you know the basic skills needed for tying several different types of flies, you have the ability to tie a whole array of patterns. The recipes included in this chapter are relatively easy to tie, durable, and most importantly, deceive fish.

You have already learned the techniques needed to tie a majority of the following flies. Now it's time to tie. After reading each recipe, think about the exact steps it's going to take to complete it, then start tying, one step at a time. Most of the following recipes list the materials in the order in which they are to be tied on the hook. Now let's get tying.

Dry Flies

These six dry flies are essential patterns to have in your box. With the skills you developed while tying the standard Adams and Elk Hair Caddis, you should have no problem figuring out how to tie the following recipes.

The Blue Wing Olive

This excellent pattern is used to match any mayfly dun with an olive body. It is used all over the country with great success.

Fish Tails

Although many fly fishermen call any fly in the Baetis family a Blue Wing Olive (or BWO, as it is often called), this is not exactly correct. Not all flies in the Baetis family have this coloring. And other mayflies outside of the Baetis family are also called Blue Wing Olives. The small olive mayfly that they refer to as the BWO is an important insect on many western rivers. The hatches are the heaviest during the early spring and late fall months, especially if the weather is overcast, rainy, or snowy. This hardy insect is so predictable on some of the western waters, you can count on using a BWO pattern any time the bad weather rolls in; or in this case, good weather.

Reel Good Advice

You will break less hackle if you align your hackle pliers with the stem of the feather instead of just the barbules. This way, you get a more secure grip.

Thread: Olive or gray 6/0

Hook: Standard length dry fly

Size: 14-22

Wing: Blue dun hackle tips

Tail: Blue dun hackle fibers

Body: Olive dubbing

Hackle: Blue dun

The Blue Wing Olive.

Black Gnat

This traditional pattern works across the entire country. It can be used to imitate black ants, midges, and dark mayflies.

Thread: Black 6/0

Hook: Standard length dry fly

Size: 12-18

Wings: Mallard quill

Tail: Black hackle fibers

Body: Black dubbing

Hackle: Black

The Black Gnat.

The Stimulator

These patterns imitate any down-winged adult fly, such as the caddis fly and stonefly. The body and thorax can be tied in a range of colors and sizes to match the naturals. These attractor patterns also work well for imitating grasshoppers.

Thread: Orange 3/0 monocord or 6/0 thread

Hook: Standard wire streamer hook, 3X long

Size: 4-16

Tail: Elk hair

Body: Orange or yellow Antron or dubbing palmered with brown hackle

Rib: Gold Wire

Wing: Elk Hair

Thorax: Amber dubbing

Hackle: Grizzly, just three or four wraps in the thorax

Catch Words

The **Stimulator** is an excellent fly pattern that can be used to mimic stoneflies, caddis flies, and grasshoppers.

The Stimulator.

The Royal Wulff

This excellent pattern is much like the royal coachman, one of the most popular flies in history, but improved. It is easy to tie, easy to see, and extremely buoyant. All and all, a great attractor pattern for beginner fly fishermen. Although this fly doesn't imitate anything in particular to eat, trout seem to love it.

Thread: Black

Hook: Standard length dry fly

Size: 10-16

Tail: Elk hair

Body: Rear (1/4) peacock herl, red floss (mid half), front (1/4) peacock herl

Wing: White calftail

Hackle: Coachman brown

Cut Bait

Be careful when wrapping deer or elk hair. If you don't pinch it to hold it in place it will spin and look sloppy.

The Royal Wulff.

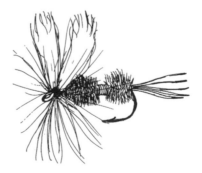

Compara-Duns

The fly patterns known as compara-duns are a relatively new addition to the wide range of flies. In 1975, two fly tying junkies, Al Caucci and Bob Nastasi, popularized these in their book *Hatches*. Depending on how the wings are tied, this family of flies imitates the adult mayfly dun or spinner. As you will notice, the flies are tied without hackle and use a fan of deer hair for the wings; an excellent imitation for highly selective trout in slow-moving water. The following recipe is for a March Brown Compara-Dun.

> **Thread:** Tan 6/0
>
> **Hook:** Standard dry fly
>
> **Size:** 12-20
>
> **Wing:** Brown coastal deer hair
>
> **Tail:** Brown hackle fibers
>
> **Hackle:** None
>
> **Body:** Tan dubbing

The Compara-Dun.

Griffith's Gnat

As far as the amount of steps go, the Griffith's Gnat is probably the quickest dry fly to tie. There is one problem, however; the hooks that the pattern calls for are tiny—usually size 18 and smaller. Although it is only tied with two materials—hackle and peacock herl—don't underestimate its powers. As you will soon learn, trout seem to have an affinity for small flies.

George Griffith developed this deadly pattern to imitate midge pupae emerging from their shucks and adult midges clumped together on the surface of the water. The fly should be presented with a dead-drift.

> **Thread:** Black, olive or gray 8/0
>
> **Hook:** Standard dry fly
>
> **Size:** 18-24
>
> **Hackle:** Grizzly
>
> **Body:** Peacock Herl

Reel Good Advice

Good lighting and magnifying glasses of at least triple magnification are essential for tying small flies (say a size 18 and smaller).

A Few Neat Nymphs

These four nymphs are some of my personal favorites. They are easy to tie, work effectively on a wide variety of water, and can take a beating.

The Griffith's Gnat.

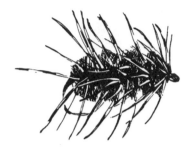

Prince Nymph

This successful winged-nymph can also be fished as a wet fly. It resembles nothing in particular, but does mimic a wide array of nymphs. It makes a great all-purpose nymph if you are not sure what to tie on.

Thread: Black 6/0

Hook: Standard, 1X or 2X long nymph hook

Size: 8-14

Tail: Two brown goose biots

Body: Peacock herl

Rib: Oval gold tinsel

Hackle: Brown collar wrap

Wing: 2 white goose biots

Cut Bait

Be careful not to crowd the front of your hook with fly tying materials. It will make it very difficult to finish the fly with a thread head or whip finish.

The Prince Nymph.

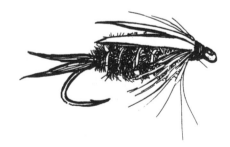

Zug Bug

Like the prince nymph, this attractor pattern also imitates nothing in particular, but the fish seem to love the peacock herl body. The Zug Bug looks very lifelike and should be included in every box of nymphs.

Thread: Black 6/0

Hook: Standard, 1X, or 2X long nymph hook

Size: 8-16

Tail: Peacock herl

Rib: Oval silver tinsel

Body: Peacock herl

Hackle: Brown

Wingcase: Wood duck flank clipped short (1/4 length of body)

The Zug Bug.

Fish Tails

Head cement has more purposes than just securing the whip finish or half hitch when you finish tying. It can also be applied to a wingcase or other fragile parts of a fly to make it more durable.

Serendipity

I have had so much success with this nymph that I just couldn't leave it out of the book. It is simple to tie and can be tied in a variety of colors to match the naturals. It fools fish as an immature mayfly, caddis fly, or midge.

Thread: Match body color

Hook: Curved nymph hook; 1X or 2X long

Size: 10-20

Tail: None

Body: Twisted Z-lon

Rib: Fine wire

Wings: None

Head: Deer body hair tied in as wings then clipped short.

The Serendipity.

Scud

The *scud* is a freshwater crustacean that thrives in still waters with aquatic vegetation. Although many fly fishermen ignore this freshwater shrimp, it should be taken to any water that houses them.

Thread: Olive or color to match body

Hook: Curved nymph fly hook

Size: 10-16

Tail: Hackle barbs; color to match body

Body: Gray, olive, tan, or mixture of synthetic dubbing

Shellback: Clear strip of plastic

Rib: Fine silver, copper or black wire over entire body and shellback

Legs: Picked out of dubbing

Catch Words

Fly fishermen call freshwater shrimp a **scud** and tie patterns to match it.

Reel Good Advice

When picking dubbing out of a nymph's body for legs, make sure they are even on both sides.

The Scud.

The Green Damsel Nymph

As I said earlier, damselflies can be one of the most important sources of food in lakes and ponds. This pattern does an outstanding job imitating these flies in their immature stages of development.

Thread: Olive 6/0

Hook: Regular wire, 3X long

Size: 8-12

Tail: Olive marabou fibers

Body: Light olive dubbing

Beard: Olive dyed mallard

Wing Case: Olive marabou tied in at head

The Green Damsel Nymph.

Streamers and Bucktails

The following flies are tied to imitate bait fish and other aquatic organisms. They are typically much easier to tie than dry flies and most nymphs, but incredibly effective for large trout. They are also tied on much larger hooks, which again, makes them easier to work with.

Muddler Minnow

The muddler minnow is one of the most effective streamer patterns invented. It can be fished in a variety of ways; dry, wet, weighted, or unweighted with much success.

Thread: Brown 3/0 monocord

Hook: Streamer; 2X or 3X long

Size: 1/0 to 10

Tail: Mottled Turkey Quill

Catch Words

A type of streamer pattern that uses bucktail for the wings is called a **bucktail**.

243

Body: Flat gold tinsel wrapped over back 3/4 of shank

Wing: Underwing is gray squirrel tail; overwings are pair sections of speckled turkey quill

Collar: Deer hair tied in as a collar

Head: Deer hair spun and clipped

The Muddler Minnow.

Zonker

The body on this streamer pattern looks more like a minnow, or shiner, than perhaps any other pattern. It is tied with a silver body that looks incredibly alive in the water.

Thread: Black 3/0 monocord

Hook: Streamer; 3X to 4X long

Size: 2 to 8

Underbody: Lead or aluminum tape; folded and trimmed to look like the shape of a minnow

Body: Silver mylar tubing over 15-20 wraps of lead wire

Wing: Rabbit fur strip tied in at head, then again in rear with red thread

Hackle: Grizzly

Black Nose Dace

This imitative pattern closely resembles the abundant minnows that feed a wide assortment of fish. Few streamer patterns match the naturals as closely as the Black Nose Dace. Thanks to the late Art Flick, here is the recipe for this incredible pattern:

Thread: Black 3/0 monocord

Hook: Streamer hook; 3X to 4X long

Size: 6-12

Tail: Red wool (short)

Body: Flat silver tinsel

Rib: Oval silver tinsel

Wing: White, black and brown bucktail bunches layered in that order

Mickey Finn

The Mickey Finn is probably the most well-known bucktail streamer ever tied. It doesn't look like any fish in particular, but looks like a lot of fish in general.

Thread: Back 3/0 monocord

Hook: Streamer; 3X or 4X long

Size: 4-12

Body: Flat silver tinsel

Rib: Oval silver tinsel

Wing: Yellow, red, yellow bucktail bunches layered in that order

Practice Makes Perfect

Like any hobby, the more you do it, the better you get. Don't be surprised if you start off tying only a few flies an hour; you will get faster very quickly!

There are several excellent fly tying books on the market that cover tips, techniques, and skills that are beyond the scope of this book. Before buying one, make sure it has the directions or recipes for the flies you want to tie. Some fly tying writers pick their favorite flies to include; these may not be your favorites.

If possible, I also recommend taking a fly tying class. Some people think fly tying is nearly impossible to learn from a book. A professional tyer will teach you tips, techniques, and short cuts that will prove to be invaluable. This is also a great way meet fellow fly tyers and fishing companions.

The Least You Need to Know

➤ The Blue Wing Olive imitates any mayfly dun with an olive body.

➤ The Stimulator is an excellent attractor pattern. It can be used to imitate stoneflies, caddis flies, and grasshoppers.

➤ The Griffith's Gnat is a great pattern to use during a midge hatch. Fish often take it as a cluster of midges clumped together in the surface of the water.

➤ Although the Zug Bug looks lifelike, it doesn't resemble any particular insect in the water.

➤ The Muddler Minnow is an extremely effective streamer. It can be fished in a variety of ways.

Part 5
Freshwater Fish

You've probably been wondering when we're going to finally talk about the fish we're after. After all, this is a book about fly fishing isn't it? Well, you're in luck. This part of the book covers the most popular freshwater fish that fly fishermen pursue, from trout to panfish.

The first chapter is dedicated solely to trout, and there is a reason. As you have probably discovered, trout and fly fishing go hand in hand. More trout are pursued with a fly rod than any other species. But don't let that fool you. Although they provide excellent game, they aren't the only freshwater fish to pursue. The remainder of this section is dedicated to the rest of the freshwater gang that are popularly fished for.

Chapter 20

The Trout Family

In This Chapter

➤ Trout habitat

➤ Leaping rainbows

➤ The wily brown

➤ About brookies

➤ High mountain cutthroat

➤ Lake trout

➤ A few honorable mentions

A certain mystique and intrigue surrounds the family of fish known as trout. If you look at the "Fishing" section at your local bookstore or library, you will find more shelf space dedicated to this small group of fish than any other species. Trout have captured the imagination and fascination of angling writers, and volumes upon volumes explore the behavior and psychology of these fish. There is even more literature discussing the "how to" of how to catch them.

This chapter is the most basic of introductions to trout. I want to begin, however, with a disclaimer of sorts. Perhaps you find it strange that there are so many books addressing the issue of trout and how to catch them. Perhaps after reading this section—and definitely after you explore a few trout streams and ponds with rod and reel—your curiosity will be heightened, and you will begin to understand the fascination.

Catch Words

Trout fever is a highly infectious malady that afflicts both beginning and expert fly fishermen. Those afflicted will spend rent money on books, and forego food and sleep, to study their elusive prey. Be forewarned!

Indeed, this is the first sign of an infection of trout fever, and I am telling you to beware. Soon you too will want to know why trout act as they do. You will wonder why the rainbows at River X went mad for a #14 Adams yesterday, but wouldn't touch it today. You will find yourself taking time off from work to explore a new pond. You will find yourself in the "Fishing" section of your bookstore perusing books and at the newsracks leafing through magazines.

Trout fever is highly infectious, so consider yourself warned. What follows are the bare bones regarding the world of trout; where they live, what they eat, and how they think. Be careful with the knowledge you are about to gain; it may change your life forever.

Trout Habitat

Trout survive in a number of environments: rivers, streams, lakes, and ponds. Different species of trout prefer different surroundings, but biologically speaking, every trout has three basic needs:

➤ **Water of the right temperature.** Trout are cold water fish. They can't survive in water that is too warm. Each species has a slightly different optimal temperature, but they all prefer comparatively cold water. This temperature preference affects where they live from season to season as the water temperature changes. For instance, trout that live in streams may move upstream in the summer months to higher elevations where the water is colder. At the same time, many lake-dwelling trout (as you will find, lake trout aren't the only trout which make lakes their home) will dive to deeper water where the temperatures remain cool even in the heat of summer. Temperatures affect their feeding patterns and habits, as well as where you will find them.

➤ **Food.** Trout live a fairly easy life. They loaf around, and they eat. I can think of many humans who would be envious of such an existence. As a matter of fact, I know many people that actually live such an existence. Like some people, trout need to live someplace where there is lots of food.

➤ **Well-oxygenated water.** Trout need oxygen. Usually, well-oxygenated water goes hand-in-hand with water teeming with insect life. Lots of insect life probably indicates an abundance of plant life (plants are at the base of the food chain, so their health affects the rest of the chain's health). And who is down at the bottom of a lake or pond pumping out oxygen? That's right, plants—the weeds, mosses, grasses, and everything green at the bottom of a body of water. Plants aren't the only producers of oxygen in water, though. Think about the bubbler in a fish tank. Like a bubbler, moving water also creates oxygen-filled bubbles. Any body of water that is spring-fed, or that contains moving water, contains oxygen. Think about some of your favorite pebbly trout streams. There may not be many plants at the bottom, but as the water tumbles it creates bubbles along the way.

Look for habitat that contains these three things and you will likely find trout.

Fish Tails

Sea run grow to larger sizes than fish who remain landlocked in freshwater. The primary food source in the ocean is the microscopic base-of-the-food-chain organisms called plankton. Freshwater contains less plankton; therefore the ocean is an exponentially more potent feeding ground. While a fish makes its sea run, it grows at a fantastic rate because of the availability and amount of food it can consume. Meanwhile, its freshwater cousins struggle to gain their nutrients from what food they catch. By the time sea runs return to their native streams, they have grown to much greater sizes.

Although trout are considered "freshwater quarry," they have a characteristic that few fish have. Trout have adapted to survive in both marine, or saltwater, and freshwater environments. Trout for whom the ocean is accessible will make a sea run. Rainbow trout, for example, are actually landlocked steelhead (see Chapter 21).

Alas, the majority of trout remain in freshwater throughout their existence. Why? Remember, most trout in commonly (and uncommonly) fished spots are transplants; they were introduced. They are stuck in this body of water and don't migrate to the seas because their home body of water doesn't spill into the ocean. In other cases, dams or pollution have blocked the route to saltwater.

This is not to say that trout don't thrive in freshwater. The opposite is true. The point is that trout have the *capability* to migrate to the sea and back, and they will do this if it is feasible. Otherwise, they survive and thrive in freshwater rivers, streams, ponds, and lakes.

Rivers and Streams

One of the most serene and rewarding fishing experiences is to fish a clear, cool trout stream. Running water, particularly that with an origin in the mountains, has exactly what trout need: oxygen, food, and cool water.

One nice thing about fishing rivers and streams is that trout don't school up. They tend to spread themselves throughout the area. (There are exceptions to this. I don't

Reel Good Advice

You will be surprised at the ability of trout to survive in small—even *tiny*—streams. Don't scoff at a small side stream as being a waste of time. Too many anglers take this attitude—and I have to salute them. It is precisely because of this attitude that small side streams continue to contain some of the best fishing!

mean that trout are absolutely evenly distributed; obviously, the seams, cuts, holes, and pools will hold more fish than open water. Also, trout that are spooked will pack together with fins trembling.) What does this mean to the angler? It means that everyone can spread out to whatever spots look good. Find what seems to you a promising spot. If it doesn't work out, you can move on after a relatively short time. Though trout tend to spread themselves relatively evenly throughout an area, the exception to this rule is during spawning season, when you will find schools, particularly at the mouth of a stream as they prepare for entry.

Our Poor Rivers

The rivers and streams of America have seen better days. Our rivers seem to be victims of nasty predators. These predators include dams, loggers, and farms. Very few streams have survived without a change resulting from these pesky predators, and trout populations have suffered. Because the survival of trout populations hang in the balance, I think it is worth briefly discussing how each predator affects rivers and streams.

➤ **Dams.** It is fairly obvious what a dam does to a river; it blocks its natural flow. A dam's effect on trout can be either blatant or subtle. Obviously, a dam can cut trout off from feeding or spawning grounds. In some cases of extremely deep reservoirs, however, some of the best trout fisheries are in the tailwaters just below the dams. These dams release cold water from the bottom of the reserve, and these releases create year-round fishing. At most dams, however, we find a different story. Some might think a small reservoir could become a deep pool—the kind at the bottom of which lunker trout like to laze around. No doubt dams create depths, but think about what the water does. It sits around stagnant in the hot sun. Stagnant water warms up, and as you now know, trout can't survive in warm water.

➤ **Farming.** It isn't farming itself that damages rivers and streams; it's irrigation. Or more accurately, *over*-irrigation. Irrigating farmland often leaves too little water to keep a river alive—let alone to keep alive all the fish, insects, plants, and so on that live in that river. The situation can come to a head in the low water months of the summer. A river gives and gives and gives via irrigation, and then it runs dry, leaving fish and scores of other living organisms literally out of water.

➤ **Logging.** For many years, loggers knocked down trees right up to rivers' edges. What we did not know was that these trees were essential for the preservation and survival of rivers and streams. Trees along a river's edge keep the river on course by preventing the erosion of the riverbank. Hindsight is twenty-twenty, but if only we had left trees within twenty feet of rivers' edges, so that the root systems could have reinforced the riverbanks! Instead, without the root systems holding the banks together, flooding washed the banks away, and what once were deep pools and undercut banks became wide flood plains that dry up in times of low water.

Cut Bait

Don't eat the fish you catch when fishing in urban polluted waters. More than likely, they are contaminated with toxins.

Fish Tails

Because of the frailty of America's rivers and streams, it is important that every individual protect them. Simply "doing your own part," however, is no longer enough. I hate to say it, but it is up to the conscientious citizens like you and me to make up for the bozos and buffoons out there who are ruining it for the rest of us. As gross as it is, we have to pick up the messes of others. Who else will? And as intimidating as it may be, we need to educate those who don't know better. End sermon.

Ponds and Lakes

Ponds and lakes are great trout pools. Alpine and glacially fed lakes can be terrific trout havens due to their cold temperatures. Many remote ponds in the middle of nowhere become great fishing spots because they are not so heavily fished. When it comes to ponds and lakes, like rivers and streams, look for the three necessities of trout subsistence: cool temperature, food, and oxygen.

It is often more difficult to know where fish will be in a lake or pond. Trout like the shallows, and they tend to feed there—until careless fishermen come crashing right up to the shoreline. If the edge of a pond or lake is covered with vegetation, expect trout to be nearby, feeding on the insects that inevitably live in said vegetation.

One option that trout have in ponds and lakes is of diving to the depths. Often the largest fish live in ponds and lakes, and they may live way down in the darkest, gloomiest, deepest places. Water temperature also plays a role in how deep trout dive. Rainbows, lake trout, and brookies will all go deep as the hot summer months warm the water. Larger lakes develop a *thermocline,* a layer in the water where a significant decrease in temperature occurs. The larger the body of water, the shallower the thermocline, because a large body of water warms up more slowly.

Spawning season also plays a role in where trout will be at different times of year. Many trout congregate at the mouths of spawning tributaries before they enter the tributary to spawn.

Different trout spawn at different times. Browns and brook trout generally spawn in the fall, rainbows and cutthroats in the spring. If you happen to be fishing during a spawn, it is important that you carefully release any fish caught. It is even more important that you don't tramp over their spawning beds as you wade.

Catch Words

Thermocline is the layer in a lake at which a significant temperature change occurs.

The mating procedure of fish is called a **spawn**.

Leaping Rainbows

In some ways, rainbow trout are like people. Have you ever noticed how people ignore a potential problem until it becomes a *big* problem before dealing with it? Rainbow trout are the same way. Different than their cousins the brown trout, rainbows are usually not discriminating or finicky eaters (except for in tailwaters and spring creeks). You might almost call them careless.

Rainbow Trout.

Until they are hooked. *Then* they attempt to make amends. They are spectacular fighters. Expect them to leap out of the water while they give everything they have to rectify the situation they could have avoided if they had examined their lunch a bit more closely.

Rainbows (scientific name *Oncorhynchus mykiss*) are among the most popular trout. One reason for their popularity, as I have mentioned, is their fighting ability. They are great sportfish. Another point in the favor of rainbow trout is that they are beautiful creatures to look at. Rainbows have black spots about their backs and dorsal fin. Their sides are a sparkling silver, with a brilliant red or pink stripe running from head to tail.

Native to the Pacific drainage, rainbows are now one of America's most widespread trout due to stocking (another reason for their immense popularity). As I mentioned, they are not finicky eaters. Their menu includes both aquatic and terrestrial insects, worms, crustaceans, eggs, and smaller fish.

Being such aggressive fighters, it follows that rainbows like fast water. Rainbows, like all trout, hang out in holding waters, but perhaps more than others, rainbows prefer to be near or in faster water. You will also find rainbows in the splashy whitewater at the bottom of pools and boils or underneath waterfalls. Anywhere the water runs briskly, but not too briskly, is ideal for rainbows.

Rainbows like cool, clear water. They are most active in water between 50 to 65 degrees Fahrenheit. Therefore, choose your spots and times. Early season rainbow fishing is a good bet, in addition to high country streams in summer. Rainbows dive to deeper waters in lakes as the shallower water warms up. Tailwaters of dams are often good year-round spots, where rainbows thrive on the cold water releases.

Rainbows are one of the most popular sportfish. Relatively easy to catch, awesome fighters, pleasing to the eye, and widespread, these fish get the adrenaline pumping everywhere.

Cut Bait

Be careful when fighting a rainbow trout; they often break off when leaping through the air. Make sure to give them plenty of slack line.

Easy Brookies

Brook trout are native to the eastern United States. When white settlers first arrived in the New World (and before), these were the only trout that people caught from New England down to Georgia. Only after the introduction of rainbows and browns, did these trout join brookies in eastern rivers.

Brook trout, *Salvelinus fontinalis*, are one of the most colorful trout, and I find them one of the most beautiful. Brownish in color, they are covered in red spots surrounded by bluish halos. Although brookies are grouped with the trout family, they are technically char.

Brook trout are even less picky about what they eat than rainbows. Brook trout remind me of a friend of mine. This guy brought me into McDonald's one day and ordered (for himself, mind you) two Big Macs, two large fries, a vanilla shake, an apple pie, and two large Diet Cokes. He explained later that he ordered "Diet" Cokes because he is watching his weight. You would think, eating the way he does that he would in fact have a weight problem. Not the case; he is a skinny 145 pounds.

Brook trout are the same way. Not only will they eat just about anything; they are constantly willing to feed. Like my friend, you would think that brookies would be fat like pigs, but on the contrary, brook trout tend to be small in size. Although the world record brook trout is over 14 pounds, most brookies seem to run no longer than twelve inches long. Part of the reason for their small size is their tendency to overpopulate a stream. When too many brook trout inhabit an area, there is not enough food for any to grow to large sizes. Because they feed so readily though, brook trout are among the easiest fish to catch. This makes them a favorite among beginners and novices.

Brook trout, unfortunately, are on the decline. Particularly in the East where they originated. Pollution and the spread of the human population have taken their toll on brook trout. These fish prefer the clearest water; as a result, they are found in the most remote streams and ponds.

This, however, makes landing a brook trout a uniquely rewarding experience, because it often means that you went to a great effort in terms of getting into a remote, far-off area in order to even afford yourself the opportunity to catch a brookie. Brook trout are found in mostly scenic, wild, obscure, and hard-to-get-to places.

Reel Good Advice

Out of all the trout species, brook trout are probably the ones to keep, if any. If you fish a stream that is overpopulated with brookies, feel free to keep a few. They're delicious!

It should be noted that anglers don't always need to reach out into the backcountry to get a shot at brook trout. Many states stock thousands upon thousands of brook trout each year. Nearly all of these fish are caught on a yearly basis, but most anglers agree that these yearlings are a far cry from the real thing. Not only are they weak substitutes, their colors are faded, and they aren't as smart. These stocked replacements don't measure up to natives, or even transplants that have become established over the course of years in out of the way places.

Consistent with their modern preference for out-of-the-way places, brook trout hang around in protected spots. Deep holes, beneath undercut banks, under logjams, near brush, rocks, or tree roots—these are places where you will find brook trout. Although they like to hide, they can, however, be easily coaxed out of hiding by a properly presented fly. Brook trout think with their stomachs.

Despite the implication of the name, "brook" trout, larger brookies live in mountain lakes. They prefer the cold water (optimal temperature for brookies is between 50 and 60 degrees Fahrenheit) of these bodies of water. As the weather warms, brook trout will drop to depths of twenty to fifty feet. Like their stream-dwelling friends, these deep divers seek out structural changes on the bottom.

Beaver ponds often become home to brook trout—particularly in remote wilderness areas. Streams running through undisturbed (by humans, that is) areas are easily dammed up by these furry engineers, and—provided the water remains cold—become perfect homes for brookies.

Brook trout fight hard, and this, combined with their relative ease in hooking, makes them another popular gamefish.

The Wily Brown

A certain mystique has surrounded the brown trout since F. Von Behr shipped 80,000 eggs from their native Germany to America. The brown is known as wily, sly, cagey, alert, and wary. Anglers have found the brown difficult to fool. Because fishing for browns is such a battle of wits—one angling mind versus a fish of superior intellect—fishing for browns is a popular pastime of experienced fly fishermen.

I don't want to burst anyone's bubble, but I have a different theory on browns. It makes catching one no less of an accomplishment, but I have to wonder about how smart brown trout are. They are, after all, fish; and fish have brains the size of a Lifesaver hole.

If you have seen the movie *When Harry Met Sally* starring Billy Crystal and Meg Ryan, you can understand why a brown is so difficult to hook. (As a matter of fact, every brown trout angler should drop everything and see this film as soon as possible.) The brown trout is Sally ordering at a restaurant. The spectacle of Sally ordering would go something like this: "I'll have the vegetarian sandwich, please." As the waiter starts away, she'll stop him. "Wait! I'm sorry, do you use low-fat mayonnaise? I see. Not low-fat. Hmm. Okay, no mayonnaise, please. Can I have mustard instead? Wait! Do you have Dijon mustard? No Dijon, just yellow. I see. I guess I'll have mayo then. And can you put extra sprouts on it? And no pickles!" And so on and so forth.

Besides coming to an understanding of why Harry's patience wore thin throughout the movie, the restaurant scenes in *When Harry Met Sally* offer invaluable insight toward the appetite of the brown trout. Browns, like Sally, are exasperatingly fussy eaters. The brown trout will not eat unless it feels like it, and unless the entree is prepared to order.

Browns will sometimes not accept anything other than what they want at a given moment in time. If a brown is hungry for a newly hatched mayfly, then a mature version of this species may not suffice. Preparing food for these fussy eaters would be an extremely frustrating endeavor, and that is where anglers come up with their theories regarding the mindsets of brown trout. But don't get psyched out! Browns aren't as wily as they are fussy. Serve them what they want and you should have some luck.

As a young boy, I wouldn't eat my grilled cheese unless it was sliced diagonally into triangular halves (versus rectangular halves). Like the three-year-old who folds his arms, furrows his brow, puckers his lips, and refuses to eat, so will the brown act who is presented with food unsavory to its present mood.

Cut Bait

Brown trout will do anything they can to snap your leader. Keep them away from any snag-likely objects such as rocks, logs, bridges, and so on.

Unlike the brook trout, browns are an extremely hardy fish in the face of adversity like pollution. They also survive in areas that are heavily fished. In a heavily fished area, for example, who will survive—the brook trout, who will eat practically anything; or the picky brown, who will pass up dinner if what is served is not exactly to its liking?

Despite their relatively picky natures, browns will eat the typical trout fare—most insects, worms, crawfish, minnows, and so forth—when they feel like it. They are known, however, to be the most carnivorous and territorial fish in the trout family. Low water conditions can offer excellent brown trout fishing; the fish get extra territorial during this time, so streamer patterns that imitate bait fish are especially effective.

Brown trout are olive-brown in color with yellowish sides. Orange and red spots, encircled by white or yellow cover the sides, while dark spots cover the back side. They are truly beautiful fish.

Another characteristic of the brown is its patience. Kids growing up in my neighborhood used to play hide-and-seek. I hid in good spots, but I had no patience. I would get bored, sneak up closer to see what was going on, and usually got caught. One kid, on the other hand, would sit in one spot for hours. He would go off, find a good spot, and stay there. One by one, all of the other kids would get caught. Finally, he would be the only one left. Then, all the kids would yell, "Come out, you've won!" He still wouldn't budge. Several hours later, after everyone would go home, I would hear this kid's mother hollering from the front door that it was dinnertime. I bet he even skipped dinner.

And so it is with the wily brown. Browns choose a spot and there they stay. Under rocks, ledges, or undercut banks. Deep, dark holes are favorite spots for lunker browns. The problem with these leviathans is that a brown becomes proportionately fussy and patient with size and age.

Reel Good Advice

Since brown trout are so carnivorous and territorial, streamer patterns that imitate bait fish can be highly successful.

Like all trout, browns prefer cool water, albeit slightly warmer than some other species. 55 to 60 degrees Fahrenheit is the optimal temperature, so as the warmer months approach, browns dive deeper in lakes. Different from other trout, browns often feed at dusk or even at night. Spawning season for browns occurs in the fall, and many rivers and streams are legendary for their autumn runs of browns.

The fighting style of the brown trout is in keeping with its cagey nature. Browns, although they are known to jump on occasion, prefer a less demonstrative fight. A brown will duke it out from the depths, while it tries to snag your line on a tree root or sunken log. If the rainbow is Muhammad Ali, then the brown is Rocky Balboa.

High Mountain Cutthroats

Cutthroats are native to the Rocky Mountains. Scientific name *Salmo clarki* (for explorer William Clark of the Lewis and Clark expedition), cutthroats display a reddish side with dark spots on the back, sides, and tail. Their distinguishing features are red or orange slash marks on each side of the lower jaw.

Cutthroats are an unfortunate example of what can happen to a fishery that is not taken care of. An early sportsman of the Colorado Territory J.W. Kelly wrote about the cutthroats he saw in the Colorado River (then known as the Grand). "The water is alive with trout… Some of these trout pass the bounds of common belief, so large are they." Today, native cutthroats are all but gone from the Colorado, as they suffered about the same plight as buffalo in the American West—over harvesting and near extinction. Today few cutthroats in the West are natives, and many are hybrids.

An interesting point about cutthroats is that they will breed with rainbows. Anyplace where rainbows and cutthroats have been introduced, there is the possibility that you may land a "cut-bow"—a cross between the two breeds.

Fish Tails

Yellowstone Lake, in early times and today, was a hot spot for cutthroat trout. Early tourists would catch cutthroats from shore, and, without even removing them from the hook, would dunk them in a nearby thermal hot spring to cook them! Finally in 1911, Yellowstone National Park outlawed the practice, citing the cruelty and inhumanity of this method of cooking trout.

Cutthroats evolved in glacial settings and, therefore, have adapted to colder water temperatures. They will feed in waters beginning at 45 degrees, with optimal temperatures being between 50 and 60 degrees Fahrenheit. Cutthroats share many of their dietary habits with rainbows and brook trout, eating insects (both terrestrial and aquatic), worms, crustaceans, and small fish.

Lake Trout—The Mac Daddies

Lake trout are big fish. Their scientific name—*Salvelinus namaycush*—contains the native American word *namaycush*, which means "tyrant of the lake." It is easy to understand why they were seen as tyrants; lakers generally run from 5 to 15 pounds, while monsters in excess of thirty pounds are also caught.

Like the brook trout, lake trout are technically not trout; they are char. Olive-green in color, their entire bodies are covered with irregular whitish spots. Their forked tail is another indication.

Lake trout do not school, and they prefer very cold water; 45 to 55 degrees Fahrenheit is ideal. Springtime—particularly soon after the ice breaks up—finds lake trout on the surface of lakes. Smaller lakers will venture into the shallows, but the big ones prefer to remain by reefs where the bottom drops off.

The diet of a lake trout consists mostly of smelt, minnows, shiners, and other bait fish. As the weather warms up, lake trout retreat to depths of over 150 feet at times, where they fumble along rocky bottoms.

Lake trout have very long lifespans. This is the reason they grow to such huge sizes, especially in light of the fact that their growth rate is not particularly fast. If you catch a trophy lake trout, it is not only possible, but *probable,* that this fish has lived and survived for twenty or thirty years. It is tempting to hang on to these trophies, but please, with these fish especially, snap a quick photo, and return them to the waters where they have lived as long as many of us.

A Few Honorable Mentions

An entire book could be devoted to the different members of the trout family. Each species has its own idiosyncrasies and peculiarities. We will just go over a few of the ones that have interesting stories and a few close cousins of trout family.

Golden Trout

Golden trout are among the prettiest fish of the trout family. Golden in color, a broad pink longitudinal stripe runs above a red stripe along the side. Black spots decorate the backside and dorsal fin.

Golden trout are native to the Sierra Nevadas of California, but are now spread more widely. They feed on terrestrial insects, small aquatic insects, eggs, worms, and small crustaceans.

Famous general and test pilot for the United States Air Force Chuck Yeager introduced one of his commanding officers, General Irving Branch, to a prime golden trout pond in the high Sierra. Thus was "Operation Golden Trout" born. Under cover of darkness, Yeager and Branch, with the help of several commandeered USAF aircraft and some New Mexico Fish and Game employees, secretly removed goldens from the fishing hole in the Sierra and placed them in special oxygenated containers in a N.M. State Fisheries vehicle. The vehicle and the trout were transported to New Mexico in a C130 cargo plane, where the trout were nursed over the winter and released into several lakes nearby where Branch intended to retire. Operation Golden Trout is the reason goldens can now be fished in New Mexico.

Apache Trout

These short, chunky trout are found only in the state of Arizona. Despite being so specialized, I list them in the "Honorable Mention" section, because of the story of how they narrowly avoided extinction. Once common to many rivers in Arizona, over-fishing wiped them out in all areas except those waters of the state's White Mountains within the Fort Apache Indian Reservation. It seems the Apaches viewed the trout as sacred, and were careful to protect it. It's a good thing they did. Since then, Apache trout have gradually been re-introduced, and, although their range isn't nearly what it once was, they can be fished on a catch-and-release basis throughout the White Mountains.

If the Apache trout's body appears to be compressed, it is; this trout has comparatively fewer vertebrae than other trout, giving them a short and chunky appearance. They have a dark backside, and their sides are pinkish-to-silver in color and covered with black spots. Their ventral and anal fins are tipped in white.

Hello, Dolly!

Dolly Varden, while an honorary member of the trout family, are, like the brook and lake trout, technically char. These attractive fish are widely found in Alaska, and to a lesser extent in northern California, Montana, and Idaho. The southern version of the Dolly Varden is greenish-brown in color, with bright orange, red, or pink spots. The northern Dolly Varden closely resembles an arctic char (the difference being the size of the spots); it is silverish-blue in color with pinkish spots. In both species, the ventral and anal fins are bordered in white.

Dolly Vardens are named for a character from a novel by Charles Dickens. Miss Dolly Varden, from Dickens' *Barnaby Rudge*, wore a pink-spotted dress.

Grayling

A distant relative of the trout family, the grayling (*Thymallus arcticus*) is found mostly in Alaska, although there are limited numbers in Montana, Wyoming, and northern California.

Grayling are dark silvery-brown in color with black spots on the forward portion of the sides. The primary feature of the grayling is the sail-like dorsal fin—much larger than the dorsal fin of any trout. The fin is dark with lighter spots.

Grayling will hit flies, as it feeds on insects, worms, and crustaceans.

Psychology of Trout

The reason so much intrigue surrounds the trout family is because fly fishing for trout involves such a high level of cerebral activity. Fly fishing for trout is a thinking game and a game that requires imagination. After all, it takes imagination to put yourself in your nemesis' shoes and try to figure out what he or she is thinking.

This is how it is with trout—trying to figure out where they will be in a tiny stream (or giant reservoir) and what they are feeding on. A trout has a brain smaller than a marble, but apparently they use what they have. I, who have a much larger brain, have put much time and effort into trying to match the wits of those small-brained creatures.

The Least You Need to Know

➤ Trout require cold water, abundant food, and well-oxygenated water to survive.

➤ Trout reside in streams, rivers, lakes, and ponds.

➤ Rainbow trout are known for their great fighting abilities.

➤ Brook trout are among the easiest trout to catch, although they live in more remote areas.

➤ Brown trout are patient, easily spooked, and finicky eaters.

➤ Although browns, lakers, brookies, and rainbows are the most common and popular trout, there are countless other trout and relatives of trout.

WHAT ARE YOU LOOKING AT?

Chapter 21

Salmon and Steelhead

In This Chapter

➤ The salmon's incredible life cycle

➤ Spawning troubles

➤ Pacific salmon in decline

➤ Atlantic salmon

➤ Steelhead—cousins of the rainbow

➤ Freshwater (landlocked) salmon

➤ Returning them alive!

It is easy to get worked up over salmon. For example, you'll get worked up when you hook one. I cannot imagine a wilder adrenaline rush than playing a huge salmon on a light fly tackle. Endless runs, long, difficult retrieves, and the aerial acrobatics of salmon make up the highest of highs in fishing.

Then there is the story of salmon and their life cycle. How they return to their native streams (wouldn't my dad like it if I had the homing instincts of salmon), struggle against seemingly insurmountable obstacles—rapids, waterfalls, and the like—to reach their spawning grounds. In the case of Pacific salmon, there they die, having given their lives, their dying efforts, to the regeneration of their species. It is a story that, although we don't completely understand the how and why, can't help but touch even non-fishing people.

On the negative side, however, the plight and downfall of salmon works me into a fury. I will not mince words when I point to humans as the responsible party in the tragic story of salmon. Salmon adapted over hundreds and thousands of years to adversity (earthquakes, floods, weather), but changes brought about by humans have decimated salmon fisheries and threaten to kill off entire species and populations of these regal, beautiful, and romantic fish. But that's not even the part that gets me worked up. The real kicker is that we have the opportunity to reverse what we have done, to save what is left, and to restore what once was. But instead we drag our feet at the most critical hour.

The Amazing Spawn

Oregon's Siletz River. October. The water appears to be on fire. But those are not flames; the water is literally packed riverbank to riverbank with scarlet sockeye salmon making their annual spawning run.

From a standpoint of regeneration, salmon are a perfect species. The creator of salmon has every variable covered. From the moment the female's egg is fertilized to the dying spawning run, everything in a salmon's life is aimed at reproduction.

While everything in the salmon's life cycle makes perfect logical sense, science is perplexed by many aspects of it. What makes a salmon return to its natal stream? Why will a salmon take a fly on its spawning run, despite having no intention of eating it? Why do Pacific salmon kill themselves in the process of spawning?

We may never know the answers to these questions, we can only speculate. However, here is what we do know about the life cycle of salmon.

Female salmon drop their eggs on a gravel river bottom. She will actually rub out a depression in the gravel before laying them. The male then ejects his sperm, or *milt*, on them. The eggs form eyes, then a tail, then fins while the fish embryo uses the surrounding yolk—just like a baby chicken—for food and nourishment. The tiny fish that leaves the gravel nest is known as a salmon *alevin*. These tiny alevin feed on even tinier insect larvae, until they grow larger when they begin to eat bigger insects. It only takes a few months before these alevin reach the size of minnows.

Parr—the insect-eating minnow-sized salmon—remain in the freshwater river for two to three years. While here, the young salmon have an insect-eating fiesta, whereby an all-you-can-eat insect buffet is held for the next two to three years. Then, suddenly, a biological change occurs.

Part of the change involves physical appearance—the first in a line of dramatic physical changes that occur throughout the life of a salmon. Parr are a dull brown in color with red spots on their sides. The spots disappear in lieu of a silvery armor-like color. These fish—between eight to twelve inches long—are now known as *smolts*, and they waste not a second in their natal stream; they immediately head for the ocean.

Catch Words

Milt is the sperm that male salmon eject onto the female's eggs. The tiny fish that leaves the salmon egg is known as the **alevin**. When alevin reach the size of minnows, they are referred to as **parr**. Finally, as they lose the reddish spots characteristic of parr, they turn silver and head to the ocean as **smolts**.

Now the real heavy feeding occurs. Smolts make smaller fish their main diet, and a salmon's life in the ocean is a bulking up experience. Salmon spend anywhere from one to six years in the ocean, and their size when they return to their natal stream is directly proportionate to how long they spent at sea.

I mentioned the salmon-creator covering all the variables. The life cycle of salmon includes several points that ensure the survival of their species. This is also where the mysteries begin. A percentage of salmon are programmed to return to their native streams and spawn after only one year at sea. There will never be a lost spawning year—barring natural (or human-caused—arghh!) disasters—because every year produces these immediate returnees. Therefore, these first year returnees and those salmon that waited two or more seasons return each year. In the case of a bad year (suppose, for example, that last year's eggs were washed away in floods or that the run was ruined by low water) this staggered return system ensures that there will always be fish coming back to spawn.

Reel Good Advice

Try to fish for salmon early in their run; the strongest members of the family seem to come up first.

The salmon that return after one season are called *grilse*, and they weigh between three and five pounds. Why are some salmon compelled to return after only one season? Nobody knows. Even more perplexing is the question of this "homing in-stinct." Salmon return to the rivers and streams in which they were born. How do they get there? Do they ask directions? Their parents are dead, so we know they didn't call home collect. One of the great mysteries of science is how on earth a salmon, who has been roaming the high seas for between one to six years makes it back to the stream in which it was born.

Catch Words

Salmon who return to their native stream to spawn after only one season in the ocean are known as *grilse*.

The staggered returns are not the only "disaster clauses" programmed into salmon. Most salmon spawn in autumn. Different than trout, however, which congregate at the mouth of their spawning stream and then enter *en masse*, salmon begin entering their native streams in spring. They come, it seems, whenever they feel like it. These offset entries into streams ensure that at least some salmon eggs get fertilized. In the event of an autumn disaster—a flood or low water, for example—some salmon are already in the stream, and they spawn.

One nice thing, from an angling point of view, is that this makes for fairly consistent salmon fishing from spring through fall. The major runs, of course, make up the pinnacle of the salmon-fishing season, but the point is that salmon runs in rivers do not necessarily correspond to the spawning season. As a matter of fact, it is common for a river or stream to have several big runs of salmon per season, and the timing of these runs varies from river to river. The only way to know when the annual runs are is to watch the river over the years (the runs tend to occur at the same time annually) or speak with a local. The locals also know which runs tend to be substantial, and which are not so big.

There are optimal conditions under which salmon prefer to enter their stream. They prefer to enter at high water or high tide. They also prefer a swift current, so expect a river to be filled with salmon following heavy rains.

The mysteries surrounding the salmon's life cycle does not end here; rather, things get even stranger. Once in the spawning stream, salmon do not eat. Even the fish that enter in the spring for an autumn spawn don't eat. Salmon that return from the ocean feed off their own fat until it is time to spawn. Part of the purpose of the time spent at sea is to fatten up for the ordeal of spawning. Eating is not part of the mating and reproducing equation.

Fish Tails

When a salmon returns from the ocean, it does not feed. It seems strange that this is when the best salmon fishing occurs. For whatever reason, salmon continue to take flies even though they are fasting.

Why is this? For one, research has shown that the effect of freshwater on an *anadromous* salmon that has been in saltwater, is to shut down the fish's digestive system. Even if a salmon ingests food—which, for reasons unknown, it sometimes does—it cannot process and digest it. This does not concern a salmon making its spawning run. Salmon undergo several biological changes when they re-enter their native stream. One such change is that they become focused on one thing and one thing only: mating and reproducing. Everything a salmon does from here on out is for the purpose of mating.

Catch Words

Anadromous fish are adapted to survive in both fresh and saltwater environments.

The mystery, then, is this: although salmon do not eat, *they will still take flies*. Don't ask why. We don't know why; just accept it! This is why we can hook salmon on their spawning runs. Would you fish for a fish that isn't hungry? A fish that not only isn't eating, but isn't even remotely interested in food? A fish that—not unlike the human male—is worried about only one thing: sex? All logic says no, but the mystery is yes. Salmon hit flies even though they don't eat them.

There are many schools of thought as to why salmon behave this way. I mean, come on. It is odd behavior to go after food when you are not eating, and not even capable of digesting. Here are some of them.

➤ **They remember.** Perhaps the most popular theory is that salmon retain some memory of their parr days when they used to eat insects all the time. This theory goes that they can't resist the old impulse to try it again. Sounds like a mid-life crisis of sorts.

➤ **Curiosity.** Hey, they can't think about sex all of the time, can they?

➤ **Irritability.** You would get irritable too if a streamer fly was swung in front of your face time and time again. Anger and the aggressive nature of salmon, or even playfulness account for this odd behavior.

Whatever the reasons they take flies, it doesn't really matter. My belief is just as valid as any of the others. I believe that salmon are simply "weird," and that's why they act the way they do. How's that for being scientific?

Anyway, salmon hang out in deep pools and other holding waters, until something clicks in their minds and tells them to start upstream. At this time, salmon undergo more physical changes. The changes vary from species to species. Chinooks and pinks turn a bright red. Atlantic salmon turn a coppery-brown. Sockeyes develop a huge hump, and their jaw twists and curls, giving them a crazy, sinister look. And then the most inspiring part of the story occurs.

Salmon head upstream, no matter what the difficulties are or how stacked the odds are against them. Stand by a waterfall in Alaska during a spawning run, and red after red will attempt to leap up and over the falls. If a fish fails, it backs up and tries again. Time after time after time. In the case of Pacific salmon, this ordeal kills them. They get to where they need to go (or they perish trying to get there), they spawn, and they die.

Fish Tails

Some Atlantic salmon don't make it from their spawning grounds back to the ocean after the ordeal is over. These nearly starved *black salmon* spend the winter under the ice sheet, and are understandably enthusiastic feeders when spring finally comes.

While Pacific salmon are programmed to spawn and die, Atlantic salmon may live to spawn another year (although why would they want to repeat this ordeal?). Still,

Atlantic salmon are completely spent when the process is over, and many do die. Many Atlantic salmon don't make it back to the ocean before winter. These fish spend the winter under the ice, and when the ice finally breaks up the following spring, these salmon are *hungry!* These weakened and thin salmon—known as *black salmon*—feed on everything until they take on their silvery armor in the ocean.

When the process is over, and the eggs have been deposited and fertilized in the gravel depression at the bottom of the river, the cycle begins again. Parr feed on insects, smolts head out to sea, and grilse and other multi-season ocean salmon return for another season's amazing spawn. The life cycle of salmon is one of nature's mysteries and triumphs.

The Sad Story

Salmon are in trouble. Before getting into the sad story, I will mention that there are places and situations where certain salmon are thriving and doing well. Landlocked salmon fishing in New England lakes is hot. The Great Lakes fisheries where Cohos and Chinooks have been introduced to these miniature inland "oceans" is also good. The health of Atlantic salmon—while precarious—seems to be relatively strong.

Pacific salmon are another story. For me, however, it is not the simple fact that the salmon are declining—and even disappearing—that makes the story so sad. Rather, it is the why. And the fact that the situation could be reversed relatively easily. If we make an effort.

As you know, the life cycle of salmon is designed to overcome hardships and disasters. Believe me, over the centuries, Pacific salmon have endured hardship. Floods, earthquakes, and weather (can you say "El Nino"?) changes affect the spawning runs of these hardy fish. But the staggered entries into rivers throughout the summer, the staggered returns to native streams over the years, and the downright dogged and determined nature of the fish themselves have overcome these challenges.

That was before the twentieth century. In the last one hundred years, salmon have faced a hurdle that threatens to wipe them out. The situation is the human-caused decimation of their habitat.

Salmon have basic needs in order to regenerate their species:

➤ Food. In the early days of a salmon's life, it lives on insects; later on, mainly smaller fish.

➤ The ability to migrate from river to ocean and back again. The life cycle of salmon, as we have seen, *depends* on this scenario. If the migration path is blocked, the species disappears.

➤ Healthy, fast-moving rivers with sheltered and protected areas in which to mate and lay eggs.

➤ Enough returning mature adults to ensure survival of the next generation.

(Note: Thanks to Save Our Wild Salmon, an organization dedicated to saving the salmon fishery of the Northwest for this information.)

The Frustrating Causes

The simple fact is that human interference has come between salmon and the accessibility of these basic needs. Consider this alarming statistic: The basin of Washington state's huge Columbia River was home to the world's largest salmon runs. One hundred years ago 10 to 16 million salmon swam up the Columbia and its tributaries to spawn. Today, this number has dwindled to a pathetic *200,000* salmon.

Fish Tails

One hundred years ago, 10 to 16 million salmon made fall spawning runs in the Columbia River basin. Today, a piddly 200,000 salmon make the same run.

What has happened, you are asking—maybe even demanding—to cause this ninety-nine plus percent decrease in numbers? Human interference has taken away the salmon's basic needs. Here's how:

Those Damn Dams

The obstacles a salmon overcomes on its pilgrimage up a spawning stream are mind-boggling. Waterfalls, rapids, and drop-offs do not deter these determined fish. If they don't make it up and over, they die trying. The fact that they prefer to make their run at high water (often after heavy rains) doesn't make it any easier. But they still try, and a surprising number succeed. But no matter how determined, or how persistent salmon are, they will not overcome a huge hunk of concrete hundreds of feet tall that human-kind plops right in the middle of their natal river. Despite fish ladders, many salmon are unable to get around dams to reach their spawning grounds.

By the same token, young salmon can't get around dams on their way out to sea. Up to 30 percent of alevin and parr that head back downstream in the direction of the ocean may die at each dam they come to. They die in the stagnant reservoir waters, they die in the dam spillways, or they get butchered in the hydroelectric turbines of the dam.

Dams are the single most fatal blow humans have given salmon populations. In addition to blocking their passage to their spawning grounds, dams create reservoirs. And stagnant reservoir waters warm up and prove fatal to salmon. Salmon thrive in water temperatures between 50 to 68 degrees Fahrenheit. They can survive outside of this range, but water above 80 degrees proves lethal, and salmon are dying in North-west reservoirs. Dams are salmon killers.

Logging

Logging up to river's edge destroys salmon habitat. Furthermore, it interrupts traditional spawning grounds. Salmon tend to frequent the same places year after year in particular rivers and streams. A particular pool or behind a certain boulder, for instance, holds salmon every year.

Salmon spawn upstream in streams with thick vegetation. Knocking down vegetation at river's edge ruins this. Furthermore, logging at river's edge is particularly detrimental to salmon, because they prefer to spawn at undisturbed places. Salmon avoid highly developed riverbanks. Even if a practical, protected, and sheltered spawning spot occurs near a highly developed area, salmon will choose a less ideal spot to spawn, a spot that offers less protection and shelter for eggs, but it is less disturbed.

> ### Reel Good Advice
>
> Because salmon tend to frequent the same spots year after year, it is a good idea to hire a guide if you are fishing a river for the first time. Different than trout, which you can think to yourself "where would be a good place to feed?" salmon don't feed. Therefore, they are more difficult to locate, and specific experience with a salmon river is the best key to success.

Agricultural Activities

Irrigation continues to take water from streams, creating a low water situation. It is often difficult for young salmon to make it out to sea in low water. Also, livestock that come to river's edge for water knock dirt and silt into a river. Salmon depend on cool, clear water. The silty results of agricultural practices make spawning more difficult.

Misguided and Misdirected Attempts to Help

Twenty years ago, the federal government implemented a program to help salmon bypass dams in the Northwest. The program involves capturing as many salmon smolts and parrs as possible, loading them into barges and trucks, and *driving* them around, or carrying them over, the dams. Are you kidding me? This is not a reasonable substitute for allowing fish to swim downstream through their natal stream to the ocean. Fish get stuck in tanks, driven, then dumped—stunned or dead—while seagulls and other trash-eating birds get ready to feast.

This misguided practice has a record of failure and has proven more detrimental than helpful. Salmon die in warm, stagnant water while awaiting transport. They go into shock at being removed from their natural environment. The practice of trucking and barging salmon around and over dams is a sad substitute for actually making an effort to return rivers to a semblance of their natural form so that salmon may make their spawning runs and regenerate their species.

Fish Tails

In the summer of 1997, 136,000 salmon smolts died at McNary Dam on the Columbia River in Washington State while awaiting transport via truck around the dam. The salmon were waiting in stagnant water that rose above 80 degrees Fahrenheit during a hot spell. The McNary tragedy, is not an isolated incident; salmon die each year waiting to be loaded in these tanks.

Pollution

Again, salmon require cool, clear water in which to spawn. Pollution clouds rivers, and, in some cases, warms them.

Overfishing

The commercial fishing industry has wiped out populations of some fish, and this nearly happened with salmon. Now, however, it seems that the commercial industry recognizes its ability to shoot itself in the foot and plays an active role in trying to manage the salmon population.

Their Unknown Future

The story gets sadder. (What? you say. How could it get worse?) The worst part is that the situation is fixable, but changes are hard to institute. And while the situation is reversible now, it may not be tomorrow. Many species of salmon are already extinct or endangered in streams ranging from California to Washington where they used to be plentiful. The situation will deteriorate if efforts are not made now. And I'm not talking about hare-brained efforts like trucking and barging.

Many organizations and conservation groups are rallying to save the salmon of the Northwest. The solutions are relatively simple, not overly expensive, and highly logical. The end of trucking and barging programs, the drawdown of reservoirs (making those warm, stagnant lakes act more like rivers), the improvement of river flows so that salmon can find their way upstream, and improved spillways so that young salmon may get out to the ocean.

Unfortunately, the logic of such ideas seems to be lost on the powers that be. For example, in Washington D.C., more than one congressman has stood up and actually called the fight to save Northwest salmon a lost cause. Again, *are you kidding me?*

Again, salmon are in trouble, and now is the critical time. A century ago, every stream in the Northwest with any accessibility had self-sustaining runs of salmon, but today this is not the case. The sad story is not this pathetic state of affairs; it is that so little is being done to head off a horrible end.

Reel Good Advice

Save Our Wild Salmon (SOS), a coalition of businesses, commercial and sport fishermen and conservationists, is trying to help the salmon of the Northwest. To get involved—or to get educated, contact SOS at 975 John St, Suite 204, Seattle, WA 98109 or by email at sos@wildsalmon.org.

The state of Alaska serves as evidence that salmon can be saved and kept strong. Although Alaska's rivers aren't dammed, Alaska recognized the threats to its salmon fisheries. Alaska not only has a huge economic stake in fishing, it also has several groups of native people whose culture centers around salmon (although salmon fishing holds huge economic implications for the Northwest, maybe their smaller stake has something to do with the lack of intelligent action). Government agencies, anglers, commercial fishermen, and conservationists work together in Alaska to carefully regulate and monitor salmon. And through this teamwork, salmon fisheries in Alaska have remained consistently strong and stable.

The story of the Pacific salmon is a sad one, but the ending has yet to be written. Hopefully in a future edition of this book I can add a happy ending.

Pacific Salmon

There are many different species of Pacific salmon that offer incredible fishing opportunities. These are worthwhile runs of salmon in some rivers along the West Coast that don't have dams.

Salmon.

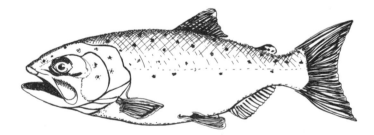

Chinook and Coho

These are the granddaddies of salmon. Chinooks grow to an excess of forty or even fifty pounds, and are therefore also known as kings. Cohos are smaller, but you can still hook a Coho of over twenty or thirty pounds. Cohos are known as silver salmon, because of their light silvery color. Their backs are covered with black spots, as is the upper half of the tail. Kings are darker in color and the spots generally cover the entire tail and often the fins.

The key to fishing for these salmon is knowing when they make their fall runs. Heavy spawning runs vary from river to river, so you need to do your research or hire a guide. Note: when the guide tells you when the fishing will be good, listen! He is not going to tell paying clients to come when the run isn't happening, because he knows you won't catch as many fish.

Remember that fishing for salmon is fundamentally different than trout fishing. Salmon are not feeding. Therefore, you will look for salmon in different places. Salmon use the current to navigate their way up a river to their spawning grounds. They put their noses into the river's main flow and swim upstream. As I said, salmon have a one-track mind at this point. They concentrate on nothing other than getting upstream to spawn. Salmon will rarely venture far from the main current. Side streams and big eddies are unlikely to hold big salmon.

Salmon will rest above and below obstructions in their route. Waterfalls and rapids require a great deal of effort to pass. Salmon will take a break before and after these obstacles. Again, they will not venture far from the main current, but they will seek out places to rest. Rocks, points, and boulders that block the current are all places where salmon may hold. Look on the lee side of these places and you may find big fish.

Chinooks and Cohos will hit a variety of flies—both wet and dry. Zonkers, Wooly Buggers, and Rusty Rats are good. Most salmon are caught on bucktails or streamers, because, coming straight from the ocean, they are used to going for bait fish.

Probably the most important thing you can do to prepare for hooking a lunker Chinook or Coho (or any salmon for that matter) is to be certain to have lots of backup line on your reel—at least 150 yards worth. It is possible that a Chinook will strike lightly, particularly if it is just "playing" with your fly. But it is more likely (and far more likely in the case of a Coho) that these massive fish will make a crazy run when you first strike. The first run of a huge Chinook or Coho is perhaps the most adrenaline-pumping event in fishing. Chinooks may make multiple runs; Cohos are known more for leaping out of the water.

Cut Bait

Be sure to have at least 150 yards of backing when fishing for salmon. They can make incredibly long runs.

It should be noted that, while Cohos and Chinooks are native to the West Coast, from California clear to Alaska, there are other substantial Pacific salmon fisheries. Chinooks and Cohos were introduced in the Great Lakes in the 1960s. They took to these miniature freshwater "seas" immediately and can be fished in tributary streams when they make their fall spawning runs and in the lake shallows in the spring when the water is cold.

Pinks, Sockeyes, and Chums—The Rest of the Gang

These are the rest of the Pacific salmon. Ranging quite a bit smaller than their Chinook and Coho cousins, these salmon also make fall spawning runs in many northwestern, Canadian, and Alaskan rivers. Techniques for fishing these salmon are similar to fishing Chinooks and Cohos. Pink salmon have pinkish-silvery sides, while sockeyes are the weirdest looking salmon. Bright red in color, they have a huge hump on their back and a curved, sinister-looking jaw. All of the Pacific species of salmon make spawning runs in western streams and rivers. Talk to a guide or do some research to find out when the fishing is most productive.

Atlantic Salmon

By law, there is only one legal way to catch Atlantic salmon in the rivers of the United States: on a fly rod. One reason for this is that Atlantic salmon are so consumed in rivers with getting to their spawning ground, that they are easily snagged or even speared. Where's the sport in that? By law, you have to make them go for a hand-tied fly.

Atlantic salmon are found in the eastern provinces of Canada and in a few rivers of the state of Maine. Atlantic salmon have a crucial characteristic that makes them different from their Pacific cousins. The ordeal of spawning doesn't always kill Atlantic salmon. Although many do perish following the spawn, and many die trying, some Atlantic salmon return to spawn two, three, four, or more times. More so than other fish, it is a good idea to hire a guide or consult someone familiar with an Atlantic salmon river as these fish tend to hold and spawn in the same spots year after year.

Salmon hit big, bright, and beautiful flies. Streamers and bucktails are most effective, but they will take trout patterns and dry flies too. The Royal Wulff, Grey Ghost, Black Ghost, Green Highlander, Rusty Rat and the Jack Scott, among others, are effective patterns that have stood the test of time.

Fish Tails

George D. Aiken was governor of the state of Vermont and the state's senator in Washington for 34 years. An avid outdoorsman, he was a master flyfisherman, known for delicate casts that, according to his widow, "did not put a single ripple in the water." The Governor Aiken fly was named for him in the 1930s while he was governor. At one point he traded one of the flies to Ted Williams for a Williams-sponsored Sears fly rod. One problem: being primarily an angler for trout, Aiken rarely used his namesake fly.

Fishing for Atlantic salmon is not appreciably different from Pacific salmon (except that you're on the opposite coast). Look for deep pools not far from the main current of a river or stream. Like their west coast relatives, Atlantic salmon prefer to enter rivers at high waters, so after heavy rains as the water clears up proves to be an ideal time.

Fish with plenty of backing on your reel, because, while Atlantic salmon do not weigh as much as Chinooks and Cohos (salmon between 2 to 20 pounds are likely, with larger fish being uncommon), they are still vicious fighters. You'll need 150 yards of backup.

Fish for salmon in Maine and Canada in autumn. Many salmon rivers in the Canadian provinces are private waters, and you'll pay through the nose for them, but more and more Canadian waters, thankfully, are being opened to the public. It should be noted that Europe's Atlantic salmon fisheries are alive and well, too, with hot spots in England, Scotland, Norway, and Russia.

Freshwater (Landlocked) Salmon

Like trout, Atlantic salmon have been introduced to freshwater lakes throughout the eastern United States. They are known as "landlocked" salmon, because they are stuck and can't migrate to the ocean. These fish can be caught on flies in lakes (these mini-seas are home to these landlocked fish) and their tributaries. Landlocked salmon behave much like their relatives in the Atlantic, except their range is significantly smaller. And fishing for them is not limited to rivers.

Their spawning runs are, of course, great times to fish for them. These runs generally occur in early fall, but, as always, they vary. Concentrate above and below obstructions, in close proximity to the main current.

In the lakes, the best fishing for these cold water fish is soon after the ice breaks up. After this, landlocked salmon, which prefer temperatures that hover around 50 degrees Fahrenheit, head for the depths. But while the water temperature is still cold, fish the shallows, inlets, near tributary streams, and sluiceways. Later in the season, although many salmon go deep, still others hang around the mouths of small streams throughout the summer while smelt and other bait fish spawn.

As always, colorful streamers and bucktails work well, in addition to nymphs, wet, and dry flies. The Mickey Finn, Grey Ghost, Joe's Smelt, and Silver Doctor are effective.

Steelhead—Cousins of the Rainbow

Like rainbow trout, steelhead are not actually a trout; they have been reclassified to the genus Oncorhynchus, which includes most Paciific Salmon. And like salmon, they make a saltwater run, and in most cases share space in rivers and streams with Pacific salmon, so I think they belong in a chapter with salmon.

Steelhead.

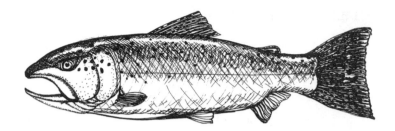

In appearance, steelhead are not so far from salmon. Named for their metallic silvery color, sometimes a pinkish hue is visible along their side—a carryover from their relation to rainbow trout. They display dark spots about the back and tail.

Different than salmon, steelhead are in a feeding mood when in the rivers, so tailor your flies to their diet: all insects, crustaceans, worms, in addition to small bait fish. Salmon and trout flies are effective when fishing for steelhead. Use a nine- to nine-and-a-half-foot rod and eight- to nine-weight fly line. Floating, sinking, sink-tips, and shooting heads are all used for steelhead fishing.

Steelhead runs vary from river to river. Some rivers boast more than one steelhead run, while others have continual steelhead runs for months, as these sea run trout continually enter the river. One unique aspect of steelhead is that they like cold water—anything down to 40 degrees Fahrenheit proves effective—and winter runs often provide the best steelhead fishing.

Steelhead hold in slow-moving water in protected areas. Undercut banks, under fallen logs, behind boulders and rocks, or near brush are favorite steelhead spots. Steelhead like the bottom, so knowing where there is structure on the bottom is helpful.

Steelhead are much bigger than their rainbow cousins, and they fight just as tenaciously. It is pretty common to lose steelhead after hooking them, so keep trying. It is common to catch steelhead up to 15 pounds, but 20 pounders are out there. They make vicious runs and they leap like acrobats. Good luck!

Returning Them Alive!

I always advocate a strict catch-and-release policy, but I cannot emphasize this enough in the case of salmon. The salmon is in trouble! We must be part of the solution, not the problem.

Think about it. When you catch a fish that is making a spawning run, you are talking about the future of a species. Females are carrying hundreds of eggs. You can't kill a fish that is actually transporting the salmon of the future! It is a freak of nature that we can have the experience of hooking these incredible fish at a time when they are not feeding. Enjoy the rush, then put them back. Return these fish alive.

The Least You Need to Know

➤ The unique life cycle and amazing spawn of the salmon is one of nature's incredible phenomena. We don't completely understand it, and that is one reason why it inspires such awe.

➤ Salmon are in trouble, but it is not a hopeless situation—yet. Get involved to ensure the future of our salmon fisheries.

➤ Salmon fishing is distinctly different from trout fishing, in that salmon quit feeding on their spawning runs. Therefore we will find them in different places than trout.

➤ Pacific salmon make their runs in rivers ranging from northern California to Alaska—usually to spawn in autumn, but at other times of year, too.

➤ Atlantic salmon make their fall spawning runs in the rivers of Maine and the eastern Canadian provinces.

➤ Landlocked salmon act like their migratory cousins, but do not make sea runs. They may be fished in the rivers and streams when they spawn, but can also be caught in the lakes early in the season and around the mouths of tributaries at other times.

➤ Steelhead are sea run rainbows, but usually frequent the same waters as Cohos and Chinooks.

Chapter 22

The Bass Family

In This Chapter

➤ The mighty game fish

➤ Big mouth!

➤ Smallmouth bass

➤ How to handle them

➤ Catch and release

If you took a poll of all anglers—not just flyfishers, but plunkers, trollers, spincasters, and so forth—undoubtedly the most popular sportfish would be bass. Despite bass fishing's widespread popularity, however, fly fishing and bass are not commonly associated. Why, I don't know.

Bass are unique fish and vicious fighters. For overall catchability (and perhaps, therefore, the slightly more popular of the two—they also run slightly bigger in size), largemouths probably get the nod. Meanwhile, smallmouths are the more prolific fighters.

In terms of behavior and preferences, largemouth bass are the polar opposite of trout. Smallmouths, in the meantime, bridge the gap between these two extremes. While trout prefer cold, clear, moving water, largemouth bass like warmer, still, and even murky, water. Smallmouths will go either way. Trout are finicky about what they eat; largemouths will inhale anything. Smallmouths—always in between—go back and forth.

Bass are worthwhile fish to get to know, from what they eat to where they live—and how to catch them.

The Mighty Game Fish

Bass have a big reputation, and they live up to it. Sportfishermen everywhere pursue this mighty game fish. And they are easy to pursue. As you will see, these aggressive fish can be found in nearly any body of water in this country.

Fish Tales

Like professional baseball and basketball players, there are professional bass fishermen. That's right, you can be a professional bass fisherman and make lots of money. As a matter of fact, the Wal–Mart FLW Pro Division winner receives a $100,000 grand prize for catching the heaviest limit of bass during the annual January competition. In 1999, the three–day event featured a $471,500 purse! Not bad for three days of work!

They're Everywhere

If you live in the continental United States, chances are you live somewhere near a stream, lake, or pond that supports a bass population. Therefore, you have no legitimate excuse for not giving fly fishing for bass a try. Native to the Mississippi River area, the Great Lakes, and the southeastern United States, largemouth bass have been transplanted all over. They now range all over the country. The native range of smallmouth bass was a bit farther-reaching—most of the eastern United States—and now they too can be found throughout the country.

Bass are warmwater fish, so the only places you won't find them is in the coldest waters. Alpine regions and mountain lakes and streams are not homes to bass, but you will find them in most low altitude lakes and ponds and even lakes in the foothills of mountain ranges.

The Popularity of the Sport

Given the far-reaching nature of these fish, it is no surprise that they enjoy widespread popularity. To be sure, fly fishing is one of the only angling forms that does not most commonly fish for bass. Bass are the most popular quarry among plunkers, live-bait fishers, spincasters, bobber fishers, and trollers.

Bass fishing is like baseball—Americans love it. The turnout at bass derbies is incredibly high. Kids like it, grownups like it, guys like it, and gals like it. Bass fishing is a popular summer pastime.

Why fly fishing isn't more often associated with bass is a relative mystery. Historically, the academia of fly fishing has looked down its nose at bass fishing, but I think this is a blunder.

There is nothing about bass to look down upon. They are handsome, strong, and powerful. Muscular fish, their sides are green in color, while their backs are nearly black. The largemouth has a bigger mouth, but specifically, its jaw extends well aft of the eye. The smallmouth's jaw terminates about in line with the front of the eye. The dorsal fin of the two fish is also different. Both fish have a spiny portion of this fin and a smoother portion. These two portions are separate in the case of the largemouth, and they are connected in the case of the smallmouth. Furthermore, the smallmouth possesses subtle stripes along its sides, while the largemouth does not.

Now that we can distinguish the two types, bass are interesting fish to get to know. So let's get to know them!

Spawning

Bass spawn twice a year, once in spring and once in fall. Like most species of fish, post-spawn and pre-spawn periods are periods of active feeding. The pre-spawn, of course, is when they gather energy for the whole spawning ordeal, sort of like filling up the tank with fuel before a big road trip. Being a *nesting* fish, after the spawn, male bass stay with the eggs. This is for the purpose of protection.

Male bass make worthy bodyguards, but they are even more aggressive during this post-spawn period than they are regularly. With this increased aggression, male bass feed even more viciously and willingly than usual, but I urge anglers not to take advantage of this feeding frenzy. Think of why we practice catch-and-release methods. To keep the species alive so that we can catch more tomorrow. Think of what you are doing when you catch a nesting bass. You are pulling him away from the eggs he is protecting. And even though you return him to the waters, the tribulation of the catch may cause him to leave his eggs. Then what have you done? There are many predators that stay away from bass eggs just because the male sticks around. Leave them alone after spawning. Think of the new bass that you will be catching next year and for years to come.

Catch Words

Nesting refers to fish that remain with their eggs for a period after spawning, as opposed to abandoning them.

Big Mouth!

Largemouths are named for just that; they have big mouths! And they use them, too. A largemouth eats just about anything that fits into its mouth. Everything about large-mouths—from their feeding habits to how to fish them—is guided by this enormous mouth, and the appetite that goes with it.

Largemouth bass.

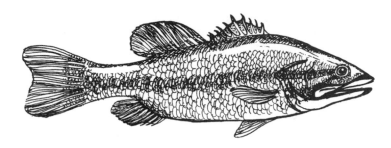

Fish Tails

Bass can swallow fish or other animals up to half the size of their mouth. Ducklings, mice, snakes, frogs—you name it—are all game for a largemouth bass.

Not Picky Eaters

Perhaps one reason for the largemouth's popularity is that they are not picky feeders. (Maybe this, conversely, is why some turn their noses up at this fish.) Therefore, they are not overly difficult to catch. Largemouth bass will eat just about anything. I mean anything! There is no doubt in my mind that if someone could tie a fly that imitated a half-eaten Oscar Meyer frank, it would be a largemouth killer.

Reel Good Advice

Fish do not have eyelids per se, but smallmouth and largemouth bass even lack the protective layer of mucus that protects the eyes of most other species. Bass, therefore, will not expose themselves to direct sunlight. Grey days, then, often become outstanding bass days. If you are fishing in sunny weather, look for areas that provide cover and protection from the bright light.

Largemouth bass will eat anything in the water. When they are small, aquatic insects make up a major portion of their diet. But these fish are pigs; as they grow (and as their mouths get bigger) they will stuff themselves with anything that fits in there. Other fish begin to make up the majority of their diet—minnows, shiners, perch, and crappie. But don't rule anything out. Largemouths will inhale frogs and other amphibians, snakes, and even furry creatures like mice that slip into the water. No creature small enough to fit into their mouths are safe if there is a largemouth bass in the vicinity.

Shades Anyone?

Some fish have a thin, but protective, mucus layer over their eyes, but bass do not. Therefore, you will not find bass basking in the sun (unless they get a hold of UV-protective fish-sunglasses). Largemouth bass hold in areas that protect them from bright sunlight. Probable largemouth spots include under lily pads, near undercut banks, under fallen logs, near underwater tree trunks, or simply in the weeds.

Why Weeds?

Protection from bright sunlight is not the only drawing characteristic of weedy, marshy areas. There are several reasons why largemouths frequent weeded areas:

➤ **Protection from sunlight** (already covered).

➤ **Oxygen.** Plants in the water produce oxygen, which largemouths obviously need. Also, the high concentrations of insect, and therefore small fish, life in weedy areas make them attractive to largemouths. These high concentrations of life are the direct result of the highly oxygenated water. Water with a high oxygen level can sustain lots of life, from the bottom of the food chain on up.

➤ **Feeding habits.** Largemouth bass lack the stamina of some other fish including smallmouths, and this affects their feeding habits. Largemouths do not run around chasing after food. Rather, they hide out until some unsuspecting prey species wanders by. Then they pounce. This sly feeding technique makes protective areas even more appealing to largemouths. Largemouths lie quietly in thick weeds, under submerged tree trunks, near fallen logs, around boulders and rocks, and behind big plants. When an innocent shiner or insect comes within range, the largemouth bursts out of hiding and strikes. Largemouths hide out under these structural steads, waiting for lunch to come rolling by.

Fish Tails

Bass have an excellent close-range sense of smell. Although they use it more for mating purposes, they also use it to find bait fish.

King of the Shallows

Largemouth bass prefer warm water. Optimal temperatures range from 65 to 75 degrees Fahrenheit—temperatures, you will notice, that make up the upper reaches of what trout will tolerate. Largemouth bass will still do well in water up to 80 degrees, but they will not feed as actively above this point. Considering the feeding habits of largemouth bass, however, even at high water temperatures, it is always worth a cast or two. As often as not, you may be able to coax them into munching on your fly.

Because they like warm water, the shallows are productive largemouth spots, especially if they are weedy. Largemouths don't seem to require as high oxygen levels as trout or even smallmouths, so they frequent water that doesn't necessarily have a current, or even any motion at all. This is not to say, however, that largemouths won't frequent streams or rivers, so long as they are warm. Largemouths tend to shut down any kind of activity when water gets too cool.

How to Fish for Largemouths

Because largemouths are so willing to hit just about anything, which fly you choose to fish is not as important as proper presentation and technique. Poppers, hair bugs, streamers, mayflies, and damselflies, are all possibilities.

With poppers, make your cast, and then let it sit. This initial pause is often critical, and I'm not talking about a few seconds like most beginners assume. Be patient and give it some time. A largemouth will often attack during this period of waiting. If you don't get a strike during this waiting period, then give your fly some action. Begin by tugging your line to produce a twitch. Remember to wait between twitches. If simple twitches don't work, be a little more aggressive; make some noise with it and splash the water a bit. Then begin a retrieve, twitching and popping it every few feet.

The key to fishing for largemouths is that it is always different. Sometimes it is the initial pause after the cast that drives them wild, while other times they refuse to strike unless your fly splashes and pops. It is critical to run your bait through all of the possibilities until you find the combination that works.

While making a ruckus with your bait is often effective, it is simultaneously critical that you maintain a low profile. If you are wading or floating in a tube, watch your waves. If you are in a boat, be quiet. Don't rattle your oars or bang your feet on the bottom of the boat. Another thing about oars: if they squeaky, you are hurting your chances. This is a drawback if you have an aluminum rowboat; I have never known one of these boats not to produce a relative din.

Because largemouths frequent weedy areas, weedless flies are invaluable. You don't want to have to clean your hook after every retrieve, and you obviously can't leave weeds all over your fly. Learn to tie a fly that does not hook weeds. Here's how:

1. While tying your fly, tie a piece of 12 or heavier pound monofilament line at the bend in your hook.

2. Tie the rest of the fly.

3. When you are done, pull the remainder of the line up to the eye of the hook and bind it there.

Cut Bait

As with other fish, it is critical when fishing for bass (this applies to both largemouths and smallmouths), not to betray your presence. Human-caused waves, noise, and commotion spook bass, erases their appetite, and sends them into hiding. Be stealthy.

What you end with is a loop of line that protects your hook from weeds. This line shouldn't interfere with your ability to hook fish, especially given a largemouth's aggressive striking tendencies.

When you hook a largemouth bass, don't railroad it. They don't make long runs, and they tire pretty easily. This is not to say they are not tenacious and powerful fighters. What I'm saying is to hang in there at the beginning of the fight, and then you should be able to land your largemouth.

Smallmouth Bass

Besides being mandibularly challenged in comparison to the largemouth, smallmouth bass have many characteristics and features distinguishing them. Sleek, fast, and fit, smallmouths are the ultimate freshwater sportfish.

Smallmouth bass.

The Sugar Ray of Bass

To illustrate just what kind of fighters smallmouth bass are, I must introduce you to a friend named Chris. Chris has been everywhere. Deep-sea fishing in the Caribbean, caribou hunting in Alaska, on safaris in Africa, and so on. He loves to go on at length about his experiences. One thing you learn about Chris, however, as you get to know him is that he is an expert on everything, whether he knows what he is talking about or not. And generally his volume level is inversely proportional to the amount he knows about the current topic. The less he knows, the louder, more argumentative, and insistent he becomes. On one fishing trip, Chris, a few buddies, and I went for steelheads on a New England lake. Chris went on at great length about the nobility of steelhead, especially in comparison to bass. Not only are trout, according to Chris, a cleaner and more admirable—not to mention smarter—fish, they are also superior fighters. Chris also bragged about his ability to discern one fish from another by the way they strike.

He was very loud and boisterous about this.

It went on (and on and on), until after awhile we had spread out a ways. Fortunately, we were not so far that we missed Chris's first strike. Chris set the hook with tremendous gusto and—with surprisingly high excitement for a fisherman who has nonchalantly landed so many fish in his day—bellowed, "Pull your lines out of the water, boys! This is one BIG steelhead! It's gonna be a battle!"

Funny thing, but throughout the fight, nobody in the group saw the signature silver flash of a steelhead. I think all eyes were drawn to Chris's dramatic yanks and tugs as, inch by inch, he worked the leviathan in. When the fish was finally in his net, Chris became notably quiet, and everyone eagerly came closer to see. The monster in Chris's net was a three quarter-pound smallmouth bass.

I don't understand the mentality whereby some in the fly fishing community continue to look down their noses at bass. If smallmouths were athletes, they would be in peak physical condition. Like the former world lightweight boxing champ, smallmouth bass have strength and stamina. They are versatile and adaptable, and possess many admirable qualities.

Weighing in at just a couple pounds, a smallmouth will give you all the fight and punch you can handle. In the South, smallmouths commonly run three pounds and as large as six pounds. Farther north, a pound or two are common, and four to five pounds is a trophy.

Reel Good Advice

The five-star dining delicacy of smallmouth bass is the crawfish, and any fly that imitates these mini-lobster crustaceans is a good start when fishing for bass.

Cut Bait

Unless you see some action, blind casting to areas with intense sunlight will most likely prove futile. Concentrate your efforts around protected, shady areas during these times.

Perhaps if largemouths win Most Popular for their eating habits, fighting ability, and ease in hooking (landing them, of course, isn't always so easy), smallmouth bass take Best All-Around. For one, smallmouths are not the gluttonous Jabba-the-Huts that largemouths can be. While they have large appetites, they are a bit more selective than their larger-apertured cousins.

What's on the Menu?

I have always noticed that smallmouths feel about crawfish the way I feel about chocolate ice cream. They love crawdads. Aquatic insects like caddis flies, mayflies, and crunchy damsels are also tasty morsels for the smallmouth. The bigger the smallmouths become, the more they concentrate on smaller bait fish for nutrition. They love shiners, minnows, chubs, and other bait fish.

Going Deep

Smallmouths prefer cooler water than largemouth bass, so their preferences compare closely with trout waters. For one, while largemouths frequent weedy areas, smallmouths are more often found on rocky shoals and ledges. The reason behind this is fairly simple: weeds and such don't fare so well in cooler waters.

Smallmouth bass will go to greater depths than largemouths, again, because they prefer the cooler temperatures. Especially towards the height of summer, smallmouths will dive up to fifty feet deep to stay in the temperatures they prefer. Fly fishing for smallmouths becomes markedly less rewarding at these warmer times of year.

Temperature preference is not the only factor that drives the smallmouth to the depths. Like largemouths, the eye of the smallmouth offers no protection from the sun. So in lieu of weedy cover (cool temperatures block lily pads and the like from flourishing in smallmouth grounds), smallmouths rely on lots of water to shield them. However, don't rule out shallow water on windy days. Even on the brightest days, a chop on the surface actually blocks much of the sunlight, so smallmouths may not go so deep to escape the sun on a breezy day.

Where and How to Fish for Smallmouths

Smallmouths have more endurance than largemouths, so their feeding habits differ. They actively pursue their prey, so rather than hiding out, you may find them out in the open. This is not to say they don't like structure. Species that also prefer structure on the bottom include the various bait fish; so by default, so do smallmouth bass. Smallmouths are not the gluttons that largemouths are, but they are still enthusiastic and frequent feeders. Large boulders, rockpiles, and holes on the bottom are good spots in cool, rocky lakes and ponds.

Smallmouth bass tend to travel in groups, so take note of where you catch one. Chances are good that there are more bass at that depth and particular area. Don't stop fishing one spot because you land a fish. Catching one is all the more reason to focus even more doggedly on that spot.

I mentioned that smallmouths like the same types of water as trout. Don't be surprised if you hook a smallmouth when fishing for trout in a stream with both species. They like many of the same stream characteristics. Riffles, pools, cuts, and runs are all prime smallmouth spots.

More so than trout—because of their sensitive eyes—smallmouths seek out protection. In streams, look for smallmouths beneath undercut banks, under logs, and in deep pools. Smallmouths generally prefer a slower current than trout, so a shaded, slow-moving, cool stream is perfect. Add some rocks under which crawdads live and you have smallmouth heaven.

As I mentioned, smallmouths bridge the gap between trout and largemouths in terms of diet. What bait you would try for either of these will also prove effective for smallmouths. Trout flies like tiny midges and nymphs, or more striking dry flies will work for smallmouths, while they may also be lured in by the streamers and poppers that are used for largemouths. Truly, smallmouths are the link between these two extremes.

Reel Good Advice

You don't need a specific fly fishing outfit for smallmouth bass. Their compact size and similarity in habits to trout and largemouths make preparation simple. Use what you were using for trout and largemouths!

The equipment you need for smallmouth fishing follows the same maxim as tackle and fly selection. Don't worry about it! Whatever you use for largemouth or trout fishing will work with smallmouths. An eight- to nine-foot rod equipped with a five- to seven-weight line works fine. You may want to use a sinking line as smallmouths have an affinity for deeper water in lakes. Again, it is no wonder that smallmouths are so popular in the non-fly fishing sectors; I do not doubt that it will catch on more.

How to Handle Them

Let's try some guided discovery learning. Go to a bookstore and find the fishing section on the magazine racks. Carefully examine the trout magazines and bass magazines. You will notice that, in both cases, the magazine covers picture proud anglers displaying big fish. How the two groups display their catches, however, is completely different. Do you see the difference?

Trout fishermen hold their catches under the belly with both hands or around the entire body, if it is a smaller fish. Bass fishermen use a different technique. Bass have an extremely tough lower jaw, so the easiest—and best—way to hold onto a bass while you remove your hook is to hold onto the lower half of the mouth. Insert your thumb into the fish's mouth just below the tongue. Hold below the lower jaw with your forefinger. The tongue will stick out and the mouth will open wide as the bass's body hangs diagonally away from your finger-hold. This technique stabilizes the fish and minimizes thrashing about, so you can remove your hook and quickly snap a photo.

Catch and Release

Like all fish, it is important to practice catch and release tactics with these fish, especially the largest ones. It takes quite some time for bass to grow to large sizes. When you do land a trophy, you are looking at a fish that has survived for years in that lake or stream. Let it be and let it continue to prosper and spawn year after year.

The Least You Need to Know

➤ In the broad scheme of things—considering the universe beyond the small world of fly fishing—bass are the most sought after fish.

➤ Largemouth bass are prolific feeders in that they will eat nearly anything.

➤ Largemouths prefer warm, still water, and weeded—almost marshy—areas.

➤ Smallmouths frequent rocky areas in water that is slightly cooler than that preferred by largemouths.

➤ Effective bass flies include streamers, poppers, hair bugs, and both wet and dry flies.

➤ Catch and release methods are critical in order to keep the species alive and well.

Chapter 23

Big, Mean, and Ugly

In This Chapter

➤ Pike on a fly

➤ Muskie

➤ Pickerel

➤ Walleye

➤ Carp—Poor man's bonefish

Just when you thought it couldn't get any meaner and any uglier, you turn to the chapter on pike. The first time you come face to face with a northern pike, I have no doubt that you will notice their most prominent feature: teeth! The teeth befit the big, mean, ugly bullies that northern are.

The muskallunge is even bigger, meaner, and uglier than the northern; only it is not as common. The pickerel is a leaner, trimmer version of the northern, but for what it lacks in size it makes up in as an active predator.

The only nice fish in this whole chapter is the walleye pike and the carp. The name "walleye pike" is actually a misnomer; the walleye is not really a pike at all. More closely related to the yellow perch, the walleye grows to large sizes at times (like pike, although not quite as big), and somewhere along the line, earned the nickname. Obviously, no relative of the northern pike could be a docile fighter like the walleye, whose fighting ability I would compare to that of a rubber boot. Walleyes do, however, have an eerie appearance with huge hollow eyes, so they fit right in with the "ugly" category.

Reel Good Advice

Talk to your local fly shop before heading out in pursuit of fish in the pike family. Fly fishing for them can be incredible but only at certain times of the year.

Being big and mean makes all of these fish (except for walleyes) great fighters, and they are therefore fun to play and catch. So get ready for a completely new experience: pike, muskie, pickerel, walleye, and carp on flies.

Pike on a Fly

Nothing could be more exciting than hooking a huge northern pike on fly tackle. From the initial splashy and violent strike, to the hard fight, to unhooking your fly from the vicinity of those huge, sharp teeth, pike on a fly is nonstop excitement.

The northern pike.

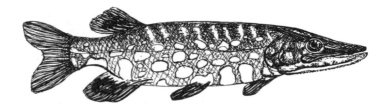

Watch Your Fingers

The best introduction I can give you to northern pike is to relate my own introduction to them. It was a cool morning and the mist was hovering over a small reservoir in Colorado. On this day, I had no intention of making the acquaintance of *Esox lucius* (the scientific name means "water wolf," an appropriate enough name); rather, I was fishing for spring rainbows. I was fishing some shallows in a weedy area of the lake—just the sort of territory (unbeknownst to me) that northerns seek out as they go into their pre-spawn feeding frenzy.

My small mayfly nymph was bouncing along the bottom, and I felt the familiar little tug at my line when a 10-inch rainbow struck and took the fly. The tip of my rod danced as the fish splashed around a bit as I worked it in. Then the mood of the pleasant little outing changed, and things turned violent.

All I really remember seeing were teeth as the three-foot long pike crashed up and out of the water like a torpedo—a wake forming behind it—and the huge splash that engulfed my little struggling rainbow. For a split second my rod doubled over. And then there was nothing. I reeled in the bloody remains of my rainbow—about two inches of fish from the nose to the bloody severed head.

I must admit that for a moment I considered throwing the fish head out as bait, but my sense of sportsmanship prevented it. I went to my local fly shop, purchased a wire leader and returned to the same spot the very next morning. Thinking I was ready for anything after the event of the previous day, I was not prepared for the excitement of tossing a popper out and witnessing not one, but *two*, 20-plus inch pike attacking my fly above the surface. That is how crazy they get before they spawn.

Landing your first northern is a humbling experience. They are just what you would expect the hoodlums and thugs of the underwater world to look like. If northerns wore clothes, they would wear leather jackets with spikes, and would carry around baseball bats.

Cut Bait

Since pike have such sharp teeth, a wire leader or thick monofilament (called shock tippet) is necessary to land them.

Sleek and trim, the northern is built for speed. The northern isn't fat; it is long and lean. Light green in color, its sides are covered with whitish to yellow irregularly shaped spots. The underside is creamy white, while the fins run from red to brown. It has a pointed snout, an absolutely huge mouth, and very sharp teeth. Watch your fingers when you attempt to remove your hook; these choppers could do serious damage.

A Voracious Appetite

Northern pike grow quickly, and their massive appetite supports this growth. Willing feeders, they eat insects and bait fish. Despite their huge mandibles, jaws, and mouth, you will be amazed at the things northerns swallow, not to mention *try* to swallow. Northerns have been known to attack mature mallards and fish one-third their size. Furry critters like otters and muskrats that swim through northern country are in great peril.

Stealth and patience are strong tools of the northern. Their greenish-yellow coloration makes perfect camouflage, and northerns are opportunistic feeders. You won't notice a huge pike hiding motionless in two feet of water until it lunges for a startled prey species. This exciting event can be extremely violent, with much splashing and with no leftovers. More often than not, northerns are members of the Clean Plate Club.

A northern pike's appetite is most always hearty, but there are times when these huge fish feed particularly actively; knowing when the big eating times are can increase your chances of catching big northerns.

Pre-Spawn Feeding

The spawning season of pike happens very early—right after ice out on most lakes. Right before the spawn and right after are big feeding periods for pike. Feeding at this time supports the upcoming spawn, which occurs in the shallows, preferably among weeds, brush, and other cover. As they move from their winter holding areas (where they are a bit more sluggish, but not altogether dormant) and into the shallows, their appetite gets bigger and bigger.

Reel Good Advice

If you know a lake or reservoir contains pike, hit it in the spring right after the ice melts. This is when northern pike go into their pre-spawning feeding frenzy—the fishing can be phenomenal.

Post-Spawn Frenzy

Immediately after the spawn is when things get crazy. Pike feed like mad immediately after the spawn. This is what was happening when the monster ripped my little rainbow in half, and when the two pike attacked the same fly. It is at this time of year when savage strikes, vicious fights, and much splashing characterize pike fishing. All pike—males and females—are worked up after the spawn, and they eat everything they see. And you don't have to worry about disturbing nesting fish; pike abandon their eggs as soon as the spawn is complete.

Ah, Summer!

Summer pike fishing is less consistent than before and after spawning time, but you can still catch big pike in the heat of summer. Pike, who prefer relatively cold water temperatures, move out of the shallows and into the depths when the water in the shallows begins to warm up.

Northerns, however, don't forget about the shallows in terms of abundant food sources. Pike frequent drop-offs with easy accessibility to the shallows. At this time of year pike pass their time in water upwards of twelve feet deep, but they keep themselves within close proximity of shallow feeding grounds.

Fattening Up for Winter

Fall is another big feeding time. Northerns are programmed to know when winter is approaching, and they plan accordingly. This means they fatten themselves up, by eating whatever food is available. Bait fish are a diet staple, as they—like all fish—grow to larger sizes throughout the summer high season. Now is when northern pike surprise you by what they can—and attempt to—fit down their gullets.

Northerns move back to the shallows in the fall as water temperatures drop. This move unfortunately does not mark a return to the kind of feeding frenzy these fish demonstrated in spring. Fattening up for winter isn't as critical for pike as it is, say, for a bear preparing for hibernation. Northerns don't stop feeding at wintertime (as a matter of fact, people land northerns with live bait through the ice on a fairly regular basis). It is a time when big northerns are looking for big bait fish. Go get them!

The Nasty Spawn

I don't want anyone to waste precious time, so make sure you know that pike do not feed during spawning. It is probably not the greatest idea to fish for any species during spawning time—this is a critical time for the regeneration of the species, and we don't want to disturb them—but in the case of pike, it would be fruitless to bother during spawning time. They won't bite!

Fish Tails

Northern pike concentrate on spawning when it is time to spawn, and they do not feed at all during this time. Their biggest feeding time, however, comes right after the spawn.

Before spawning, northerns move into the shallows and prepare for the spawn by feeding very actively. You will probably know whether fish you land at this time is a male or female; females are much larger. The spawn itself is pretty violent and fairly nasty. Lots of splashing (remember, it takes place in the shallows, sometimes in as little as a few inches of water) marks the spawn of the northern. The female tries to choose a weedy spot with lots of cover in which to drop her eggs. The male ejects his sperm on them, and then thrashes about violently to spread it out.

In perfect accordance with their mean personality, northern promptly abandon their eggs. Maybe this is one reason northern grow up so mean—they were abandoned by mom and dad as eggs! Northern pike are the behavior problems of the waters. Maybe they could use counseling.

Fighting and Landing Them

Now that we know where to find them, how do we hook and land big pike? The first step is to be adequately equipped. If you fish with trout-sized gear, you will be disappointed. But you will learn quickly. How many broken leaders and lost fish can it possibly take?

A strong leader is perhaps the most important piece of the puzzle. As I said, northerns possess a nasty set of choppers, and they will bite and break a small leader every time. Wire leaders or at least a 30-pound test monofilament is required for the last foot of your leader.

Pike flies are bright and big. Pike have big mouths and big appetites, so present them with big breakfasts, lunches, and dinners! The largest Wooly Buggers, streamers, and poppers have the most success—most in the 2/0 to 3/0 size range. A warning: your flies will take an absolute beating. Pike are rough on gear; bring backup flies. If your fly survives one fight with a thrashing northern who drags your fly through mud, weeds, and trees, you are lucky. It won't survive the second.

Because pike flies are big and heavy (most tied 3 to 7 inches long!), you will need line and a rod that can handle such gear. Heavy line and a big, heavy-duty rod are necessary for pike fishing. You need an eight- to ten-weight, nine- to nine-and-a-half-foot rod, and a weight-forward fly line that matches to cast these enormous flies. Then you'll need a big reel that can hold this style line. These are big fish, you fish with big bait, and you need big equipment to hold up.

Mix up your tactics when fishing for northerns. Often a slow retrieve works; other times you need to speed it up. One noteworthy point is that the eye placement on the head of northern pike results in a blind spot in front. If you notice a northern following a couple feet behind your fly, don't be surprised when it doesn't strike. It probably just lost sight of your fly. Help it keep your fly in its line of vision by speeding up your retrieve or tugging your fly to one side or the other.

Reel Good Advice

Since flies take such a beating from pike, tie them with durable materials such as rabbit strips and bucktail.

When your quarry strikes, be ready for the fireworks. The initial strike is madness, complete with a huge splash and much splashing about. Hard, sudden runs characterize the fighting technique of northern, but hang in there. Like largemouths, northerns lack stamina, so their fighting ability, while powerful and strong, will not last too long.

After landing a northern pike, holding it is a two-handed endeavor. Use one hand just behind the gills—and nowhere near the teeth! With the other hand, control the thrashing tail. Once landed, these monsters have the ability to inflict much damage and pain. Watch their teeth; watch your gear. Use long-nosed pliers or large hemostats to remove the hook. I don't care how many northerns you hold; you will always be apprehensive. Like a dog that bears its teeth when you go to pet it, northern pike are mean and vicious, and you want to keep this in mind.

Cut Bait

Be careful when handling northern pike; they have sharp teeth and big mouths.

Muskie

While northerns are the loose cannons of the pike family, tiger muskies are a little more controlled and reasonable. This is not to say they don't fit into the "big, mean, and ugly" category. These fish hold their own in the shady, dangerous neighborhoods! For one they are huge. Just when you thought you were reaching the upper limits with northerns, along come muskies, which are even bigger. Four foot long, thirty pound muskies are common.

As far as ugly goes, these fish aren't winning any beauty contests. Huge teeth give them a sinister look, and tiger stripes complete the aura.

As far as their personality goes, it is far from nice. First off, we have to mention two types of muskies: tiger muskies and muskellunge. Muskellunge are nearly as big as tigers, but they will sometimes mate with northern pike to produce tiger muskies. Tigers are the largest fish in the muskie family, and they are unfriendly. They don't even pair up at spawning season, because, for the tiger muskie, there *is* no spawning season. These fish do not reproduce.

Tigers

Tigers serve an important purpose in the scheme of things in a lake environment. They are sort of like the United Nations peacekeeping forces around the globe. Like the U.N., which goes into strife-ridden nations, but doesn't actually take over, muskies control fish populations but don't overrun lakes. They feed on big bait fish and some rough species. They keep other species populations under control, but they don't take over because of their inability to reproduce. This lack of reproduction is also a reason for their huge size. Tigers don't compete with one another for food, and their food sources are never depleted by overpopulation. Therefore, they feed casually, but still get what they need to grow to huge sizes. Mother Nature is amazing; she thinks of everything.

Fish Tails

Tiger muskies are a cross between northerns and muskallunge. They feed on large bait fish and other predators, but they are barren. Tiger muskie don't take over because they are unable to reproduce.

Take the Muskie Challenge

You will notice how much these tigers demonstrate their meanness once you hook one. More often than not, you will lose a muskie. These fish have more endurance, more size, and more power than a northern. Impossible! you say. Once you hook one, you'll believe.

Muskies make great sportfish because it's relatively difficult to catch them. First off, muskies don't have the voracious appetites of northerns. For a monster fish, muskies have dainty eating habits. They pick and choose. How muskallunge grow to be so huge, I don't know. But they are not the vicious and constant feeders that northerns are. Tiger muskies, on the other hand, don't have the spawning ordeal to worry about. They slowly but surely eat and grow to a fantastic size. The meals that these huge fish select tend to be large; they don't waste their time eating tiny flies and small fish. Muskies eat big bait fish.

Muskies, like northerns, ambush their prey. They prefer weedy, protected areas, and their eating habits mirror those of largemouths. They hide out in the weeds, until a smaller fish appears. Then BLAMO! they strike. That, by the way, is when they feel like it. Just as often, the muskie glides out of its hiding spot and tails the prey around, until it loses interest and doesn't eat it. That is one reason why fishing for muskies is a challenge. Making them bite is often difficult.

The other half of the challenge is the fight. Part of the problem is that it is easy to lose concentration while these monsters hesitate to bite. Once you get used to actually watching these huge fish follow your fly, but not bite, as you retrieve it half the time when they do actually strike, you aren't ready. Patience and persistence are critical. You have to be ready for the rare hit, because the key to landing muskies is in setting the hook. These fish are master leapers; muskies leave the water perhaps more than any other fish. You can imagine the thrill of a three to four foot fish leaping high above the water. Repeatedly. It isn't surprising that a high percentage of muskies get off. They spend so much time in the air, that a perfectly set hook is the only way to keep them on your line. Anything less, and muskies will get off.

Reel Good Advice

Remember to bow to a muskie and give it some slack line when it gets air-bound. Otherwise, it will snap your tippet.

Where and How

Although tiger muskies don't spawn, both muskallunge and tigers feed actively around spawning time. Like northerns, muskies move to the shallows soon after ice out. These fish prefer warmer water than northerns, so muskie fishing starts slowly until temperatures warm up. I don't know why tigers feed around spawning time. They don't exhibit any spawning activities like pairing up, but they do feed more actively. The reason, perhaps, is genetic programming? Nobody knows.

Because they prefer warmer temperatures, muskies remain in the shallows longer than northerns, but as summer reaches its height, they too retreat to deeper waters. Another good spot for muskies before temperatures warm up is around warm feeder streams.

Use the same equipment for muskies as you use for northerns. Heavy fly lines and long rods are necessary, not only to play these large fish, but to cast the heavy line and tackle. Remember that muskies eat sporadically, but they eat big. Use large flies, like with northerns. Muskies, sometimes, tend to prefer less colorful presentations—more grays, blacks, and whites, and fewer bright colors.

Muskies like wooded and weeded areas. Again, this adds to the challenge. It takes experience and practice to fish around heavy debris, but the end result makes the trials and tribulations worthwhile.

Pickerel—Mighty Predators

Chain pickerel (*Esox niger*) are hoods just like their larger cousins. Lean and mean, pickerel look similar to pike, except for the chainlike markings along the sides, and the scales that cover the entire cheek and gill cover.

The feeding habits of pickerel mirror those of northerns more than muskies. Pickerel are active fish with a seemingly high metabolism. They feed on a wide range of food, from insects (both aquatic and terrestrial) to crustaceans, frogs, and bait fish. Pickerel are versatile fish that can survive and thrive in a wide range of conditions and temperatures.

The temperature range is perhaps one of the most impressive characteristics of pickerel. Commonly caught through the ice by bait fishermen, pickerel remain in weedy shallows all summer long. This means pickerel survive in the coldest water and the warmest water.

They range throughout eastern Canada and the United States, where they are most often found in slow water with lots of weeds. A weeded cove in a quiet lake is perhaps the best place for the pickerel seeker.

Pickerel move quickly, so a swift retrieve often works best. Streamers, bucktails, and poppers are the best flies for pickerel. They will strike wet and dry flies, too. Anything used for trout or bass has a chance with pickerel.

The same is true of equipment. Use the same gear as your bass and trout setup, but they have teeth so you need a wire leader. Pickerel run significantly smaller in size than northern and muskie. Most pickerel you catch will be under three pounds, but they do grow to as large as five or six. While they put up an active fight, it isn't hard to land a pickerel. Many times, when nothing else is biting, you can find pickerel that are willing feeders.

Walleye

As I mentioned, walleye are not official members of the pike family; they were dubbed "walleye pike" somewhere along the line, and that is how they gained entry into this chapter. Scientific name *Stizostedion vitreum vitreum*, walleye commonly run two to four pounds and as large as 10 or more.

Dark green to gold in color, walleyes have huge eyes. Their eyes appear hollow and empty. Their big eyes enable them to feed when other species can't see. Nighttime and murky waters—conditions that hurt fishing for other species—are ideal for walleyes. By the same token, walleyes are extremely light sensitive, so don't fish for them in the bright sun.

Walleyes are native to Canada and some northern portions of the United States. They are very popular elsewhere now too, although they are fished with flies less commonly than live bait and trolling. Through stocking programs, however, they can be found all over the country.

Fish Tails

Walleyes possess a membrane known as the *tapetum lucidum* that creates the reflective sheen characteristic of the large eyes of these fish. This membrane serves to gather light, thereby permitting walleyes to see in dark murky waters. The membrane also makes walleyes sensitive to bright light.

Walleyes eat worms, some insects, and small fish. Early in the season they seek out shallower areas, although not as shallow as most pike. Shallow for walleye means at least several feet deep (different than pike who will feed in just a few inches of water). Walleye look for darker places, and they feed actively at night.

As the water warms up, walleyes move to deeper water. Walleyes seek water between 65 and 75 degrees Fahrenheit. They will put into shallower water at night, when the temperatures may become a bit cooler.

Walleyes move from the depths back into the shallows in the fall, but they continue to avoid sunshine. As long as there is good cover away from the sun, walleyes will bite.

When they do hit, they dive. Walleyes pull downward. They are not big fighters in the sense that they don't tug, leap, and yank. They are strong fish, however, and the larger walleyes are sometimes difficult to identify as fish. Many times I have gotten a strike, set the hook, and then thought that I was snagged on a big old stick. Don't give up; you may still have a lunker walleye on your line!

Carp—The Poor Man's Bonefish

Carp get a bum rap in this country. When I was in Europe, I could not believe the attitudes in restaurants regarding these fish: carp is a delicacy. One black tie eating establishment went as far as to list carp as their specialty of the house.

Carp.

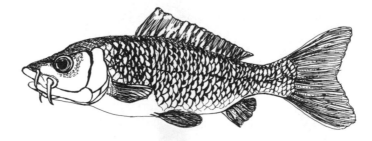

In America, the prevailing attitude is quite the opposite. The attitude regarding carp is best described by the instructions offered in one of my favorite books, *The River Why*. David Duncan James gives these instructions regarding the best way to cook a carp:

1. Clean the fish.

2. Place it on a cedar shingle.

3. Cook it with butter over an open flame until the carp turns a golden brown.

4. Throw away the carp and eat the shingle.

Believe it or not, carp were introduced in this country. Their original habitat included eastern Europe and Asia—China in particular. They were introduced throughout Europe, and had made it to England by the time Walton wrote his *Compleat Angler*. Their introduction to America occurred in the 1830's when they were raised in a pond. The carp escaped from the pond and into the Hudson River. It didn't take long before carp began to surface throughout this huge river drainage.

It isn't surprising that carp not only made it, but thrived. Carp are extremely adaptable. They can tolerate extreme temperatures—from upwards of 90 degrees to even being frozen for a short time. Most fish like it at either the cold end or the warm end, but not both. Carp go either way.

Carp are often used to stock manmade bodies of water or decorative fountains. Golf courses use them. Buildings with fountains use them. They are simply durable fish; they are low maintenance, and they eat anything.

While they are bottom feeders, carp will eat a variety of foods: crustaceans, insects, worms, eggs, plants, fish, and so on. If you have seen carp, the impression etched in your memory is probably one of a carp moving along the bottom with his mouth on the bottom searching for plantlife.

Carp don't chase food like other fish. You have to cast your fly right up in front of carp. Carp sort of amble along, coming across food as they go. Midges, gnats, nymphs, and other flies may prove effective. I have heard of anglers tying green flies that imitate vegetation as carp are omnivores. Try an olive Woolly Bugger or a green popper.

Carp—being different anyway—act different than most fish when it comes to spawning. First off, given their propensity to survive at such a wide range of water temperatures, there is really no set time when carp spawn. They will spawn at a variety of water temperatures and at different times of year.

Catch Words

Carp eat a variety of foods. They are **omnivores**, which means they are both *carnivores* (flesh-eaters) and *herbivores* (non-meat-eaters). Carp eat everything from insects and bait fish to vegetation.

Carp spawn in shallow and weedy areas like pike, but, different from pike, their pre-spawning period is not marked by a feeding frenzy. Carp become aloof as they get ready to spawn. After the spawn, there is no consistent behavior to speak of. Some carp feed, and others don't. Try fishing in muddy, weedy water.

I think that the personality of the carp—or lack thereof—is the main reason for their lack of popularity in this country. As a whole, Americans are outgoing and personable. Not so with carp. Carp don't seem to care what anyone thinks of them. They do their own thing and nothing more.

One way to address fish characteristics is to try to compare them to people. For example, the brown trout is like Sally from *When Harry Met Sally*. Everyone knows someone like Sally. I can't say I know too many people like carp. They don't have much of a personality. They don't seem to care where they live or have a favorite water temperature. They eat just about anything. They grow to enormous sizes and live for a long time—upwards of 20 years in ponds and lakes (much longer in captivity). What kind of a person could I even begin to compare them to? Humans just aren't that easy to please.

Carp get awfully big, with eight to 12 pounders the norm and 20 pounders caught all of the time. When you fish for carp, use whatever rod you have handy. Like sunfish, don't go out and buy a "carp outfit." A nine-foot, five- to nine-weight fly rod will work well. Just make sure your reel has plenty of backing. Carp are powerful fighters; they simply don't come to you and will often take you into your backing.

Cut Bait

Make sure you have a smooth drag mechanism when fishing for carp. They are powerful fighters and will often take you into your backing. If the drag jerks or stops, they will surely break you off.

When it comes to choosing a leader, we have a bit of a dilemma. Carp tend to be somewhat leader-shy; however, they are so big and powerful, they will break a leader that is too light. Use the lightest leader you can get away with—without spooking them. I'm sorry I can't be more specific, but trial and error will prove invaluable here.

Carp fishing in the United States is taking off. Carp are finally gaining acceptance in this country as a legitimate gamefish. And rightly so; carp are dogged survivors, a challenge to hook, and powerful fighters. Because their behavior is so odd in comparison to other fish, carp are somewhat of an anomaly, and this is what presents such a unique challenge. Go ahead, and check this challenge out. Go out and test the waters (excuse the pun), and see if you too can hook and land these strange fish that inhabit so many of the waters of this country.

The Least You Need to Know

➤ Pike have huge appetites and are willing to bite nearly anytime.

➤ Pre- and post-spawning is the ideal time to go for most all pike.

➤ Muskies are more difficult to hook and to land than any other pike.

➤ Walleyes aren't really pike, but you can find them in dark, cool water.

➤ Carp—while they are not often pursued in America—are considered a dining delicacy in other parts of the world. They are a challenge to hook and will give you a good fight.

Panfish

Panfish are among the most fun fish to catch—simply because you can catch lots of them. These are the fish that little kids go out after with coffee cans of worms and catch by the hundreds. If you find the right spot and the right time, you too can become a kid again. You are likely to catch extraordinary numbers of these fish on fly tackle.

Panfish include bluegill sunfish, crappie, perch, rock bass, and so on. The biggest selling point about them is that they are easy to catch. If it's a slow day, and fish don't seem to be hitting, these are the fish to resort to. We've got to get our excitement somehow, don't we?

These fish are plentiful and they reproduce in large numbers. As a matter of fact, in many cases overpopulation is a problem. Panfish constitute the only instance where catch-and-release doesn't necessarily apply.

Is It Game?

Panfish are everywhere. Most species are quick to take a fly and put up a good battle—especially for their sometimes minute sizes. This makes them a perfect starting point for the beginning fly fisherman. Why set yourself up for defeat and frustration by going for the wily brown trout in a tight, wooded stream? Don't be surprised when your tangles, hooked branches, and hours of fishing without hits prove to be the norm, rather than the exception when you're first learning. As a novice, it makes sense to fish for quarry that hit willingly, live in open water, and are known, not for wariness and fussiness like the brown, but for ease in fooling like sunfish or rock bass. Believe me, the thrill of the first few strikes and hooked fish will not matter; whether they are crappie, brook trout, or bass, it will cause shivers, tingles, and a rush of adrenaline. I don't care what kind of fish you hook into in your initial fly fishing efforts. It won't be the fish getting hooked by your line so much as it will be you getting hooked by an incredible new sport.

One noteworthy characteristic regarding panfish is their reproductive prowess. These fish spawn actively and effectively. Like their relative the bass, these are nesting fish, and they see their young through to survival. What happens, however, is that panfish often become overpopulated, and this causes harm to the overall well-being of panfish. When a fish population approaches or surpasses the capacity of habitat, the individual fish begin to have to compete for food. Average health and size of the species declines.

Reel Good Advice

If a lake or pond is overly populated with panfish, don't release your quarry. An abundance of small fish is a good indication of an overly populated pond or lake.

What can anglers do to help? Throughout this book, I have advocated catch-and-release methods. I don't necessarily insist upon catch-and-release with panfish. There are lakes in the United States that actually ask anglers to kill what panfish they catch in order to preserve habitat for other species of fish. Some panfish, like yellow perch and bluegill, are actually good eating.

Take note of the fish you are catching. Are most of them tiny and in the same size range? If so, there is a population problem. And anglers can help ease the burden on the habitat.

Bluegill

I have caught lots of bluegill sunfish in my day; especially when I was just learning how to fly fish. When other fish don't hit, you can still catch sunfish. In the heat of summer with the sun beating down on a lake, sunfish are willing feeders. If you are learning to fly fish, and you want to catch fish, bluegills are the answer.

Bluegill.

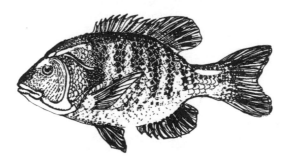

Bluegills, *Lepomis macrochirus*, are small, round fish with a turquoise spot on the gill cover. Most of their body is green, but their throat is orange. Bluegills are closely related to pumpkinseeds and green sunfish, two smaller, but equally fun, panfish.

You will find bluegill sunfish in lakes all over the United States, and you will find lots of them. In most cases, bluegills don't have a very specific spawning time. They spawn anytime from spring through summer. Bluegills do many things that ensure plenty of new generation fish. For one, a female is capable of laying 40,000 eggs. The math is simple; the more eggs you lay, the more young fish will survive. Secondly, sunfish are nesting fish. The male stays with the eggs to protect them from predators. These fish are copious spawners.

Being so effective in the area of reproduction, however, sometimes produces adverse effects. Overpopulation of bluegills and their related sunfish is a common problem. Too many fish creates a feeding problem. Too many fish means not enough food. You end up with tons of small bluegills, because their growth gets stunted.

Fish Tails

Bluegills are effective spawners. Females can lay up to 40,000 eggs and males stay with the eggs for protection.

It is important, therefore, that predator species control sunfish populations. Muskies, pike, and bass come into play here. Without predator species controlling the bluegill population, an entire ecosystem could suffer. With a population explosion of bluegills, it isn't just the bluegill population that experiences ill effects. Every species in an ecosystem (like a lake) is closely and tightly interwoven. Because bluegills feed on some of the same things as many other species, the exploding bluegill population will make food-finding difficult for bass, pike, trout, and so on. Soon, all the fish in the ecosystem will begin to exhibit signs of an unhealthy population—namely, decreased sizes and weights. It is critical that something preys on these panfish to keep down their numbers.

When the population stays under control (in other words, bigger fish or even anglers are preying on them), then healthy bluegill can grow to impressive sizes. In a healthy population, half-pound bluegills are most common, but one to two pounders make great fighters and exciting quarry. These lunker sunfish are not the norm, and they don't usually travel with the rest of the schools.

Sunfish that grow to upwards of a pound, however, didn't get there by luck. Bear in mind that a one pound bluegill is probably in the neighborhood of 10 years old, because bluegills don't grow very quickly. Accurate casting, proper fly selection, and stealthy approaches are all necessary to catch the trophy bluegill.

Bluegills feed on worms, insects, crustaceans, and minnows. The smaller bluegills feed more predominantly on insects and the smaller crustaceans like scuds, while the larger bluegills will go after bait fish. Don't, however, rule out insects and so forth for the big ones. Especially when overpopulation is the rule, these fish will take advantage of whatever is available.

Bluegills like to hang around structural changes. A boulder or submerged stump or log provides good habitat. They also look for cover of some sort and just about always travel in groups. Once you hook one bluegill, get ready; your fun is just beginning.

Cut Bait

Be careful not to trash bluegill spawning beds when wading through shallow water (unless of course, an exploding population needs to be controlled).

Don't overcomplicate things when talking about a fish like bluegill. Yes, they do act differently depending on the season and where they are in relation to their spawning time. But bluegill are so abundant, sometimes it's tough to avoid them!

Bluegill like to spawn in shallow water with a variety of bottom surfaces. They prefer gravel or sand, but will settle for anything—even densely weeded bottoms. The male digs out a nest using his fins and tail. The nests are a couple of inches deep and as much as a foot wide. The nests actually serve as landmarks for good sunfish grounds. Find a nest—or several nests (it is common for the nests to be very close to one another)—and chances are bluegills will not be far away. The female lays her eggs in the nest, and the male ejects his milt.

Like bass, the male nests with the fertilized eggs. During this time he is extremely aggressive and will attack just about anything that comes near him, whether it makes sense or not. A male bluegill nesting over eggs will assault a grasshopper, a minnow, or a four-pound largemouth bass. Look out! Again, bluegill spawn throughout the summer, so know where their spawning beds are, and check back at those spots often.

After spawning, bluegills tend to move into slightly deeper water and back to the structural changes they prefer. Summertime, if accompanied by a significant temperature change in the water, can push bluegills into deeper water and out of fly fishing range. Don't despair! Chances are there are other bluegills preparing nests in the spawning areas and getting ready to feed like mad.

Although matching the hatch can provide outstanding fishing, you very rarely need to when fishing for these indiscriminate feeders. Dry flies like Irresistibles, Humpies, Variants, and just about any Adams pattern works well for these fish as well as small terrestrials such as ants, beetles and hoppers. A variety of streamers and wet flies work well too. Bluegill are not discriminating eaters, and that's exactly what makes them so much fun!

Your fishing outfit should not be complicated. Don't go out and buy a new rod and reel (your "sunfish outfit"); whatever you use for trout is fine—maybe even overkill. Use a light leader and your trout flies, and have fun!

Crappie

When you have become a sunfish master, it is time to graduate to crappie. Crappie are a bit more discriminating in their eating habits than bluegills. They feed more specifically on minnows. For this reason, streamers like Mickey Finns or Woolly Buggers work well.

I have to mention, for those new to the sport of angling, the pronunciation of the word "crappie." I remember reading about and fishing for crappie long before I heard their name spoken, so I must admit to being a bit turned off. Who wants to go after crap? "Crappie," however, is pronounced "croppie." For me, this simple fact alone makes them a more attractive animal.

There are two species of crappie—the white and the black. They are nearly identical, except that black crappie have a few more black spots throughout the sides. Black crappie prefer clear water and rocky bottoms, while white crappies frequent murkier water surrounding sunken brush piles and the like. You will find crappie in lakes throughout the continental United States and southern Canada.

It isn't uncommon to find black and white crappies together in a given area. These fish travel in schools and are not so vastly different that they will not intermingle. Also, don't put feeding for insects past them. They are panfish, remember, and one characteristic is that they are easy to catch.

On the panfish scale, however, crappie rate a "more difficult" in terms of catching them. If you learn their feeding habits and their preferred feeding times, however, you can catch scads of crappies. This is the main difference between crappie fishing and bluegill fishing. It is difficult to pinpoint a specific spawning time or temperature with bluegills, because bluegills tend to spawn throughout the summer. Spawning times and feeding schedules for crappie are specific.

Catch Words

The correct way to say **crappie** is "croppie." Be careful how you pronounce it.

One reason for this is their tendency to follow bait fish. When summer heat warms water temperatures, bait fish move into deeper water. Again, crappies feed primarily on bait fish, so when these prey species make their move out of the shallows, crappies follow. Once they make this move into the deeps, don't bother. Fish in the deeps are out of range with most fly tackle. Before this, however, get ready for lots of crappie fun.

Reel Good Advice

Crappies can usually be found in the shallow water just after the ice melts. The water is warm and there is an abundant supply of food.

Crappies move to the shallows in the springtime after the ice melts. They search for warmer water, minnows, and plankton—another piece of the crappie diet. (Unfortunately, I don't know anyone with fingers adept enough to tie microscopic plankton flies; I wouldn't want to hook crappie through the gill rakers anyway.)

Crappies spawn in the spring in water somewhere in the neighborhood of 65 degrees Fahrenheit. Crappies make their nests in a variety of bottom surfaces. Their preference is gravel, but you will find crappie nests in sand, brush, or weeds. Crappies don't make the clean, easy-to-spot nests that sunfish make (what do expect with a name like "crappie," a tidy homemaker?). Like sunfish, the male digs out the nest, and the female deposits her eggs. The male fertilizes them with his milt, and then nests until they hatch. All told, the process takes about five or six days.

The best crappie fishing runs until the end of the spawning period. During this time, the shallows are productive, and the fish are feeding heavily after the winter and in preparation for spawning. Also, like sunfish, nesting males are big feeders. Use your wet flies and streamers to catch these fish. While they are more discriminating feeders than sunfish, they are still very catchable at this time.

It isn't until summer when they head for the depths that crappies become more elusive. If you do choose to fish for them in the height of summer, keep track of where and how deep you catch them. Crappies travel in schools, so where you catch one, you will undoubtedly find more.

Fish with your smallmouth setup when you go for crappie. You will catch lots of tiny crappie, but half pounders are common. A one pound crappie is a monster. Crappies, unlike bluegills, grow comparatively quickly and do not live long. The highest life expectancy for these fish is five years.

Use a nine-foot, six-weight fly rod outfit equipped with a floating line. If you're going after the deep-diving crappies during the summer, a sinking line is necessary to get to the depths.

Yellow Perch

If you can't catch anything else, you ought to be able to find willing yellow perch. I can't say I have noticed a season that is hot for perch; yellow perch feed all year long. I also can't really say I have found a particular time of day when yellow perch hit best; morning, high noon, evening—they are all good. Perch don't seem to have a preference.

Yellow perch are pretty fish with about six vertical dark green stripes over a lighter green side. Their bottom is white and they have two orange ventral fins. They travel in schools, and feed on a variety of bait. Mainly minnow chasers, perch will also eat insects and small crustaceans.

Fish Tails

Perch hit pretty consistently at all seasons, including winter. When you drive by a frozen lake in the middle of February, and you notice shanty villages out on the ice, there is a good chance these anglers are fishing for perch.

Fish for perch with standard wet fly and streamer patterns. When a perch strikes, it is unmistakable. You get a few nibbles while it checks out your fly. Once it actually takes your fly, you need to set the hook. Then you get the rapid, successive tugging characteristic of perch.

Perch spawn early in the season—often beginning in March and throughout the spring. Water in the 45 to 50 degree Fahrenheit range is the optimal spawning temperature for perch. Perch, being potent reproducers, face the same issues regarding overpopulation as their panfish cousins. As the perch population explodes, the perch in a given ecosystem begin to decrease in size, and the food stores become depleted, not just for perch, but for other fish too.

Again, it is therefore permissible—and often *helpful* for the population—to ignore catch-and-release tactics for these fish. With perch, perhaps more than other panfish, this is a fact worth taking note of. Perch are the best eating panfish. They run small (a half pound perch is large; I saw a three-quarter pound monster once), so it takes lots of perch to make a meal. But remember, we are talking about panfish. You can catch scads of these fish. Indeed, once you get one, chances are, you won't be able to *avoid* catching a bunch more. Perch taste good, so simultaneously treat yourself to a tasty meal while you help the health of an ecosystem in your local lake.

Reel Good Advice

Since perch may nibble at your fly before actually taking it, don't prematurely set the hook—wait until you feel the fish swallow the fly.

It isn't hard to catch lots of these panfish. It is good practice for the beginner, and loads of fun.

White Perch

White perch are a long narrow fish and whitish to silver in color. They are found in streams and bays along the East Coast, and actually prefer salty, brackish water. Some of the larger Atlantic coastal bays of the southeastern United States house great numbers of these fish.

White perch feed on a variety of foods: worms, minnows, small crustaceans, grubs, and aquatic and terrestrial insects. They spawn in rivers and streams during the spring and feed heavily during this time.

Fish Tails

White perch and yellow perch—although they share the same name, are not relatives. White perch are related more closely to white bass and stripers, while yellow perch are aligned with walleyes.

Depending on the time of day and weather conditions, the depth of water in which they hold varies greatly. Most daylight hours are spent in the depths and out of range of fly tackle, but as evening approaches they move to the surface to feed. Get your rod ready during this time!

White perch like to cruise in search of food, so they can be tough to find. But they travel in huge groups, so when you do find them, you may have some incredible fishing. You will know when you have stumbled into one of these large schools. The entire surface of the water will be boiling with rises. This usually happens around sunset.

The Least You Need to Know

➤ Panfish overpopulation is a common problem and results in lots of fish with stunted growth.

➤ Panfish occupy lakes in great numbers and are especially active feeders—for the most part—around their spring spawning times.

➤ Bluegills are colorful fish that—while their spawning time focuses in spring—may spawn throughout the summer months.

➤ Crappie are spring spawners that retreat to the depths when water temperatures warm up.

➤ Yellow perch are the best eating panfish. If you come to a pond or lake with an over-population problem, host a perch-fry for dinner.

➤ White perch frequent the coastal streams and bays along the Atlantic coast, and travel in huge schools.

Part 6
Saltwater Fly Fishing

The planet earth is 75 percent water, covering 138 million square miles of ocean. With all of this water, just think of all the fly fishing to be had!

Well, people in coastal areas all over the country are beginning to figure this out. All of a sudden, fly rodders are realizing that you don't have to live near a trout stream to fly fish. And as my last trip to Florida proved, some of these fly fishermen couldn't figure out why freshwater anglers devote so much time to trout.

After all, they said, "They're much more difficult to catch, and a good-sized trout is not much larger than the bait fish I am imitating. I'm used to fishing for big fish that like to fight. Not puny little fish on puny little tackle."

Well, for whatever reason you're thinking of taking up saltwater fly fishing, this part of the book is for you. We'll start at the very basics: how to get started, where to go, and the equipment needed, and then ease into what techniques and flies to use, and the fish you will be pursuing.

Chapter 25

Why Salt and What to Bring

In This Chapter

➤ The beauty of saltwater fly fishing

➤ How to get into the sport

➤ Saltwater fly fishing equipment

➤ What to bring

Whether you are an avid freshwater fly fisherman looking to broaden your horizons or an old crusty marine angler looking for a new way to catch fish, making the transition to saltwater fly fishing isn't difficult. And if you are just learning about the sport and have no prior fishing experience, there are many aspects of saltwater fly fishing that are easier to learn than its counterpart—the fish aren't usually quite as finicky and you don't have to learn about all of the aquatic insects. As a matter of fact, a few patterns will carry you through most saltwater fly fishing excursions. Effective distance casting, on the other hand, may take a little longer to learn, but is no reason not to take up the sport.

Whatever the reason you decided to take up saltwater fly fishing, you are in luck. An overwhelming proportion of the earth is water, and most of it is salty.

The goal of this chapter is to persuade you to take up saltwater fly fishing and explain the exact gear and tackle you will need. Good luck on your journey!

The Exotic Sport of Saltwater Fly Fishing

Why are so many anglers taking up saltwater fly fishing? Well, the answer isn't so simple. There are a variety of reasons why saltwater fly fishing continues to be on the boom.

Cut Bait

Fly rods have the tendency to "disappear" when packed underneath an aircraft. Always carry your fly rod with you so you know where it is at all times.

➤ **Escape the crowds.** Many of this country's rivers and lakes have become crowded with fishermen. Since there is so much more saltwater on this planet, it's much easier to escape the crowds, especially on a boat.

➤ **As the saying goes, there are many more fish in the sea.** There are hundreds of species of saltwater fish and any fish that can be caught on regular tackle is fair game on a fly rod.

➤ **The fish fight harder.** Matched inch for inch, pound for pound, most saltwater fish are much stronger and faster than their freshwater counterparts.

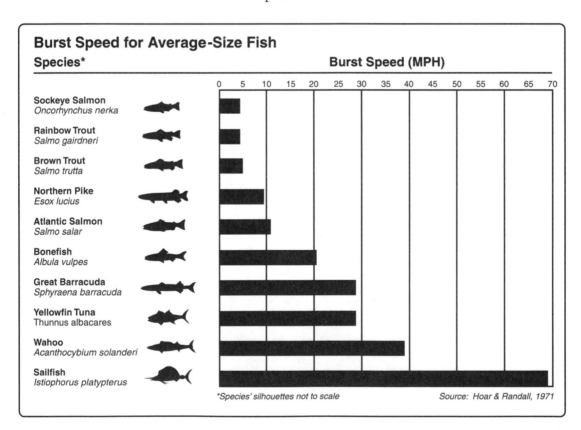

Burst Speed for Average-Size Fish

Bursting speed for average size fish.

➤ A good portion of this country's citizens live along the coast where there are endless fly fishing opportunities (fortunately, not everyone lives near a gurgling trout stream).

➤ You don't have to worry about figuring out what's public and what's private—oceans haven't been privatized like many freshwater rivers and lakes.

➤ It takes you to exotic places such as Belize, Costa Rica, Christmas Island, Australia, and New Zealand.

➤ It's challenging. Not only do you have to spot an often well-camouflaged fish, you also have to make an accurate cast and present your fly as naturally as possible.

Well, what are you waiting for? Get reading. With all of these reasons to take up saltwater fly fishing, you don't have time to waste before your next vacation.

Getting into Saltwater Fly Fishing

I highly recommend hiring a guide on your first few saltwater fly fishing trips. They will save you countless days of searching for fish; which can be quite intimidating and frustrating in such a large body of water. Experienced guides seem to have a sixth sense. It's incredible how some of these guides know when and where each species of fish is holding. And their ability to spot individual fish at a distance in the flat shallow water is even more impressive.

Fish Tails

Many high-end fly shops in the United States have arrangements with fishing lodges and guide services in other countries. They may even offer pre-booked packaged trips with set dates. One of the shop's employees (who has probably visited there before) usually goes on the trip and acts as the liaison.

As you will soon learn, the gravitational pull of the sun and the moon has a major influence on the daily tides, which, in turn, influences the fishing. A knowledgeable guide knows exactly when and where to pursue the species you are after.

Before you go out on a guided trip, I advise you to thoroughly practice the double haul. Saltwater fly fishing guides are expensive, especially if you hire one with a boat. It's not worth spending precious (and expensive) fishing time with a saltwater fly fishing guide working on your double haul when you can practice it just as easily before you go. Believe it or not, many fishing guides in foreign countries don't know the first thing about fly fishing anyway. They simply know how to find and spot fish—the rest is up to you. And don't be surprised if they don't speak much English; telling someone the location of a fish is universal in all languages.

If you are not sure where to book a fly fishing trip abroad, pay a visit to your local fly shop. They will be able to give you a whole list of destinations. Many quality shops also have arrangements and package deals with lodges and guide services in other countries. This is a great way to visit remote, exotic fishing locations. More than likely, you will go with a small group of people with the same interests—catching fish on the fly. It is also a great way to break the language and safety barriers that may accompany a trip on your own.

Equipment

If you already have a fly fishing outfit, you may be able to use it in the saltwater. This of course, depends on what type of equipment you have. If your only rod is an eight-footer, equipped with a three-weight line, your options will be severely limited. But if you have a seven- or eight-weight fly rod that you usually use for bass or pike fishing, there is no reason not to use it in the saltwater.

Fortunately, the cost of saltwater fly fishing equipment is comparable to freshwater, perhaps a bit more. But once you've made the big purchase, it could last a lifetime. Due to heavy competition, most fly rod manufacturers offer lifetime warranties on their fly rods. But of course, if you're like me, you will soon fall for the inevitable "technological break-through" that will forever change the rods, reels, and lines of yesteryear. Whatever the case, a good rod and reel should last you at least five or ten years, depending on how often you use it (or abuse it). More than likely, you will snap your rod in a boat, or in a car door anyway, in which case you'll probably get a new one under warranty.

Reel Good Advice

Saltwater fly fishing equipment needs to be thoroughly washed with freshwater and a mild soap after every use, dried thoroughly, and the reels relubricated.

We have already gone over the basic equipment and gear for basic fly fishing. I will spare you another lengthy discussion on fly rod lengths and weights, line tapers and types of reels. Just flip back to Chapter 2 for reference. I'll just tell you what you need to get started.

Saltwater Fly Rods

Saltwater fly rods aren't too much different than freshwater fly rods, only a little bigger and heavier. Unlike freshwater rods, which are primarily designed for their casting efficiency, saltwater fly rods also have to be designed to lift a large, heavy fish to the boat. Some are even powerful enough to lift a 188-pound tarpon (the world record for tarpon, which of course, will probably be broken by the time this book comes out).

Fish Tails

Make sure that the fly rod you are shopping for comes with a lifetime warranty. With all of the traveling and abuse they are put through, they break or get damaged very easily. Of course, this won't help you out when you finally get to your hideaway in Belize; that's why I recommend always travelling with two rods to foreign countries. And make sure you bring extras of all the essential gear (leaders, shock tippets, flies, etc.). You won't find them there.

Like with any hobby, sport, or luxury, there is an ideal way to get into it and a realistic way. For instance, I would *ideally* like to have a new four wheel drive pick-up truck for the mountains, a Porshe Carrera for road trips, and some sort of float-plane for Alaskan fishing trips. But in *reality*, I have a truck from the 1980s with almost 150,000 miles (hopefully a newer one when I get paid for this book), no sports car, and of course, no plane.

The same is true with fly fishing. If cost (or debt) isn't an issue, I would suggest:

➤ A nine-foot, six- or seven-weight for smaller saltwater fish.

➤ A nine-foot, eight-weight for snook, bluefish, and bonefish.

➤ A nine-foot, ten-weight for permit, tarpon, and dolphin (also called dorado or mahi-mahi)

➤ And a nine-foot, 12- to 14-weight for giant billfish such as marlin and sailfish.

This wide assortment of rods is, of course, not realistic for too many people. Like when buying a freshwater fly rod, you first have to weigh your needs. Are you primarily going to be fishing for bonefish in the flats or out in the deeper water in pursuit of marlin and sailfish?

If you are going to start off with just one all purpose saltwater fly rod, and aren't sure what you'll be fishing for, I'd recommend getting a nine-foot rod for an eight-weight line. Very few beginner saltwater fly fishermen start out fishing for huge billfish like sailfish and marlin. A nine-foot, eight-weight graphite rod can be used for a variety of species in a variety of conditions all over the world. It has enough backbone to land a nice sized fish, yet is still light enough for a good fight on a smaller fish. And since saltwater fly fishing takes you to such exotic places, I also recommend buying a multi-piece rod. If you do decide to take a guided trip for the monsters in the deep water, your guide will probably have a heavier fly fishing outfit you can use for the day.

When shopping for a saltwater fly rod, you will quickly notice that many of them have an *extended butt section* with a small rubber ball or cork. These butt extensions serve two purposes. First of all, they keep the spinning handle away from your body, which has the potential to do severe damage otherwise. Butt extensions are also larger and don't dig into your abdomen or chest as much as the butt on a freshwater rod. If you buy a rod with a removable butt, keep it on when fishing for large species. It's nearly impossible to attach during an intense battle.

Salty Reels

Single action reels are by far the most popular for saltwater fly fishing. *Multiplier reels* (one turn of the handle produces more than one revolution of the spool) are an option, but more of a novelty than anything; many serious fly fishermen laugh at them. They are much more expensive and have many more moving parts. As most fly fishermen know, the more moving parts something has, the greater the chance of a part breaking or malfunctioning.

You also have the choice between direct drive and anti-reverse reels. They are both single action reels but differ when releasing line from the spool. A direct drive reel is the most popular for all around fly fishing—the handle spins backwards when line is released. This makes it easy to judge when to start retrieving line, as you can see and feel when the tension decreases. The only problem with these reels is that the spinning handle can be lethal. Keep your fingers, chest, stomach, eyeglass cords, or anything else away from a quickly spinning reel handle. Anti-reverse reels were designed to alleviate this problem. The handle on anti-reverse reels remains stationary while line is peeled from the spool. This alleviates the bloody fingers and knuckles often associated with savagely spinning handles. The choice is a toss-up on reels designed for larger species though. If you will be fishing for small species on light tippet, stick with a direct drive reel; with the drag set lightly, anti-reverse reels can slip when you reel line in (making it more difficult to retrieve line).

Cut Bait

Don't try to attach a butt extension while you are fighting a large fish. Either keep it on at all times or don't use it.

Whatever type reel you choose, an efficient drag system is crucial for saltwater fly fishing. Most of the fish you will be pursuing in the saltwater are much stronger and faster than their freshwater cousins, and require a smooth drag for the battle. Just about all premium saltwater reels come equipped with an efficient drag system.

Saltwater fly reels come in many different sizes. Like freshwater reels, they are sized according to what weight line they will hold. More importantly, large saltwater reels boast a greater diameter of line on the spool. Think about it, the greater the diameter of line on the spool, the more line you will reel in per revolution. This is crucial for trying to fight large fish that may run several hundred yards; it would take forever trying to bring one in on a small reel. The smallest reels, often called bonefish reels, are designed to hold an eight or nine weight fly line equipped with 200 yards of 20-pound-test backing; perfect for bonefishing. The middle size reel is designed to hold a twelve or thirteen-weight fly line equipped with 250 yards of 30-pound-test backing. Since this is a perfect set-up for tarpon, it is often called the tarpon model. Strong fighting fish like billfish require the largest size reel. These over-sized reels can house a fly line and over 400 yards of 30-pound-test backing. Again, they were designed with such a large spool diameter to make it easier to retrieve great lengths of line.

Unlike most freshwater reels, saltwater reels must be made out of corrosion resistant materials to fight the harsh elements. Most are made out of stainless steel and anodized aluminum materials but this is still not enough. If you want your reel to last a long time, thoroughly clean it after every outing. Use an old toothbrush to scrub your entire reel (not just the outside rim) with warm *freshwater* and a mild dish soap, camping soap, or dishwashing detergent. Rinse thoroughly after each cleaning, let it dry, then relubricate.

While we're on the subject of reeling in a fish, you will soon notice that many experienced saltwater fly rodders cast with their strong hand, and retrieve with it as well. It may seem a little odd switching hands for the fight, but you'll have a greater understanding of this wisdom on the very first large fish you fight. More than likely, you will instinctively switch hands anyway; your strong hand can simply reel in line faster than your weak hand. It also doesn't fatigue as quickly.

Backing and Fly Line

Depending on the species you are fishing for, either 20- or 30-pound-test Dacron or Micron backing is commonly used. These materials lay flat on the

Reel Good Advice

When fighting a large fish, try reeling it in with your strong hand. You will be able to reel it in much faster and you will not tire out as quickly.

spool and stretch very little, making it easy to pump a fish during a battle. The strength of the backing you use needs to be much stronger than the tippet used or you risk losing your entire line if a fish snaps you off. Although rare, I have heard of this happening. To play it safe, use 20-pound-test backing on tippets up to about 12-pound-test and 30-pound-test backing when fishing with tippet any heavier. Depending on the size of your reel, it should house anywhere from 200 yards of 20-pound-test backing to over 400 yards of 30-pound-test backing for the largest models. Again, the greater the diameter of the spool the easier it is to retrieve line.

Fortunately, you have a lot less options when it comes to fly line tapers than you do with freshwater fly fishing. Saltwater fly fishermen either use a weight forward (WF) fly line or a shooting head or shooting taper (ST) fly line. These lines were designed for ultra-fast, accurate presentations; a huge benefit for most saltwater circumstances. Because of their increased versatility, weight forward fly lines are much more popular for saltwater fly fishing. There are several different types of specialty weight forward fly lines that are each designed for specific uses. For instance, some companies make a

Cut Bait

Always make sure your tippet is the weakest link in your system. If it is stronger than your backing or fly line, you risk losing your entire line if a fish breaks you off.

saltwater taper, a bonefish taper, a tarpon taper, a billfish taper, and a special wind taper. Each of these specialty lines vary in total length, color, and amount of weight forward properties.

If you are in pursuit of a variety of saltwater species, I recommend sticking with a saltwater taper. This versatile taper is easy to cast and is made with a very thin running line for distance casting in a just about all weather conditions (great for windy days).

Saltwater fly lines also come in either floating, sinking, or sink tip lines. Remember, there are many different types of sinking lines to choose from: regular-sinking, fast-sinking, and extra-fast-sinking. Again, it depends on the type of fishing you are going to be doing. If you were to only own one fly line for all of your saltwater fly fishing needs, I would have to recommend an intermediate fly line. But if you could splurge on two lines, I would also get a floating line. Floating lines work great in the flats and for manipulating popper flies.

Remember what you learned in Chapter 2 about intermediate fly lines? Well if not, I'll give you a quick rundown so you don't have to keep flipping back and forth. Intermediate fly lines are slightly denser than water and sink very slowly, perfect for fishing the shallows for tarpon and bonefish. They are also ultra thin, which means they have very little air resistance when casting; ideal for windy days (they cut right through the air). And since intermediate lines sit just below the surface, they work great for avoiding choppy water or surface waves.

Saltwater Leaders

Two basic types of leaders are used for most saltwater fly fishing: tapered leaders and leaders with a shock tippet. The tapered leaders are virtually the same as freshwater tapered leaders, just a bit stronger and stiffer. These pre-made knotless tapered leaders are available at any fly shop that caters to saltwater fly fishermen. These leaders are most often used for delicate presentations and smaller fish. They are not to be used on fish with razor sharp teeth or gill plates, such as barracuda, shark, king mackerel, or sailfish.

Thankfully the only two knots you need to know when using a knotless tapered leader are the Surgeon's Loop for the leader to fly line connection and the Palomar Knot for tying the fly to the tippet. Refer back to Chapter 4 if can't remember how to tie these knots.

If you are pursuing larger species, or smaller fish with sharp teeth or mouths, you will need to use a leader with a *shock tippet*. The shock tippet is stronger and more abrasion resistant than regular *class tippet*. It is made out of either wire (coated or single strand) or heavier monofilament (anywhere from 30- to 150-pound test) and should be less than 12 inches in length. This classic leader has three sections; the butt section, which is roughly one-half to two-thirds the total length of the leader; the *class tippet*, which is the middle section, and the shock tippet on the end. For instance, say the leader is six and a half feet long. The butt section may be four feet of 25- to 40-pound test, the class tippet two feet of 12- to 20-pound test, and the shock tippet six inches of 30- to 150-pound test. Why do we need a weak link in the leader? Well, if a fish were to snap you off, it's better that it breaks you off at your class tippet rather than somewhere in your backing.

Catch Words

Shock tippet is a short piece of wire or heavy mono attached to the end of your leader and is used for pursuing game with sharp teeth or mouths.

There are almost a dozen different knots that are used to construct a standard saltwater leader (butt section, class tippet, and shock tippet). Since you've already learned several knots in Chapter 4, I won't throw many new ones at you; many of them will work for saltwater leaders as well. The Blood Knot and Surgeon Knot are the most popular knots used to construct a tapered leader. Knot opinions differ greatly, but here is how I suggest building a standard saltwater leader:

Reel Good Advice

Use a pair of pliers to tighten heavy mono (especially shock tippet). It is nearly impossible to tighten it by hand.

1. You have a variety of options for the butt section to fly line connection. The Nail Knot (coated with rubber-based cement) and the loop-to-loop connections you learned in Chapter 4 both work well, though the loops will prove to be much easier for changing leaders.

2. The butt section to class-tippet section can be attached with a variety of knots. Again, I prefer to use either the Surgeon Loop or the Perfection Loop so I can quickly change the leader. Other knots include the Bimini Twist or a Spider's Hitch equipped with a Surgeon's Knot. Remember to always test your loop knots with a firm object before testing them on a fish.

3. The shock tippet can also be attached to the class tippet with a variety of knots. The Albright Knot is probably the most popular, but the Surgeon's Knot also works (and you already know to how tie it).

4. The fly can be tied to the shock tippet with a variety of knots as well. Some people prefer loop knots for the lively action they give the fly while others prefer a knot that gets rid of the movement and cinches the fly to the tippet. The Non-Slip Mono Loop and the Perfection Loop both work well for loops. If you would rather not use a loop knot for the fly connection, use an Improved Clinch Knot

(unless you're using over 12-pound test) or the Trilene Knot, a much stronger knot. Shock tippets made from single strand wire should be attached to the fly with a Haywire Twist.

Since you already know some basic knots that will work for each of these connections, I will spare you (and my artist) directions on the other knots commonly used. If you really have a desire to learn all of the types of knots, get a book dedicated to knots or ask someone to show them to you and follow the directions very closely.

Catch Words

A **stretcher box** is a fly box designed to hold flies that are already tied to the tippet or leader.

Many saltwater fly fishermen construct their leaders with the fly attached *before* they even hit the water. This is a great idea if you use loop to loop connections for your leader knots. A *stretcher box* is a type of fly box designed to hold tippet sections with flies already attached. The beauty of the boxes is that they keep the shock tippets straight and ready for action. If you happen to break off while on the water or need to change flies quickly, all you have to do is swap one loop for another and you're ready to go!

The Hook on Saltwater Hooks

Saltwater flies are large. Depending on the fish you are after, hooks range in size from about a size 8 all the way up to a 4/0. Because of the size of these hooks, it is extra critical that they be sharpened before every outing. Files seem to work best on these large hooks and always remember to file away from the point of the hook—toward the bend. If you file the wrong way, it only weakens the point and increases the risk of a break-off, especially if you make the point too long when sharpened.

If you tie your own saltwater flies, use light wire hooks rather than heavy wire. Although they are not quite as durable and don't sink quite as fast, they penetrate a fish much easier than the larger diameter heavy wire hooks. And don't forget you can always add lead wire (weight) around the hook before tying the fly.

Cut Bait

Make sure you file a hook from the point toward the bend. If you do it the opposite way, you will weaken the point and risk losing a fish.

You will also have the choice between stainless steel and carbon steel hooks. Stainless steel is rust proof while carbon steel rusts. That makes the decision easy, right? Go with stainless steel. Well, it's not that easy. Many conscientious anglers switch to carbon steel precisely because it does rust. If they happen to lose a battle from a strong game fish (which happens often in fly fishing), they have the peace of mind knowing that the hook will soon rust out. Who knows how long a stainless steel hook will last in a fish? Furthermore, stainless steel hooks are softer than carbon steel and are known to bend during a long, hard fight.

Other Essential Saltwater Items

Though not quite as gear intensive as freshwater fly fishing, there are several items that are essential for saltwater outings. Depending on where you go, always bring the following gear:

➤ **A hat and polarized sunglasses.** The harsh sun and saltwater fly fishing go hand in hand, especially in tropical climates. These two items protect you from the sun's harmful rays and help cut glare. Like I mentioned earlier, a good pair of polarized sunglasses are a must for spotting fish.

➤ **Breathable rain gear.** Even the most gorgeous morning of the week might turn into a day of rain, no matter where you are. Bring light colored rain gear (both top and bottom) on all saltwater outings. If you can splurge on breathable materials such as Gore Tex, go for it. They are much more comfortable than sweating to death under a rubber suit.

➤ **Hip boots or waders.** Hip boots or waders are essential for cold water in-shore fly fishing. If the ground is slippery, studded, felt soles are often necessary.

➤ **Long nosed pliers with wire cutters.** A good pair of pliers with built-in wire cutters will come in handy on any saltwater outing. They will be used to release a hook from a landed fish and to cut wire and heavy mono. Sorry, nail clippers won't quite cut it for saltwater fly fishing (pun intended).

➤ **A catch and release glove.** It's not that fish are slimy or anything, it's just that species like snook, striped bass, tarpon, and Jack Crevalle have spiny fins or abrasive scales. Trust me on this one: always have at least one glove ready for handling fish.

➤ **Stripping basket.** Stripping baskets can be essential pieces of equipment for saltwater fly fishing. They are used to store long lengths of shooting line next to you while in search of your next quarry and to keep line from getting tangled around your legs or gear on the boat. They can be purchased from a fly shop or made on your own. A small plastic dishpan works well when tied around your waist with a bungee cord.

Reel Good Advice

A good way to keep track of your line when fishing from a boat is to fish barefooted or with a pair of socks, but no shoes. This way, you can feel when the line starts creeping around your feet. Just make sure you wear sunscreen if you go barefooted.

➤ **Booties.** Booties help protect your feet from sharp objects while wading and the harmful rays of the sun.

➤ **Other small items.** Don't forget sunscreen, water, extra flies and leaders, and a good camera.

The Least You Need to Know

➤ Since saltwater fly fishing takes you to exotic destinations, buy a multi-piece fly rod for easier travel.

➤ Saltwater corrodes fly fishing equipment. Be sure to clean your reel extra thoroughly with warm water and mild dish soap after every outing.

➤ The double haul cast is essential for getting the distance needed for saltwater fly fishing.

➤ Intermediate fly lines are probably the best all around fly line for saltwater fly fishing. Floating lines, however, are easier to handle for beginner saltwater fly fishermen.

➤ A sharp hook is essential for saltwater fly fishing. It can be the difference between catching a fish and losing a fish.

Chapter 26

Where to Go and the Tides to Fish

In This Chapter

➤ Understanding tides

➤ Different saltwater types

➤ Where the fish are holding

➤ Follow the birds

➤ On-the-water safety

The most intimidating part about saltwater fly fishing is figuring out where the fish are. After all, the ocean is a very big place, covering more than three-quarters of the earth's surface. If you are fishing in the Pacific Ocean, you are fishing in a body of water that lies in between the east coasts of Asia and Australia and the west coasts of North and South America. I understand where your intimidation comes from.

This chapter will help you dissect these massive oceans and turn them into small bodies of water, each requiring their own special techniques. But before we begin dissecting the oceans, we must first have an understanding of how the ocean works, or moves.

Understanding Tides

Before we discuss the different types of saltwater, you must first have a general understanding of the rising and falling tides in the ocean water. Even if the ocean environment is new to you and you've never left your adobe deep in the Arizona desert, I'm sure you've heard of the ocean having high tides and low tides. Right? Well, whatever the case—keep reading. A general understanding of the tides is very important for saltwater fly fishing.

The Mighty Moon

Tides are created by the gravitational pull of the sun and the moon. Since the moon is so much closer to the earth, it has a much greater impact (2.17 times greater to be exact). As you may have noticed, certain times of the month have higher tides than other times. This is because the moon orbits the earth in approximately 28 day cycles and at certain times within this cycle, the moon and the sun align directly with the earth; hence, the gravitational pull is the strongest. These higher tides, or stronger currents are called *spring tides* and happen during the full moon and new moon; twice every 28 days. This is when the variation between the tides is the greatest.

Catch Words

Spring tides have the greatest variation between high and low tide. They happen during the full and new moon. **Neap tides**, on the other hand, don't have much of a variation. They happen when the moon is in its first and third quarter phases—when the gravitational pull is the weakest.

Since the sun and the moon are not aligned with the earth during the moon's first quarter and third quarter phases, there isn't as much gravitational pull. The tides are called *neap tides* during this time and the variations between high tide and low tide are at their smallest.

You will also notice that the ocean has two high tides and two low tides every day. That is because the earth rotates around its axis one full time each day. When the surface of the water passes beneath the moon, the moon's gravity pulls on the water and creates a high tide. Since the moon's gravity also pulls on the solid earth below the water, the earth on the opposite side of the moon gets pulled away from the opposing ocean and creates a second high tide. Since the earth spins one full rotation each day, you see both tides. I guess it's not too important for you to know why the tides keep changing, just be aware that each day sees two high tides and two low tides.

The Powerful Wind

Winds can also affect the size of a tide. The amount of influence greatly depends on the velocity of the wind and the direction in which it is blowing. If there is a powerful onshore wind, the tide will be higher than usual. Likewise, if there is a strong offshore wind, the wind could keep the tide lower than usual. Since large storms are often accompanied by fierce winds, the tide is greatly affected.

Predicting Tides

A tide chart is the most accurate way to predict a tide. But don't worry if you don't have one. You don't have to be a rocket scientist to figure out how to predict the tides on your own. Since the moon rises approximately fifty minutes later each day, so does the tide. This is influenced, however, by a number of variables. Which phase the moon is in, time of year, and current weather patterns all affect the daily tides.

Why Does All of This Matter?

What does all of this matter for fishing? Well, to tell you the truth, it may not matter at all. It all depends on where you go. Some types of water aren't too affected by tides and offer good fishing all of the time. Other areas are slow during *slack tides*, the time in between high and low tide when the water is at a standstill. Many areas, however, are best fished in the few hours after a high tide, which is called *high outgoing*, or the first few hours after low tide—when the water is rising—often called *low incoming*. You see, these tidal changes create currents that move bait fish and make them vulnerable to the predators we are after.

Reel Good Advice

Since tides can have such a major impact on the fishing, buy a tide chart—it can be an invaluable tool.

I wish I could tell you the exact tides to fish wherever you go, but depending on the tide, each type of water fishes a little differently. As with most aspects of fly fishing, time on the water is the best way to figure it out.

Types of Water

Like freshwater, there are many different types of saltwater to choose from. As a matter of fact, there are probably even more. But how could that be, you may ask? You either fish from the beach or take a boat out to the deeper water, right? Well, not quite. As you will see, the options are almost endless and constantly change depending on the tides. But since most saltwater fly fishing is done inshore, we will keep it simple and discuss the five basic types of inshore fly fishing. But just in case you get the itch for an offshore battle, we will cover blue water as well.

Fishing from the Beach

Although the powerful water crashing turbulently against the beach may seem like an unlikely place to fish, the *surf* can offer incredible fly fishing. And fortunately, there are thousands of miles of shoreline bordering the earth's land masses that provide access for this fast-growing sport.

One of the most crucial things to keep in mind when saltwater fishing is figuring what the fish are feeding on and where that food is. Most of the time, the food is smaller bait fish and the patterns don't have to be exact.

Depending on a number of variables, these bait fish are greatly affected by changing tides, especially when fishing from the beach. Because of the faster currents and deeper water associated with high tide, the fishing is usually best (on an open beach) one to two hours before high tide, and one to two hours after high tide. During this time, holes and depressions in the beach get filled with deep water. These holes and depressions offer easy holding water for both bait fish and the game fish that feed on them.

Cut Bait

Practice extra caution when fishing during high tides, especially on steep beaches.

The strong currents associated with high tides also stir up sand crabs and seaworms, both of which make easy meals for predatory fish. Bait fish also lose one of their biggest defenses when a strong current breaks up their school—strength in numbers. When a school of bait fish stays together, it is more difficult for a predator fish to narrow in on one meal. Strong currents break up these schools and make individual fish easy targets. Other large game fish, however, simply swim through a school of bait fish and inhale whatever they can get their mouths around. Game fish that zero in on a particular target are usually much easier to catch.

Although the surf can be a pain in the neck to deal with when fly fishing, it does have its advantages:

1. Waves help outline holes and depressions along the beach where bait and game fish are likely holding—just look for the dark blotches of water.

2. Waves help give your fly lifelike action when being retrieved.

3. Waves make game fish strike more aggressively. In calm water, they have time to inspect the fly before striking.

4. Waves help bring game fish and bait fish closer to the shore.

These advantages, of course, hold only when the waves aren't too large. Fly fishing is nearly impossible when the surf is high because the fly line becomes uncontrollable.

Undoubtedly, the hardest part for most beginner saltwater fly fishermen when fishing from the beach is figuring out how to read the water. Depending on the layout of the beach, there are a variety of places to start:

➤ **The deep water after sand bars.** The surf causes sand bars to form either parallel to the beach or at an angle. This shallow water is where the waves break. The water then usually forms another wave that crashes on the shore. The water in between these waves, just after the sandbar, is usually the deepest and calmest; hence, houses the most fish. This is a great place to concentrate your casting. Make sure you vary the speed of your retrievals, the angles at which you cast, and depth of water you present your fly.

➤ **Fish the cuts.** Cuts are often formed in between sandbars to allow water to return to the ocean. Concentrate your efforts around these cuts as game fish often lie in ambush for weary bait fish.

➤ **Washes or troughs.** Try to locate washes or troughs along steep beaches. They vary with wave size but are typically located where the receding wave meets the ocean.

➤ **Rocky areas.** Rocky areas along a shoreline offer great holding water for fish.

These are just a few spots to start with when you hit the water. Hopefully, you will get turned on to the signs and symptoms of a feeding frenzy soon thereafter.

Jetties

This isn't exactly a type of water, but you don't usually fish *jetties* from the beach. *Jetties* are manmade structures built to combat erosion on beaches and to prevent river mouths from filling. They vary in size depending on the needs of the area, but are usually made out of wood or rock.

Although jetties are manmade, bait fish quickly capitalize on the small nooks and crannies that are typical of their disposition. This provides excellent feeding stations for the larger fish that feed on them.

Catch Words

Jetties are manmade structures built to protect a river mouth or beach.

Although some are better than others, jetties can be fished at any time of the day and during all tides. An outgoing tide is often the best though, because it flushes bait fish out into the open water where they are more vulnerable to feeding fish.

Fishing should be concentrated around the *rips,* or the current that is formed at the end of a jetty and the white water around a jetty. The most productive spots are often within a few feet of the jetty.

Fishing jetties can be done from a boat, but boating experience and local knowledge is essential. The best way to fish a jetty is while standing in a safe spot where you can easily land a fish. This may be tough, depending on the tide, the size of the jetty, and the surf, but it is possible.

Estuaries

Estuaries are much like the tributaries of a large river, only in this case, the large river is the ocean. They occur when rivers, freshwater tidal creeks, or bays, intermingle with the ocean and create a backwater. Like the confluence of two rivers, estuaries create a sheltered zone that provides great holding water for both game fish and bait fish. This type of water, (usually *brackish*, or a mixture of fresh and saltwater) can offer incredible fly fishing possibilities because it is the home and breeding grounds to a wide array of foods.

Since the natural flow of creeks and rivers pours fresh water into the ocean, the current is severely interrupted when the tide rises. Incoming tides alter the flow of water and may create an upstream current in the mouth of the river. This increase of water floods out the estuary and brings an abundance of fish with it. Bait fish thrive during this time as the high water creates an abundance of hiding places and fills the marshes.

Once the water begins to drop, however, their hiding places become sparser and they are forced into deeper, moving water. This is when they are most vulnerable to game fish and when the fishing is usually the best. Look for any structure in the water where game fish can hide, waiting to ambush their prey. For instance, if there is a sudden drop off next to a shallow marshy area, you bet there will be game fish waiting to ambush their next meal.

Fish Tails

Experienced fishermen often pay a visit to estuaries and river mouths during low water just to get a glimpse of the structure—holes, cuts, drop-offs, rocks, and so on, and remember them for later. When they come back to fish during the falling tides, they know exactly where to fish even though the structure is underwater.

Rivers and estuaries usually have a main channel extending to the open ocean. This is usually the deepest water in an estuary and has the most current; current that is greatly affected by the tide. The main channel is easy to spot—it is usually a different color than the side water. And if these channels are navigable, you can't miss them—they will most likely be marked with rock pilings or channel markers.

Channels offer excellent fishing. They are the main passageways for both bait fish and game fish. Large game fish often wait in the main channel and ambush their prey along the shallower edges.

Channels can either be fished while wading from their edges or from an anchored or drifting boat. Whatever the case, be careful—there is usually a drop-off at the edge of a channel. This poses opposite hazards for wading fishermen and drifting boats. Wading fishermen can accidentally walk into the strong current of the main channel while boaters can get stuck in the shallows.

Cut Bait

Play it safe when wading around channels. Be on guard for steep drop-offs and powerful currents.

Coral Reefs

Coral reefs can offer some of the most intriguing fly fishing opportunities in the ocean. They house more species of fish than anywhere else in the ocean and are usually found in warm climates—often surrounding tropical islands—a good combination if you ask me. Reefs also provide more structure than any other type of water and an abundant source of food for bait fish, which in turn, bring in the game fish that we are after. Fish ranging from shark to grouper, barracuda to snapper and almost everything in between, can all be caught around a coral reef.

Since they require such intense sunlight to survive, coral reefs are only found in shallow water, making them ideal for fly fishing. Furthermore, coral reefs are found in some of the most exotic vacation spots in the world.

Sounds like paradise, right? Well, it is, but it does have its drawbacks. Depending on the layout of the reef, wading can range from easy to just about impossible. Coral is very fragile and gets damaged if you step on it—not to mention what its sharp edges does to your skin. This means that you must only wade in sandy areas and wear durable shoes. The only problem, is that there are sometimes no sandy areas around a reef.

Fishing from a boat is sometimes the best option but the water surrounding a reef is often too rough to navigate. Furthermore, only experienced boaters can pick their way through a reef without bottoming out. Depth finders are virtually useless in this type of water.

Since coral is so sharp and abrasive, it can take a serious toll on fly fishing gear. Fish seem to capitalize on this and, if allowed, will make a quick dash to the nearest corral head, snapping your leader in the process. A heavy fly rod (at least a nine or ten weight) is essential for bossing these fish around. To protect your gear and not lose the fish, it is imperative that you keep them away from any coral heads or snags. A floating fly line also works best for avoiding the sharp coral and fraying your fly line.

If possible, hire a local guide for your first few outings. They will show you the appropriate techniques and direct you to the hot spots.

Fly Fishing the Flats

The *flats* are shallow sections of water with uniform depth. They vary in size, depth, current, and structure and although most fly fishermen associate flats with the tropics, they can be found in many different types of water. They are often located next to a point or reef, in the back of an estuary, adjacent to the mouth of a river, or surrounding part of an island. Whatever the case, flats can provide outstanding fly fishing opportunities.

Flats can be fished either by wading or from a boat. They each have their pros and cons. Wading fishermen spook less fish but can't see as many as a fly fisherman standing in a boat, or *skiff* or *ponga*, as these shallow water boats are often called. Wading muddy bottomed flats can also be dangerous. I sank to my waist a few years ago while wading through a flat in the Yucatan. Luckily, I was able to free myself and learned a lesson the easy way.

There are no set rules when it comes to the effect tides have on flats; it simply depends on the layout

Catch Words

A **skiff** or **ponga** is a type of boat used for the flats because they draw very little water.

of the flat. Some flats aren't influenced at all while others dry up at low tide. It is up to you to figure out what tide, if any, offers the best fishing for each particular flat.

Fighting a fish in the flats can be one of the most exhilarating types of fly fishing. Since the water is shallow, they don't have any room to dive. The fish simply run, some at incredible speeds, across the shallow water until tiring out. Bonefish, probably the most sought after flats fish, reach incredible speeds as they try to free themselves.

Since flats are so shallow and often clear, blind casting is highly ineffective; it does nothing more than spook the water and tire your shoulder. Spotting the fish before they sight you is the key to successful flats fishing. This makes it essential to remain as stealthy as possible. Once you have found a target, a good presentation with the right fly is critical.

Although difficult to see, there are a variety of signs and symptoms used to locate these well-camouflaged fish:

➤ **Tailing fish.** If the water is shallow enough, many species of flats fish feed on the bottom, leaving their tails exposed through the surface of the water.

➤ **Seeing a wake.** Some fish cruise the surface of the water and leave a highly visible wake just behind. Always cast ahead of waking fish so the fly lands in front of them. This can be difficult because the fish often swim by very quickly.

➤ **Cloudy water or "mud."** This can be a great sign of feeding fish. Since the water is usually clear in the flats, a cloudy or muddy section usually indicates bottom feeding fish (such as bonefish) kicking up sand or mud as they feed. If this is the case, cast a bottom-dwelling imitation in the middle of the cloudy spot and retrieve. Make sure the imitation gets to the bottom quickly and you should have some luck. Since the visibility is lousy, you may not spook the other fish as well and have a chance to catch more than one. If the muddy or cloudy water seems to be moving, the fish are more than likely moving with it. If this is the case, cast your fly in the same direction and wait for the cloud of murky water to reach it before retrieving. You should be rewarded with a hook up.

Reel Good Advice

Look for nervous water in the flats. It can be a great indication of feeding fish.

➤ **Nervous water.** *Nervous water* is a great sign for fish. But unlike freshwater, the nervous water you are looking for in the flats is created by fish swimming or feeding near the surface. Although sometimes hard to decipher, this ruffled water can be a great indication of a fish's whereabouts.

➤ **Hearing the feeding fish.** Fish feeding on the surface often make pop and splashing noises. This can be very easy to hear on still water flats.

Blue Water—Going Deep

All of the previous types of water are considered inshore fishing. *Blue water*, on the other hand, is considered offshore fishing. It is most often associated with trolling for big-game fish like marlin, sailfish, and tuna. But as the saying goes, where there's a will, there's a way. And believe it or not, fly rodders have recently found that way. Just a few short decades ago, fly fishermen would have laughed at the idea of fishing this type of water. Nowadays, however, although not a large number, blue water anglers as well as curious fly fishermen are hopping in boats and cruising to this deep, mysterious water with fly rods in hand.

As you have probably guessed, this type of water is much different than any of the other types. First of all, the water is deep—really deep, beyond a thousand feet in some places. Wading, of course, is out of the question. As a matter of fact, you need a good sized boat just to negotiate the strong currents and immense waves in this type of water. The fish are also really huge; the fly line world record for marlin is just under 200-pounds—that's right, almost 200-pounds reeled in with a fly rod! And of course, some of the tactics used to fool these fish are much different than any other type of fly fishing.

Blind fishing borders on insanity in this type of water—there is just too much of it. Like when fishing the flats, you must first pursue the fish. Of course, you aren't quite as stealthy when cruising the seas in a motor boat, but you do what you can. There are several excellent signs that can help alert you to the fish's whereabouts.

➤ **Birds.** That's right, it can be as easy as following the birds. Like freshwater fishing, birds can be a great indication of available food. Since birds and game fish both eat bait fish, birds can tell you where the game fish are. If you see birds diving into the water after bait fish, you better believe other fish are dining as well. From a distance, cast your fly right in the center of the ala-carte and wait for the strike of your life.

➤ **Floating wood, buoys, and weeds.** If you don't see much bird activity, narrow your search to objects floating in the water. Floating logs, weeds, buoys, and lifejackets (only kidding) can provide a sanctuary for bait fish. In this big-fish-eat-little-fish world, game fish lurk just beneath waiting for their chance to attack.

➤ **Spotting the fish.** Although you may sometimes see large game fish jumping through the air, you will more than likely see small bait fish fleeing for safety. If you see bait fish jumping through the air, there are probably game fish feeding on their brothers and sisters not far below (they're not just trying to catch a glimpse of the outside world).

Cut Bait

Never drive your boat directly into a feeding frenzy. This will only spook the fish and halt the feeding.

333

If you are having no luck finding game fish, there are several ways to attract them. However, some of these tactics are highly questionable for many fly fishermen.

One of the methods used to attract fish is by trolling. This can be done with either regular lures or *teasers*—lures without hooks. Some deep-sea anglers troll the water in search of big game fish. Once a fish strikes, a fly of similar color and size is offered to the rest of the school in hopes of some action. Unlike the trout you may be used to, many gamefish travel in schools in search of food. Once one fish finds a meal, or lure in this case, the others get excited and search for food as well. Some angling "teams" just fish with conventional tackle until someone hooks up. Then, the other buddy switches to fly tackle and takes advantage of the other trailing fish.

The technique is a little different when using a teaser. Once a fish gets "turned on" to a teaser, the teaser is retrieved and a fly is cast in its place—just in front of the teased fish. This often ignites huge strikes.

If this isn't your cup of tea, *chumming* probably won't be either. As a matter of fact, some of my fly fishing friends think it is comparable to throwing a jar of salmon eggs or a can of worms into a lake before trout fishing. Actually, it's not too much different. *Chumming* is when you throw parts of fish, or entire fish, into the water to attract fish. They are often thrown in a mesh bag and tied to the boat. While their oils and scents get spread throughout the water, the "fly fisherman" presents his chum looking fly to the awaiting fish.

Reel Good Advice

If you have never fly fished in the blue water before, get a guide for your first few outings. They will help find the fish and teach you the appropriate techniques.

Although these methods are much different than what you may be used to, they can be highly effective and often necessary for successful blue water fly fishing. There is often just no other way (yet known) to find big game species like marlin and sailfish.

Blue water fly fishing for big game species can undoubtedly be some of the most exhilarating fly fishing around. The only downside is its cost—you need a good sized boat to get out there. If you have never fished in the blue water before, I highly recommend hiring a qualified guide for your first few outings.

Playing It Safe

Like with any risk taking venture, preventative measures go a long way. But accidents happen and it's important to know what to do in case of an emergency. The first thing to remember is to not panic. I know this can be difficult, but it only worsens a situation.

Each type of water has its own inherent risks and dangers. It is important to respect the power of the ocean and know your limits within it. Here are some things to watch out for when fishing each type of water.

➤ **Fishing from the beach.** Large surf and powerful currents can take you down in a heartbeat. But with a little respect for the ocean's power, it can easily be avoided. Don't wade too far out into the surf, especially on steep beaches! If you do take a swim, don't panic. If you can't stand back up, don't try to fight the current—there is no way you will win. Save your energy and swim to the side of any holes or cuts. The next wave should help you reach shore without much of a struggle.

➤ **Fishing the flats.** The most dangerous part about fishing a flat is probably getting stuck in the muddy bottom; they're not very dangerous places. Many unwary fly fishermen also get badly sunburned and dehydrated. Always carry plenty of water. It is also important to always know where you are and what tide it is when wading. If you wade out during a low tide and the water is rising, you may be forced to swim to shallow water—which can be tough with fly rod in hand, especially if you're not a good swimmer. If possible, remember the route you took in and where the deepest water was.

➤ **Blue water.** Sea-sickness is a common occurrence in the blue water. Several medications, like Dramamine or Scopolamine, work well as a preventative measure. Before venturing far from shore, it is also important that you have proper boating and navigational skills. One of the biggest dangers, however, is landing these sometimes massive, sharp, toothy, fish. If you are going to boat them, make sure they are sufficiently tired out before you bring them in. Otherwise, they might flop around and harm you, your boat, your equipment, or themselves.

➤ **Reefs.** Be careful when wading around sharp beds of coral reef. These objects are extremely fragile and will crush when stepped on. They can also take a toll on your fly fishing gear. Only experienced boatmen with local knowledge should attempt to boat around these fragile reefs.

Cut Bait

Be aware of stingrays and sea urchins when wading the flats. The best way to avoid stingrays is to let them know you're coming. Instead of picking up your feet when you walk, shuffle them through the sand. This will usually alert a stingray and send them away. If you happen to bump one, don't worry. As long as you don't step on its stinger you won't get stung. Once you bump it, it will take off. The best way to avoid a sea urchin puncture is to not wade barefoot.

The Least You Need to Know

➤ A *flat* is a shallow sand or mud-bottomed area with consistent depth. Flats are ideal for fly fishing because they are easy to wade and the fish are highly visible.

➤ When fishing channels, thoroughly cover any rock pilings and channel markers; they make great hideouts for bait fish.

➤ Fish when the tide is either rising or falling. A slack tide is the still water in between tides and usually offers the worst fishing.

➤ Birds are a great indication that there are bait fish in the vicinity; hence, predator fish as well.

➤ When fishing the blue water, look for any floating objects that may provide habitat for bait fish.

➤ Respect the strong currents when fishing from the beach or near a channel.

Chapter 27

What to Use and What to Do

In This Chapter

➤ Saltwater fish food

➤ Successful fly patterns and their recipes

➤ Hooking the fish

➤ The big fight

➤ How to land them

Figuring out what fly to use is without a doubt the biggest quandary for most fly fishermen, beginner to expert. Books filled with hundreds of fly patterns dot the shelves of just about every large bookstore. You will hear names such as the Surf Candy or Lefty's Deceiver coming out of the mouths of most saltwater fly fishermen. As this chapter will demonstrate, there is no need to be intimidated—a few patterns will do for most circumstances. Choosing a saltwater pattern shouldn't be stressful (although this is just about the most stress you will encounter on any given day on the water).

We've already discussed what to do if the pattern you've chosen doesn't work, but what do you do when it does? What should you do if you do get a strike? Well, fear no more. We will discuss exactly how to hook a fish, how to win the big fight, and how to safely land it all without losing it.

Choosing the Right Fly

Choosing the right pattern for saltwater fly fishing can be as complex as choosing the right fly in the freshwater. Luckily, there are a few major differences. First of all, saltwater fish aren't nearly as picky. Although there are thousands of species of fish that get eaten, most game fish are *opportunistic eaters*. That is, they will take advantage of any food source that may come their way.

Fortunately, many species of bait fish look alike; one pattern can work in a variety of circumstances. Of course, the fisherman who knows the exact source of food the fish are feeding on and who has the ability to imitate it with a lifelike pattern, will have more success than the fisherman who doesn't change flies or tactics throughout the course of the day. But all in all, game fish couldn't give a hoot as to what species of mullet or herring they are eating. As a matter of fact, they couldn't give a damn if they were eating their nephews and nieces, let alone their own offspring. As long as the fish looks lifelike and isn't too big, it's fair game—there are no rules.

If you can't find any bait fish in the area you are fishing, choose a pattern that matches the surroundings. That is, if the bottom is dark—choose a dark imitation, if the bottom is light—choose a light imitation. Mother Nature gave bait fish the ability to blend in with their surroundings. This ability to adapt helps them avoid a wide array of predators.

If you can identify what the fish are feeding on, you will have a major advantage. Rather than getting caught up in trying to figure out exactly what species of bait fish you should imitate, try to get an idea of the fish's size, coloring, shape, and behavior. If you can match these attributes with the appropriate fly and present it like the naturals, you should be in for some incredible fishing. Let's take a look at each one of these characteristics:

➤ **Size.** Match the size of the bait fish you are imitating. Of course, this has it's limitations. Bait fish greatly range in size—some more than two feet long. This of course, is too big of a fly to cast but with a heavy rod, an eight- to ten-inch fly isn't out of the question. It's important to realize though, that the larger the fly, the more difficult it is to cast.

Reel Good Advice

Size and shape should be two of the most important things to think about when choosing a saltwater fly pattern.

➤ **Shape.** The shape of the fly can be important when matching the naturals. Wide-bodied fish, like mullet and mackerel should be imitated with wide-bodied flies. Thin or narrow fish, like needle-fish, sand eels, smelt, and sardines should be imitated with patterns of similar shape.

➤ **Behavior.** Try to match the behavior of the food you are imitating. For instance, most bait fish swim through the water with a darting motion. Study the swimming motion of the bait you are imitating and mimic this action. Experiment with your retrieve; vary the length of each strip from a few inches to a foot and vary the time paused in between each strip until you start hooking up.

These are some basic characteristics to think about when choosing an appropriate pattern. But as with freshwater fishing, presentation outweighs everything. No matter how perfect you think your imitation may be, you won't catch fish if you spook them or can't cast your fly quickly and accurately to get it to them.

The Dirty Dozen Flies

The following dozen flies and recipes have been proven successes over and over. These are, of course, just a few recommendations out of the more than 350 popular saltwater fly patterns regularly used today.

Although most of the recipes are relatively easy, many of the required techniques are quite different than the ones we discussed earlier. The best way to learn how to tie these saltwater flies is by taking a class, watching an expert, watching videos, or reading specialized books on the subject.

These popular flies are regular producers and should be carried in just about every fly box. They have been proven time and time again to be extremely effective patterns. Don't be afraid to make small changes when you tie these flies. Experiment with materials and colors until you find a good producer.

Some All-Purpose Patterns

These few patterns can be used to imitate just about any bait fish in the ocean. They are general all-purpose patterns that are widely used all over the world. No fly box is complete without several variations of each of these flies.

Fish Tails

The Lefty's Deceiver is probably the most widely used pattern by all saltwater fly fishermen. Invented by Lefty Kreh, a household name among just about all fly fishermen, the Lefty's Deceiver has turned into a whole family of fly patterns. It can be tied on a wide variety of hook sizes with a wide array of materials in just about any color.

Lefty's Deceiver

Designed by fly fishing legend Lefty Kreh, this all-purpose fly is the most popular saltwater fly ever used. Depending on the materials used, how it is tied, and the size of the pattern, deceivers can be used to imitate just about any species of bait fish around the world. It can be tied in a variety of hook sizes and several different deceiver patterns should fill every saltwater fly box.

Lefty's Deceiver.

Here is the recipe for the White-Grizzly Deceiver, which in Lefty Kreh's book *Saltwater Fly Patterns*, he claims is his favorite. It is just one of several deceiver recipes listed:

Thread: Red

Hook: Standard length, straight eye

Size: 6 to 3/0 are most popular, but it can be as large as a 7/0 for larger species of game fish.

Wing: White saddle hackles with a natural grizzly feather secured on the outside. Several strands of rainbow or pearl Crystal Flash on both sides.

Beard: Red

Topping: Either green Crystal Flash or strands of peacock herl

Collar: White bucktail, with a short natural grizzly hackle on each side.

Head: Red

Black Deceiver

This excellent pattern, as well as most black colored flies, seems to work well in whitewater or off-colored water. Here is the recipe for the Black Deceiver:

Thread: Black

Hook: 6 to 3/0

Wing: Black hackle with black Crystal Flash or Flashabou on each side

Collar: Black calf or bucktail

Head: Black

Catch Words

The **Clouser Minnow** is a famous fly designed by Bob Clouser.

The Clouser Minnow

This legendary fly was created by Bob Clouser. It has evolved into a whole fleet of fly patterns used to imitate several different species of bait fish. Here is just one of several recipes that works well for imitating bait fish:

The Clouser Minnow.

Thread: Gray

Hook: 6 to 6/0 for the blue-water fishing

Eyes: Metallic (lead, pewter, brass, and so on)

Wings: White bucktail with pearl Crystal Flash. Green or gray bucktail as the upper wing

Head: Gray

Surf Candy

With small modifications, this lifelike imitation can imitate just about any bait fish in the ocean. Bob Popovics invented this popular fly to imitate anchovy, mackerel, sardines, and many other bait fish. The most effective patterns are two to four inches long. Here is the recipe:

Thread: Many colors will work but usually white

Hook: 2 to 2/0

Wing: Various colors of Ultra Hair blended together with flash for the tail and body. A light coat of five-minute epoxy is used to form the body and hold its shape.

Eyes: Prismatic stick-on eye

Gills: Red markings with a permanent pen on the epoxy

Head and body: More epoxy over the entire body

Sand Eel Patterns

This pattern represents a major food source for game fish—sand eels. These long, eel-like fish, also called sand lance, are found in just about all inshore water types in the north and mid-Atlantic and Pacific coasts. They bury themselves in the sand overnight, then form heavy schools during the day. Fish go into feeding frenzies over these easy to catch meals. Sand eel imitations should be two to five inches long and tied very sparsely. A slow retrieve with a short dashing motion works well for imitating these fish. Here is the recipe for a Clouser Minnow Sand Eel:

Cut Bait

Be careful not to tie sand eel patterns too bulky—the naturals are very thin fish.

341

Clouser Minnow Sand Eel

Another pattern out of the Clouser family of flies, this fly is a regular producer.

Thread: Gray

Hook: 4-1

Wing: Long white and gray bucktail with some pearl Crystal Flash

Eyes: Painted silver (smallest size)

Head: Gray

Reel Good Advice

When fishing in an area with large schools of bait, present your fly to the side or below the school. Game fish love solitary fish.

Sand Eel

This sand eel pattern doesn't look much like the natural when dry, but it is deadly when wet. It is tied with long wings that should breathe when retrieved. Here is one of several sand eel recipes:

Thread: Tan or brown

Hook: 1/0 to 3/0

Body: Silver Mylar piping

Wing: FisHair or Ultra Hair, white and olive-green

Head: Tan

Eye: Painted white with black pupil

Shrimp

Like humans, game fish enjoy feasting on these delicacies. Shrimp are an important source of food in just about any shallow water, especially estuaries and flats. When active, shrimp swim in an upward motion. Imitating this behavior is similar to imitating many freshwater nymphs and emergers. Let the fly sink to the bottom, then lift it towards the surface and repeat the process. When frightened, shrimp quickly dart in short bursts. Short, fast retrieves work well for imitating this behavior.

Crazy Charlie

Although there are several excellent shrimp imitations that are widely used, Clouser Minnow patterns will work (as they work well to imitate almost any bait). Some shrimp patterns are tied on hooks with the point facing up, also called *bend-back* flies. These are used to prevent your fly from getting snagged in weeds or rocky shorelines. Here is one of several Crazy Charlie recipes, a very popular fly invented by Bob Nauheim.

The Crazy Charlie.

Hook: Size 2 to 6; 4 is very popular

Thread: Pink

Body: Clear monofilament wrapped with pink Flashabou then wrapped again with clear monofilament

Wing: Pink Crystal Flash

Eyes: Lead (red eye with black pupil)

The Snapping Shrimp

The snapping shrimp is a major food source for bonefish. This snapping shrimp pattern was invented by Chico Fernandez. Here is its recipe:

Thread: Brown

Hook: 2 to 6

Body: Light tan synthetic dubbing or yarn with a small band of orange dubbing at the bend of the hook

Wing: Brown Fish Hair

Head: Brown

Eyes: White with black pupil

Crabs

Crabs are a delicacy for a number of game fish including: bonefish, permit, spotted sea trout, cobia, redfish and snook, among others. They are found along open beaches, shorelines, estuaries, and in the flats.

Del Brown's Permit Fly or Crab Fly

There are several different patterns tied to imitate these creatures but the most popular is perhaps Del Brown's Permit Fly or Crab Fly (since permits eat crabs almost exclusively). Pick a pattern that resembles the size, body shape and color of the crabs in your favorite water and you should have some luck. Here is the recipe for Del Brown's Permit Fly:

Hook: 2 to 1/0

Tail: Pearl Flashabou with flared ginger hackle tips (roughly six)

Legs: Rubber bands tied to the hook shank

Body: Tan and brown yarn tied with bright green thread

Eyes: Lead eyes

Bonefish Special

This deadly pattern was developed by Chico Fernandez, a world-renowned fly fisherman.

Hook: Size 2 to 6

Thread: Black

Tail: Orange Marabou

Body: Clear monofilament wrapped with gold Mylar or Flashabou along the full length of hook

Wing: White calf tail or bucktail with a grizzly saddle tip on each side

Head: Black

Poppers

Poppers are surface patterns that are used to attract fish. They are tied to imitate a wounded bait fish, fighting relentlessly in an effort to make it for cover. A good popper pattern should imitate this commotion on the surface of the water. It should make splashy noises when retrieved and leave a small wake on the surface of the water.

Catch Words

Poppers are patterns that float on the surface of the water to attract fish.

Dahlberg Diver

Like most saltwater baits, a few patterns are all that's needed to cover most situations. Here is a recipe for the Dahlberg Diver, first created by Larry Dahlberg. It is usually tied with a weed guard.

Thread: Color to match fly

Hook: 2 through 3/0

Tail: Marabou with Crystal Flash on either side

Body: Thread body

Head: Spun deer hair trimmed with a taper nose and a flared-back collar

The Popping Bug (or Skipping Bug)

These successful patterns were created by Bill Gallasch, of Richmond, Virginia. They can be tied in a variety of sizes and colors. Here is one of many recipes for Bill's Popping Bug:

Hook: Long shank size 4 through 7/0 (for large blue water species)

Tail: Bucktail with some flash

Body: Either foam or cork, tapered or pre-shaped. After the tail is tied in, glue or epoxy the body on to the hook. It can then be painted a variety of colors including red and white, black, blue and white, yellow, cream, or silver.

Reel Good Advice

The size of a popper should match the depth of the water. That is, small poppers should be used in shallow water and larger patterns used in deeper water.

Setting the Hook

Now that you should have a good idea as to what flies to use, it's time to learn how to set the hook. Like newcomers to freshwater fly fishing, this is one of the hardest things for beginners in saltwater fly fishing. Fortunately, many of the same rules apply to both fishing situations. The most important thing to remember is to let the fish take the fly. That is, don't set the hook prematurely.

Depending on the circumstance, each species of saltwater game fish takes the fly a little differently. Some fish take the fly very nonchalantly while others strike with such aggression you may be scared to land it. And how hard a fish strikes is no indication of its size. Even big fish, like tarpon for instance, can take a fly very gently while smaller fish may strike with a vengeance. Whatever the case, make sure you let the fish actually take the fly before setting the hook.

It is just as important to remember not to set the hook too hard. This is a hard habit to kick with most beginner fly fishermen, especially if they have a spin casting background. But remember, setting the hook to hard will do one of two things:

1. Pull the hook right out of the fish before it penetrates.
2. Snap your leader.

Like I said earlier, sharp hooks can be the difference between catching a fish and losing a fish. Make sure you properly file the hook every time it is used and check it periodically while fishing. Hooks become dull very quickly in the saltwater.

There are a few different methods used to set the hook. Some saltwater anglers don't use the rod at all. They actually hold the rod underneath their casting arm and keep it low and pointed at the fish. Then they use both hands to strip line in. This works very well and allows you to strip line at an incredible speed. I admit, it looks a little funny and it's hard to believe you can get enough power to hook a fish, but you can. The beauty of this technique is that if you miss a strike or a fish refuses your offering, you simply continue to retrieve line and you don't spook the fish. You also don't have to make another cast to get it there like you would otherwise.

Cut Bait

Never have more excess line next to you than you need. It will only increase the chance of it getting snagged around your legs, the butt of your rod, or other fishing gear.

Another way to set the hook is to sweep your rod to the side of your body. This serves the same purpose as the two hand retrieve—if you miss the fish, you get a second chance on the same drift. The most common method, however, is to strike with a straight pull with your line hand.

Whatever method you employ, you must know what to do when you do hook a fish. Rather than getting caught up in the excitement of the fish, think about where your excess line is. If you're not paying attention, you will often find it wrapped around your leg, caught on the boat, or strung around the butt of your fly rod just after the fish snaps off. Trust me, unfortunately it has happened to me enough to be an expert on the subject. Not until you've cleared all of the excess line is it time to start thinking about the fight.

The Big Fight

The biggest thrill in saltwater fly fishing is, of course, the fight. Most saltwater fish are strong and powerful and fight like Mike Tyson. And these fish are large. As a matter of fact, most of the trout you may have caught in freshwater are not much bigger than the bait fish you will be imitating in saltwater. This is one of the main reasons why the sport is booming and much of the growth is from freshwater fly fishermen. Stories of fighting bonefish, tarpon, and permit tease any fly fisherman who has never fished for them before.

For all practical purposes, the fight doesn't really start until you have the fish on the reel. That is, until all of your slack is fed to the fleeing fish and your drag kicks in. If you lose a fish before this point, it doesn't really count as a fight. Unfortunately this happens quite frequently—your spare line gets caught on something and the fish snaps you off. Sure it was exciting, but more of a tease than anything.

There are a few things to remember once the fish in on your reel. First of all, their first run is almost always the most powerful. Not only does the fish realize it just got hooked, it also has the most energy. Don't try to tame the fish at this point—it will only break off. Instead, let the fish run under a light amount of pressure. Whenever a fish makes a fast run, point your rod directly at the fish and keep the tip close to the water. What you do next depends on two things:

1. If the fish swims back toward you after a run, either reel in the excess line or strip it in as quickly as possible.

2. If the fish just slows down after its initial run, bring the fish closer to you by *pumping* the rod.

Catch Words

Pumping the rod is a technique used to bring a fish closer to you.

Pump That Fish!

Pumping the fly rod is an excellent technique used to bring a fish closer to you. To do it, simply lift the rod tip up to bring the fish in and let it back down to reel in the excess line. It should be done with a fluid motion, not a snapping motion. In order to win the battle, you need to keep constant pressure on the fish.

Start the pumping action with your fly rod aimed directly at the fish. Keep the tip low—just above the surface of the water—and raise your rod tip with enough force to steer the fish in your direction. Now lower the rod tip, but make sure you still have pressure on the fish (the tip should still be bent) and reel in the excess slack. If the fish makes a run, quit pumping and point the rod-tip directly at the fleeing fish. This will reduce the amount of drag that is applied and let the fish run more easily. Once the fish slows down, the pumping action resumes. As you will notice, your reel is only used to bring in slack line, not to fight the fish. This is the rod's job.

Like rainbow trout, many species of saltwater fish like to get airborne—only there is a big difference. Unlike rainbows, some saltwater fish catch big air—I mean greater than 10 feet high! Like we discussed earlier, in order to give them the slack they need, it is important to bow to these fish. With out appropriate slack, they will surely break you off.

Reel Good Advice

When fighting a fish, never give it a chance to relax. This will only give it a second wind and increase its chances to win the battle.

Landing the Fish

The two most common times to lose a saltwater fish is before the battle—when your excess line gets snagged, and after the battle—when you're ready to land the fish. It happens for the same reason both times—the leader snaps from too much pressure. The key to fighting and landing a fish is to keep constant pressure on your leader. That is, don't give the leader any slack or it will snap when abrupt pressure is applied.

The techniques used to land a fish depend on what type of water you are fishing. If you are fishing from the beach, you can use the surf to help bring the fish in to the shore. That is, use an incoming wave to more or less surf the fish in. As the wave recedes, release some pressure and allow the fish to recede with it. If you have its head pointed toward you, any struggle will only bring the fish closer to you.

Fishing from a boat is a different story. Chances are, the fish will make one final run when you get him close to you or your boat. Often, it will dash underneath the boat in an effort to snap the leader. Don't worry if this happens—it can still be landed without too much difficulty. To keep the leader from snapping, simply submerge the point of your fly rod in the water. Even bent, a nine-foot fly rod will help clear the line and leader away from your boat. Now, with the rod still pointed down in the water, try to steer the fish back towards you. If it that doesn't work, carefully walk around the *stern* (back) or *bow* (front) of the boat with your tip in the water and continue to tire out the fish. Once the fish surrenders, which may take a while, it must be landed. But be careful, a fish will often make one final attempt to escape—respect its desire and feed line out if necessary. Otherwise, it will simply snap you off.

It usually requires a team effort to land a large game fish from a boat—they are nearly impossible to net or gaff on your own. Always stand behind the guy with the net and steer the fish into it head first. This way, if it struggles, it will struggle right into the net.

It is extremely important that you tire out any game fish that you plan on bringing on board a boat. I have heard stories of restless fish flipping around on deck and smashing gear, rods, and people.

Cut Bait

Brightly colored nets have the tendency to spook fish. Purchase a net that is as color-friendly as possible. That is, one that blends in with the natural environment.

Steer the Fish

When fighting saltwater game fish, it is important to steer its head in the right direction in order to bring it closer to you. If you are fishing in an area that has lots of obstructions or weeds, you must have a plan of attack for when you hook up. Coral, weeds, jetties, buoys, boats, and so on can all snag your line or snap your leader in a heartbeat. And like the wily brown trout, saltwater fish use these obstructions to their advantage. They will wrap around any obstructions in the water, trying to snap the leader in the process.

Releasing Your Catch

Like when freshwater fishing, it is good practice to release the majority of your catch. Although the ocean is a huge place, fishermen do have an impact on the fish. When releasing a fish, exercise the same principles that you apply in freshwater.

There are two important things to remember in order to increase the odds a fish will survive.

1. The less a fish is handled, the greater its chances of survival. Fish have a protective coating that gets removed when handled. To minimize this, be sure to wet your hands and net before handling a fish.

2. The less tired it is when released, the greater its chance of survival. If you plan to release a fish, bring it in as quickly as possible.

Getting the hook out depends largely on the size of the fish. Keep smaller fish in the water and use hemostats or pliers to remove the hook. Larger fish must be netted or a release *gaff* must be placed in the fish's jaw while the fly is released. If the fly is too deep, cut the leader as close to the fly as possible before releasing the fish.

Catch Words

A **gaff** is a long device with a hook on the end commonly used on boats to land a fish.

Watch It—They're Dangerous

You must practice extra caution when handling saltwater game fish. Most of them have either razor sharp teeth, spiny bodies, sharp gill plates, or sharp tails. Some species, like bluefish for example, seem to have excellent vision out of the water and are known to bite after being landed. Use gloves and common sense when handling these fish.

The Least You Need to Know

➤ Choosing the right saltwater pattern isn't as tricky as choosing the right freshwater pattern. For the most part, the fish aren't nearly as picky.

➤ A few all-purpose flies, such as the Deceiver and Clouser's Minnow, can be used to imitate just about any bait fish.

➤ Saltwater flies should match their surroundings. Dark color flies work well in dark bottomed areas and light patterns work well in light areas.

➤ Always keep constant pressure on a fish in battle; otherwise, it will snap your leader.

➤ Always wear gloves when handling saltwater fish. Many species have sharp teeth, spiny bodies, or sharp tails.

Chapter 28

There Are More Fish in the Sea...

In This Chapter

➤ Popular saltwater game fish

➤ Where they live

➤ The equipment used

➤ Handling concerns

Although you have probably heard the expression "There are more fish in the sea," more often than not, it's when someone gets dumped by a girlfriend or boyfriend. It is true, however—there are more fish in the sea. And, fortunately, most of them are catchable with fly tackle.

This chapter is a list of the most commonly sought after saltwater fish, some of their characteristics, and special considerations each one may have.

Saltwater fishing is quite the adventure, and hooking some of these fish—particularly the real fighters—can be the experience of a lifetime.

The Saltwater Lineup

Here is a list of some of the most common saltwater game fish. All of these will take a fly, and they can all be landed—with varying degrees of difficulty—on fly tackle. So without further ado, here's the saltwater lineup.

Tarpon

Tarpon make the top of the saltwater game fish list because they have it all. They grow to large sizes, they're incredible fighters, and they are very commonly sought after (and caught). Small tarpon, also called *baby tarpon*, are up to fifty or sixty pounds. The larger adults, however, grow to upwards of 150 pounds. They eat a variety of foods but primarily schooling bait fish such as sardines, mullet, and anchovies. They will also eat a wide array of crustaceans.

Tarpon.

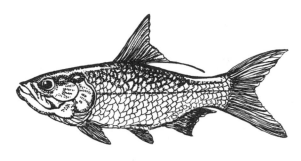

Catch Words

Since tarpon can grow to such huge sizes, tarpon smaller than 50 or 60 pounds are called **baby tarpon**.

Cut Bait

Tarpon are large fish, and playing them can be treacherous. As they approach your boat, beware of their ability to actually jump aboard and cause considerable damage. Also be aware of their size, strength, and their potential to pull you into the water!

Another reason tarpon top the list is their willingness to take flies. A mystifying quality of tarpon is that even the biggest ones have a strong tendency to take small (for saltwater fish) flies. Fishing from a skiff (a type of boat) with a guide or wading the flats and waiting for the fish to pass are the most popular methods for tarpon fishing. These monstrous fish thrive in tropical and warm coastal waters. They inhabit relatively shallow water—12 feet is about the maximum for the largest, while you'll find the smallest tarpon in as little as shin-deep water in the flats.

Tarpon are among the hardest fighting fish. They will jump nearly ten feet in the air and ten feet side-to-side. They make vicious runs in excess of a hundred yards. Obviously, back your line up! There are considerations to make when fighting tarpon. The larger variety do not tire easily (as a matter of fact, I would venture to bet that you will tire much more quickly than they will!), so the fight may not end when the fish is boated. The gill plates and scales of tarpon are very abrasive and capable of inflicting horrible injury and damage. Likewise, as you get your tarpon close to the boat, beware of the fish's ability to leap up and into your craft and wreak havoc upon your equipment and you! All the while, a big tarpon is quite capable of pulling a fisherman into the water.

Because of their large, up-turned lower jaw, tarpon are easy to identify. They cruise around in small schools when feeding, and can be spotted at a distance (the schools get larger during spawning). A tarpon in clear water may be seen as a dark spot in the water. You may see them rolling about on the very surface. When you do spot them, cast ahead of them and pull your streamer in with steady pulls.

Since tarpon vary in size, it's difficult to recommend one fly rod outfit for tarpon fishing. If you are after baby tarpon, bring a nine-foot, nine- or ten-weight fly rod outfit. A twelve-weight fly rod outfit will be needed for the larger species.

Sailfish—Younger (Smaller) Brother of the Marlin

Moving along in the category of "exciting saltwater fish to catch," sailfish are sleek fish that even *look* fast. Everything about these rocket-shaped animals suggests speed. Larger sailfish can move through the water at over 60 miles per hour. The two varieties—the main difference being their size and where they are found (Pacific sailfish are found in that ocean, while Atlantic, obviously, are found in the Atlantic)—have blue-black backs and silvery sides. Their nose is a long, thin bill like a saber and a huge black fin like a sail adorns their back. The smaller of the two, the Atlantic sailfish, tops out at about 130 pounds and eight feet long. The Pacific sailfish, on the other hand, grows up to 10 feet long and weighs in at up to 240 pounds.

Sailfish.

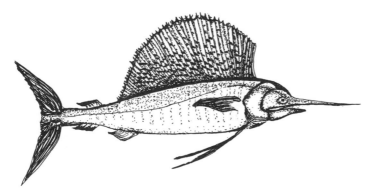

Most sailfish that are caught run about fifty to seventy pounds, although they occasionally exceed one hundred. Like the tarpon, sailfish are exceptional leapers. These fish will jump well above the water's surface, shake about up there for awhile, and finally fall over sideways. It is quite a spectacular sight.

Sailfish eat a variety of foods. Squid, octopus, mackerel, bonito, tuna, and smaller bait fish make up the majority of a sailfish's diet. Although they don't grow to the huge sizes of some of their relatives like marlin, sailfish eat quite a bit. Being as powerful and strong as sailfish takes energy, and, for a fish, energy is food.

Reel Good Advice

When fishing for billfish like sailfish and marlin, you must set the hook several times in order to penetrate their hard mouths.

These prize-fighting game fish are spread throughout the world's tropical and warm water seas. Fly fishing is done from a boat in the blue water with eight and a half to nine-foot fly rods equipped with 12- to 14-weight lines and 300 yards of 30-pound backing.

Marlin—Remember Santiago

If you have read *The Old Man and the Sea*, then you already have some experience with marlin. If you haven't read Hemingway's classic, put this book down right now, go to the library, and read it! You want to be an angler, right? *The Old Man and the Sea* (and this book) are required reading for every fisher.

Hemingway's hero, named Santiago, manages to hook one of the larger species of marlins—probably a blue marlin, which, at their largest, weigh in at over a ton. Hopefully, you will be better equipped than Santiago, with his hand lines. (It should be noted, also, that Hemingway's old man did not hook his monster on a fly; he was using live bait.) Maybe you will, like the old man, see the shape of a fish on the end of your line pass under your boat, and whisper to yourself in shock: "No, it can't be *that* big!"

Marlin look, eat, and act like sailfish, except for one thing: they are bigger. The smaller species of marlin—the white—grows up to 200 pounds, while the striped grows to almost 700. The larger species of marlin—the black and the blue—grow to almost 2,000 pounds! The largest sizes yet landed with fly tackle are just under 200 pounds.

These are awesome fish. Like the sailfish, they are fighters. Marlin are known for their acrobatics and leaping ability and for their powerful runs through the water. Many more marlin get hooked than caught, which makes them that much more sporty.

If you have the fortune—good or bad—to hook a marlin, remember it. You are in for one of the most incredible experiences (and exhausting battles) of your life.

Fly rod outfits should range between eight and a half and nine feet long. They should be equipped with 12- to 14-weight fly lines. Like sailfish, marlin are caught from boats in the blue water.

Barracuda—Armed and Dangerous

Barracudas are mean fish that have mean teeth to match. The largest of these fish grow up to over 100 pounds, and they are fighters. If you plan to fish for these, be careful. Their teeth are razor sharp, and they are aggressive by nature.

Barracuda.

Everything about them suggests bully. Barracuda eat injured or smaller young barracuda, in addition to bonefish, needlefish, mullet, and a variety of other bait fish. They are very quick. The run of a barracuda can be over two hundred yards, and they can be incredibly fast. They do, however, tire out very easily. Again, the teeth on these vicious fish are extremely dangerous, so take caution!

Barracuda are found in just about all water types, from shallow flats to the blue water. They should be fished with nine-foot rods equipped with an eight- or nine-weight fly line and a wire shock tippet to combat their sharp teeth.

Cut Bait

Beware of the extremely sharp teeth of the barracuda. They have powerful jaws equipped with large canine teeth for grabbing their prey and a row of very sharp teeth used to shred it.

Bonefish

Bonefish are perhaps the most popular saltwater fly fishing quarry; especially in the shallows. They are known for their incredible speeds and amazing stamina. Stories of landing bonefish on a fly kicked off the saltwater fly fishing boom. They are found in tropical and subtropical waters worldwide and are willing takers of artificial flies. They are most often fished for in shallow flats with muddy or sandy bottoms.

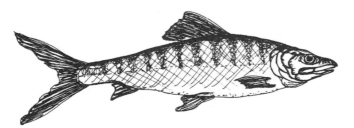

Bonefish.

Grayish-silver in color, most bonefish caught are in the two to four pound range though they have been known to grow to over 19 pounds. To date, the largest bonefish caught on a fly rod weighed 14.8 pounds and was taken in Islamorado, Florida.

Bonefish live in the shallow flats and feed on shrimp, crabs, mollusks, worms, sea urchins, and small bait fish. They usually feed on the bottom and often stick their tail out of the water. This tailing behavior is a great indication of their whereabouts. Large adult bonefish cruise in alone, or in small schools. The younger ones however, form much larger schools.

Bonefish are not fish that you toss your fly in the water and wait for a hit. With bonefish, you must first locate your quarry, and then make your cast. Lead the fish by several feet. It is now that you learn whether the bonefish liked your presentation or not. Like the wary brown trout in freshwater fishing, there is not much margin for error with bonefish. These fish get spooked very easily when presented with a sloppy cast or a loud vibration in the water.

Once hooked, the fight of a bonefish is not marked by thrashing or jumping, but their initial strike and run is very spirited. Bonefish are hardy fish that will not simply swim to the boat.

Reel Good Advice

When fishing for bonefish, you don't cast and wait. You must wait until you see one, then cast to it. Bonefish will not come looking for your bait; you need to present it right to them.

Bonefish like crunchy food. Mollusks, shrimp, crab, as well as small fry of other fish are tasty morsels to the bonefish. Bonefish are specially equipped to handle this type of fare, and this is something you will want to take note of when it comes to handling these fish. Bonefish are equipped with crushers in the back of their mouth, designed specifically for crushing the shells of crustaceans and the like. Do not put your hand in their mouth!

A nine-foot fly rod loaded with an eight or nine-weight floating fly line is most commonly used for bonefish. Shrimp and crab fly patterns are usually the most productive.

The Elusive Permit

Permit are more difficult to catch than most saltwater fish. Let me rephrase that. Permit are probably the most difficult fish in the ocean to catch (besides some of those cryptic deep-living dwellers that we can't reach). Permit inhabit the same waters as bonefish, but are extremely finicky in their eating habits—especially when it comes to imitation food. This is why fly fishing for permit has become extremely popular in recent years—fly fishermen crave a challenge and this fish is it. Besides being difficult to fool, permit are also difficult to land. Some people claim that inch for inch, they are the strongest fish in the ocean.

Permit.

Permit are fairly large, ranging in size from five to 50 pounds. Unfortunately, most landed permit weigh in at around ten pounds. Silver to green in color, the permit wins the award for "largest forehead."

Very similar to fishing for bonefish, you must first spot a permit before casting your fly. Since they are often feeding on crabs on the bottom in shallow water, you can often see their tails sticking through the surface of the water.

Crab is the mainstay in a permit's diet, and this single-minded culinary interest makes them difficult to hook. Permit spook even more easily than bonefish, and it is this characteristic that makes catching one a feat. Hooking a permit isn't the only hard part; they are fighters, too. The initial run of a permit is strong. The fight's tone changes when the permit turns broadside towards you. This makes it extremely difficult to work a permit in. As noted above, permit can be very large—usually ranging in the 10-pound range, permit grow to over 50.

Permit are single-minded fish in that they concentrate on looking for food. If you don't make accurate casts to get your fly right in front of them, your chances are slim. Use flies that mirror their favorite food: crabs.

A nine-foot fly rod loaded with a ten-weight floating fly line is most often used for permit fishing in the flats.

Bluefish

Bluefish are a great saltwater quarry simply because they have such an insatiable appetite and the willingness to take flies. These popular game fish will also put up an incredible battle. Once hooked, expect lots of acrobatics and short, hard runs.

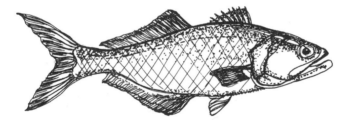

Bluefish.

Bluefish generally range between five to fifteen pounds, but are known to reach sizes of up to fifty pounds. These migratory fish roam the seas in large schools in search of bait fish. Once they find a school of bait fish, look out—they go into an absolute feeding frenzy and will eat just about anything in sight. As a matter of fact, I have heard stories of bluefish coming close to shore and biting swimmers in the ocean with their sharp, triangular teeth during a feeding frenzy. Keep this in mind when landing these nasty fish, and keep your hands away from their mouths and use long pliers to remove the hook while firmly holding the fish.

Since bluefish travel in such large groups, once you catch one, be ready for the fun to begin—most likely you will catch many more.

Cut Bait

Be careful when unhooking a bluefish. They have razor sharp teeth and are known to bite when out of water. Use long pliers to release the hook while holding the fish firmly in place.

357

These fish are indiscriminate in their food preferences and will attack a large array of artificial flies. They feed on various bait fish, including herring and silversides but will attack just about any fish in sight. Since most bluefish landed on a fly rod are in the five to 15-pound range, you don't need a super heavy fly rod outfit to land them. A nine-foot, eight or nine-weight fly rod works well for these fish. Due to their toothy mouths, it's necessary to use a shock tippet.

Stripers—Sittin' by the Dock of the Bay

Striped bass, or "stripers," frequent the bays and inlets of the Atlantic and Pacific coasts. Commercial fishing threatened to wipe these fish out 25 years ago, but, fortunately the situation has been reversed, due to strict regulations regarding minimum-sizes and seasons.

Striper.

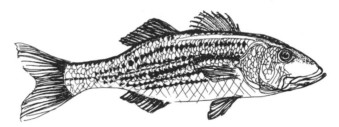

Stripers feed on smaller fish like herring and silversides, in addition to other bait fish, squid, crab, and shrimp. These are one of the few saltwater game fish that can be so selective in their eating habits you feel like you're fishing for trout. You often have to "match the hatch" to have any luck when fishing for stripers; that is, match the exact bait fish they are feeding on with an imitation. At other times, however, they will hit whatever is offered.

Reel Good Advice

When fishing from a boat, once you've found a school of feeding stripers, cut the engine and let the boat drift into a good casting position. Don't drive the boat right into the action—this will only spook the fish.

Like their freshwater counterparts, striped bass seek out structure. They can be found hanging around rock piles, rocky shorelines, jetties, channels, and so on—anywhere they can ambush bait fish. They can also be found on the flats in bays, estuaries, and river mouths but are most often fished for in the surf. They can tolerate extremely rough water and have adapted well to the rolling surf where they actually chase bait fish right up to the shoreline. Stripers were introduced to many freshwater reservoirs and lakes in the United States and seem to be doing very well.

Stripers are big fish; 20 pounders are common, and they grow to over 60. Stripers are light silver with darker horizontal stripes that run along their sides. They have sharp dorsal fins and gill plates so be careful when handling them.

The type of tackle you use depends on the size stripers you are pursuing. If you are after the small ones, also called *schoolies*, a heavy outfit is not needed. However, if you are going after the big boys in the 20 to 30 pound range, you'll need a nine-foot, 10-weight fly rod outfit. A shock tippet may also come in handy—the fish's sharp dorsal fin and gill plates may snap a tippet when the fish thrashes about.

Redfish

Redfish, also known as Red Drum or Channel Bass, have a reddish coloration and one or more dark spots at the base of their tail.

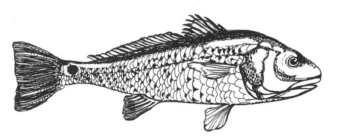

Redfish.

They aren't known as particularly hard fighters and probably won't give you an acrobatic show, but they do grow to respectable sizes. While smaller fish in the five to 10-pound range are often caught, red drum grow to sizes of 75 pounds or more.

Red Drum frequent some of the same waters along the Atlantic coast as bonefish and permit and often tail when they feed. When you see one, cast several feet ahead of it. Like bonefish, if you have tied on the right fly—and it's what the "redfish" (as they are often known) wants, it will probably strike. They are easy to spook but may not immediately take off like bonefish. They may hold their spot with no intention of feeding and tease you while you try to make the perfect presentation.

Red Drum frequent weedy, grassy, flat areas, channels and coves, and certain tidal rivers. They patrol these areas for a variety of food, including crustaceans like crab and shrimp, and a variety of other bait fish.

Like bonefish, red drum present the problem of the crushers at the back of the mouth. This characteristic enables them to crush the shells of the crustaceans they make their food, and it is critical that your hands stay away from this dangerous feature.

Catch Words

Red Drum, Redfish, and **Channel Bass** are all different names for the same fish.

Cut Bait

Be aware of the crushers at the back of a red drum's mouth. Keep your hands clear when handling the fish.

The ideal fly rod set up for most Red Drum would be a nine-foot fly rod equipped with a floating eight or nine-weight fly line.

Spotted Sea Trout

Spotted Sea Trout are not relatives of freshwater trout. The speckles about the spotted sea trout's back and sides resemble some of the markings of their freshwater counterparts, but they share no direct lineage.

Spotted Sea Trout.

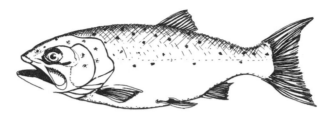

Sea trout live up and down the Atlantic coast and into the Gulf of Mexico. Look for them close to shore in the grassy areas that are home to lots of shrimp. Mullet, crabs, and bait fish make up the rest of the spotted sea trout's diet.

Like many of the other saltwater fish mentioned, it is important to avoid the crushing teeth in the larger species. Handle these fish with care when removing the hook.

Deceiver's and the Clouser Minnow are old standbys for Spotted Sea Trout, as are many other shrimp and crab imitations. Typically at about two to three pounds, these are not the biggest fish you will pull out of the ocean, but they are known to exceed ten pounds at times.

A nine-foot fly rod equipped with a seven or eight-weight floating fly line works well when fishing for Spotted Sea Trout.

Weakfish—Relative of the Spotted Sea Trout

Weakfish are not necessarily weaklings. Steady fighters, weakfish got their name because of the soft, or weak, and fleshy mouths—a feature to consider when playing these fish. If you try to pull a weakfish in too quickly when landing it, you will more than likely rip the hook out of its mouth.

Weakfish.

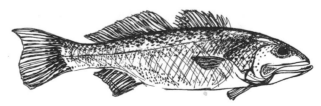

Weakfish can be found in just about all water types, but they are best fished for in the shallows or smaller creeks where they will put up a decent fight. Rather than hard-running fish, weakfish are head-shakers. That is, they will violently shake their heads in an effort to dislodge the hook. Unlike most of the other species mentioned, there aren't many handling concerns to worry about with weakfish. They don't have spiny gill plates or sharp tails or teeth. They do, however, have large canine front teeth that they use for snacking on bigger bait fish but they don't pose much of a threat to the fisherman as long as pliers are used to release the hook.

Weakfish eat worms, crabs, shrimp, and bait fish, and they are found around the southern Atlantic coast and the Gulf of Mexico. A nine-foot, seven to eight-weight fly rod works well for weakfish fishing.

Reel Good Advice

Weakfish are not named for their strength or lack thereof. They are named because their mouth is soft—a characteristic that brings up special considerations as to how to strike and play this fish.

Snook

This popular game fish has a history of being loved to death. Both private and commercial fishermen have always loved this tasty white-fleshed fish and caught it in great numbers. Some harvesting restrictions and other protections finally saved this weird looking game fish and they are making a comeback. Although they are extremely tasty, I highly recommend letting them go—at least until their populations have fully bounced back.

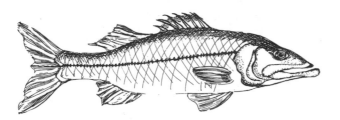

Snook.

Besides being a delicacy, snook are also known for their excellent fighting abilities. They jump, run, dive—everything that makes a great fighting fish. Just be careful of their sharp gill plates when handling them.

Snook resemble a pike with their elongated lower jaw and aggressive eating habits. They average between five to eight pounds, but some are much, much larger—reaching over 50 pounds. They have a single black lateral stripe that reaches their tail.

Like bass, snook ambush their prey from well-protected areas. Look for them around any structure in the water; docks, bridges, rock piles, tree roots, and so on and cast accordingly. They are opportunistic feeders and will hit just about any well presented fly that resembles a bait fish, shrimp or crab. Although they are most often caught in coastal areas, they also inhabit mangrove swamps, creeks, and inland rivers and canals.

They prefer warm waters (above 59 degrees), so they are found only in the southern-most American waters and down. A nine-foot, eight-weight fly rod is ideal for the average snook.

Shark

If you want to raise some eyebrows, say you're fishing for sharks. If you want to get a good laugh, say you're fly fishing for them. Believe it or not, however, you can catch sharks on a fly.

Shark.

Don't take the endeavor lightly, of course. Sharks bring with them several safety issues. Sharks stretch to as long as fifteen feet and can weigh hundreds of pounds, so you want to be prepared before bringing one on board. The first, foremost, and most obvious consideration regarding sharks are their teeth. Rows of sharp teeth fill their mouth. Sharks also have extremely abrasive skin—like a high-grade sand paper—so wear gloves when handling them. It is never wise to bring a large fish of any kind—especially sharks—onto a boat without assistance.

Fish Tails

Sharks are one of the most ancient fish in the ocean. Rather than having a skeleton of bones like most animals, they have cartilaginous skeletons. The whale shark is the world's largest fish and is thought to grow to over fifty feet and 77,000 pounds!

In the case of a shark, someone needs to hold the head tightly from behind, while someone else works the hook free. In the case of exceptionally large sharks, don't bother bringing it on board. Cut your leader, and let it take your fly.

Sharks eat other fish. The adage that blood attracts sharks is mostly true; sharks will most definitely feed on injured fish. Sharks can be found in just about every water type. Larger species are most often fished for in the blue water but smaller sharks also provide excellent fly fishing opportunities in the flats and channels.

The fly tackle used to land sharks obviously depends on what size shark you are pursuing. Small sharks in the flats can be landed with a nine-foot, eight to nine-weight fly rod outfit. Of course, larger sharks in the deep water require much heavier tackle. Long, huge streamers, including Lefty's Deceiver and Tarpon Glo, work well for catching sharks.

Tuna—Not from the Can

Tuna come in various forms (and I'm not talking about in oil or water), ranging in size from the blackfin at 40 pounds to the bluefin at over 1500 pounds. Only the smaller species of tuna, those up to about 100 pounds, are affordable with a fly rod.

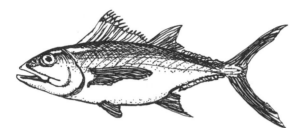

Black Fin Tuna.

These fish are strong; among the strongest game fish in the ocean. I will never forget watching my dad play a blackfin (or should I say, *holding on* to my dad while he played one), while it took us for a ride. Back and forth and back and forth, his tuna made run after run, until it finally tired out. Their stamina is even more impressive than their strength.

These are hard, strong fish, capable of damaging you and your gear. They are found in temperate and tropical waters all over the world and are a popular commercial fish as well as game fish. As a matter of fact, the commercial industry dwindled the numbers of certain species of tuna, along with many other popular game fish, with their huge drift nets. Fortunately, international agreements have placed certain restrictions on harvesting tuna with these nets and the fish have made a comeback.

Tuna eat all kinds of creatures: shrimp, octopus, flying fish, bait fish, and certain game fish. A variety of large bait fish and popper patterns work well for fooling these strong fish.

Smaller species of tuna, such as the Blackfin, can be landed with a nine-foot, nine-weight fly rod. Larger fish require a much larger outfit to have any luck. The largest species aren't possible to land on today's fly gear but who knows what the future has in store.

Snapper

Snappers are hard fighters. The fight of a snapper is typically marked by a ferocious initial strike followed by a hard first run.

Red Snapper.

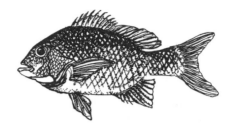

There are several hundred kinds of snappers—red, gray, cubera, lane, mutton, and so on. Mutton snapper are probably the most commonly pursued by the fly fishermen. They are easy to identify by a blue stripe running below each eye and a small dark spot on each side. They range in size from five to 10 pounds, although the largest exceed 25 pounds.

Snapper are most often found in tropical seas, though a few species are found in warm-temperate waters. Mutton snapper are regularly fished for throughout the Caribbean and off the southern coast of Florida. They actively feed in the flats, coral reefs, tidal channels, and creeks and put up an incredible fight once hooked.

Snappers feed on bait fish, shrimp, and crab, so streamers and poppers will prove effective. Once you land a snapper, you want to be very wary of its sharp teeth and powerful jaws.

A nine-foot fly rod equipped with a ten-weight fly line is necessary to fight these hard running fish. A heavier outfit with a tight drag mechanism may be desired when fishing near coral reefs. It will help overpower the fish and prevent snags and damage to your line.

Cut Bait

Snapper have incredibly strong jaws—use extra caution when unhooking your fly!

Mackerel

The hard runs of mackerel make for exciting fights. Their long stream-lined body and powerful tail and fins made for swift attacks make them the perfect game fish—as does their tasty flesh. Once hooked, they can be very difficult to land. The various types of mackerel range from two pounds to over 150 pounds.

Mackerel.

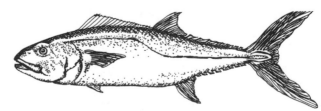

Mackerel are found in just about all parts of the ocean. They are fly-fished for in the reefs, surf, river mouths and inlets, and in the blue water with much success. Many species of mackerel, such as the king and Atlantic mackerel form huge schools as they roam the ocean in search of food. You can often see them close to shore feeding ravenously on smaller bait fish.

Fish Tails

Some species of fish in the mackerel family are able to fold their fins flush against their bodies into indented slots. This makes them more streamlined (hydrodynamic) and allows them to swim faster.

They eat all kinds of bait fish, so basic fly patterns work well. They are not known to be the most discriminate eaters but a good presentation is a must. They have very sharp teeth so practice extra caution when handling these fish—always use long-nosed pliers to release the hook and hold the fish firmly in place.

The tackle you use largely depends on the fish you are seeking. Since these fish vary so much in size per species, I can't recommend one fly fishing outfit.

Jack Crevalle

These funny-looking, broad-foreheaded fish in the jack family provide excellent fly fishing opportunities as they put up incredible fights for their sizes. Averaging at just a few pounds (although they have been known to reach over fifty pounds), their size is very deceiving; you will think you had hooked a fish twice their size when you finally bring it to shore. Their great power and remarkable speed make them an excellent fly rod quarry.

Jack Crevalle.

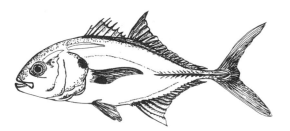

Jack Crevalle live in just about every type of tropical or warm temperate water. They can be caught in the flats, in the blue water, river mouths and channels, estuaries, and in the surf, where they are most often fished for. They can even be found up freshwater creeks and rivers where many other saltwater fish can't tolerate.

These fish form large schools and are typically seen quickly cruising the shoreline in search of bait fish. Once they find a school of bait fish, they'll herd it to the surface and make a commotion no fishermen could miss. Cast your popper (Jack Crevalle are a sucker for loud and obnoxious poppers) or streamer imitation right in this feeding frenzy and you will surely get a hit. Jack Crevalle also feed on crustaceans such as shrimp or crab and their imitations work as well as searching patterns.

There are many species of fish in the jack family, some much larger than the Jack Crevalle. The Almaco jack, for example, frequently weighs in at over 100 pounds while the greater Amberjack can reach over 150 pounds.

Be cautious when handling any members of this family; they have sharp spines and an abrasive tail. Also, seek local advice before eating these fish. Although some species can be tasty, others can give you a lethal dose of food poisoning.

Despite their small size, a nine-foot fly rod equipped with a seven or eight-weight floating fly line is ideal for muscling in these strong fish. A heavy shock tippet will also come in handy for combating their sharp teeth.

The Least You Need to Know

➤ You must practice extra caution when handling most species of saltwater fish. Many of them have sharp teeth, abrasive skin, and skin-puncturing gills.

➤ Tarpon are among the best fighting game fish. They usually reward you with a great acrobatics display.

➤ Sailfish can be as large as 250 pounds and can swim through the water up to 60 miles per hour!

➤ Bonefish are responsible for the boom in saltwater fly fishing. They are a strong running flats-fish that require a stealthy hunt as well as precision casting.

➤ Like bass, stripers seek out structure in the water to ambush their prey.

➤ Pound for pound, tuna are probably the strongest game fish in the ocean. Today's fly tackle can only handle tuna up to the 100–pound range.

Glossary

Action   Used to describe the flexibility or stiffness of a fly rod.

Anadromous Fish   Species of fish that have adapted to survive in both freshwater and saltwater environments.

Angler   One who fishes with a rod and reel.

Aquatic Insect   An insect that hatches and develops below the surface of the water. Most aquatic insects spend their adult lives out of the water.

Arbor   The center of a fly reel's spool.

Arbor Knot   A commonly used knot to apply the backing to the arbor of the reel.

Backing   Attached to the fly reel before the fly line. Backing serves two purposes. If a strong fighting game fish makes a run to the end of the fly line, the backing will give it more distance. It is also used to take up space on the fly reel. This increase in diameter makes the fly line easier to reel in.

Bait Fish   Any fish (usually in the minnow family) that is of primary prey for a larger fish.

Bank   The shoreline of a body of water.

Barb   A sharp point on the hook used to prevent a fish from slipping off.

Barbless Hook   A hook without a barb. Many catch and release fly fishermen smash the barb of the hook down to avoid injuring the fish.

Brackish Water   A mixture of both freshwater and saltwater.

Bucktail   A type of streamer that is tied with the hair from a bird's tail. Bucktail patterns are used to imitate bait fish.

Caddis Flies   An aquatic insect that goes through complete metamorphosis. Adult caddis flies have tent shaped wings. They are excellent sources of food for trout and a variety of other species.

Catch and Release   The act of releasing a fish after it is caught. The term is often used to describe water that has strict catch and release regulations.

Channel   A recession in a river, lake, or tidal area. Channels are usually formed by the main current of water.

Char   A popular gamefish that is a cousin of the trout family. A brook trout is actually in the char family.

Chum   Bait that is chopped up and thrown in the water to attract other fish.

Crustaceans   An animal that has a hard shell. Crustaceans are often found in both freshwater and saltwater; for example, shrimp and lobsters.

Current   The natural flow of water.

Damselfly   Resembling the dragonfly, damselfies are aquatic insects most often found in lakes and ponds. They are an important source of food for many species of fish.

Dapping   A fishing technique that uses very little, if any, line on the water. It is used to eliminate drag and present the fly to fish that hug the bank of a river.

Dead-Drift   When your fly drifts downstream with the natural pace of the current.

Drag   Drag has two definitions that pertain to fly fishing: (1) When your fly drifts in the water in an unnatural manner; (2) A device inside the reel that puts pressure on the fly line.

Dragonfly   A large predatory aquatic insect that usually matures in ponds and lakes. A close relative of the damselfly.

Dressing   The materials used to tie a fly. Dressing is also a liquid that is used for maximum fly buoyancy.

Drift   An artificial or natural fly's movement affected by the current of the water.

Dry Fly   An artificial fly tied to float on the surface of the water.

Dun   A stage of life in the mayfly's lifecycle. Duns hatch out of the surface of the water and offer an important source of food for many species of fish, especially trout.

Eddy   A spot in a section of moving water that hits an obstruction in its natural flow. Water in an eddy usually swirls in the opposite direction of the main current.

Emerger   An aquatic insect that emerges toward the surface of the water to hatch. It is also a type of fly that imitates this behavior.

False Cast   Casting the line back and forth to dry off the fly, feed line out for distance, or more accurately hit the target.

Floatant   A liquid or powder applied to a fly, fly line, or leader to increase its buoyancy.

Flat   A shallow section of water most often associated with saltwater. Flats can offer incredible fishing.

Fly   Any artificial bait tied on a hook with both natural and synthetic materials to imitate insects, fish, animals, worms, and so on.

Gaff   A long pole used to land a fish. Gaffs are most often used when fishing from a boat in the ocean.

Inshore Fishing   Refers to saltwater that is close to the shore, such as channels, estuaries, flats, coral reefs, and the surf.

Grilse   Salmon that return to their natal stream to mate after only one year in the ocean.

Guides   The wire loops on a fly rod that allow line to pass through.

Haul   A casting technique used to get more power on the fly line.

Hook Keeper   A small metal loop on some fly rods that is used to attach the fly when not in use.

Hook Shank   The top of the long section of a hook.

Jetty   A man-made structure designed to combat erosion on beaches and to prevent river channels from filling up.

Jigging   A technique used to bounce a fly on the bottom of the water.

Knotless Leader   A tapered leader that is manufactured from one single strand of tapered nylon. It is the link between the fly line and the fly.

Larva   The immature stage of an aquatic insect that goes through complete metamorphosis. *Larvae* for plural (pronounced *larv-ee*).

Leader   The tapered link between the fly and the fly line.

Leader Straightener   A patch of rubber used to get the kinks out of a leader.

Leech   An aquatic worm or a pattern tied to imitate it.

Marabou   A fuzzy feather used for fly tying.

Mayflies   A type of aquatic insect that provides food for a variety of fish. Mayflies have upright wings in the shape of a sail.

Mending   A technique used to reduce or avoid fly drag.

Midge   A small aquatic insect that thrives in just about all aquatic environments. Midges provide an excellent source of food for fish.

Milt   The secretion of a fish for reproduction.

Monofilament   A nylon line used in fly leaders.

Neap Tide   During the moon's first quarter and third quarter phases when the variation between high and low tides is very small.

Nesting   When a fish remains with its eggs for a period of time after spawning.

Nymph   An aquatic insect during its immature stage of development while underneath the surface of the water. *Nymph* has also become the generic term used for any fly pattern fished below the surface of the water, even if the imitation is not of the nymph stage of an aquatic insect. Fishing in this manner is called *nymphing*.

369

Offshore Fishing   Fishing from a boat away from land.

Panfish   A generic name for small freshwater fish.

Pocket Water   A small piece of water that usually sits behind a rock or other obstruction. Pockets provide excellent holding water for trout.

Pool   A slow moving, deep stretch of a stream or river.

Popper   An imitation fly that is used on the surface of the water. Poppers make a popping sound and splash the water to attract fish.

Pumping   A technique used when fighting a large fish.

Pupa   An immature stage of development for an aquatic insect or an imitation fly pattern that imitates this stage of life.

Reel   The device attached to a fly rod that is used to store, distribute, and recover fly line.

Riffle   A quick running, shallow choppy section of a river or stream.

Rise   When a fish rises to the surface to take either a natural or imitation fly.

Roll Cast   A method of casting that doesn't involve the back cast. It is an efficient technique in tight areas where a back cast isn't feasible.

Run   A smooth stretch of running water in a river or stream. Also, a term used to describe a hooked fish that is trying to flee.

Running Line   The thin part of a fly line made to thread easily through the guides of a fly rod.

Shock Tippet   A short piece of heavy monofilament or wire that is used on the end of the leader when fishing for toothy fish.

Shooting Head   A section of fly line designed for distance casting.

Sink Tip   A fly line designed so the tip sinks underneath the surface of the water while the rest of the line floats.

Skiff   A type of boat designed for very shallow water. Also called a *ponga*.

Slick   A smooth spot in the choppy water of a river or stream, usually caused by a large rock on the bottom of the water.

Spawn   The mating of fish.

Spent   A term used to describe a dying insect after it lays its eggs.

Spinner   The reproductive stage of a mayfly. Also a pattern that matches this adult insect.

Split Shot   Round balls of metal attached to a leader used for fishing below the surface of the water.

Spook   To scare a fish. Once spooked, a fish usually takes off and seeks shelter elsewhere.

Spring Tide   When the sun and the moon align directly with the earth and the gravitational pull is the greatest. This is when the variation between high and low tides is the greatest.

Steelhead   A rainbow trout that is born in a freshwater stream, migrates to an ocean or large lake, and comes back again to spawn.

Stoneflies   An aquatic insect that prefers cold, well-oxygenated, clean water.

Streamer   A fly pattern used to imitate a bait fish.

Strike   When a fisherman tries to set the hook into a fish. Also a term used when a fish bites the fly. To the dismay of the fisherman, strikes don't always end up in hook-ups.

Strike Indicator   A piece of material attached to the leader that floats on the surface of the water and is used to detect a striking fish.

Strip   The action of pulling line from either the water or the reel.

Surface Film   The surface of the water that often traps emerging insects.

Tailwater   The moving water below a dam.

Terrestrials   Land-borne insects such as ants, crickets, and beetles that can provide an abundant source of food for fish. Also a pattern that imitates these land-borne insects.

Tippet   The end part of a leader that attaches to the fly.

Waders   Waterproof boots worn to keep an angler dry when walking through the water. They come in various sizes, from waist-high to chest-high.

Wading Staff   A long pole or walking stick used to gain balance in moving water.

Weed Guard   A piece of monofilament tied to a hook to prevent it from getting snagged on weeds.

Wet Fly   A fly pattern that is used to imitate creatures below the surface of the water.

Fly-Fishing Books

There have been dozens and dozens of excellent books written on the subject of fly fishing, perhaps more than any other sport. This is a brief list of just a few of the books that dot the shelves of my fly-fishing library.

Art Flick's Master Fly-Tying Guide by Art Flick; Crown Publishers, 1972. This book is full of tips and techniques from some of the world's best fly tyers.

Beyond Trout by Barry Reynolds and John Berryman; Johnson Books, 1995. An informative how-to guide to fly fishing for freshwater fish other than trout.

Black's Fly Fishing; Black's Sporting Directories; JFB Inc. An annually updated guide to fly fishing tackle manufacturers, instructors, guides, and destinations.

Fly Fishing in Saltwater by Lefty Kreh; Lyons & Burford, Publishers, 1987. This must-have book gives excellent tips and techniques for saltwater fly fishing.

Fly Patterns of Umpqua Feather Merchants by Randall Kaufmann; Umpqua Feather Merchants, 1998. As my friends and I call it, this is "The Bible" of fly patterns and fly recipes (1,500 to be exact!). A must-have book for any serious fly tyer or any fly fisherman who wants to learn the various patterns of flies.

Inshore Fly Fishing by Lou Tabory; Lyons & Burford, Publishers, 1992. This informational book covers the basics of inshore fly fishing, including an abundance of tips and techniques. It is geared mostly to the northeastern fly fishermen, but the information can be used on any inshore fly fishing trip.

Longer Fly Casting by Lefty Kreh; Lyons & Burford, Publishers, 1991. This how-to guide will help you master long-distance fly casting and correct your casting ailments.

Lou Tabory's Guide to Saltwater Baits and Their Imitations by Lou Tabory; Lyons & Burford, Publishers, 1995. As its title implies this small handbook covers the different saltwater baits and successful patterns that are used to imitate them.

McClane's New Standard Fishing Encyclopedia and International Angling Guide, edited by A.J. McClane; Holt, Rinehart and Winston, 1974. The most complete and reliable encyclopedia on fishing information.

Practical Fishing Knots by Mark Sosin and Lefty Kreh; Lyons & Burford, Publishers, 1991. This handy guide has clear instructions for every fishing knot you'll ever need to know, and more.

Prospecting For Trout by Tom Rosenbaur; Dell Publishing, 1993. This book will teach you how to dissect a trout stream and figure out how and where the trout are feeding when they aren't rising to the surface.

Reading Trout Streams by Tom Rosenbaur; Lyons & Burford, 1988. This how-to book will teach you how to locate trout in new water.

Talleur's Basic Fly Tying by Dick Talleur; Lyons & Burford, 1996. This hands-on, how-to book gives clear and concise directions for tying a number of fly patterns.

Essential Magazines

Check out the newsstands for these and other periodicals pertaining to fly fishing.

American Angler, a bimonthly magazine published by Abenaki Publishers. It is devoted solely to fly fishing and fly tying.

Fly Fisherman is published six times a year by Cowles Magazines, Harrisburg, PA. This is the largest magazine in the industry devoted entirely to fly fishing and fly tying.

The Fly Fishing and Tying Journal is a combination of Frank Amato publication's two previous magazines, *Western Fly Fishing* (formerly *Fly Fishing*) and *Western Fly Tying*. This seasonal publication comes out four times a year and covers information for both avid fly fishermen and fly tyers.

Fly Rod & Reel is another bimonthly publication dedicated entirely to fly fishing. Formerly *Rod & Reel,* the magazine changed its name to *Fly Rod & Reel* in 1989 and now exclusively covers fly fishing.

Fly Tyer is a must-buy magazine for any fly fisherman, beginner to expert, who tie their own flies. It gives step-by-step directions for the newest and hottest fly patterns along with interesting articles about the flies you're trying to imitate.

Saltwater Fly Fishing, as its name implies, is for saltwater fly fishermen. This magazine contains excellent articles on tips and techniques and gives some great saltwater fly fishing destinations.

Warmwater Fly Fishing, a new magazine dedicated to the recent warm water fly fishing boom, covers fly fishing for bass, panfish, pike, and more.

Fly-Fishing Associations and Organizations

Fortunately, there are many fly-fishing associations and organizations that work to protect our fisheries. The following non-profit organizations are dedicated to saving our natural resources and ensuring the sport of fly fishing for future generations. I urge you to pick one or more of these organizations and help protect our dwindling resources.

American Rivers
1025 Vermont Ave., NW Suite 720
Washington, DC. 20005
(202) 547-6900
Fax (202) 347-9240

American Rivers is the nation's leading river conservation organization. Their mission is to protect and restore America's river systems and foster a river stewardship ethic in the United States.

American Sportfishing Association
1033 N. Fairfax St. #200
Alexandria, VA 22314
(703) 519-9691
Fax (703) 519-1872

The American Sportfishing Association is a nonprofit industry association dedicated to ensuring healthy and sustainable fishery resources, increasing sportfishing participation, and providing valuable services to its members.

The Federation of Fly Fishers
502 S. 19th, Suite 1
P.O. Box 1595
Bozeman, MT 59771
(406) 585-7592
Fax: (406) 585-7596

The Federation of Fly Fishers is an international non-profit organization dedicated to conservation, restoration, and education through fly fishing.

FishAmerica Foundation
1033 N. Fairfax St. #200
Alexandria, VA 22314
(703) 548-6338
Fax: (703) 519-1872

The FishAmerica Foundation provides funding for community-based projects that directly improve fish populations and water quality. Since 1983, FishAmerica has assisted over 400 groups in North America to complete such hands-on projects as stream habitat improvement, sediment control, construction of marine and freshwater artificial reefs, fish stocking, hatchery construction, and shoreline stabilization.

International Game Fish Association (IFGA)
1301 E. Atlantic Blvd.
Pompano Beach, FL 33060
(954) 927-2628
Fax: (954) 941-5868

The IFGA is a non-profit organization that maintains and promotes ethical international angling regulations and compiles world game fish records for saltwater, freshwater, and fly fishing.

Trout Unlimited
1500 Wilson Blvd. #310
Arlington, VA 22209
(703) 522-0200
Fax: (703) 284-9400

With around 100,000 members, Trout Unlimited is America's leading trout and salmon conservation organization, dedicated to conserving, protecting, and restoring coldwater fisheries and their watersheds.

Index